THE PALAEOLITHIC ORIGINS
OF HUMAN BURIAL

Humans are unique in that they expend considerable effort and ingenuity in disposing of the dead. Some of the recognisable ways we do this are visible in the Palaeolithic archaeology of the Ice Age. *The Palaeolithic Origins of Human Burial* takes a novel approach to the long-term development of human mortuary activity – the various ways we deal with the dead and with dead bodies. It is the first comprehensive survey of Palaeolithic mortuary activity in the English language.

Observations in the modern world as to how chimpanzees behave towards their dead allow us to identify 'core' areas of behaviour towards the dead that probably have very deep evolutionary antiquity. From that point, the palaeontological and archaeological records of the Pliocene and Pleistocene are surveyed. The core chapters of the book survey the mortuary activities of early hominins, archaic members of the genus *Homo*, early *Homo sapiens*, the Neanderthals, the Early and Mid Upper Palaeolithic, and the Late Upper Palaeolithic world.

Burial is a striking component of Palaeolithic mortuary activity, although existing examples are odd. This probably does not reflect what modern societies believe burial to be, with modern ways of thinking of the dead probably arising only at the very end of the Pleistocene. When did symbolic aspects of mortuary ritual evolve? When did the dead themselves become symbols? In discussing such questions, *The Palaeolithic Origins of Human Burial* offers an engaging contribution to the debate on modern human origins. It is illustrated throughout, includes up-to-date examples from the Lower to Late Upper Palaeolithic, including information hitherto unpublished.

Paul Pettitt is Senior Lecturer in Palaeolithic Archaeology at the University of Sheffield, UK. He has degrees from the universities of Birmingham, London and Cambridge, and was Senior Archaeologist in the Radiocarbon Accelerator Unit at the University of Oxford and Research Fellow and Tutor in Archaeology and Anthropology at Keble College, Oxford. His research interests focus on the European Middle and Upper Palaeolithic. He has published over 190 papers in scientific journals and edited volumes, including chapters on the Neanderthals (in the *Oxford Handbook of Archaeology*) and the rise of modern humans (in Scarre (ed.) *The Human Past*). In 2003 he co-discovered Britain's first examples of Palaeolithic cave art at Creswell Crags, where he currently excavates.

THE PALAEOLITHIC ORIGINS OF HUMAN BURIAL

Paul Pettitt

Routledge
Taylor & Francis Group

LONDON AND NEW YORK

First published 2011
by Routledge
2 Park Square, Milton Park, Abingdon, Oxon OX14 4RN

Simultaneously published in the USA and Canada
by Routledge
711 Third, New York, NY 10017

*Routledge is an imprint of the Taylor & Francis Group,
an informa business*

© 2011 Paul Pettitt

Typeset in Garamond by
Florence Production Ltd, Stoodleigh, Devon

British Library Cataloguing in Publication Data
A catalogue record for this book is available
from the British Library

Library of Congress Cataloging in Publication Data
Pettitt, Paul.
The palaeolithic origins of human burial / Paul Pettitt.
p. cm.
1. Paleolithic period. 2. Burial—History.
3. Human remains (Archaeology) I. Title.
GN772.P48 2010
393'.1—dc22
2010017943

ISBN 13: 978-0-415-35489-9 (hbk)
ISBN 13: 978-0-415-35490-5 (pbk)
ISBN 13: 978-0-203-00155-4 (ebk)

ISBN 10: 0-415-35489-7 (hbk)
ISBN 10: 0-415-35490-0 (pbk)
ISBN 10: 0-203-00155-9 (ebk)

CONTENTS

FIGURES

The following were reproduced with kind permission. While every effort has been made to trace copyright holders and obtain permission, this has not been possible in all cases. Any omissions brought to our attention will be remedied in future editions.

TABLES

ACKNOWLEDGEMENTS

A number of colleagues have been exceptionally helpful during the production of this book, and it is a pleasure to acknowledge their help, professionalism and friendship. For reading various draft chapters I am particularly grateful to Andrew Chamberlain, Bill McGrew, Erella Hovers, Jörg Orschiedt, Alexander Verpoorte and Mark White. All of them had much to say on what they read, and the book is much improved as a result of their kindness. Numerous colleagues put up with requests for information, clarification and the like, and were also instrumental in tracking down elusive references. I hope I have not left anyone out when I thank sincerely (and alphabetically) Leslie Aiello, Jim Anderson, Pablo Arias Cabal, Paul Bahn, Lawrence Barham, Nick Barton, Wayne Bennett, Eugène Bonifay, Richard Byrne, Andrew Chamberlain, Jim Chatters, Robin Dennell, Claire Fisher, Yolanda Fernandez-Jalvo, Vincenzo Formicola, Dominique Henry-Gambier, Erella Hovers, Tatyana Humle, Tetsuro Matsuzawa, Bruno Maureille, Dani Nadel, Pia Nystrom, Jörg Orschiedt, Marylène Patou-Mathis, Ralf Schmitz, John Shea, Andrei Sinitsyn, Martin Street, Jiří Svoboda, Chris Stringer, Thomas Terberger, Alexander Verpoorte, Lyn Wadley and Joao Zilhão.

If it weren't for the ambitious project on the dating of Paviland cave, which Stephen Aldhouse-Green very kindly invited me to join, I would probably never have begun thinking of burials at all, and I am grateful to Stephen for his kindness, and for sharing his ideas on the 'Red Lady'. Similarly, I shall never forget the phone call from Joao Zilhão with the news of the discovery of the Lagar Velho burial, and I am grateful to him for inviting me to participate in the post-excavation analysis.

I owe a great debt to Lalle Pursglove and Matthew Gibbons at Routledge for their help, enthusiasm and, most of all, patience for the project. I warmly thank Julia Mitchell and Jane Fieldsend for their professionalism in the production of the book. In Sheffield, Robin Dennell provided the opportunity to discuss issues on several occasions; these were always informal, enjoyable and profitable, and I am grateful for his friendship. Maureen Carroll educated me about death in the Roman period, helped with Italian translation, made the odd cup of tea, and most importantly put up with me during the long process of writing the book. It was partly researched during study leave in 2007, and I am grateful to Sabine Gaudzinski and colleagues at the Forschungsbereich Altsteinzeit, Römisch-Germanisches Zentralmuseum, Schloss Monrepos, Germany who made my stay there during that time so enjoyable and profitable. Also during the study leave, Christine Neugebauer-Maresch and Maria Teschla-Nicola extended wonderful hospitality in Vienna and very kindly allowed me to view the newly excavated infant burials from Krems-Wachtberg. Margherita Mussi and Alexander Verpoorte in particular have shared their ideas with me over the years and continue to do so to this day. Their friendliness in Rome and Leiden is much appreciated.

Part of Chapter 5 appeared as an article in Volume 1 of the journal *Before Farming* and I am grateful to the editor, Lawrence Barham, for permission to reproduce this. I have in all cases sought permission to reproduce figures, and in almost all cases I was astounded by the kindness and helpfulness of a number of colleagues who provided photographs and illustrations and permission to reproduce them, or helped me obtain these. I am especially grateful to Takeru Akazawa, Juan-Luis Arsuaga, Nikolai Bader, Ofer Bar-Yosef, Eugène Bonifay, Laurent Chiotti, Angiolo Del Lucchese, Francesco d'Errico, Vincenzo Formicola, Giacomo Giacobini, Bill Kimbel, Israel Herschkovitz, Erella Hovers, Tatyana Humle, Don Johanson, Margherita Mussi, Dani Nadel, Roland Nespoulet, Christine Neugebauer-Maresch, Jörg Orschiedt, Marylène Patou-Mathis, Antonio Rosas, Ralf Schmitz, Andrei Sinitsyn, Ralph Solecki, Jiří Svoboda, Maria Teschler-Nicola, Javier Trueba, Eligio Vacca, Bernard Vandermeersch, Marian Vanhaeren, Carole Vercoutère, Pierre Vermeersch, Joao Zilhão; and the following institutions: Elsevier, Madrid Scientific Films, LVR-LandesMuseum Bonn, and the Soprintentenza ai Beni Archeologici della Liguria.

To everyone my warmest thanks.

1

INTRODUCTION

Death and the Palaeolithic

A death in a storm

It was obvious that the baby was very ill indeed. All his four limbs hung limply down and he screamed almost every time his mother took a step. When Olly sat down, very carefully arranging his legs so as not to crush them, Gilka went and sat close to her mother and stared at the infant. But she did not attempt even to touch him.

Olly ate a couple of bananas and then set off along the valley, with Gilka and me following. Olly only moved for a few yards at a time and then, as though worried by the screams of her infant, sat down to cradle him close. When he quietened she moved on again, but, of course, he instantly began to call out so that, once more, she sat to comfort him. After travelling about a hundred yards, which took her just over half an hour, Olly climbed into a tree. Again, she carefully arranged her baby's limp arms and legs on her lap as she sat down. Gilka, who had followed her mother, stared again at her small sibling, and then mother and daughter began to groom each other. The baby stopped screaming and, apart from occasionally grooming his head briefly, Olly paid him no further attention.

When we had been there some fifteen minutes it began to pour, a blinding deluge which almost obscured the chimps from my sight. During that storm, which went on for thirty minutes, the baby must either have died or lost consciousness; when Olly left the tree afterwards he made no sound and his head lolled back as limply as his arms and legs.

(Goodall 1971)

You'll have guessed that this observation is about chimpanzees. It was witnessed by Jane Goodall, among the chimpanzees of Gombe, Tanzania. But omit the one reference to chimpanzees in the last paragraph (and perhaps the tree climbing) and this could easily be describing humans. In this touching observation, we recognise many of the ingredients of suffering and loss;

1

we empathise and sympathise both with Olly and her dying infant, and we find touching the mother's attempts to avoid causing additional suffering to her child by carefully arranging its limbs so she does not sit on them. We share the curiosity of the dying baby's sister, Gilka, and perhaps see in mother and daughter's mutual grooming some attempt to console each other.

This book is about what links us with them in terms of our responses to death. Among humans, organised and cultural responses to death are universal, and over a century and a half of archaeology and anthropology has given us a burgeoning archaeological record attesting to the remarkable inventivity that humans have applied to dealing with the dead. The authors of an anthropological survey of mortuary habits captured this inventivity:

> What could be more universal than death? Yet what an incredible variety of responses it evokes. Corpses are burned or buried, with or without animal or human sacrifice; they are preserved by smoking, embalming, or pickling; they are eaten – raw, cooked, or rotten; they are ritually exposed as carrion or simply abandoned; or they are dismembered and treated in a variety of these ways. Funerals are the occasion for avoiding people or holding parties, for fighting or having sexual orgies, for weeping or laughing, in a thousand different combinations. The diversity of cultural reaction is a measure of the universal impact of death. But it is not a random reaction; always it is meaningful and expressive.
>
> (Huntington and Metcalf 1979)

There are two concepts contained in the last sentence of this quote, which in a way encapsulate the issues addressed by this book: behaviour that is *meaningful* and *expressive*. As we shall see, the responses of chimpanzees to death are certainly expressive, although from a Palaeolithic perspective the question is at what point in human behavioural evolution did responses to death become culturally meaningful?

Here, I seek to provide a long-term picture of the development of human mortuary ritual, spanning the entirety of the Palaeolithic. This is, of course, a somewhat arbitrary archaeological category. It is defined at its earliest end by the appearance of stone tools that, beyond facilitating the dismemberment of corpses, has no meaning for a study of mortuary activity, and there is no reason why proposed responses to death of the first Oldowan communities should differ from those of contemporary or earlier Plio-Pleistocene hominins who did not knap stone. I therefore begin my review of hominin mortuary activity before the currently recognised appearance of the archaeological record. At the other end, the Palaeolithic 'ends' with the beginning of the Holocene, although as archaeologists have long realised this has little to do with the development of late hunter–gatherer and early agricultural groups who, in many areas of the Old World, show considerable continuity from Late Pleistocene 'Palaeolithic' peoples to Early Holocene 'Mesolithic' or 'Neolithic' ones. I am, however, guilty of perpetuating this long-held semantic distinction, as I draw a hard (albeit arbitrary) line at the end of the Pleistocene, simply for reasons of space and lack of expertise. This book should, I hope, be taken as a celebration of the contribution of our pre-Palaeolithic and Palaeolithic forebears to the development of human mortuary ritual.

Why another book on Palaeolithic burials?

Several useful surveys of Palaeolithic mortuary activity exist, although they don't crop up that frequently. Binford's oft-cited 1971 paper 'Mortuary practises: their study and potential' did much to establish the interconnectedness between mortuary activity and social status, and stimulated a number of developments in earlier and later prehistory. Few investigations of mortuary activity neglect to refer to it, and although most works reflect its tenet that the social persona of the deceased, filtered through the medium of the cultural 'system', will determine what specific mortuary rites will be brought to bear, few address its specific tenets. I am guilty of this neglect; the Palaeolithic mortuary record is simply not robust enough to test hypothetico-deductively generated predictions derived from systems theory, although sufficient data exist as to facilitate intuitive observations and generalisations. Such intuitive approaches could be said to characterise much of the literature on Palaeolithic mortuary activity, and this is not a weakness. Excavators of Middle Pleistocene sites that may represent the shadowy beginnings of archaeologically visible funerary activity have speculated in recent years on the implications of their sites. Several specialists have provided surveys (and critiques) of the evidence for Neanderthal burial, and popular articles on death in the Palaeolithic occur from time to time. Three excellent French language surveys of burials exist: Binant's (1991) survey of European Middle and Upper Palaeolithic burials; Defleur's (1993) survey of European and Levantine Middle Palaeolithic burials, and May's (1986) survey of European Upper Palaeolithic burials. Riel-Salvatore and Clark (2001) produced a critical comparison of Middle and Early Upper Palaeolithic burials (in English), and Wüller (1999) a useful survey on Magdalenian burials (in German). An excellent popular survey of funerary activity from the Middle Palaeolithic to the Mesolithic was published (in French) as an entire volume of *Dossiers d'Histoire et Archéologie* 66 in 1982. The surveys, which attempt gross analyses of burial patterns are of great use, although as Zilhão and Trinkaus (2002b) note, these surveys are discrepant in detail, completeness and agreement. The surveys do not explicitly interpret the burials for which they provide so much compelling data and, furthermore, several burials have been discovered in the time subsequent to their publication, notably the Lagar Velho child and the Dederiyeh Neanderthals. Existing studies have tended to concentrate on the act of burial, whereas new analyses of human remains in recent years have done much to improve our understanding of the complex variety of human funerary rituals in their widest sense.

There has been a lack of an English language survey of Palaeolithic mortuary activity, and that forms the first justification for this volume. It is intended to provide an up-to-date survey for the Anglophone world, but, I hope, somewhat more. As Parker Pearson (1999, 148) has noted, debate as to the origins of the 'awareness' of death, and especially of funerary activity, has largely been restricted to the archaelogical record of the last 100,000 years. To some extent this is probably because burial has come to be seen as an item on the 'trait list' of 'modern' human behaviour (e.g. Mellars 1989). This view, I believe, is no longer sustainable. Available observations for chimpanzees alone indicate awareness of death and provide a number of examples of the reaction of individuals and groups to death, opening up the possibility for a long-term view of the development or hominin and hominoid mortuary activity. I thus seek to integrate the known mortuary record into a long-term model of development of mortuary behaviour among the Hominidae, beginning by elucidating how one might expect early hominins (and even hominoids) to have behaved in response to death. To my knowledge this has not been attempted before. In order to do this I review the existing literature on our closest relatives, chimpanzees. These are, of course, not behaviourally fossilised Miocene hominoids but evolved social creatures in their own right, although exploring the diversity of responses to death among these fascinating hominoids, I argue, can provide clues to what our 'core' responses to death may have been in the dim evolutionary past. This serves as a starting point from which more complex (and ultimately archaeologically visible) mortuary behaviour arose. I then proceed through the Pliocene and Pleistocene, organising the chapters in terms of themes of carcass processing and aspects of visible mortuary ritual.

Some caveats

This is a book about the long-term development of human mortuary activity, not a general book on Palaeolithic archaeology or human evolution. Where necessary I contextualise the mortuary evidence I am dealing with in wider behavioural issues, at least on a site-by-site basis, but where I do not feel that such contextualisation is necessary or informative I make no apologies for excluding it. In fact I exclude a lot. I am not interested here in ancient DNA sequences, controversies in taxonomic identification, Pleistocene hominin dispersals and issues as to how, when and where 'modern' behaviour arose. The taxonomic categories I use are just that – taxa – and while there may be some validity in comparing hominin taxa I make no judgement that biological differences need equate with hard-and-fast behavioural differences in the mortuary realm. In the biological sense I interpret as I find, and it should be remembered that when different biological taxa are treated in separate chapters or sections they could indeed be part of the same behavioural processes, for example the earliest inhumations of *Homo sapiens* and those of *Homo neanderthalensis*.

This is not a book on human mortuary activity in general. Mortuary 'generalists' – if such a person exists, and given the variability one has to deal with simply in certain periods of the Palaeolithic I suggest they should not – will find the following pages largely mute about overarching themes. I do, however, define some general terms below, which I use as an heuristic to approach the record and to try to rein in the data in a definable way. These terms span what I argue are the extremes of mortuary activity: the fragmentation and dissolution of the individual body at one extreme, and the collective sequestration of the bodies of many individuals in cemeteries at the other. Burials, as the book's title suggests, feature strongly. I do consider other aspects of mortuary activity as well as other behaviours that I consider to be linked to burial, although I am, of course, dependent upon the preservational vagaries of the archaeological record. I will make the point several times in the book that whatever 'normal' or 'routine' mortuary practices were employed in the Palaeolithic, they are invisible; abandonment, exposure or for that matter floating bodies off down rivers will leave no traces, and I acknowledge that I am dealing with a small and biased fraction of behaviour (Figure 1.1). However small and biased it is, it is nevertheless informative, at least about those odd circumstances that required odd mortuary solutions. I shall argue, for example, that for most of the Palaeolithic what we define as 'burials' were probably very different to what we in the modern world think of as burials.

But that is jumping the gun, and these ideas will be developed in the core of the book and are summarised in the concluding chapter. The book is fairly unbalanced, yet I am unapologetic about this. Some chapters are rather brief, and others are fuller; in the latter, where I am on more familiar ground, the data are more abundant and, I believe, simply more can be said. If one were to judge the book by the length of chapters it could be said that it is about chimpanzees, Neanderthals and Gravettians, although (forgive the pun) this would be a grave insult to the dead of Skhūl and Qafzeh caves, of the shores of Lake Mungo, or of the Late Upper Palaeolithic and would, in addition, understandably horrify my primatologist colleagues. This is not a book in the main about chimpanzees, Neanderthals and Gravettians but it is a testimony to the wealth of data available for these subjects. I have drawn the book to an end arbitrarily: it ends with the end of the Pleistocene and the onset of interglacial conditions – a somewhat arbitrary point in itself. While the mortuary developments that I discuss towards the end of the Pleistocene certainly herald in a new form of funerary organisation (the 'cemetery' as I define it *sensu stricto*) that continues on into the Holocene as part of the behavioural repertoire of the Mesolithic, I do not pursue it. The Mesolithic literature is vast; I am not a Mesolithic specialist, and I therefore shy away

Figure 1.1 Open air cremation of the dead, Pashupatinath, Katmandu, Nepal. After
the body is largely destroyed the remains are floated off down the river.
Note another body ready for the pyre. Although cremation seems to have
been practised very rarely in the Palaeolithic, rivers and other natural
features used for their deposition would ensure that they do not come
down to us (photo: author).

from this in order not to add my Mesolithic colleagues to the primatologists
as those on whose tarsals and phalanges I have so rudely trodden. Similarly,
I am not an Epipalaeolithic specialist and the literature is again vast for several
regions of the African continent, the Near East and Australasia, and here I
end simply with a 'taster' of developments in mortuary variability. I therefore
draw the book to an end using a mixture of general survey papers, some s
pecific papers, and information provided by a number of kind and helpful
colleagues. I apologise unreservedly to them, and to the Iberomaurusians,
Capsians, Natufians and many, many more complex societies who I have so
unfairly summarised in few words. In order to grasp – however cursorily –
funerary developments at the dawn of the Holocene I have decided, however,
that in this case a little is better in than out.

Death: the final frontier

As modest as I like to think I am, it would be unfair and incorrect to say
that I know nothing. To paraphrase a great thinker, I know at least one thing;

6

that I am going to die. It may be some comfort, though, that I am constantly told that when my physical body dies, my soul, mind or essence will continue to exist. I cannot prove or disprove this belief, but the possibility that things will not be finished for me when my body gives out should offer me comfort, and many of the specific ideas about exactly what should happen to my soul after death certainly do offer me occasional amusement. Herein lies the metaphysical nub of the problem: we cannot prove anything positive or negative, and while logic determines that life-after-death is improbable, our emotional responses retain the notion for our own comfort. I hold no beliefs about what will happen to me after death; I regard myself as an intellectual agnostic (sensibly I cannot demonstrate that gods, spiritual realms and spirits do not exist) but an emotional atheist (my gut feeling on logical grounds is that they don't). This does not prevent me from entertaining notions of what my life was or will be like both before and after the proverbial three score and ten. Here I rapidly encounter contradiction. I find the notion of reincarnation illogical and biologically impossible, but at the same time I am attracted to the idea that I may once have been Nelson or Ghengis Khan (or Cleopatra – why do we assume that our gender remains the same over this spiritual cladogenesis?). Likewise, I do not believe that the dead really continue to exist, yet whenever I do anything naughty the image of my grandmother looking down at me from the clouds springs rather disconcertingly to mind, chastising me in her kind, calm way. When I was young this thought stopped me from stealing a Paddington Bear pencil top from a well-known stationers, and were it not for the improving spiritual agency of this ancestor I might have developed into a master criminal. There are, admittedly, better examples of the social agency of the dead, but at least this one is personal.

Paddington Bear does not concern himself with life-after-death (or did not: has he died, or will he ever?). I envy him his single-minded pursuit of marmalade sandwiches. But herein lies a serious question: at what evolutionary point did hominoids or hominins begin to develop a 'sense' of death, and a sense that something may lie beyond it? I remember when I was very young trying to imagine what it would be like *not existing*. For some reason I imagined this as floating slowly and silently along in the universe, alongside other diverse and sundry non-existing items such as, unsettlingly, double-decker *Routemaster* London buses. Why I should associate death with *Routemaster* buses I do not know, but it is, perhaps, an association no more eccentric than many beliefs about death and the dead that anthropologists have observed the world over. What a peculiarly inventive species we humans are! When we are not killing each other, putting our evil cunning to great effect in spreading vast swathes of misery to millions, and generally messing up the planet, we have put considerable effort into creating cosmological beliefs that, while considerably varied the world over, share one thing: they all put forward inventive (and sometimes complex) notions and beings that have never been experienced (as far as one can tell) in objective reality. They are in this sense purely imaginary, and surely evolved, like my non-existent *Routemaster* buses, as by-products of our modern hominin brains (Atran 2006; Boyer 2008).

It is this inventivity – in this case in the mortuary sphere – that is the subject of this book. Several chapters cover particular periods that, as I explain in the concluding chapter, comprise developmental phases in mortuary activity. These 'phases' are snapshots in time, and do not link together in a continuous narrative. The Palaeolithic record is not continuous and I see no reason why the long-term model I develop here should be either. I see the development of hominin mortuary activity – like many other aspects of hominin behaviour – as regionally variable and discontinuous, but in the long term essentially cumulative in nature.

Death and mortuary activity: some concepts

It has long been recognised that funerary practices form part of a wider set of transitions or rites of passage that are marked by ritual activity. Robert Hertz and Arnold van Gennep, both based in France and active in the first half of the twentieth century, did much to contextualise mortuary practices in wider social currents, notably emphasising funerals as major rites of passage whether for positive (Hertz) or negative (van Gennep) reasons. Although both published their major works in 1907 and 1909 respectively, both went largely unnoticed in the Anglophone world until they were published in English in 1960 (Hertz 1960; van Gennep 1960). Van Gennep originated the concept of *rites de passage*, which became a major heuristic for the interpretation of funerals. Now, they could be seen as transitions, marking the journey of the deceased into new worlds, and providing a structure for mourning and the renegotiation of society after the removal of a social agent. To Hertz, death transformed individuals, although they retained social agency as ancestors and thus assisted the perpetuation of the over-arching collective society.

The mortuary activities discussed in this book form part of the human responses to death in these wider perspectives. As archaeologists we recognise only points in time – the material remnants of specific acts – that fit somewhere on the complex ritual sequences that form the physical expression of these transitions. In order to compare them, and if one is at all able to attempt a study of their development, an heuristic is required in which specific definitions of recognisable mortuary phenomena are possible. The major examples referred to in this book are as follows:

- *Curation*. The carrying around of the dead, either of an entire corpse, or of preserved body parts. Corpses and body parts may be accorded social agency and used accordingly, in which case they can be defined as *relics*.
- *Morbidity*. An enquiring concern with the injured, diseased or dead body, whether or not this derives from a desire to understand the nature or cause of death of an individual.

- *Cronos compulsions.* A physical extension of morbidity: the urge – for whatever reason – to dismember, injure or consume parts of the bodies of one's conspecifics. Named after Cronos (Roman Saturn), who consumed his children. This concept links nutritional and ritual cannibalism, processing of the body such as scalping and dismemberment, and any other examples whereby physical changes are brought about to the corpses of the dead. Funerary processing and secondary burials can arise from such 'compulsions'.

- *Abandonment.* The simple act of leaving a helpless individual to die. This, for example, is the default mechanism of infanticide (Hrdy 1999, 298). Also, the abandonment *in situ* of a corpse.

- *Structured abandonment.* The deliberate placement of a corpse at a certain point in the landscape, for reasons amounting to no more than simple concerns such as protection from scavengers.

- *Funerary caching.* The structured deposition of a corpse, or parts of a corpse, in a chosen place, without modification of that place, such as at the back of caves, in natural fissures, etc. Also the use of pits originally created for purposes other than burial. Unlike structured abandonment, however, the place is given meaning beyond prosaic concerns such as corpse protection. Concepts such as 'places of the dead' may arise from funerary caching.

- *Cairn covering.* The creation of a cairn – a pile of stones – over a corpse. This differs from funerary caching (whereby a corpse is taken to a natural feature and placed within it) as natural materials are brought to the corpse and used to cover it. The resulting space is part-natural, part-artificial, and in this sense similar to simple inhumation.

- *Formal burial or inhumation.* The creation of an artificial place for the purposes of containing a corpse. This is at least a three-stage process involving 1) the excavation of an artificial pit or trench intended to serve as a grave; 2) the interment of a body within the grave; and 3) the covering of the body with the extracted sediment. Without the inclusion of humanly made grave goods, the result is part-natural (in that only natural phenomena are used) and part-artificial (as they have been repositioned). Formal burial may be distinguished from ritual deposits that include human remains, as with burial, the *interment of the body* itself is the prime object of the process.

- *Place of multiple burial.* From the Middle Palaeolithic, a number of sites are recognisable in which several individuals were buried in several graves. This phenomenon can be recognised for *Homo neanderthalensis* and for early *Homo sapiens.* Numbers of individuals recognised from these sites is usually low, typically in the order of ~6–12, and although grave cuttings typically do not disturb previous burials the general sense at these sites is of brief phenomena in which several individuals were buried sequentially, without any overriding organisational principles or long-term persistence that

9

would define the site formally as a cemetery. In addition to this, places of multiple burials typically occur within settlement contexts, that is, they are not separated from the world of the living, the dead interred amidst the waste of prosaic occupation.

- *Cemetery.* By contrast to places of multiple burial, cemeteries *sensu stricto* are places given over in the main or entirely to the dead, with little or no evidence of settlement. Although there is inevitably overlap with multiple burial locales, the number of burials in cemeteries tends to be larger (>20) and a degree of spatial organisation is in evidence. In some cases they can persist for long periods of time.
- *Detachment.* The weakening of existing social bonds between the living and the dead. This is a *process*, which may occur simply through the attrition of time, unembellished by any cultural acts, such as with primates. Alternatively, it may be governed by rules, embellished by ritual practice, material culture and the like, in which case it is a *detachment ritual* (Gamble 1999).
- *Commemoration.* To preserve the memory of an individual, either through the expression of energy (story, song, dance and other ritual acts, deposition in a special place) or as material culture (e.g. grave goods, grave markers, etc.).

These concepts will be used as I believe they are recognisable in the archaeological record. It will become evident that several blend into each other, and at some sites, for example, funerary caching and formal burial were practised alongside each other. In the last chapter I am concerned with the evolutionary development of funerary behaviour, and in particular at what point one might sensibly call funerary activity 'symbolic'. This reflects the concern with the origins of symbolism as perhaps the main cognitive characteristic of 'modern' behaviour in current palaeoanthropological research. But first, it is the modern world that will furnish us with a set of core responses of the living to the dead. Not the modern world of *Homo sapiens*, but the modern world of chimpanzees.

2

PRIMATE ROOTS FOR EARLY HOMINID MORBIDITY AND MORTUARY ACTIVITY

Why begin with chimpanzees?

In addition to their genetic relatedness to extant humans (Friday 2000; Marks 2000, 2003; Sibley 2000), chimpanzees have often been seen as extant behavioural reflections of earlier hominids, perhaps even of a Late Miocene common ancestor (Goodall 1990). In addition to this, my rationale for beginning with chimpanzee morbidity and mortuary activity is rooted in their numerous similarities with extant humans such as organisation in large social groups, a high degree of sociality, a theory of mind and potential language use. In particular, the apparent 'cultural' variation in tool use and other behaviours noted in chimpanzees (e.g. McGrew 1992; Boesch *et al.* 1994; Whiten *et al.* 1999) and orang-utans (Van Schaik *et al.* 2003), which apparently varies independently of environmental and ecological contexts, makes higher primates a particularly useful source of background data from which to begin an enquiry of this nature. Only for chimpanzees is there a suitable body of observation from which generalisations can be made.

I am fully aware that chimpanzees are not a biologically and behaviourally frozen hominid, and as such do not preserve the behaviour of what one might expect of the earliest hominins. I do, however, believe that, whether or not by convergent evolution or by sharing of generalised hominid/hominoid behaviour, they do offer a general behavioural model that might be taken as a baseline for the origins of mortuary activity in the Homininae. Similarly, I am aware of the dangers of making arguments by simple analogy. I appreciate that, even in situations where chimpanzees behave in remarkably similar ways to us, the derivation of such behaviour may come from radically different mind sets (Povinelli 2003). I am, however, not concerned per se with cognition, concepts of mind or related matters. Rather, I am concerned with establishing some basic parameters of the physical responses or behavioural acts towards death and the dead body. These are presumably finite and limited in number, and my reasoning is that if the core behaviours on which behavioural evolution operated in the hominid lineage are identifiable today, then they will most likely be found in our nearest genetic and behavioural relatives. Given that there are, in fact, a relatively limited number of things one can do with the dead body at the simplest levels of organisation without complex belief systems to guide behaviour, I feel that using chimpanzees as a basic heuristic is, in this case, justified. The challenge, of course, will be to link meaningfully these physical responses to death with the emergent belief systems that from some point in evolutionary time begin to underpin them.

The purpose of this chapter is to use the behavioural record of chimpanzees in order to establish the core elements of morbidity – attitudes towards the dead – and the treatment of the dead body. Given that in small-scale societies the worlds of the living and the dead are rarely separated (e.g. Binford 1971), I approach this issue in two ways. After a brief consideration of the factors that bring about death among chimpanzees I first look at how individual chimpanzees on occasion play an active role in the death of their conspecifics and consume them. Second, I examine evidence of compassion and other phenomena that accompany the treatment of the dead. From an interweaving of these two extremes of behaviour I construct the core elements of morbidity and mortuary behaviour that I suggest pertained in various forms for early hominid societies. The point at which the record changes and additional mortuary behaviour enters the record forms a point of departure for the next chapter.

Mortality in chimpanzee communities

Social dynamics will, of course, have an interactive, two-way relationship with population demographics. If deliberate mortuary behaviour occurs within a given population, it will to a large degree relate to demographics and social organisation. It follows that a three-point relationship should exist between social organisation, demography and mortuary activity. As a result, any discussion of mortuary activity, at least that beyond the most simplistic treatment of the corpse, is to an extent a reflection of social organisation.

Chimpanzee societies may be generally described as multi-male, multi-female, which remain relatively stable for a number of years despite fission–fusion fluctuation, and in which individuals may travel alone and mothers form strong bonds with their young. Hostility often occurs between neighbouring groups, particularly between competing males with a drive for domination (e.g. Goodall 1977, 1986; Wrangham 1999; Mitani *et al.* 2002). Despite an apparent population stability, fluctuations are evident that relate to changing birth and death rates in addition to female immigration and emigration. The Taï Pan troglodytes community of Ivory Coast, for example, varied between 29 and 82 individuals with an average of 60 over a 16-year span (Boesch and Boesch-Achermann 2000, 21). Death rates will vary accordingly and at Taï were actually lowest when the community was at its demographic extremes, that is, largest and smallest. Although small degrees of variability in mortality patterns are observable between groups, no simple rules appear evident. A degree of difference may exist between wild and captive chimpanzee groups (with lower degrees of survival in the wild), although both witness relatively high mortality among infants and an otherwise attritional pattern at which the chances of survival decline as years of age progress towards a maximum age of around 30 years (Courtenay and Santow 1989; Hill *et al.* 2001). Inbreeding, particularly in captive populations, may well account for a degree of the high number of infant deaths.

A degree of caution is necessary in using chimpanzee mortality data to make wider inferences. As most chimpanzees usually just disappear (from the point of view of the human observer at least) and death and its causes therefore need to be assumed (Goodall 1986, 109), it follows that the data that are actually available form a small subset. This having been said, in addition to sound observations a satisfying number of reasonable assumptions can be made to allow a general picture of chimpanzee mortality to be constructed. Dunbar (1988, 71ff.) lists four main causes of primate mortality in the wild: starvation, disease, temperature stress and predation. Of these, disease and predation are cited as the dominant causes of chimpanzee mortality, although Goodall (ibid., 111) found not one case of predation to be responsible for 51 logged deaths. It seems that the contribution of predation to death may, in fact, be exaggerated, as it is rare among documented causes of death (W. McGrew pers. comm.). In addition to active agents of death, the relative dominance of mothers will affect the survival chances of their offspring. High-ranking females live longer and may offer their offspring more protection against predation, whereas infants of low-ranking mothers showing far greater degrees of mortality than higher-ranking ones among the Gombe community (Pusey *et al.* 1997). Of the three intra-community infant killings observed at Gombe by 1975, all were the offspring of low–medium rank disabled mothers and the killings were perpetrated by either one high-ranking mother or her daughter.

Although disease may on occasion have a notable effect on population structure (Goodall 1986, 92ff.; Matsuzawa *et al.* 1990), despite the lack of clear evidence, predation is often cited as the biggest killer of chimpanzees. As noted above this could be exaggerated; Dunbar (1988, 74) saw 'animals as large as chimpanzees as all but immune from predation'. Without citing observations, Boesch and Boesch-Achermann, for example, note that 'predation on chimpanzees by big cats *probably* happens throughout their sympatric range in undisturbed habitats' (2000, 33, my emphasis). Leopard aggression, often resulting in the deaths of subadult and adult chimpanzees was said to be common at Taï (Boesch and Boesch-Achermann 2000, 30–1), where it was listed as the primary cause of death, albeit again without observations. Lions were similarly noted as causing high numbers of deaths among the Mahale chimpanzees (Tsukahara 1993), but only one observation was logged in 44 years of study, and predation furthermore played no real role in mortality at Bossou, Budongo, Kanyawara or Ngogo (W. McGrew pers. comm.).

Whatever the importance of predation, inter-community aggression can be the cause of significant numbers of chimpanzee deaths. At Gombe, for example, strangers or part-strangers, especially immigrant infants, are particularly at risk (Goodall 1986, 331), strangers (incoming individuals) especially caused infant deaths at Mahale (Nishida *et al.* 1990). Human predation has certainly been observed as a cause of death among chimpanzees, both directly (by rifle) or indirectly (by snares). It can, on occasion, have dramatic effects on population structure. Indirect predation can affect infants in particular, who seem incapable of freeing themselves from the grip of snares (Boesch and Boesch-Achermann 2000, 36). As with human societies, illness will also take its toll. At Taï, for example, poliomyelitis, influenza, pneumonia and monkey pox were observed causes of death (Boesch and Boesch-Achermann 2000, 35–6), and a suite of respiratory diseases in particular caused death at Gombe (Williams *et al.* 2008). More widely, Ebola and the simian immunodeficiency virus SIVcpz (the direct precursor to HIV-1) have particularly pronounced negative effects on wild chimpanzee mortality (W. McGrew pers. comm., Keele *et al.* 2009), and the diseases so far documented as causing chimpanzee mortality are probably a significant underestimate (Boesch 2008).

Unlike inter-community aggression, intra-group aggression between individuals, which was common at Taï, was generally the only cause of minor injury even during changes of the alpha position, and rarely resulted in death (Boesch and Boesch-Achermann 2000, 33). Death by accidents, such as falling from trees, was also rare at Taï (Boesch and Boesch-Achermann 2000, 30). Similarly, at Gombe, aggression between adults in agonistic situations rarely caused more than minor injuries (Goodall 1986).

Overall, it is important to remember that causes of death may vary significantly from time to time and from population to population (Dunbar 1988, 74). New agents of death, whatever they are, may cause profound slumps in population levels. At Taï, this can be seen clearly within two contrasting periods of observation, both of which saw pronounced population declines due to different causes. In the former, 76 per cent of deaths were attributable to leopards or illness, whereas in the second period, Ebola alone accounted for 66 per cent. Disease, predation, inter- and intra-group aggression variously account for the majority of chimpanzee deaths. Infants are particularly at risk. While to human observers many deaths are simply recorded as individuals who disappear; a number of these occur in circumstances that heavily imply the role of other chimpanzees. Cases of infanticide in particular, even the manner in which this is undertaken, may well have a cultural element. These issues will be discussed below.

Cronos compulsions: infanticide and cannibalism

If we look back to an extremely remote epoch, before man had arrived at the dignity of manhood, he would have been guided more by instinct and less by reason than are savages at the present time. Our early semi-human progenitors would not have practised infanticide, for the instincts of the lower animals are never so perverted as to lead them regularly to destroy their own offspring.

(C. Darwin, *The Descent of Man*, 1871, 134)

Infanticide – the killing of dependent offspring – is widespread in the animal kingdom, despite individual occurrences within groups (i.e. rates) being relatively rare (Van Schaik and Janson 2000). Among primates, the apparently deliberate killing of infants by adult members of the same species has been reported in several species of monkeys and apes in the wild (see Goodall 1977 for a useful summary). Some statements are controversial; Hrdy (1999, 243), for example, saw vegetarian gorillas as highly infanticidal, although no observations exist to attest this. Chimpanzees however – a highly social primate – are relatively carnivorous and indulge in infanticide, usually as a group (multi-female or multi-male) activity. Equally, the consumption of individual conspecifics (i.e. cannibalism) is widely observed in the animal kingdom and again among primates. I refer to infanticide and cannibalism – potentially deep-rooted urges to kill and/or consume the body of ones' conspecifics – as Cronos compulsions.[1] I am concerned here with their relationship to each other and to the corpse in general.

Here, I use the phenomena of infanticide and cannibalism among higher primates as a point of departure for investigating the social dynamics that underlie the deliberate removal of individuals from a social group. What factors affect or stimulate the killing of an infant? There are, in fact, a number observable among mammals – infanticide is even more common among langurs and lions than higher primates (W. McGrew pers. comm.). I shall argue below that the social factors that underlie choices of when and who to remove from society also underlie whether or how the corpses of individuals are afforded attention in death. If this connection is assumed, it follows that observations of the factors affecting infanticide and killing of individuals – put another way the *creation of death* – may be used as an heuristic to investigate potential factors behind variable mortuary activity. This could certainly have been a factor underpinning Mid Upper Palaeolithic burials, as discussed in Chapter 6. Above all, I shall argue that as Cronos compulsions are observed in our closest relatives, they have probably played an important role in death among the Hominidae. As Hrdy (1999, 243) has suggested, human infanticide may well be attributed to the common heritage of chimpanzees and humans.

The observation that infanticide plays an important role in ecology is not new. Although Darwin speculated that 'some competent observers have

15

attributed the fearfully common practice of infanticide partly to the desire felt by the women to retain their good looks' (1871: II, 344), he was aware of its overriding importance to the Malthusian struggle for survival. As he observed in *The Descent of Man* (1871):

> Malthus has discussed . . . several checks [on population] but he does not lay stress enough of what is probably the most important of all, namely infanticide, especially of female infants . . . These practices appear to have originated in savages recognising the difficulty, or rather the impossibility of supporting all the infants that are born.

Furthermore, he suggested that 'wherever infanticide prevails the struggle for existence will be in so far less severe, and all the members of the tribe will have an almost equally good chance of rearing their few surviving children' (1871, 363). Continuing the theme of the widespread human indulgence in infanticide, Darwin's friend, Sir John Lubbock (Lord Avebury) mentioned several examples of the practice in his account of 'modern savages' in *Pre-Historic Times* (1865).

In a seminal overview of infanticide among animals, Hrdy (1979, 14) suggested that it can be explained as occurring for one of five reasons. Four of these assume that the practice in some way favours (i.e. is adaptively advantageous for) the perpetrator – exploitation, resource competition, parental manipulation and sexual selection. The fifth – social pathology – does not assume that infanticide is adaptively advantageous, but rather that it results from the aberrant behaviour of the perpetrator. Exploitation relates to situations in which the death of an infant will be in some way advantageous to the killer, either directly (e.g. to remove competition) or indirectly (e.g. as an incidental bi-product of 'play mothering' or during agonistic (combative) behaviour. Circumstances of parental manipulation include the killing of disabled or otherwise debilitated offspring or use of the offspring as a (nutritional) resource in situations of environmental or other pressures (Hrdy 1979, 17). Aside from adaptively advantageous factors, although infant deaths may occur simply through mistakes or other social pathologies, these are difficult to test objectively and do not explain infanticide as clearly as other, adaptive factors (Hrdy 1979, 20).

The function of infanticide among mammals has been debated heatedly since the 1960s. Certainly, numerous factors might affect the risk and rates of infanticide, as summarised in Table 2.1. Today, however, the notion developed by Hrdy (1979, 1999) that it primarily functions as a strategy for sexual selection, particularly among primates, has largely been accepted as the main, if not the sole, stimulus for the practice (Van Schaik and Janson 2000, 2). Hrdy suggested that males deliberately employ it as a reproductive strategy, given that females whose offspring are killed will return to fertility rapidly. Equally, infanticide may function to reduce population size, reduce levels of

Table 2.1 Some factors affecting infanticide among higher primates

Cause	Explanation	Sphere of influence	Source
Rate of breeding male replacement	The greater the turnover of dominant males, the greater the rate of infanticide, assuming newly dominant males are infanticidal	Infanticide rate	Janson and Van Schaik 2000
Sexual dimorphism	The larger males are relative to females, the easier it is for them to kill female offspring	Higher rates of infanticide where males are significantly larger than females	Janson and Van Schaik 2000
Female dispersal	Dispersal of females reduces the strength of female alliances that protect against infanticide or greater mobility of females allows them more choice of successful male protectors	Female dispersal may limit the impact of male replacement on infanticide rates	Janson and Van Schaik 2000 Nishida and Kawanaka 1985
Single vs multi-male groups	Higher male replacement rates in multi-male groups	Greater replacement rates equals greater infanticide rates	Janson and Van Schaik 2000
Diet	Infanticide more common among folivorous primates than frugivorous	Possible need to limit group size in folivores, thus higher infanticide rate. Males may dominate mating more in folivorous species as their time-budgets are less constrained	Hrdy 1979 Janson and Van Schaik 2000
Population disturbance	Disruption of male–female ratios affects female abilities to counter infanticide	Male–female disequilibrium affects infanticide rate	Janson and Van Schaik 2000
Predation pressure	May select for greater female or greater male numbers within groups	Grater female numbers = higher rates of protection and thus lower infanticide rates: greater males may increase male–male competition and turnover thus raise infanticide rates	Nunn and Van Schaik 2000
Female–female competition	When intra-group resource competition increases, so does female–female competition	May increase infanticide rate by females	Nunn and Van Schaik 2000
Male–male competition	Aggressive male displays involve potentially lethal activity	Infanticide possibly employed to remove future competition	Harnai et al. 1992

inbreeding and stabilise population levels well below environmental carrying capacities, at least in the case of hunter–gatherers (for these and other notions see Lee and DeVore 1968 and Dunbar 1994, 257ff.).

In terms of individual sexual selection the destruction of another individual's offspring can be seen as an advantageous (and indirect) effect of male takeovers. A recent examination of the male-perpetrated sexual selection explanation concluded that infanticide by males in a number of species is best explained as a reproductive strategy albeit with exceptions; that there are predictable correlates of infanticide risk and rates among primates such as life history variables, social organisation and ecology; that females have evolved a variety of strategies to reduce the risk of infanticide; and that females do kill infants, if not generally as commonly as males (Janson and Van Shaik 2000). There is a two-way relationship between infanticide and social organisation, as each will affect and cause modification of the other. For example, as infanticide is costly to females, it follows that higher rates of the practice lead to increased female counterstrategies and thus new social relationships (Nunn and Van Schaik 2000). Such counterstrategies seem to be highly variable, and possibly relate to ecological contexts.

There are clear variables observable in infanticide across species. Given this, primates, particularly apes, obviously form the most appropriate focus for the origins of body interaction in the Hominidae. Among primates the context of infanticide is more homogeneous than in other species (Van Schaik and Janson 2000). The greater majority of cases are perpetrated by males (although females also indulge – see below), and most infants killed are unrelated to their killers. Variability is, however, still observable, and Hrdy (1979, 14) has concluded that infanticide 'cannot be understood as a unitary phenomenon'. In exceptional circumstances, infants can even be killed by members of their own group, by their own parents and even by other infants (ibid., 14). In the context of the discussion here, it may be these relatively exceptional cases of infanticide that are more germane to understanding the social factors behind killing and social organisation.

Multiple cases of chimpanzee infanticide have been observed in the Budongo Forest, Tanzania (Suzuki, quoted in Goodall 1977), the Gombe National Park, Tanzania (Goodall 1977), and the Mahale Mountains, Tanzania (Norikoshi 1982; Takahata 1985; Hamai et al. 1992). At Gombe, one infant was forcibly torn from her mother and mortally wounded (Goodall 1977, 260), and Goodall (ibid.) has noted that the violence displayed towards mothers, which abates after their infants have been seized, suggests a deliberate desire to obtain (and kill) the infants. At Mahale, the perpetrators were always adult males (Hamai et al. 1992) and their targets were infant males, suggesting that one aim of the infanticide was to remove potential future competition for their sons (Takahata 1985).

The most obvious form of infanticide is extrinsic, that is, males from neighbouring groups killing individuals of groups in which they have inserted themselves and assumed a dominant role. This would not count for chimpanzee males who do not emigrate, but could apply for example, to baboons (W. McGrew pers. comm.). Violence on such occasions may be extreme, and resulted in the complete extermination of a whole group at Gombe, and probably at Mahale (Mitani *et al.* 2002, 18). Bygott (1972, 410), for example, noted a violent encounter between two separate groups of Gombe chimpanzees, and the killing and eating of an infant by a dominant male (Humphrey) following a violent encounter with adult females. Goodall (1977, 262) reported extrinsic killing and cannibalism among the Kasakela community at Gombe. Not that infanticide arising from inter-group aggression can be held to be universal, however. The rarity of infant deaths through this cause is made clear in a discussion of the only observed case of infant cannibalism among the Taï Forest chimpanzee community:

> The only case of cannibalism we saw at Taï . . . is not very conclusive. The student who witnessed the event . . . arrived at the site when several females were already eating a dead infant. The adult female Poupée kept the dead infant all the time but shared some meat with the other females. We do not know for certain whose baby it could have been, although a young mother appeared 27 minutes later without her newborn baby. Curiously she showed no signs of tension or distress, as we would expect if her own baby were being eaten in front of her. The location of the event . . . does not allow [us] to exclude an inter-community interaction. It remains a puzzling case, particularly as we never witnessed any sign of aggression aimed at infants in all the inter-community encounters we observed.
>
> (Boesch and Boesch-Achermann 2000, 33–4)

While extrinsic infanticide is understandable from the point of view of the establishment of dominance and removal of potential future competition, intragroup infanticide is potentially more revealing about the social aspects of the practice. Goodall (1977, 266ff.) reported three cases of the intra-community killing of infants among the Gombe community. Of these, two were the offspring of a low-ranking and partly disabled female. The third was the offspring of a medium-ranking but also disabled female. In all cases the killer was one high ranking female or her adolescent daughter.

Unlike extrinsic examples, within groups, rival mothers may on occasion be at the heart of infanticide, in a number of social mammals in addition to chimpanzees. In the words of Hrdy (1999, 52) 'we now know that, *given the opportunity*, a more dominant female chimp will kill and eat babies born to other females' (emphasis original). At Gombe, at least ten infants were killed by females. Hrdy (1999, 86) also suggests that offspring killed by males of neighbouring communities are more likely to be males, although in terms of sexual selection infanticide seems to occur mainly through male–male

19

competition over female choice (W. McGrew pers. comm.). Although there have been no observed cases of infanticide in bonobos, this may be due to the strength of female–female bonds acting as a protective measure, rather than a genuine absence of this behaviour among this species.

Fossey (pers. comm. to Hrdy, quoted in Hrdy 1979, 15) reported that cannibalism among wild gorillas was also attributable to dominant females. Some of the first systematically reported examples of cannibalism among chimpanzees involved the acquisition (as to how is unclear) of infant corpses by adult males at Budongo, Uganda and Gombe (Bygott 1972). Bygott (ibid., 411) saw predatory aggression at the root of cannibalism, arguing that it arises 'from a situation of extreme aggressive arousal such as that preceding the Gombe infant killing'. In 1983 an infant male was killed and eaten, again by high-ranking males, at Mahale, Tanzania (Takahata 1985).

Among human societies, as with other higher primates, infants are usually killed while they are at early life-history stages that demand maximum amounts of parental investment (Hrdy 1979, 18). Unlike nonhuman primates, however, humans make conscious decisions about whether or not an infant will be kept following birth. If it is to die, this will be facilitated as quickly as possible: in human traditional societies almost all infanticide occurs immediately following birth and grief is apparently greater if the act occurs after naming ceremonies or equivalent *rites de passage* (Hrdy 1999, 470). Although to some extent this relates to conceptions of the humanness (or not) of the newly born, it also relates to the sensible notion that neonaticide is safer for the mother than a late stage abortion. A notable distinction between nonhuman primates and humans is the lack of aggression during infanticide in the latter. Among humans, it is accompanied by grief, regret, or, at worst, nonchalance and detachment. Compared to this, Bygott's (1972) observations of aggressive killing and cannibalism among chimpanzees, and the apparent link between aggression in hunting and infanticide among Mahale chimpanzees (see below) stand in stark contrast.

Hrdy (1979, 20ff.) discussed intraspecific variability of infanticide, noting that it ' . . . is not equally likely to occur in all populations'. It follows that, as with nut-cracking and other object manipulation, infanticide among higher primates, especially chimpanzees, may have group, that is, cultural, variation. Hrdy seems to favour an environmental correlation at least for hanuman langurs, that is, that ' . . . so far as langurs on the Indian subcontinent are concerned, animals . . . reared in similar environments would exhibit the same range of behaviour' and that langurs raised under different environmental conditions should be ' . . . genetically different and exhibit corresponding differences in behaviour'.

Following this, it is interesting that a number of cases of infanticide were undertaken by biting to the head. At Gombe, an adult female isolated a mother from her infant, chased her off, and then 'sat down and bit deliberately into the frontal bones of her victim, killing her instantly' (Goodall 1977, 267).

The following year the unfortunate mother gave birth to a son. As if she had not been unlucky enough the first time, the same adult attacked mother and son. After seeing off the mother, the attacking female 'seized the baby, ran off with him, and *bit into his forehead and face several times*' (ibid., 268, my emphasis). In a third incident – a disturbing *modus operandum* is emerging – an infant was seized during fighting with the protective mother. As the mother was held off 'Pom pulled the baby towards her and *bit into its head and face*, probably killing it' (ibid., 269, my emphasis). At Mahale the fatal injury was a bite to the face in two of three cases, and the first parts eaten of killed infants were the face and head, in addition to distal limbs (Hamai *et al.* 1992). The facilitation of infanticide by head-biting has even been observed among langurs (Hrdy 1999, 237). Given that other methods of killing infant-sized prey (as well as colobus monkeys and other typical prey species) include bashing against trees, biting of limb extremities, tearing and general feeding, the concentration of the head area is surprising. It is tempting to view this as a culturally varying behavioural trait.

To my knowledge, all observed cases of chimpanzee cannibalism arose out of infanticide. Because of their vulnerability infants are obvious targets of killing and cannibalism, but these phenomena are by no means restricted to them among higher primates in general. There are straightforward benefits to the practice of cannibalism, which at the same time results in the gaining of a meal by the perpetrator as well as the potential removal of competition. Goodall (1977, 279) cites four examples of cannibalism among three nonhuman primates. Two of these were observations (red tail monkeys and chacma baboons, both of which involved the consumption of infants) and the remains of a gorilla infant were found in the faeces of two other gorillas. In addition, Goodall reported cannibalism among male and female chimpanzees at Gombe. Interestingly, the behaviour of the cannibalistic chimpanzees differed from the behaviour they exhibited when eating from the corpses of other species. Only a few individuals present participated. In addition, 'abnormal patterns' of behaviour were observed (ibid., 279) that involved repeated charging at the body and flailing of it, which typically occur during the capture and killing of normal prey but not beyond its death. Other common aspects of such 'abnormal' behaviour include the poking and examination of the dead body (see below); pounding of its chest or head with fists; playing with or grooming of the body and abandonment of the body after relatively little of it has been consumed. The bodies of non-chimpanzee prey species, by contrast, tend to be utilised to the full. Once again there may be regional, 'cultural' differences here: at Mahale, individuals' behaviour around killed infants did not differ from that at normal prey kills, including prolonged consumption of the corpse, sharing and tolerated scrounging (Norikoshi 1982) and more consumption of the corpse occurred. Here, infanticide occurred mainly in the morning, following periods of intensive feeding and possibly stimulated by failed attempts to hunt other animals (Hamai *et al.* 1992). The elements of abnormal behaviour here I define as *morbidity*. Among the Gombe community at least they set apart the chimpanzee corpse from other prey, eliciting a very different set of behaviour among the living. It is such a separation in the behavioural realm around the corpse of a conspecific to which I shall return below, as the root of a core set of morbidity and mortuary behaviour.

The dead remaining with the living

A remarkable observation among the Bossou chimpanzees (Guinea, West Africa) by Tetsuro Matsuzawa in 1992 affords a glimpse of the transition of a young female from the world of the living to the world of the dead. Matsuzawa was able to observe the infant – the two-and-a-half-year-old Jokro – and her community for 16 days prior to her death and 27 days after, recording events on film (Matsuzawa 2003). Jokro's health deteriorated over the 16 days prior to her death. Some behavioural abnormalities were observed over this period of deterioration, notably relatively long periods spent grooming her mother, Jire, despite infants rarely engaging in grooming for long periods. As her illness progressed Jokro spent increasing amounts of time prone, and at one point her sister, Ja, tugged at her legs and tried to pull her up, trying to get her to play.

Jokro died on 25 January 1992. in the days prior to her death her mother had carried her on her back, Jokro barely finding the energy to hold on. The fascinating observation is that Jokro was not abandoned in death; Jire continued to carry her corpse for an entire month. On the day of her death, Jire carried Jokro's corpse in the same way she had carried her in life, with Jokro 'riding' on her back. After two days, when decomposition had begun, Jire had resorted to carrying Jokro face up on her back, swatting away flies that were attracted to the corpse, and three days after death, her body emaciated, she was being carried in the unnatural upside down position. Four days after death the corpse took on an unnatural shape, gases distorting the belly and signs of mummification appearing, yet Jire still carried her as if she were alive, in the prone position with her right side up. Several individuals showed curiosity about the corpse: the alpha male, Tua, sniffed it, and in the periods when Jire put it down numerous individuals peered at it. No individuals showed any signs of aversion or fear, and Jire began to pick fly larvae off of it. Even when climbing a tree Jire retained the corpse by wedging its wrist between her neck and shoulder.

By 15 days after death Jokro's corpse had completely dessicated, but Jire was still carrying it carefully, and still swatting flies away. Once, having set the body down, she lifted its head and peered into its face, then carefully groomed it as if Jokro were still alive. Later that day (9 February) an intriguing event occurred that again is reminiscent of the treatment of Jokro as if she were still alive. A six-and-a-half-year-old male, Na, played with the corpse

22

while the adults were taking a rest. He climbed a tree with the corpse, swinging it and allowed it to fall to the ground, whereupon he rushed to it, picked it up and once again carried it up the tree, dropping it once more. This curious activity was repeated a number of times, and appeared to Matsuzawa similar to two chimpanzees playing chase. Jire was watching this throughout yet made no attempt to intervene.

At this time Jire had resumed her menstrual cycle as she was no longer suckling Jokro. Twenty-one days after Jokro's death she was in oestrus, yet still did not abandon the corpse despite being the recipient of a courtship display by a five-and-a-half-year-old male. On 17 February – 23 days after Jokro's death – her corpse was used as part of an aggressive charge at Matsuzawa by an adult male. Normally, dead branches were used in such displays. These were usually treated carelessly, yet the aggressive male carefully changed the hands in which he was holding Jokro's corpse when he turned, finally abandoning the body, which was retrieved by Jire.

This use of the corpse for the same function as branches – both adjuncts to display – is of interest in the context of another observation made prior to Jokro's death. On 16 January, when Jokro was already displaying signs of illness, her sister, Ja, carried a log aloft in a tree, either on her shoulder or under her arm. Occasionally she stopped, set the log down, and patted it gently. Clearly, some association with the log was occurring in Ja's mind, and to Matsuzawa, this recalled the use of logs as dolls by local children. The use of objects as dolls by apes is well documented (W. McGrew pers. comm.). Whether or not the log was symbolic of a living individual is, of course, impossible to ascertain, but these two observations reveal a latent identification with inanimate objects and an association between these and a corpse, each 'assisting' aggressive display.

Further carrying of dead infants by their mothers was observed at Bossou in 2004 (Biro et al. 2010). A respiratory epidemic killed, among others, two infants, whose mothers continued to carry them for 19 and 68 days after death, during which time their bodies mummified (Figure 2.1). Responses to each of the dead were similar and reflect those that have been seen for Jokro, such as grooming of the corpse, chasing away of flies, and aspects of morbidity including touching, poking, handling and sniffing the corpses. In this fascinating case, two mothers from the same group were carrying their dead infants at the same time.

These compelling observations – the curation of the corpse for an entire month after death, and episodes of morbidity and use of the corpse in social situations – show very clearly that death was not necessarily the end, and that some individuals at least could retain a form of social agency for several weeks after death. One might explain the simple curation of the corpse either as the result of habit (W. McGrew pers. comm.) or as a relatively unconscious result of a mother's deep attachment to her dead child. Either of these could carry profoundly different meanings, but I suggest that the intellectual curiosity

Figure 2.1 The mummified corpse of infant Veve being carried by her mother Vuavua at Bossou, Guinea, in 2004. Vuavua carried this infant for 19 days after her death (photo courtesy of Tatyana Humle).

of others and the use (by others) of the corpse as a focus for social activity suggests that there is real meaning behind these observations. Further support for this notion comes from the fact that continuing to treat a corpse as if it were still alive could in some cases be risky, especially if it died of a contagious disease. Several other observations of the treatment of the dead among chimpanzees have been made, and we can now consider these in order to develop the notions of morbidity and simple mortuary activity.

Compassion: the roots of morbidity and mortuary activity?

As Boesch and Boesch-Achermann (2000, 250) state, there are '. . . many examples suggesting that chimpanzees evaluate their companions' state, anticipate their actions, and adjust their own behaviour to these social evaluations'. In stark contrast to the Cronos compulsions, chimpanzees are capable of displaying clear degrees of compassion towards the ill, injured, dying and dead, at least on occasion. In this sense, two extreme emotional states contribute to the emergence of morbidity, from emotions of aggression and compassion. Familial ties are strong in chimpanzee societies, often leading to the care of orphaned siblings and the injured that amounts to a degree of compassion (Goodall 1986). It appears that some understanding of the emotional state of other individuals underlies these examples (ibid., 385–6). As the bond between

24

mother and infant is particularly strong, it is not surprising that the disruption of this bond by death can lead to significant behavioural disturbances that may last several months (Goodall 1986, 101). Whether it is correct to ascribe a degree of this change of behaviour to a state of 'mourning' rather than to other biological and social reasons is debatable, but it demonstrates at the very least that the occurrence of death may cause profound changes in the social order, particularly among individuals with a close relationship to the departed. At Gombe, infants who lost their mothers, for example, displayed numerous symptoms of behavioural disorders in the physiological and behavioural realms, all of which began with signs of clinical depression. Some of the infants gradually recovered and reverted to normal behaviour, others didn't. The specific responses of these infants are summarised in Table 2.2. The premature loss of play activity and general lethargy are notable. I interpret these responses as expressions of mourning activity of a kind found among modern human groups. They certainly fall into the remit of definitions of mourning, grief and sorrow as defined by various English dictionaries.[2] Although for chimpanzees one need have recourse to no more complex an explanation than an outpouring of emotion following death, it is such behaviour, I argue, that would later evolve into formal (i.e. rule-regulated) mourning in human societies.

Table 2.2 Physiological and behavioural responses of infants to the death of their mothers among the Gombe chimpanzee community

Individual (infant)	Age at mother's death	Physiological symptoms	Behavioural symptoms
Sorema	14 months	Lethargy	Ceased playing
Cindy	3 years	Lethargy. Grew pot belly	Ceased playing
Pax	4 years		Whimpered when left behind during travel
Beattle	4–5 years	Grew pot belly	Play decreased. Whimpered when left behind during travel
Beethoven	4–5 years	Delayed scrotal development	Delayed sexual interest in females. Violent reaction when sibling mated
Merlin	4–5 years	Lethargy. Grew pot belly. Developed sunken eyes and grew emaciated	Significantly decreased play. Rocking, hair pulling, hanging upside down. Deterioration of social responses
Skosha	5 years	Grew pot belly. Delayed sexual maturation	Decreased play. Unusually fearful. Never carried an infant
Kristal	5 years	Lethargy	Significant decrease in play
Flint	8.5 years	Lethargy. Loss of appetite. Sunken eyes. Gastric trouble	Significant decrease in play. Nervous with large males

Source: Data from Goodall 1986, table 5.8.

Goodall (1971, 1986) reported on the death through illness of a newly born baby at Gombe, an excerpt from which I discussed in Chapter 1. The mother, Olly, had been carrying the ill infant, occasionally allowing her daughter, Gilka, to groom the infant, which she had not previously allowed while the infant was healthy. As the infant was clearly in pain, Olly paid careful attention to avoiding crushing the infants legs when she sat next to it. When he screamed in pain she would cradle him closely, moving on only when he fell quiet. When the infant died, during a storm, Goodall was 'amazed at the complete change in Olly's handling of her baby' (ibid., 196). Although she would carry the dead infant around the day after its death, her attitude was now careless, for example, flinging the limp body over her shoulder and occasionally allowing it to fall heavily to the ground. As Goodall observed 'it was as though she knew he was dead'. In addition to this, on six occasions at Gombe an elder sibling carried and/or cared for its younger relation after their mother died (Goodall 1986, 383). Such observations seem to suggest that chimpanzees are aware that death has occurred, perhaps even as soon as the event occurs (Teleki 1973, 92). If this is the case, it is difficult to see the numerous examples of morbidity as simply relating to efforts to test whether or not the individual is still living. They must mean more than this. Not that injury and death need always be met with compassion, however. At Gombe, several individuals behaved aggressively towards the elderly, incontinent male, Mr MacGregor, who had become paralysed from the waist down (Goodall 1971, 199–204). While individuals could, on occasion, groom the old male, they would also display near him and even attack him, despite the fact that he was helpless. No attempt was made to slow down for him either, and as he could only move by pulling himself along by his hands or by a peculiar somersaulting action, this meant that he was left behind much of the time. One can only guess at the stimulation for such behaviour; perhaps his bleeding, smelling, fly-ridden presence was a factor.

At Taï, compassion largely revolved around the apparent recognition that wounded individuals were in pain, which resulted in wounds being tended, usually by licking, occasionally for months or years after the attack that produced them (Boesch and Boesch-Achermann 2000, 247–8). Even more remarkable indications of abnormal behaviour that may be taken to include forms of compassion occur at deaths. For example, the death of an infant, Bambou, occasioned carrying, cradling, carrying of the body and soft calls:

Bambou's death

[On] the 23 March 1991, at 10.45, Bambou, a two-year-old male, died, probably by breaking his neck when he fell from a tree. His mother, Bijou, immediately carried him against her chest making loud alarm calls for 10 minutes. She climbed into a tree to avoid the arriving displaying males, who all climbed behind her to smell the motionless body. Bambou presented no visible wound. After 30 minutes, one hour after Bambou's death, she started to lay him on the ground for short periods of time, but continued to carry him all day long. On 24 March, the body of Bambou was swollen and smelling, but Bijou still carried him against her chest.

The next morning, she was eating in a tree, having left Bambou on a branch, when Kendo started warming up for a display against her. Brutus, in anticipation, came and took the dead Bambou in his arms. Bijou did not hurry to retrieve him and Brutus brought him to the ground, where he rested with him near Macho and Ulysse, who both smelled at the body.

At 9.20 the body was so swollen that the skin tore in several places and flies started to swarm. At 14.30, after a long rest, the group started to move and Bijou, hesitatingly, looked alternately at the group and at Bambou's body. Then, Mystère, Goma, Belle, Agathe, and Ondine came back to Bambou. Mystère and Serène, Ondine's infant and preferred playmate of Bambou, climbed a small tree above the body, looking down on it. Ondine, Mystère, Goma, and especially Serène made a few soft 'hou' calls. Then, they all left silently. At 14.56, leaving Bambou behind, Bijou started to catch up with the group. Brutus, Macho, Kendo, Fitz, and Ali were silently waiting for her. After 8 minutes, Bijou, alone, came back to Bambou and carried him over 20 metres. She hesitated in this way for another 80 minutes, until she left him definitively behind.

(Boesch and Boesch-Achermann 2000, 250)

The authors discuss the potential significance of the soft calls made by the females who returned to Bambou's corpse. As they note, if Ondine, Mystère, Goma and Serène were all aware that they would not see Bambou again, their behaviour makes sense. If they were not, then it is puzzling. Could it be that the apparent empathy that resulted in their action lies at the heart of this touching scene? As Boesch and Boesch-Achermann speculate (ibid., 250) empathy could well improve the chances of survival of wounded individuals. Care of the wounded would certainly contribute towards survival rates, but the investigation of the wounds of the dead may inform about causes of death. In this sense, this *morbidity* plays itself out through *compassion* arising out of *empathy*, and may ultimately relate to *survival strategies*.

The social activity occasioned by Bambou's death affected the behaviour of at least 14 individuals, that is those observed to interact with Bijou and her dead child. At least 16 individuals among the Gombe chimpanzees were observed interacting with the death of Rix (Teleki 1973). Rix was lying motionless in a small clearing, having died instantly from a broken neck as he fell from a fig tree. As Teleki (ibid., 84) notes, 'we are for some time uncertain whether he is dead or simply unconscious'. It is worth repeating in full much of the observations from the moment of his death, taken on 22 November 1968:

8.38 [am]. After travelling close on the heels of about 8 chimpanzees who walk for about 1 kilometer along trails through dense undergrowth, both observers arrive at a small clearing beneath riverine forest, near Kakombe Stream, as a number of chimpanzees explode into frenzied activity and raucous calling, including shrieks, cries, screams, waa barks and wraah calls. (These plus others that soon arrive comprise the large group of 16 individuals). A few stragglers rush forward to the site, where 6 males charge about in complex display sequences – their hair erect, swaggering bipedally, slapping and stamping the ground, tearing and dragging of vegetation, and throwing large stones. The high speed action and vocal din indicates extreme excitement and agitation in the entire group; the activity appears randomly directed, a melee of criss-crossing individuals, but actually concentrates around a small gully in which Rix's body is sprawled among the stones littering the dry stream bed. Continuous vocalisations, high in pitch and volume, and involving at least half the group at any one moment, blankets all other sound in the area, the clear wraah calls echoing off the steep valley walls. One or another individual occasionally pauses to stare down at the corpse, then launches again into long series of waa barks or wraah calls. Several adult males brush repeatedly past the body (without hard contact) in short but vigorous displays, Charlie and Godi [two of four young adult males] are among the most persistent vocalisers, while Hugo [past-prime adult male] and Humphrey [prime-adult male] perform displays most consistently. Amidst all this, individuals interact by embracing, mounting, touching and patting one another while making grin, whimperface, and other expressions. Aggressive, submissive and reassurance actions are performed at high frequency and intensity by nearly everyone present, with many swift shifts in demeanor. Charlie copulates with Melissa [the group's only mother with infant].

8.42. Intense group vocalization continues without pause, squeaks, screams, waa barks and wraah calls being predominant. After a brief lull in activity, Mike [the top-ranking prime-adult male], Humphrey and Hugo resume their vigorous displays, Hugo throwing several large stones (some at least 15 cm in diameter) in the general direction of the body, but not hitting it. Hugh [a prime-adult male] mates Melissa.

8.45. The excitement abates somewhat as displays and vocalisations become more sporadic. Mike, Goliath [the second past-prime adult male], Godi and others tensely approach and sit within a few meters of the body, some on the ground and others in the vines, thickets and trees nearby. Godi stares intensively at Rix and wraahs persistently; the others simply gaze at the corpse. Erecting his hair, Hugo walks closer and sits on a rock, looking at but not touching Rix, and is soon joined there by Hugh. Hugo then steps closer still, stands right next to the body, and peers down at it for several minutes; he then launches into a vigorous display away from the corpse. Hugh and Mike also charge away in different directions, ripping down vegetation as they run. Meanwhile, Godi and Sniff [an adolescent male] have been steadily wraahing while staring fixedly at the body from a distance of several meters; others join in the calling more sporadically. The three males return from their displays, soon followed by others, and at least 12 individuals now gather around the body, forming a rough circle of about 5–8 m diameter; all but Godi, who wraahs steadily, sit in silence and stare at Rix.

(Teleki 1973, 83–4)

The first signs that the group are calming down occur from 8.57am, nearly 20 minutes after Rix's death. A few individuals resume sporadic grooming and feeding, but there is more to come:

The silence is soon disrupted by screams from Willy [described as a paralytic adult male], whose interest in copulation is ignored by Melissa; Charlie and Godi then charge at Willy, who retreats into the bushes, and others add waa barks. Charlie afterwards mates and then grooms Melissa. A few resume to groom intermittently, but most sit and silently stare at the corpse.

(Ibid., 85)

Various examples of grooming and mating follow over the remaining two-and-a-half hours that the group remain in the clearing (one has at this point some sympathy for Melissa, who is the only female to be mated throughout the observation; by 11.27 am she has been mated with 18 times by 11 males!). Over this period individuals begin to leave the vicinity of the corpse and resume other activities, but there are still numerous examples of morbidity and social display:

9.08 . . . individuals [who aren't grooming or mating] continue to sit around the body, their attention occasionally wandering to other points . . . 9.15 . . . most attention still focuses on the corpse . . . Winkle [adolescent female] stays near the body, watching it consistently and intently . . . 9.32 . . . Humphrey stands on a branch, looks intently at Rix for some minutes, then climbs higher. Godi immediately replaces him, sits and looks fixedly at Rix, whimpering softly, hair erected. Suddenly, Godi stands and stamps briefly along

29

the [tree] limb with both feet, only to sit again and intersperse long whimpers with series of waa barks while staring at Rix . . . 9.37 . . . Godi descends and walks within a few meters of the body, looking intently at it while whimpering and waa barking, then does a long series of wraah calls; he appears extremely agitated, more so than any of the others. Several chimpanzees shift their attention back to Godi and/or the body. Sniff approaches and stares, walks hesitantly within a metre or so of the corpse, still staring, then steps slowly forward, leans close, and examines or sniffs Rix's head. Godi watches intently, now silent, and is joined by Satan [adolescent male] just as Sniff hurriedly retreats into a nearby tree, where he lies down, facing the body.

(Ibid., 85)

By 9.45 most individuals are once more engaged in other activities, although none are farther than 35m from the corpse. Several individuals still watch the body and other corpse-related activities still occur:

9.50 . . . Godi leans down from his [tree] limb, still watching the body, and again whimpers repeatedly. Humphrey pants to him, then displays through a tree, shaking and slapping branches . . . Godi displays briefly, stamping and flailing a branch towards the corpse . . . 9.55 . . . Godi, Satan and Winkle remain nearest the body, watching it silently.

(Ibid., 86).

From 10.00am various individuals (particularly Godi) continue to stare at Rix, and other individuals seem to stare at those investigating or watching the corpse, whereas activities apparently unconnected to the corpse increase in frequency. By 11.27 only Godi remained with the corpse. Departure occurred over some 25 minutes, with various individuals glancing or pausing for longer looks at the corpse. At 12.11 Godi is the last chimpanzee to inspect the corpse and at 12.16 the last individuals depart. The process of detachment has occurred over three-and-a-half hours.

Teleki presents an interesting analysis of this fascinating observation, noting that the specific reactions of individuals varied with age. Past-prime and prime adult males showed an immediate reaction but lost interest more rapidly than younger chimpanzees, who showed less initial reaction but showed interest in the corpse for longer periods. Most of the visual (and perhaps olfactory) morbidity was undertaken by four individuals – Satan, Godi, Sniff and Winkle – and *at no time was the corpse touched*. Adolescents seemed to show more of a tendency to investigate the corpse and thus morbidity may to an extent relate to age, although Godi, the male adolescent who showed by far the most interest in the corpse, was frequently in the subgroup that included Rix. The wraah calls were the most distinctive of numerous vocalisations noted, all others of which occur in many social contexts. The wraah calls, by contrast, were typically observed when two groups meet and when chimpanzees are disturbed by unfamiliar humans, and have also been noted on other occasions when they have seen dead baboons or chimpanzees. Teleki (ibid., 89) notes that these 'high-pitched, repetitious, plaintive wails . . . convey an intense emotional state which cannot be adequately communicated in words . . . [but which] . . . can be intuitively interpreted as danger and distress in most of the known contexts'. Intriguingly, however, wraah calls have not been recorded when the body of an infant is carried by its mother.

To a large extent, as Teleki (ibid., 91–2) notes, the cycles of interest (as expressed by vocalisation and display) and apparent distraction (as expressed by grooming and rest) follow a 'domino effect' in that the stimulus from one chimpanzee spreads rapidly to others. Teleki concluded that chimpanzee groups

Adult death

- were capable of swift and vigorous responses to the death of a familiar individual;
- may stay with a corpse for several hours after death, orienting much of their attention to the body;
- vary their individual responses depending on social standing and relationships;
- indulge in repeated examination of the corpse (i.e. morbidity);
- engage in persistent and intense vocalisation when a death is observed, among which wraah calls may have particular significance;
- may temporarily heighten group interaction and cohesion when exposed to death of a familiar individual.

Although such fascinating observations are very rare, this is not a unique observation. The peaceful death of a 50-year-old female, Pansy, in the midst of her captive social group at Blair Drummond Safari Park in Scotland was observed by Anderson *et al.* (2010). This included aspects of pre-death care by several group members as Pansy flagged, close inspection and what is interpreted as testing for signs of life at the moment of death, male aggression towards the corpse, all-night attendance on Pansy's corpse by her adult daughter, cleaning of the corpse and avoidance of the place of death despite the fact that it had hitherto been used frequently. Among the Taï chimpanzees very similar activities have been observed relating to the death of a chimpanzee that were recorded after a young female died following a leopard attack. At Taï, deaths from such attacks were fatal in four cases. The chimpanzees' reactions to these deaths are described as 'strikingly similar and different to their reactions to wounded individuals' (Boesch and Boesch-Achermann 2000, 249–50). The similarity between all four cases revolved around the dominant adult group members who appeared to 'require respect towards the dead of

31

other group members and particularly so of youngsters . . . [who were] . . . chased away when they came close'. In contrast to wounded individuals, the wounds of the dead were never licked. From these observations, Boesch and Boesch-Achermann (ibid., 250) conclude that 'chimpanzees differentiate between injured and dead individuals: the injured need to be tended, but dead ones do not'. The death of Tina, a young female, and the activity around the corpse, is worth detailed attention:

Tina's death resulting from a leopard attack

This anecdote is so extraordinary that we wish to give it here in detail. Tina was a 10-year-old juvenile female who had lost her mother some four months earlier. Together with her 5-year-old brother, Tarzan, she was since that time seen to be regularly associated with the dominant male, Brutus. Obviously, Tarzan wanted to be adopted by Brutus and he was even seen to share his night nest. Tina was more careful with Brutus, and followed him at a certain distance. Regularly, Brutus was seen in the forest followed by Tarzan, the Ali who Brutus had adopted some five years before, and finally by Tina.

On the 8 March 1989, at 7.45, Grégoire Nohon, a field assistant, was following the female named Bilou when he heard unusual calls nearby. Rushing to the spot with Bilou and the alpha male, Macho, he saw Brutus encircling the body of motionless Tina, some of whose viscera were visible through a cut she had on the belly. We can only guess how the attack had happened: the hidden leopard possibly let Brutus pass, followed by Tarzan and attacked Tina who was lagging behind. Brutus immediately reacted and the leopard fled. However within the first seconds of the attack, the leopard had killed her by biting through her neck, breaking the second cervical vertebra, as we could confirm later when examining the body. When Grégoire arrived, already four males and several females had gathered around Tina and there were loud calls.

We arrived at 8.17 and found six males and six females sitting silently near the body. The males showed some aggressive behaviour by displaying nearby and by dragging the corpse over short distances. Ulysse hauled it over two metres and Brutus pulled it back to where it had been before, about five metres away from the place where the attack had taken place. Kiri, Poupée, and Ondine, all high-ranking females, were nearby as well, and the smelled Tina's wounds and some leaves on the ground. Ulysse rapidly inspected one of Tina's hands, holding it. Four females arrived and very carefully approached the body, which was now guarded by the males and Ondine, the alpha female. Malibu smelled the body, while the infant Lychee was

32

chased away as she approached. Malibu, as had done all the others, smelled the body near the wounds, but did not lick them. At 8.30, Macho lay down and started to groom Tina for the first time. Brutus did the same from the other side. Ricci, a low-ranking female, smelled the body, but Ondine and Brutus chased her away. During a period of 1 hour and 20 minutes, Ulysse, Macho, and Brutus groomed Tina's body for 55 minutes. This was unusual because neither Ulysse nor Macho were ever seen to groom Tina alive and other males rarely did so for a few seconds. Salomé, the beta female, came and smelled the wounds and the genitals of the body.

Nearby, subadults and low-ranking females inspected with great intensity the place where the attack had taken place and where the ground showed clear traces of a fight with traces of blood. In contrast to what had happened when Ella was wounded by a leopard, not a single drop of blood was licked. Goma and Héra approached and they were allowed the smell the wounds, whereas their two infants were chased away by Odine and Brutus. At 9.07, Brutus gently tapped Tina's chin, while looking at her face. Macho and Ulysse later softly shook one of her hands and legs, looking at her face. It looked as if they were testing for some kind of reaction. Also, for the first time, Brutus and Ulysse started to play briefly together with their hands, showing a distinct play face, and then groomed her. Brutus played with Ulysse, Macho, and Ondine in this way several times, always very close to Tina and generally grooming her afterwards. It looked as if some tension among the guardians of Tina's body had to be released and this could explain the short duration of the play along with strong play face and laughter. Xérès wanted to approach, but Brutus chased her away and she fled screaming. Following some alarm calls by Kiri in the north, they moved on a bit and for the first time no chimpanzee was within two metres of the body.

From 10.10 onwards, the flies on the body were numerous and started to be a nuisance for the chimpanzees. They waved them away frequently and removed the eggs laid in the nose, eyes and wounds of the neck. Two hours thirty-eight minutes after Tina's death, Tarzan came to smell gently over different parts of the body and he inspected her genitals. He was the only infant allowed to do this. Then, Tarzan groomed her for a few seconds and pulled her hand gently many times, looking at her. At the same time, Brutus chased away Xérès and her juvenile daughter Xindra. 11.45: most chimpanzees stayed at 5 m from the body due to the impressive number of flies, the males coming closely intermittently to wave them away. Many chimpanzees left the site for a while to feed and came back later. All females of the community came back to look at the body, the males stayed generally for longer and Brutus remained without interruption 40 hours and 50 minutes, except for 7 minutes. In all, there were chimpanzees constantly with the body for 6 hours and 50 minutes.

After having inspected and weighed the body, we left it at the sites and checked regularly for the passage of a leopard or other scavengers. Two days after the attack, on the 10 March in the afternoon, a leopard had come and eaten part of the body. That day, the flies that had been covering the body, were gone. The leopard had cut the body in two through the lower back region and carried the lower part (with no open wound and relatively free of maggots) 15 m away and eaten it.

(Boesch and Boesch-Achermann 2000, 248–9)

Although this is a singular example, this fascinating episode is a useful heuristic with which to begin constructing core aspects of morbidity and mortuary activity. Several elements stand out in this case that deserve attention:

- unusual calls;
- Brutus at the corpse;
- several individuals gather around the corpse and make loud calls;
- several individuals sit in silence around the corpse;
- aggressive displays from males;
- dragging of the corpse over short distances (again by males);
- high-ranking females smell and investigate Tina's wounds and leaves on the ground, but do not touch or lick them;
- various inspections of the corpse;
- chasing away of low-ranking individuals;
- grooming of the corpse;
- playing, play-faces and laughter: relief of tension?
- removal of insects' eggs from nose and wounds;
- males generally stay longer at the corpse than females.

Some behavioural aspects may be ascribed to simple irritation (removal of insects' eggs from the corpse). Others, or greater interest, relate to communication (loud calls). Here one reaches an interpretative impasse: does this communication represent the expression of arousal and nothing else, or were the living actually communicating about Tina's death, the presence of her body, or their emotional reactions to these, in ways very similar to the responses of the Gombe chimpanzees to Rix's death? This is as yet impossible to ascertain, but for the purposes of the origins of morbidity and mortuary activity it is not so important; the point is that certain behaviour is elicited around the corpse. In time, it is such behaviour, from the starting point perhaps of an unconscious expression of arousal, that becomes coded with meaning and thus turns into deliberate cultural activity. It is interesting, however, that

34

most of the behaviour – and it is very varied and persisted for several hours after Tina's death – relates to social display and the investigation of the corpse that I have termed morbidity, to which I shall now turn.

Acknowledge of death

Morbidity

A number of individuals investigated Tina's corpse. High ranking females paid particular attention to her wounds, but unlike wounded individuals did not lick them, as if they were perhaps aware that this would do no good. Males, who seemed to use the occasion as a stimulus to social display, dragged the corpse over several metres. Several high-ranking individuals – those allowed access to the corpse – groomed it. Occasionally the tension is broken, by apparently deliberate play, play faces and calls. It is difficult to explain all of this behaviour as a simple attempt to check for signs of life. Dragging, inspection of wounds and grooming do not relate to this. Additional abnormal behaviour such as sitting around the corpse in silence, displaying, and the chasing away of lower-ranking individuals suggests that something very different is occurring at this death site.

Tina's body seemed to occasion two types of behaviour at Taï. On the one hand, the corpse seemed to stimulate the living into social displays – the death site became a social theatre. Perhaps this is not surprising, given that death brings the living into the context of the unknown. In doing so it offers the prospect of renewal and renegotiation of social relationships, assertions of power. Reading the account of activity around Tina's corpse at face value, it seems that access to the corpse – who gets to groom it, even if they didn't bother while she was still alive – is a central component of this social negotiation. A number of further examples of behaviour around the death of infants by infanticide or the corpses of chimpanzees killed by other agents suggest very strongly that the act of killing or the presence of a corpse occasions displays, vocalisations, grooming and other indications of a death-focussed social theatre. At Mahale, for example, during the consumption of an infant killed by adult members of the same group, spectating females intermittently groomed each other and vocalised (Norikoshi 1982, 69). Here, infanticide arose in a number of cases from male–male competition (Hamai *et al.* 1992) and in this sense it is perhaps no surprise that elements of social display are an integral part of the act.

In addition to the corpse-focussed social theatre among the living, there are also numerous indications of intense interest in the corpse. Dragging, smelling, staring into eyes, pulling of hands and investigation of wounds are commonly observed. Even some of the earliest recorded observations in this light attest to the amount of variability expressed in the realm of morbidity. For example:

Each [chimpanzee] spent only a few minutes nibbling meat [from the body of an infant chimpanzee], and few mainly on other foods

35

while *holding the carcass*. Figan played roughly with it, flailing and shaking, but Satan spent many minutes *gently examining and grooming it*. When Satan finally abandoned the infant, 6 h[ours] after the kill, only the legs, one hand, and the genital region had been eaten, although the carcass had changed hands six times. This suggests that the prey was less attractive as a food object, and *more an object of curiosity*, than other animals that Gombe chimps have been seen to eat.

(Bygott 1972, 410, my emphases)

Following the death of one infant at Gombe, its mother carried the corpse around, and, when the corpse had begun to smell, its sister carefully groomed it, put on a play face, and tried to play, putting the dead infant's hand on a ticklish spot on her neck (Goodall 1971, 197). Another example of active morbidity occurred during the case of cannibalism observed at Budongo, in which males 'showed great interest in touching and peering at the infant, which was apparently still alive' (Bygott 1972, 410). In another observation of cannibalism, this time at Gombe, Bygott (1972, 210) reports that after some two hours' of eating of an infant by two adult males, closely observed by three younger males, the powerful male, Humphrey

by now stopped eating and was playing with the carcass. In an exploratory manner he *peered, sniffed and poked at the carcass, groomed it, and often shook it by a leg or tapped its chest with his knuckles*, such activities often increasing in intensity to culminate in violent punching, biting, or flailing the carcass against the ground. There were frequent lulls when Humphrey lay back and rested and the other individuals *tentatively handled, groomed or nibbled the carcass*, though if too persistent they were mildly threatened by Humphrey or Mike.

(Bygott 1972, 410–11, my emphases)

Later, Humphrey having abandoned the carcass, 'Figan played roughly with it . . . [and] . . . Satan spent many minutes *gently examining and grooming it*' (ibid., my emphasis). The co-occurrence of apparently contradictory behaviour arising out of both compassion (grooming, gentle examination) and more Cronos compulsions (violent punching, biting) demonstrates that the emotional responses of the living to the corpse range between two extremes. In a second incident at Budongo, reported by Goodall (1977) two adult male chimpanzees (Figan and Jomeo) were encountered holding the body of a dead infant. A third adult male was chewing the hand of the infant. Following this,

Jomeo began to pull at the flesh with his teeth, but soon Figan seized the body and began to *display with it*, dashing it repeatedly against the ground and tree trunks. Next he sat down and pounded on its head with his fists, time and again. *He pushed his hands into the thoracic cavity, withdrew and sniffed it*, then wiped his hand on the ground. Then he abandoned the body. It was picked up by an adolescent male (Goblin) who slapped at it a few times then left it lying on the ground. A young female approached, *sniffed the body, and briefly groomed it*. Satan dropped the hand and it was picked up by Goblin who nibbled at it but seemed to eat a mere scrap, if anything. After this the chimpanzees moved away, leaving the remains on the ground.

(Goodall 1977, 264, my emphases)

Here, one can observe the behaviour of one individual (Figan) ranging from display and aggression to investigation of the thoracic cavity. Another (Goblin) exhibits aggression and minor cannibalism (nibbling 'a mere scrap'). A young female investigates the body before grooming it.

At Gombe, an aggressive female sat and watched as her mother and infant shared the carcass of an infant she had helped to kill. The unfortunate mother of the infant also watched the macabre feast, and 'once, she picked up some intestines which had been laid over a branch: she sniffed them and then carefully put them back' (Goodall 1977, 269). At Mahale, Nishida and Kawanaka (1985, 276) note that during an episode of infanticide and cannibalism, one unfortunate mother, Chausiku, 'stayed close to Kasangazi, and *watched intently* as he ate her offspring' (my emphasis).

During a case of adult aggression against an infant at Kasakela, no cannibalism was observed. Rather,

Satan approached [the mortally wounded infant], picked her up, *groomed her, and then gently put her down*. She was then 'rescued' by a 4 year old male . . . who *carried her around* for over an hour, constantly supporting her since she was too badly wounded, and probably too shocked to cling unaided.

(Goodall 1977, 266)

Following this, the infant is put down and picked up by other individuals, being carried for another hour and 40 minutes before finally being abandoned in some thick bushes. Was it just coincidence that the infant was abandoned in thick bushes? Or was it deliberate? An obvious interpretation was that the bushes would offer a degree of protection, at least from some predators. Can one see in this example a deliberate concern for the deposition of a wounded individual in a place of shelter and safety? If this is the case, then it may be seen as an example of structured abandonment, as defined in Chapter 1. If this occurs for the wounded and dying, it would not be unreasonable to expect the dead to be placed in such positions, at least on occasion. It is plausible that structured abandonment has deep roots.

Given that chimpanzees appear to be aware that death has occurred, probably at the time of the event or very shortly afterwards, instances in which corpses are carried as if they were still living infants, as opposed to being dragged over several metres, are surprising. As Hrdy (1999, 178) has noted,

> a monkey or ape mother will carry for days the limp, even decomposing, body of an infant that has died. Ever so gently, the mother lays the corpse on the ground while she feeds, fetching it when she is ready to move on. Gradually the distance between the mother and the object of false hope extends. She moves farther and farther away to feed. Elapsed time between visits to the now dessicated corpse grows longer until, reluctantly, one day, with obvious ambivalence, the mother leaves behind the fattened strip of fur.

At Gombe, after a group of adult males ate the flesh of a newborn infant for over two hours, the group moved on, with the dominant male carrying the carcass (Bygott 1972, 410). Similarly, after an infant's death through female aggression, Goodall (1977, 269) noted that the mother 'carried the body all the next day'. After an infant died of a short illness a mother carried it around the day after its death, although admittedly without the due care and attention she showed to it during its last days (Goodall 1971, 196). For much of the day this was the case, until when Goodall caught up with the small group the baby had gone – obviously abandoned.

If mothers and siblings are aware that infants are dead, yet continue to carry around their corpse with care, either they require additional time to release themselves from the boundaries of habit (in this case of carrying offspring) or they are participating in the expression of mourning. It is plausible that the latter is more likely; as infants generally cling to the fur of their mothers, this cannot in my opinion relate simply to the thoughtless retention of mothering instincts. Instead, I suggest that this is an act of *detachment*, occurring over several days. The origins of such detachment could arise from habitual activity, and one need invoke no particularly sophisticated development of this among chimpanzees, but a new form of behaviour has clearly emerged. Admittedly it occurs without any obvious cultural embellishment and is thus not a detachment *ritual,* but already represents a significant degree of mortuary activity.

Developing a model of core morbidity and mortuary activity

From the observations discussed above, some generalisations can be made that, I argue, form core elements of morbidity and mortuary activity. These are:

- *Cronos compulsions* of infanticide and cannibalism, either by males (inter-group), or females (intra-group), often arising from social tensions and possibly varying culturally;

- clear manifestations of *morbidity* by individuals with a close relationship to the deceased, including grooming of the corpse;
- manifestations of *mourning* including signs of depression, calls and carrying of corpses as an act of detachment;
- *social theatre* around the corpse, including controlled access to the corpse and display. These involved behaviour that is not witnessed in other circumstances (i.e. in the presence only of the living) and may therefore be termed 'funerary gatherings'. In addition, corpses may be used socially, for example as adjuncts to display such as in the case of Jokro.

It is clear how much of this behaviour is still practised among modern human populations, which, in my opinion, demonstrates the strong evolutionary link between these basic realms of morbidity and mortuary activity and their importance to the Hominidae. In particular, they can be separated into three overlapping realms. The realm of communication (calls, laughter, play) facilitates the flow of information about the corpse, individual and group responses to it, in addition to serving to alleviate the tensions that arise around deaths. The realm of social theatre relates to the living and facilitates the renegotiation of social ties in the new context presented by the removal of the dead individual from the living. The realm of morbidity arises out of an interest among the living about the dead body. Figure 2.2 divides up observed instances of abnormal behaviour based on the account of Tina's death discussed above. Ultimately this set of behaviours may be divided into those that belong to the realm of the living (the life sphere), and those that relate to an interest in and communication about the dead body (the death sphere). Interaction between the realms of communication, social theatre and morbidity will focus either on the living (i.e. the group) or the corpse, and will be mediated by the social personae of interacting individuals.

Given that the expressions of the basic behavioural realms seem to be found in differing chimpanzee groups as well as among most living human populations from diverse cultural settings, it seems justified to suggest that these represent deep-rooted core elements of morbidity and mortuary activity. While their expression would presumably vary specifically and regionally within populations (i.e. culturally), I suggest that these may be taken as an essential blueprint for the earliest manifestation of such behaviour among the earliest members of the Hominidae. It is very tempting to see in the grooming of corpses and other expressions of compassion, the investigation and dragging of the body and other aspects of morbidity, and the occasional aggressive actions that create deaths in the first place, the early emotional responses to the greatest metaphysical problem faced by humans: what happens beyond death. In this sense, herein lies the root of all cosmology and religious belief. In the next chapter, I examine aspects of the early hominid record for indications of when additional responses to death may have appeared, assuming these core elements were in some form or another in place since the Late Miocene.

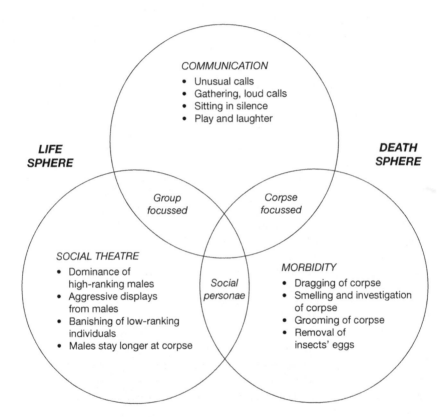

COMMUNICATION
• Unusual calls
• Gathering, loud calls
• Sitting in silence
• Play and laughter

LIFE
SPHERE

DEATH
SPHERE

Group
focussed

Corpse
focussed

SOCIAL THEATRE
• Dominance of
  high-ranking males
• Aggressive displays
  from males
• Banishing of low-ranking
  individuals
• Males stay longer at corpse

Social
personae

MORBIDITY
• Dragging of corpse
• Smelling and investigation
  of corpse
• Grooming of corpse
• Removal of
  insects' eggs

Figure 2.2 Developing a model of core morbidity and mortuary activity. Chimpanzee
actions around a corpse have been divided into the realms of communication, social interaction, and bodily interest, showing means of integration
(based on data from Boesch and Boesch-Achermann 2000).

3

FROM MORBIDITY TO MORTUARY ACTIVITY

Developments from the australopithecines to *Homo heidelbergensis*

Pliocene and Early Pleistocene core mortuary activity

In the last chapter I used chimpanzees as an heuristic to develop core elements of morbidity and mortuary activity, and suggested that these could extend to all hominids, given a degree of regional and chronological variability. The main elements of this core include Cronos compulsions, morbidity of the corpse, mourning and social theatre around corpses. I shall make the assumption here that one might expect various expressions of these for most or all of the genera and species of early hominids from the Late Miocene onwards. Thus, one might envisage elements of these being played out by *Ardipithecus ramidus* in the forests of Aramis, by *Australopithecus anamensis* around Lake Turkana, *Paranthropus boisei* in the grasslands of Olduvai, and *Australopithecus africanus* in the forests around Sterkfontein.

I appreciate that, as these core behaviours are largely non-material expressions of energy, or if physiological do not affect skeletal parts, searching for them in the palaeontological and archaeological record is futile. In this chapter, I shall endeavour to ascertain whether any other developments in mortuary activity may be detected for the earliest African hominids. I suggest that one element can – the movement and structured abandonment of corpses at particular points in the landscape, notably away from areas of intense activity. Perhaps it is too much to link this apparent concern with removing corpses from intensely used areas to the modern concern for the *rest* of the dead, but it may at least reflect some conscious desire among early hominids to afford the dead some special last resting place or minimise the chances that in death they become the meal of a scavenger.

[handwritten margin notes: "Among the oldest known hominins"; "-some evidence of bipedal but still arboreal"; "Next step past Ardipithecus - Almost fully bipedal - A lot of tremors and some master and threat twitch"; "Large bodied Australopithecan"]

41

The bodies on the hill: a case for structured abandonment in the Pliocene

The Hadar hominid sites are situated in Ethiopia's western Afar depression, spanning ~4myr to ~2.5myr in time (Aronson and Taieb 1981: see Figure 7.14) with important fossil material classified as *Australopithecus afarensis* dating to ~3myr to ~3.5myr (Johanson *et al.* 1982). Most hominid fossils at the Hadar sites are isolated and fragmentary, although generally bear minimal weathering suggesting that they have not been transported far (Johanson *et al.* 1982). Two localities, AL-288 and AL-333, stand out in preserving major associated hominid cranial and postcranial material. At Hadar locality AL-288, the partially complete skeleton of a small ~3.3myr-old *Australopithecus afarensis* adult usually identified as female (Al-288-1 'Lucy') is virtually unique in terms of the representation of nearly all anatomical parts (Johanson and Edey 1981; Johanson *et al.* 1982). Lucy came to rest in the sandy channel of a low energy stream. The lack of weathering on her remains, and the presence of only one carnivore gnaw mark (a depressed puncture on the pubic symphysis), indicate that it was not long before she was gently buried by sediment. Although the discoverers have speculated that she may have floated down the stream under gentle conditions before reaching her final resting place (Johansen *et al.* 1982, 380), the site yielded only a background fauna, which is not indicative of the locality being a major accumulation area. It is entirely feasible that Lucy came to be deposited on the edge of the sluggish stream, and was quickly covered by its overbank flood deposits. Such an interpretation could be forwarded for many of the partially complete hominin skeletons that span the Pliocene and Early Pleistocene, but it is admittedly impossible to eliminate any of these competing hypotheses. A more promising example of structured abandonment at Hadar can, however, be found at site AL-333, which deserves careful scrutiny.

Locality AL-333/333w at Hadar lies on a steep hill slope, the palaeotopography of which was similar during the Pliocene to how it is today. It has yielded from surface and excavated contexts ~200 hominid fossils representing an MNI of 13 individuals assigned to *Australopithecus afarensis* (Johanson *et al.* 1982) (Figure 3.1). Of these, nine are adult, two juvenile and two infant, and were recovered as a 7m spread within an excavation and collection area of 33m^2 (Aronson and Taieb 1981, 189). In terms of the numbers of individuals the site is remarkable, given the general rarity of hominid remains relative to other mammalian taxa at the Hadar localities (Aronson and Taieb 1981, 187). Pre-fossilisation weathering is minimal on all AL-333 hominid fossils, and is restricted to long-bone fracturing, which suggests that the carcasses laid around the site for only a few months before being covered with low-energy fluviatile deposits (Johanson *et al.* 1982; Radosevich *et al.* 1992). In terms of skeletal parts, preservation varies from single elements (e.g. the youngest individual, assuming modern human developmental patterns, is

Figure 3.1 AL-333 site under excavation (photo courtesy of Don Johanson).

represented only by the AL-333x-25 deciduous incisor) to closely associated and articulating postcranial elements such as finger phalanges, suggesting that multiple taphonomic processes were at work (Johanson *et al.* 1982, 380).

The hominin fossils were recovered from a sedimentologically diverse matrix, including silty clays and carbonate-nodules stratified 2m beneath the Denen Dora member, and date to ~3.2myr BP. One specimen, the cranium of an infant, was recovered from a fine sand matrix, and another was covered in an accumulation of carbonate balls of unknown origin (Aronson and Taieb 1981, 190). In all, the sedimentological matrix indicates that the hominid remains accumulated on a deltaic plain (ibid.; White and Johanson 1989) in the context of a stream-side woodland (Radosevich *et al.* 1992). A very low number of faunal remains were recovered from the site, far below the general background number of fauna typical of Hadar. Those that were consist solely of a few unidentifiable fragments, two crocodile teeth and several fish and rodent bones. The recovery of owl pellets suggests that this animal may have been responsible at least for the deposition of the latter. In short, a picture emerges from the palaeontology of an area of the landscape in which activity of any form was very minor. Despite the lack of gnawing marks on the bones, the disarticulated nature of most of the remains and their elongated scatter pattern within the 7m spread suggest that some scavenging of the corpses may have occurred prior to burial (Aronson and Taieb 1981, 190: although see below). If this did occur, however, it must have been very minor in nature, and the condition of most of the bones and the articulation of some of them

Even though scattered by chances animals. What are the chances the animals only killed hominids

indicates that carnivores were not the agents of deposition of at least 13 *Australopithecus afarensis* individuals. Given the intriguing lack of other animal remains, Johanson and Shreeve (1989, 87) note that AL-333 is 'just hominids littering a hillside'.

Controversy has surrounded the interpretation of this unique site. The large number of individuals represented here, the close association of postcranial elements, and the lack of fauna have suggested to some the notion that a single event accounted for the death and subsequent preservation of a single hominid group. This view derives from the assumption that as 'they had all lain in close proximity . . . [they had] . . . presumably died together' (Johanson and Edey 1981, 214). Preliminary interpretation of the AL-333 site was thus that the hominids had accumulated as the result of a flash flood (White and Johanson 1989, 98), but this became less tenable as the geology of the site was more clearly understood (Johanson *et al.* 1982). By contrast, Lewin (1987, 170) suggested that it is more likely that the individuals accumulated separately over 'a long period of time', although this interpretation fails to account for the taxonomic composition of the sample (White and Johanson 1989, 98). In addition, the lack of any other indications of animal or hominid activity at the site, the similar state of weathering of all of the fossils, and their restriction to a 7m spread makes this interpretation, in my opinion, highly unlikely. Given the absence of carnivore modification of the bones White and Johanson (ibid., 98) concluded that 'mammalian carnivores probably had little to do with the accumulation of hominids at site AL 333'. Aronson and Taieb (1981, 187) suggested that 'a hominid group was overcome, buried, and preserved by a Pliocene sedimentation-related event'. They speculated that, of the possible causes of death of the group, 'among the many possibilities, the group could have been either directly drowned and buried with little scattering by currents, or the group could have become bogged down while trying to cross the wet plain' (ibid., 191). Given the low-energy fluviatile activity indicated by the sedimentary matrix, a flood event powerful enough to kill a whole group including nine adults is difficult to envisage. Hypothetically, if this did occur, it is difficult to see how a catastrophic event so powerful could produce a scatter of at least 13 individuals including adults and infants within only a 7m spread, especially as the site is on a hill. It is also difficult to see how a group could become 'bogged down' on a wet plain only to die together. If the carcasses were indeed subjected to minor scavenging, then clearly the scavengers themselves did not become bogged down as their remains are not preserved at the site. As the hominid remains seem only to have lain on the site for a few months before sediments covered them, and as carcasses remain as a viable nutritious and non-toxic resource for a matter of only a few days (A. Chamberlain pers. comm.) the environmental conditions that prevailed as the hominid carcasses were deposited presumably would have prevailed during any scavenging episode/s. Thus, if scavengers did utilise parts of the carcasses they would have to have done so

Huge flaw in this : deg

during waterlogged conditions. Clearly then, they were able to vacate the site, and it may therefore be reasonably inferred that the hominids could have vacated it too.

For these reasons I reject depositional models invoking a single catastrophic event or localised bogging. In other words, I see no clear indications that the reason why at least 13 hominids came to rest at the site were out of the control of the hominids themselves. Thus, although the bodies came to rest in the open air and were not tucked into a naturally constrained locale such as a cave, this behaviour, if correctly interpreted, still fulfils the definition of funerary caching in that the bodies have been moved to the site of deposition, and in this case were still 'hidden' albeit in tall grass.

Cronos compulsions: cut marks from the australopithecines to *Homo heidelbergensis*

In Chapter 1, I defined the notion of 'Cronos compulsions' as the physical extension of morbidity to the extent of consuming parts of hominin carcasses, and discussed the various 'reasons' for this activity. There are no reasons, however, to believe that the 'Cronos compulsions' evident in the African and European Lower Palaeolithic relate specifically to ritual. There are severe interpretative limits to cut marks on hominin skeletal material, in that all one can demonstrate is that muscle is being removed from bone, or that the latter are being smashed or snapped. What happens after that must remain speculation. It need not follow that the soft parts removed from a corpse are consumed; it could be that defleshing per se was the desired activity, perhaps to 'clean' the bones for funerary purposes or disposal. If the intention was to consume the soft parts, then several reasons might lie behind such cannibalism, as noted by Fernández-Jalvo *et al.* (1999). Synthesising their list with non-cannibalistic reasons to deflesh corpses or parts of corpses, possible reasons for this activity are numerous and are listed in Table 3.1.

The Stw 53 partial skull from Sterkfontein provides evidence of carcass processing in the Plio-Pleistocene (Pickering *et al.* 2000). This takes the form of a partial cranium and associated mandible, excavated from Member 5 which is assigned to a late Pliocene date, and is taxonomically assigned either to *Homo* cf. *habilis* or to a late species of *Australopithecus*. Three sets of short striations occur on the right zygomatic and maxillary bones that are consistent with stone tool cut marks left by variously oriented deep incisions consistent with the severing of the masseter muscle. Pickering *et al.* rule out excavation damage, chewing damage and other activities, and suggest (ibid., 581) that the most likely explanation for this is the removal of the mandible from the cranium and therefore that Stw 53 was deliberately disarticulated, although they note that it is impossible to infer the reason for it; 'reasonable hypotheses include cannibalism, curation, mutilation and/or funerary procedures'. Other evidence of processing among archaic *Homo* groups is elusive. The partial

Reasons for canibalism

Table 3.1 Possible objectives, rationales and functions of conspecific defleshing. For the objectives behind removal of soft body parts see discussion in Fernández-Jalvo *et al.* 1999

Primary objective of defleshing	Main rationale	Example functions
Exposure/isolation/ cleaning of bone	Non-mortuary	Cleaning, purification Rationalisation (minimalising) for disposal
	Mortuary	Cleaning, purification and/or rationalisation for secondary burial Preparation for use in mortuary ritual Preparation of portable relics
Removal of soft body parts	Non-mortuary	Nutritional: occasional (e.g. response to stress) Nutritional: regular (e.g. hominins are part of the diet) Pathological: individuals are compelled to consume (e.g. mental disease) Aggressive social: e.g. victory display, intimidation Passive social: e.g. to obtain the strength/ nature of consumed
	Mortuary	Detachment ritual retaining element of attachment Detachment ritual involving element of transformation Means of ritual curation of the dead

remains of several individuals classified as *Homo erectus* recovered from Zhoukoudian Locality 1, China, bear marks that have often been seen as indicative of cannibalism although they are entirely consistent with carnivore breakage and bioturbation (Boaz *et al.* 2004).

Cannibalism and Cronos compulsions

The concept of Cronos compulsions – defined in Chapter 1 – is of use here, I argue, as it applies to the morbid interest in defleshing carcasses whether or not the primary reason for doing so is to clean bones as part of a mortuary ritual, or to remove soft parts for consumption. Dichotomies of this nature may well describe adequately the differing reasons why hominins defleshed carcasses, but they will not capture the subtle emotional rationale for such behaviours, which after all need not be mutually exclusive. The concept is intended to elaborate this notion of interconnectedness of the reasons for processing bodies, a number of which are noted in Table 3.1. Even if the original reasons for defleshing lie in nutritional cannibalism, other 'non-prosaic' reasons could easily arise out of these, particularly given the levels of morbidity one might expect for early hominins based on the chimpanzee analogies discussed in Chapter 2. These could simply relate to an unconscious 'compulsion' to taste part of a corpse, perhaps in the context of morbid exploration of a fresh carcass, to nutritional cannibalism. It is easy to see how, ultimately, ritual use of the practice would arise, and as I argue in Chapters 6 and 7 this had certainly arisen in the European Mid and Late Upper Palaeolithic. As Hovers and Belfer-Cohen (in press) have noted, 'it is possible that the concept of treating the bodies of dead conspecifics was ingrained in the behavioural repertoire of Middle Pleistocene ancestors that gave rise to both Neanderthals and AMH [anatomically modern humans]'.

Feeding: Cronos compulsions at the Atapuerca Gran Dolina

Cronos compulsions are clearly in evidence in late Lower Pleistocene deposits at the Gran Dolina at Atapuerca, Burgos, Spain (Bermúdez de Castro et al. 1997, 2004; Fernández-Jalvo et al. 1999). In contrast to the single example from Sterkfontein, several hominin remains from the Gran Dolina bear indications of processing, and therefore provide a better opportunity to explore the possible meaning of soft tissue removal among early hominins. The remains of ten individuals assigned to Homo antecessor have been recovered scattered randomly over a space of ~7m² within the 30cm thick Aurora stratum of the TD6 stratigraphic unit, in association with Oldowan-like stone tools and a faunal assemblage representing an MNI of 22 large mammals (Bermúdez de Castro et al. 1997, 2008). These were stratified one metre below the Brunhes-Matuyama palaeomagnetic boundary and thus pre-date 780,000 BP, and are most probably close in age to 800,000–850,000 BP on the basis of supplementary ESR and U-series dating and micromammalian biostratigraphy (Parés and Pérez-González 1999; Falguères et al. 1999). As with the faunal remains, most of the hominin material from the TD6 stratum bear hominin-induced damage. Percussion, chopping, and 'peeling' – similar to bending back and snapping a twig – are in evidence on a number of bones that were recovered scattered through the deposit in association with stone tools and fauna remains. In an exhaustive study of the hominin material, Fernández-Jalvo et al. (1999) identified fractures, snapping ('peeling'), percussion marks on long bones relating to the removal of marrow and cut marks relating to dismemberment and the removal of muscle, on both cranial and postcranial elements. The location and form of these marks are very similar to those left on faunal remains at the site (Díez et al. 1999), and Fernández-Jalvo et al. note that the Aurora stratum is characterised by analogous butchery patterns for both fauna and hominins, similar techniques for marrow extraction and similar patterns of discard (i.e. random scattering), and conclude that the modifications represent butchery practices aimed at the removal of meat and marrow, that is, to the practice of nutritional cannibalism (ibid., 620).

Clearly, one need not invoke any specific mortuary concerns to interpret what is best explained as a case of nutritional cannibalism, whether for the purposes of short-term survival or as a longer-term element of the diet. Bermúdez de Castro et al. (2004, 38) favour the regular incorporation of hominin meat in the regular diet of *Homo antecessor*, given that the temperate climate that prevailed during the period of deposition as well as abundant available game suggests that resource-stress is unlikely, although such a broad interpretation does not take into account short-term crashes in game populations, or seasonal stress. As they note, however, it can be seen as a feeding site (ibid., 38). Whatever the case, one need not interpret this as deliberate structured abandonment; like the faunal remains at the site, the hominins are best explained as having been disposed of as the remains of feeding. One can take interpretation a little further, however. It is of interest that several hominin individuals show signs of processing. These are found at several distinct stratigraphic levels of the Aurora stratum rather than as one depositional event, and although one cannot estimate the actual number of times carcasses were processed at the site or how much time elapsed between these events, one may at least assume that cannibalism was practised repeatedly at the site, possibly over a considerable period of time (Bermúdez de Castro et al. 2008). Thus, however imprecise the chronological data, the processing at the site cannot be explained simply as a 'one-off' (and thus perhaps unique) event; some degree of repetition is in evidence that suggests that the behaviour was more structured in the regional society of *Homo antecessor*. Cronos compulsions seem to have been deeply and perhaps routinely embedded in the subsistence behaviour of at least one hominin group at this time. Clearly, this behaviour required an intimate knowledge of the hominin body, its musculature and other soft tissues, as well as the ability to remove these with the skills used routinely on faunal remains. Given this, one might sensibly suspect that other aspects of Cronos compulsions as well as a degree of morbidity at least were practised from time to time. Small beginnings, but it should be clear from this how aspects of the core elements of morbidity could, on occasion, result in behavioural patterns that are visible in the archaeological and palaeontological record and that could, given sufficient cultural stimulus, become elaborated in a relatively simple fashion. It would be incorrect to draw any hard lines between simple (albeit repeated) feeding behaviour at such sites, and more formalised mortuary activity, but it should at least be clear enough that one might lead to the other. The morbid interest in the corpse – in the case of the examples discussed here rather than in Chapter 2, which focussed on tissues, their nature, their removal and use as a resource – is inseparable from the social reorganisation that occurs after death. Unless the individuals that were processed at the Gran Dolina derived from a rival social group and therefore required or elicited no mortuary activity, one must envisage a situation at the site where social activities of the likes observed among chimpanzees in Chapter 2 occurred alongside the more prosaic

48

concerns of meat removal and consumption. It is in such complex interactions – quite literally of the physical and theatrical consumption of the corpse – that a base for more recognisably 'human' mortuary activity arises. *to Neandrtal*

heidlebursensis → precursor

Archáic Homo sapiens *and defleshing*

Evidence for defleshing around 600,000 BP occurs on the Bodo cranial remains, from the Awash river valley, Ethiopia. These have a well-established Middle Pleistocene antiquity and are associated with Acheulian artefacts (White 1986). The specimen has usually been seen as an archaic *Homo sapiens* with some indications of a transitional status from the *Homo erectus/ergaster* grade, and is often classified as *Homo heidelbergensis*. At least 25 linear cut marks are recorded in 17 different locations on the frontal part of the cranium, notably on the left zygomatic, the orbits and the left supra-orbital area, and wear on several areas of the cranium may well have obscured further marks. White (ibid., 508) argues that the symmetry and direction of cut marks in the frontal region suggests intentional defleshing of the Bodo individual by a hominin using a stone tool, and was able to match these to the location and nature of cut-marks on the crania of gorillas that had been defleshed with steel knives in the nineteenth century. As with the Stw 53 cranium, it is impossible to distinguish between several interpretations of this defleshing; it merely provides another point in time, enough to suggest that hominin soft tissues were deliberately removed at various points in time during the Lower and Middle Pleistocene.

Caching the dead: the origins of funerary space at Atapuerca?

From the discussion above it is clear that episodes of carcass processing occurred from time to time throughout the Lower and Middle Pleistocene, during which one might expect at least simple aspects of morbidity and even mortuary activity to have occurred. But, as we have seen, the data are limited and ambiguous; they are open to several interpretations and it would be unwise to infer much from the existing material. From the point of view of archaeo-logical visibility, identifying the point in time when such activities became structured in space may be more profitable. In such a case, the repeated use of a specific point in the landscape for these activities, and the robust repre-sentation of these activities on separate occasions and for several individuals, in a context where other interpretations can be eliminated, would make a more convincing case that structured mortuary activity was employed as a cultural practice. This situation arises, I suggest, after 500,000 BP, once more in the karst environment of Atapuerca.

More than 4,000 fossils representing at least 28 individuals assigned to *Homo heidelbergensis* have been recovered from a Middle Pleistocene silty clay within the Sima de los Huesos (Pit of the Bones) at Atapuerca (Arsuaga *et al.*

1997a, 2003; Bermúdez de Castro *et al.* 2004) (Figure 3.2). These have been interpreted as evolutionary forebears of the Neanderthals (Arsuaga *et al.* 1997b). Original U-series and ESR measurements suggested an age of 300–400 kyr BP but U-series dating of a speleothem overlying the hominin remains suggests an age in excess of 480kyr BP at 2σ, at least if assumptions about the stratigraphic relevance of the speleothem are correct (Bischoff *et al.* 2003). The dates are consistent with biostratigraphic data from the same context such as lion *Panthera leo fossilis* and a large wolf *Canis* (cf. *mosbachensis*) (García *et al.* 1997), and from an overlying mud breccia that contains the remains of the Middle Pleistocene bear *Ursus deningeri*. Whatever the age of the material (400,000–500,000 BP) the site forms an important Middle Pleistocene sample highly relevant to the development of mortuary activity.

The hominin remains were recovered from the silty clays from several areas of the cave, both on an inclined ramp (the 'rampa') and from a more horizontally bedded deposit in the Sima itself, but refitting of fragmentary hominin remains from several areas shows that the remains derive from the same broad sedimentological context (Arsuaga *et al.* 1997a). Based on the justified assumption that dental maturation rates were similar to those of modern *Homo sapiens*, the age profile of the hominins is skewed towards adolescents and prime-aged adults, with a low representation of adults and children (Bermúdez de Castro and Nicolás 1997), and the variable morphology of mandibles suggest that at least 12 male and 8 females are represented (Bermúdez de Castro *et al.* 2004, 36). The sample seems originally to have derived from relatively complete skeletons, and four shafts that were the potential sources of the hominin material are known, of which three are nowadays blocked (Arsuaga *et al.* 1997a; Andrews and Fernández-Jalvo 1997).

How the hominin remains accumulated and what this implies for the function of the site is debatable, but many factors can be eliminated. The noticeable lack of stone tools recovered from the site shows that it was not a prosaic camp or feeding site (Arsuaga *et al.* 1997a). The one biface recovered from the shaft – an amygdaloid-shaped, plano-convex form on quartzite – has been interpreted as ritual in nature but it is impossible to verify this claim, and as this natural trap clearly claimed a large number of animals there is no surprise that it might also have claimed the odd non-organic item from the landscape above where prosaic hunting and butchery presumably were taking place. Neither was the accumulation due specifically to carnivore activity, as the remains of carnivores were remarkably low, restricted to *Vulpes vulpes* (MNI=23), *Panthera* sp. (MNI= 4), *Lynx pardina spelaea* (MNI=2), *Felis sylvestris* (MNI=2), *Martes* sp. (MNI=3) and a small mustelid (MNI=2) (García *et al.* 1997). Of these, only *Panthera* or *Felis* could potentially have accumulated prey as large as hominins, and if carnivores were responsible for the accumulation one might reasonably expect the presence of herbivores, which are, however, completely absent (Andrews and Fernández-Jalvo 1997). As carnivores were apparently able to remove some of the smaller hominin skeletal elements

Figure 3.2 Skull 4 under excavation in the Sima de los Huesos, Spain (copyright Javier Trueba/Madrid Scientific Films and with thanks to Juan-Luis Arsuaga).

it seems that the site did not function as a one-way natural trap in which hapless bears and hominins found themselves and were subsequently unable to seek exit (Andrews and Fernández-Jalvo 1997, 215). Neither did the hominins simply fall down a hole in the landscape: the extremely high degree of breakage of the hominin remains – far in excess of breakage patterns observed experimentally – demonstrates that the fragmentary state of the remains is not simply due to their having been thrown down the 13m-deep shaft (ibid., 215). If this were the case one might also expect a more complete representation of all skeletal parts, in addition to clearer preservation of anatomical articulation, but instead smaller bones are missing and the whole assemblage is jumbled (Fernández-Jalvo and Andrews 2001, 230).

Andrews and Fernández-Jalvo (1997) undertook a taphonomic investigation of the hominin fossils excavated from the Sima's undisturbed sediments. The greater majority of the hominin fossils are broken, with an essentially even representation of green (fresh) and dry-stick breaks, the latter having occurred probably not too long after deposition. This is not a site at which cannibalism was practised: cut marks are completely absent (scrape marks on some of the hominins' anterior dentition were caused by accidental scraping with stone tools in life, probably when cutting meat held between the hands and teeth; Fernández-Jalvo and Andrews 2001, 229; Lozano-Ruiz *et al.* 2004). In addition to the breaks, the most abundant surface modifications on the fossils are pits and punctures that derive from carnivore activity, and 50 per cent of these are found on long bone shafts. The size distribution of the marks is very close to that left by foxes on the bones of sheep in modern samples. This is perhaps not surprising as fox is the dominant carnivore in the deposit, although the presence of larger size of puncture marks on some of the more robust bones shows that another, larger carnivore, probably lion, also had access at least to some material (ibid., 208).

Clearly, this scavenging occurred after the hominin carcases were deposited at the site, and bears no relation to the cause of their accumulation. Bermúdez de Castro *et al.* (2004, 36) see the sample as neither attritional (as it possesses a high percentage of adolescents) nor catastrophic (as it almost completely lacks infants and children and as it has an abnormally high percentage of adolescents and prime adults). Assuming that the remains were deposited over a relatively short period of time, and that they represent a random sampling of the original life population of the area, Bocquet-Appel and Arsuaga (1999) suggested that they display a catastrophic mortality pattern, arguing that the extreme under-representation of juveniles that one would otherwise expect to be represented in a catastrophic mortality profile relates to site taphonomy, that is, to the differential destruction of relatively fragile bones and, as Andrews and Fernández-Jalvo (1997) noted, the marks of scavengers – particularly *Vulpes vulpes* – are present on 50 per cent of the hominin remains. Bocquet-Appel and Arsuaga emphasised the dominance of adolescents and prime adults in the sample, noting that 'the sample of individuals comes from a segment of the age-pyramid whose members, at first sight, are physically resistant and mobile . . . normally able to run away from the impact area of a catastrophe' (ibid., 335), and thus concluded that the sample represents a group of physically fit individuals who were 'on the run' from a catastrophe of some form, who 'under severe privation . . . stopped in the shelter exhausted' (ibid., 336) and died. They reached a similar conclusion about the accumulation of Neanderthal remains at Krapina that will be discussed in Chapter 5. What this catastrophe was is unspecified (it could have been inter-group violence, disease or a crash in resources, for example) and in this sense its nature is irrelevant: the point is that, according to Bocquet-Appel and Arsuaga, the population lucky enough to escape the catastrophe found themselves at the cave, exhausted, and ultimately doomed.

It is important to note that theirs is an interpretation of a demographic profile, not a theoretical exploration of a taphonomically complex site at which hominin remains accumulated in relatively exclusive circumstances. Critical to their argument is the assumption that the hominins 'all died together at the same time' (ibid., 335). Taphonomic studies of the bones suggest that this was, in fact, not the case: 'un témoignage des fractures de bords pui suggère un mélange d'os fossils et fraise incompatible avec la mort simultanée des 32 individus' (Fernández-Jalvo and Andrews 2001, 230). As noted above, one can also eliminate on taphonomic grounds the possibility that the hominin carcasses were thrown down the shaft. The age profile of the SH bears – of which the greater majority accumulated later in time – appears to be catastrophic (García *et al.* 1997), but in contrast it does appear that the hominin profile is not. On the basis of differing stages of weathering of the hominin fossils it seems that they were accumulated on a number of occasions, over a time span of perhaps as much as several thousand years (Y. Fernández-Jalvo pers. comm.). It is, however, generally agreed that the hominin remains were accumulated anthropogenically (Arsuaga *et al.* 1997a; García *et al.* 1997; Andrews and Fernández-Jalvo 1997), albeit over a potentially long period of time. If this was for funerary purposes – and I shall come to this below – one certainly cannot talk of the use of the cave as some sort of proto-cemetery. Given the varying stages of weathering of the bone surfaces, the significant fracturing of all remains, the presence but not abundance of indications of carnivore processing and the absence of evidence of serious carnivore accumulation, the most sensible interpretation is that the hominin carcasses were brought to the cave or its exterior (perhaps its original entrance – which remains to be discovered (Fernández-Jalvo and Andrews 2001)) and were left exposed in or near the shaft, and on occasion at least foxes and lions had access to them when they were still a scavengeable resource. These activities would have begun the process of carcass disarticulation; it would have continued as the remains were dragged or fell further into the cave system, and the process would have been further intensified by mud flows within the cave itself (ibid., 232). The result would have been the jumble that is recognised today.

This interpretation certainly differs from the image of a number of dead adults being thrown down the shaft followed by a single biface (Bermúdez de Castro et al. 2004), and one cannot demonstrate therefore that this was a site of collective disposal of the dead or its associated rituals. Bermúdez de Castro et al. (ibid., 37) have suggested that 'the finding of this unique tool together with the corpses of 28 individuals is difficult to explain as a natural accumulation, that occurred without human intervention', but really forward no case other than its 'exceptional characteristics' (i.e. it is well made: ibid., 37) as to why this should be so. While one cannot rule out the possibility that this as yet unique find was in some way a deliberate (and therefore possibly ritual) deposit, to argue that it should be so on the case of its uniqueness and on the grounds that it is well made (as thousands of Lower Palaeolithic bifaces were) is unconvincing. One should certainly isolate discussion of the biface from the accumulation of the hominin remains: there is no a priori reason to associate it with the fossils, and a parsimonious explanation of its presence could simply be that it was in the pouch of one of the dead who were brought to the site or a chance loss from one of the living who left them there. As Fernández-Jalvo and Andrews (2001, 230) conclude, the Sima de los Huesos 'ne pouvait être un site magique', noting instead that several reasons could have resulted in the deposition of the carcasses in the cave's entrance, such as a need for hygiene. New research on the fossils is showing that a large number of them show evidence of pathologies – possibly relating to unpleasant, painful and disfiguring disease (Y. Fernández-Jalvo pers. comm.) – which may explain a desire to dispose of the corpses at a specific place and in a way distinct from usual processes of abandonment or disposal. The frequency of tempero-mandibular joint (TMD) disease in the sample is indeed high, but high frequencies of TMD disease are not unusual in skeletal samples of different ages and there is, as yet, no compelling reason to assume that the levels of TMD disease observable in the Sima sample would have caused significant pain, perhaps only some discomfort such as clicking of the jaw whilst chewing (A. Chamberlain pers. comm.).

Whatever the specific reason for why the dead came to rest in the Sima, can one fully discount the possibility that this place in the landscape was associated over a long time period with the disposal of the dead (or at least some of them)? It could potentially reflect a number of isolated occurrences of structured deposition of carcasses – individual caching events – resulting from the cultural association of a specific place with an opportunity to dispose of the dead. If this is correct, the Sima may provide a critical clue as to how humans came to dispose of the dead in certain places and thus brought about a geographical element to mortuary activity. It is easy to envisage how hominins may become aware of this natural trap in the landscape; the relatively few carnivores recovered from the site were presumably attracted to it as a place of scavenging opportunity, attested by tooth marks on both bear and hominin remains. It was clearly known to the Homo heidelbergensis groups operating in the area, although the lack of stone tool cut marks on the bones suggests that its importance to them was not mainly for scavenging. Perhaps it may even have become known as a place of death of other animals such as bear, and perhaps this is why it came to be a place of hominin death. If this is correct, the origins of places of funerary caching is as places of *disposal*: liminal, unpleasant and possibly dangerous places, associated with decay and disease; places to be avoided, but places where the dead can be removed from the ordinary places of life. When this point is arrived at, the landscape has become dichotomised: places of life, and places of the dead.

Further funerary caching by early Neanderthals at Pontnewydd Cave, Wales?

A similar possibility can be found, intriguingly around the same (very broad) time, on the northwestern periphery of the early Neanderthal world. The partial remains of at least five and possibly up to 15 Neanderthals were deposited at Pontnewydd Cave, Wales somewhere before 225ka BP, that is, in MIS7 (Aldhouse-Green 2001). They were mostly male and under 20 years of age. Aldhouse-Green reasons that it is pushing interpretation to see carnivores depositing this amount of human material, and is 'more inclined, therefore, to see these remains at Pontnewydd as arising from a conscious deposition of the dead in the dark recesses of the cave' (ibid. 116). It is of course impossible to establish this with any confidence, given the highly fragmentary and incomplete nature of the remains, although one should remember that the Sima de los Huesos material discussed above – which is widely seen as an anthropogenic accumulation – is dominated by teeth and phalanges (Andrews and Fernández-Jalvo 1997).

Castel di Guido, Italy

Seven fragmentary remains representing 2–6 hominins have been recovered from the edges of a brook or lake at Castel di Guido near Rome (Mariani-Costantini *et al.* 2001). These bear archaic (*erectus*-like) and progressive (Neanderthal-like) features, and are associated with Acheulian lithics and a temperate faunal assemblage that can be assigned to Marine Isotope Stage 9 (~300,000–340,000 BP). Six of the fragments bear incisions, and particularly deep, v-sectioned incisions are visible on the outer surfaces of a parietal and an occipital fragment. Carnivore gnawing (which also appears on the bones) and sediment wear (again, visible on the bones) cannot account for these clearly delineated marks, and they bear close resemblance to those produced by stone tools. Their location indicates the removal of major muscles and ligaments, particularly in the temporalis area. One fragment – a femur – bears no such marks, and it therefore seems that the cut marks represent the defleshing of the head.

Summary: the development of morbidity and mortuary activity through the Lower and Middle Pleistocene

Two axes of change mark the development of mortuary activity from the earliest hominins through to the early members of the genus *Homo,* focussed on the body (as increasingly varied expressions of morbidity and thus Cronos compulsions) and on space in the landscape (as the development of funerary caching). Examples of body processing are noticeable from the earliest hominin record and it is probably fair to assume that these represent a modest elaboration of the morbidity witnessed among chimpanzees and expected among Miocene and Pliocene hominids and hominoids. If the interpretation of AL-333 as a place of deposition of bodies in long grass is correct, this would indicate that the specific association of *places* with the dead has an exceptionally long antiquity. Perhaps this is not surprising; early hominins were, after all, repeatedly attracted to other locales such as water holes and other areas where foraging opportunities were available, and we have seen in Chapter 2 how chimpanzees avoid certain aspects of sites where their conspecifics have died, and behave differently towards the wounds of the dead than towards those of individuals who have survived injury. In this sense there is probably an inevitability among hominins at some point in their evolutionary history to invest certain locales with meaning about the disposal of the dead. It thereafter remains to seek specific locales where the dead can be hidden away, or even to create small spaces where they can be hidden, and these developments can be traced to the earliest populations of *Homo sapiens* and to *Homo neanderthalensis,* as I shall argue in the next chapter.

Not just treatment of bodies but of the idea of place

4

FROM FUNERARY CACHING TO THE EARLIEST BURIALS OF EARLY *HOMO SAPIENS*

Introduction

In Chapter 3 I discussed the perpetuation of Cronos compulsions and the unfolding of funerary caching among pre-Neanderthal archaic humans. The practices differ, in the sense that the first concentrates on the body and arises out of morbid interest, and the second involves the deliberate movement of the body to a locale identified as a place of disposal, which at some point in time would become meaningfully associated with the dead. It seems to me quite likely that the repeated deposition of at least 28 individuals around the Sima de los Huesos indicates that such meanings were already in existence around half a million years ago. From this point, however, little further variability in funerary activity can be identified in the archaeological record until after ~120,000 BP, when the first examples of simple inhumation – the *deliberate creation* of a space in which to deposit and cover a corpse – are evident. In this chapter I explore the early inhumations of *Homo sapiens*, from the earliest examples down to later forms ~50,000–60,000 BP. This is a long period of Upper Pleistocene time and it would be premature to link these together as a strong and meaningful tradition, but it seems at least fair to group them together for heuristic purposes. Geographically, the pattern takes us from the fringes of Africa as far east as Australia. Given this range, the chronology and dispersal patterns of our own species, it is possible that simple inhumation, at least at times, was a fundamental part of the behavioural repertoire of *Homo sapiens* as it dispersed out of Africa for the first time. The processing of body parts – Cronos compulsions – continues alongside this practice.

Dating of specimens discussed in this chapter is somewhat more precise than for those of the African and Eurasian Middle Pleistocene. The 'archaic' *Homo sapiens* skeleton of Skhūl 9 may be the oldest burial known as yet (Stringer 1998) although it is conceivable that the Tabun C1 Neanderthal is as old as 120ka BP (e.g. Grün *et al.* 1991; McDermott *et al.* 1993) and in any case the dating of the entire Tabun sequence is a fiercely debated issue (e.g. Millard and Pike 1999).[3] With the exception of the Sima de Los Huesos sample from Atapuerca discussed in Chapter 3, it is only from the substages of MIS5 that near-complete human remains are found on enclosed sites in Eurasia, and only from late MIS3 and MIS2 (i.e. the Mid Upper Palaeolithic) that they are found on open sites. Prior to this, as Gamble (comment to Gargett 1989) has noted they are 'truly bits and pieces'.

Cronos compulsions

Isolated human remains from Klasies River Mouth, South Africa

Fragmentary remains of a number of sexually dimorphic individuals assigned to *Homo sapiens* have been recovered from Middle Stone Age occupation deposits in the Main Cave at Klasies River Mouth, South Africa. These include several partial mandibles, cranial fragments, and several isolated postcranial elements from long bones and feet (Singer and Wymer 1982 and papers cited in Rightmire *et al.* 2005). The human remains span at least 10,000 years, from the oldest level (LBS, MIS5d ~110,000 BP) to the overlying SAS member from which most derive (MIS5c >90,000 BP), although the clustering in the SAS member is of interest. A parsimonious interpretation of the data suggests that most or all of the remains come from the SAS U sub-member ~100,000 BP (Rightmire and Deacon 2001).

The fragmentary human remains from the Main Cave represent a small number of individuals, scattered across the occupation site as a result of 'an episode of cannibalism' (Rightmire and Deacon 2001, 538). Whatever the reason for the processing of body parts of several individuals and their deposition amidst food waste at Klasies, it is clear that humans – or parts of them – would, from time to time, be disposed of visibly and even in central activity areas.

Herto, Ethiopia

Partial crania of two adults and one juvenile from the Herto member of the Bouri formation in the Middle Awash, Ethiopia, have been attributed to *Homo sapiens* (subspecies *Idaltu*) and dated to ~150,000–160,000 BP on the basis of ^{40}Ar/^{39}Ar dating of their sedimentary contexts (Clark *et al.* 2003; Gibbons 2003; White *et al.* 2003). These were recovered from a lake margin in association with abundant lithic assemblages bearing both late Acheulian and Middle Stone Age elements, and abundant faunal remains of large mammals, particularly hippopotami, many of which bear evidence of butchery. While these apparently do not represent the remains of burials, they do bear cutmarks that the excavators believe to be 'indicative of mortuary practice', that is, defleshing that does not relate to cannibalism (Clark *et al.* 2003, 751). The more complete adult individual, tentatively seen as male, bears the least amount of such modification – a vertical cut mark on its right parietal. Several fragments of the second adult bear cut marks – some very deep – and scrape

[handwritten marginalia: Good to note but cannot rule out]

[handwritten note at bottom: – Abundant lithic + faunal remains → evidence of butchering]

marks that are probably the result of soft tissue removal (ibid., 751). The juvenile cranium bears cut marks left by a very sharp stone tool and again indicative of defleshing, probably after the removal of the mandible. Some of the edges of the cranium are smooth and polished, probably due to post-mortem manipulation and curation (ibid., 751). As similar marks were found on the Middle Pleistocene Bodo cranium (see Chapter 3) it is conceivable that the Herto remains represent a late manifestation of a Middle Pleistocene African tradition of post-mortem curation of crania. *Explination*

Early inhumations of *Homo sapiens*

There is no reason to believe that the few fragmentary human remains from Africa that pre-date 100,000 BP such as the cranial and postcranial elements of Omo I represent inhumation (Pearson *et al.* 2008). The earliest known burials of *Homo sapiens* are not African, but from the 'gates of Europe' (Hublin 2000). In recent years the literature has focused on the age of these burials, notably from the point of view of the relationship between these populations and Near Eastern Neanderthals and their relevance to the issue of the earliest demographic expansion of our own species. Today, in the light of emerging evidence of early forms of personal ornamentation (McBrearty and Brooks 2000; Kuhn *et al.* 2001; Henshilwood *et al.* 2004; Vanhaeren *et al.* 2006; Bouzouggar *et al.* 2007; Bar-Yosef Mayer *et al.* 2009; Henshilwood and d'Errico 2009; Henshilwood *et al.* 2009) these burials and other associated funerary activity can be seen in the context of emerging 'modern' human behaviour. At present, a parsimonious reading of the chronometric data suggests that, with a few possible exceptions discussed in Chapter 5, these burials pre-date those of the Neanderthals elsewhere in the Near East and Europe.

Skhūl, Israel

Excavations in the 1920s and 1930s in the Mugharet-es-Skhūl, Mount Carmel, Israel – usually referred to in the Anglophone literature as Skhūl Cave – yielded the remains of ten individuals initially classified as *Palaeoanthropus palestinensis* but now assigned to early *Homo sapiens* (McCown and Keith 1939; Day 1986). A number of these are complete or near-complete, and at least four can be considered to have been buried. There is no reason, however, why the remaining six partial skeletons, although highly disturbed, cannot also be considered as burials. At least ten individuals therefore seem to have been buried in the cave between 100,000 and 130,000 BP on the basis of ESR and U-series dates on the teeth and bones of the burials respectively and TL dating of burnt flints associated with them (Mercier *et al.* 1993; Grün *et al.* 2005). Not all of these can be regarded as formal inhumations. While some were lain in artificially excavated grave cuttings such as Skhūl I, IV, V and IX and therefore are burials as I define them (Garrod and Bate 1937; Belfer-Cohen and Hovers

Naturally laid so wasn't because [handwritten margin note]

1992; Figures 4.1, 4.2, 4.3), the partial Skhūl VIII hominin seems to have been lain in a natural (probably water-worn) channel, and thus should formally be defined as an example of funerary caching. Infants represent 30 per cent of the sample (Tillier 2008).

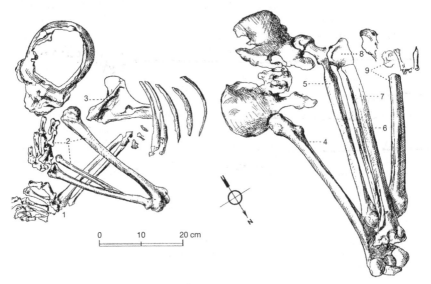

Figure 4.1 Plan of the Skhūl IV burial (from McCown and Keith 1939).

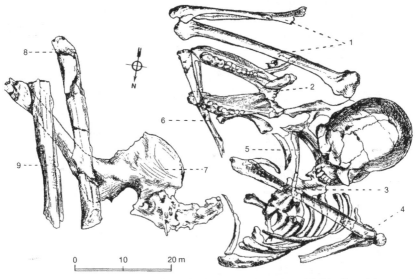

Figure 4.2 Plan of the Skhūl V burial, showing orientation, highly flexed legs and location of the mandible of *Sus* sp. (from McCown and Keith 1939).

Figure 4.3 Photo of Skhūl V burial (from McCown and Keith 1939).

The identification of burials at Skhūl is reliant upon preservation and articulation of skeletal parts, although some seem to have been simple inhumations into shallow natural and artificial pits, lain on their side in a foetal or sleeping position (Belfer-Cohen and Hovers 1992). The heads of Skhūl V, VI and possibly IV were recovered facing the valley (i.e. north), otherwise no clear pattern of orientation is observable. Two interesting burials occur, however, although the relatively limited excavation techniques with which the remains were recovered, and the lack of some documentary information, does not enable a confident clarification of the situation. As Defleur (1993, 131) has noted, the Skhūl V burial was squeezed into a small (90 × 50cm) oval grave cutting of relatively small dimensions, resulting in highly flexed legs, arms drawn up towards the chest and face and a head

good
evidence

61

tucked low – essentially a foetal position. The inclusion in the grave of a large mandible of *Sus* sp. is a rare example of a deliberate grave inclusion for the Middle Palaeolithic, seen also at Qafzeh (discussed below) and paralleled in the burial of the Amud 7 Neanderthal infant (discussed in Chapter 5). This is due to its size (nearly 20cm in maximum dimension), completeness, and location. It was recovered in a natural triangle formed by the left forearm and right upper arm, aligned parallel to the latter, and with its right mandibular ramus located *under* Skhūl V's left radius and ulna. This is the only convincing argument for deliberate grave inclusions at Skhūl; other examples, such as the lithic debitage recovered with Skhūl I and the bovid cranium with Skhūl IX are almost certainly intrusive, due to use of excavated sediments to cover the burials (Skhūl I) or to disturbance (Skhūl IX).

It is interesting to note the proximity of the adult Skhūl VII, usually interpreted as female, and the partial remains of the Skhūl X child, which were found very close to the head of Skhūl VII. Although both are highly disturbed, the original excavators thought that the Skhūl X child was buried first and was therefore disturbed by the subsequent burial of Skhūl VII, but no detailed sedimentological observations have been recorded and no known plans or photographs exist; this is a shame, as if it could be demonstrated that Skhūl VII and X were buried at the same time and in the same excavation, this would be the earliest known example – by as much as 100,000 years – of an adult buried with a child. A similar limitation – this time for a potential double or triple grave – exists at Qafzeh (see p. 68).

It is possible that mollusc shells were associated with some of the Skhūl burials. Five shells of four distinct species that seem to have been used as personal ornamentation (Vanhaeren *et al.* 2006) were recovered during the original excavations, although it is impossible today to associate these definitively with the burials (Bar-Yosef Mayer *et al.* 2009).

The stratigraphic position of the burials, and close spatial association of several of them, suggest that they were emplaced within a relatively restricted period of time, although one cannot rule out that Skhūl IX is older than most (see discussion in Grün *et al.* 2005). Ronen (1976, 33) has argued that there may have been two periods of inhumation as individuals I, II and III were stratigraphically higher than the rest and because individual VIII had been disturbed, although there is no reason to believe that a considerable period of time separates the two phases. A parsimonious interpretation of the Skhūl remains would see from four to ten simple inhumations emplaced in a relatively discrete time period and on occasion close in time, probably all without deliberate grave inclusions or orientation. If, on the other hand, it could be demonstrated beyond reasonable doubt that Skhūl V contained a deliberate inclusion, and/or Skhūl VII and X represented an associated adult and child burial, then in terms of funerary activity the Skhūl *Homo sapiens* population was behaving – at least on two occasions – in a similar manner to some Neanderthals, as will be discussed in the next chapter.

- could possibly be earliest adult buried w/ child but we can't know when they were buried

Qafzeh, Israel

Excavations in the 1930s, 1960s and 1970s in the Djebel Qafzeh, near Nazareth, Israel – usually referred to in the Anglophone literature as Qafzeh Cave – yielded the remains of 13 complete or nearly complete hominins classified as *Homo sapiens* (Neuville 1951; Vandermeersch 1981; Defleur 1993; see Table 4.1). Of these, five nearly complete skeletons were recovered during the earlier excavations (Qafzeh 3–7) and eight from the later (Qafzeh 8–15), in addition to which a number of isolated remains are known (Qafzeh 1–2, 16–22), although it is unclear as to whether these represent disturbed burials or individuals with more complex post-mortem taphonomies. As Tillier (2008) has noted, the relative abundance of non-adults (60 per cent of the sample) is striking.

All of the hominin remains derive from the Lower Palaeolithic levels, and date to 90,000–100,000 BP on the basis of ESR dates on the bones of the burials themselves and TL dates on burnt flints from the same levels (Schwarcz *et al.* 1988; Valladas *et al.* 1988). Although the layers into which the graves were emplaced contained bones, lithics and hearths, the lithic assemblages are rather homogeneous and seem to indicate that the site at this time was not functioning as a general purpose camp but a task-specific site, possibly for burial (Bar-Yosef and Vandermeersch 1993). While the funerary specialisation is unclear, the site certainly does not seem to have acted as a prosaic camp at this time (E. Hovers pers. comm.). All of the hominin remains seem to have derived from the same stratum, Neuville's Bed L (Qafzeh 3–7) and most of Vandermeersch's stratum XVII, which can be confidently equated with each other, with the exception of the Qafzeh 11 adolescent which derived from the lower stratum XXII. The sediments of these levels accumulated rapidly; this, and the homogeneity of the lithic assemblages argue for a relatively tight chronology for the burials, and the spatial clustering near the cave's entrance and near to its southern wall of burials discovered since the 1960s certainly supports the notion of a 'tradition' of emplacement in this area rather than the fortuitous association of burials emplaced widely over time in this large cave.

Given that the Middle Palaeolithic occupation of the cave continued beyond the period of deposition of the burials, the lack of human remains from the later Middle Palaeolithic layers XV–III is of interest. As the amount of lithic artefacts remains similar throughout the sequence one cannot argue that the cave was used less or by fewer individuals later in time, and thus the lack of funerary activity seems to reflect a true change in the use of the cave. Clearly, the cave ceased to have a funerary function, possibly indicating that the early modern humans of the region made cultural decisions about when and where to bury their dead. This observation is further reinforced by the rarity of hearths and burnt sediments and flints in the upper levels, which Hovers *et al.* (2003, 508) ascribe to a real behavioural difference.

Table 4.1 The Skhūl and Qafzeh hominins

Hominin	Age	Chronology	Position, grave, associations	References
Skhūl I	Child 4–6 yrs	100–30 kyr BP (TL and ESR)	Close to entrance of cave. Remains in anatomical association, corpse lying on left side. Possibly male. Numerous unretouched lithic debitage in grave fill but probably fortuitous	Garrod and Bate 1937; McCown and Keith 1939; Day 1986; Defleur 1993; Zilhão and Trinkaus 2002b
Skhūl II	Adult	100–30 kyr BP (TL and ESR)	Fragmentary remains not in anatomical association on the terrace, probably female. Probably a disturbed burial, conceivably of one individual also represented also by nearby Skhūl 3	Garrod and Bate 1937; McCown and Keith 1939; Day 1986; Defleur 1993; Zilhão and Trinkaus 2002b
Skhūl III	Adult	100–30 kyr BP (TL and ESR)	Emplaced outside a small alcove to east of terrace, somewhat disturbed (partial leg bones only), conceivably one individual represented also by nearby Skhūl 2. Probably male	Garrod and Bate 1937; McCown and Keith 1939; Day 1986; Defleur 1993; Zilhão and Trinkaus 2002b
Skhūl IV	Adult	100–30 kyr BP (TL and ESR)	Probably male, located just behind rock overhang. Laid on right side, head inclined towards the left shoulder, highly flexed legs and hands lain in front of the face with wrists and hands supine. Flint scraper found between hands but possibly fortuitous association	Garrod and Bate 1937; McCown and Keith 1939; Day 1986; Defleur 1993; Zilhão and Trinkaus 2002b
Skhūl V	Adult	100–30 kyr BP (TL and ESR)	Probably male, located in a central position. Laid on the right side with legs highly flexed with a mandible of wild boar placed in the angle between the left forearm and right arm, possibly a deliberate inclusion	Garrod and Bate 1937; McCown and Keith 1939; Day 1986; Defleur 1993; Zilhão and Trinkaus 2002b
Skhūl VI	Adult	100–30 kyr BP (TL and ESR)	Partial skeleton near to Skhūl V and IX, probably the remains of a highly disturbed burial. Probably male	Garrod and Bate 1937; McCown and Keith 1939; Day 1986; Defleur 1993; Zilhão and Trinkaus 2002b

Specimen	Age	Date	Description	References
Skhūl VII	Adult	100–30 kyr BP (TL and ESR)	Partial skeleton, probably female, located in a central position. Arms and hands drawn up towards the face, legs highly flexed. Probably the remains of a highly disturbed burial. Note proximity of partial remains of Skhūl X	Garrod and Bate 1937; McCown and Keith 1939; Day 1986; Defleur 1993; Zilhão and Trinkaus 2002b
Skhūl VIII	Child 10 yrs	100–30 kyr BP (TL and ESR)	Partial (lower) skeleton in articulated position, located to the east of the terrace. Probably a highly disturbed funerary cache within a natural (water?) channel. Possibly female	Garrod and Bate 1937; McCown and Keith 1939; Day 1986; Defleur 1993; Zilhão and Trinkaus 2002b
Skhūl IX	Adult	100–30 kyr BP (TL and ESR)	Highly fragmentary elements of (generally upper) skeleton located in centre of terrace. Fortuitous associations include the cranium of a large bovid. Possibly male	Garrod and Bate 1937; McCown and Keith 1939; Day 1986; Defleur 1993; Zilhão and Trinkaus 2002b
Skhūl X	Child 5 yrs	100–30 kyr BP (TL and ESR)	Partial skeleton (mandibular and humeral elements only) recovered near to the head of Skhūl VII, probably disturbed by the interment of the latter. Possibly male	Garrod and Bate 1937; McCown and Keith 1939; Day 1986; Defleur 1993; Zilhão and Trinkaus 2002b
Qafzeh 1	Adult	90–120 kyr BP (TL and ESR)	Isolated frontal bone	Neuville 1951; Vandermeersch 1981; Day 1986; Defleur 1993; Zilhão and Trinkaus 2002b
Qafzeh 2	Adult	90–120 kyr BP (TL and ESR)	Highly fragmentary (calotte, mandible, teeth only)	Neuville 1951; Vandermeersch 1981; Day 1986; Defleur 1993; Zilhão and Trinkaus 2002b
Qafzeh 3	Adult	90–120 kyr BP (TL and ESR)	Partial skeleton, possibly laid on left side, located in Neuville Bed L	Neuville 1951; Vandermeersch 1981; Day 1986; Defleur 1993; Zilhão and Trinkaus 2002b
Qafzeh 4	Child	Probably 90–120 kyr BP (TL and ESR)	Highly fragmentary (palette, mandible, teeth only). Not with main cluster of hominins: found against wall in NE corner of terrace excavation (as Qafzeh 5) in Neuville Bed L. Possibly from same skeleton as Qafzeh 4a	Neuville 1951; Vandermeersch 1981; Day 1986; Defleur 1993; Zilhão and Trinkaus 2002b

continued . . .

Table 4.1 continued

Hominin	Age	Chronology	Position, grave, associations	References
Qafzeh 4a	Child	Probably 90–120 kyr BP (TL and ESR)	Highly fragmentary (pelvic and cranial fragments only). Possibly from same skeleton as Qafzeh 4	Arensburg and Tillier 1983; Day 1986; Zilhão and Trinkaus 2002b
Qafzeh 5	Adult	Probably 90–120 kyr BP (TL and ESR)	Highly fragmentary (calotte, palette and teeth only). Not with main cluster of hominins: found against wall in NE corner of terrace excavation (as Qafzeh 4) in Neuville Bed L	Neuville 1951; Vandermeersch 1981; Day 1986; Defleur 1993; Zilhão and Trinkaus 2002b
Qafzeh 6	Adult	90–120 kyr BP (TL and ESR)	Very fragmentary (cranial elements and teeth only): cranial elements possibly laid on left side, located in Neuville Bed L	Neuville 1951; Vandermeersch 1981; Day 1986; Defleur 1993; Zilhão and Trinkaus 2002b
Qafzeh 7	Adult	90–120 kyr BP (TL and ESR)	Very partial skeleton (cranial elements, teeth, mandible, clavicle and phalanges) found associated with Qafzeh 6 in Neuville Bed L	Neuville 1951; Vandermeersch 1981; Day 1986; Defleur 1993; Zilhão and Trinkaus 2002b
Qafzeh 8	Adult	90–120 kyr BP (TL and ESR)	Burial in vestibule (main cluster of burials). Partial skeleton, lain on the right side with semi-flexed legs. Large stone block with cupule and scrape marks found in close proximity to feet, and two worked flints and several fragments of ochre found close to the skeleton	Vandermeersch 1981; Day 1986; Defleur 1993; Zilhão and Trinkaus 2002b
Qafzeh 9	Adult	90–120 kyr BP (TL and ESR)	Burial in vestibule (main cluster of burials). Partial skeleton laid on left side, with flexed legs and arms in lap, within excavated grave. Found in close proximity to Qafzeh 10	Vandermeersch 1981; Day 1986; Defleur 1993; Zilhão and Trinkaus 2002b
Qafzeh 10	Child, 6 yrs	90–120 kyr BP (TL and ESR)	Burial in vestibule (main cluster of burials). Near-complete child (feet absent), found at the feet of the Qafzeh 9 adult. Partially on its back, head resting on its back, left arm over the head and right parallel to the body, strongly flexed	Vandermeersch 1981; Day 1986; Defleur 1993; Zilhão and Trinkaus 2002b

Qafzeh 11	Adolescent 12–13 yrs	90–120 kyr BP (TL and ESR)	Child deposited in a sub-rectangular grave 1 × 0.6m and 0.6m deep. Large blocks of limestone may have been used to line and/or mark the grave. Body placed on its back, head against the edge of the grave cutting, large limestone block placed on top of skeleton. Fallow deer antler found in proximity to hands and head	Vandermeersch 1981; Day 1986; Defleur 1993; Zilhão and Trinkaus 2002b
Qafzeh 12	Child 3–4 yrs	90–120 kyr BP (TL and ESR)	Fragmentary remains found just in front of cave entrance. Possibly highly disturbed burial	Vandermeersch 1981; Defleur 1993; Zilhão and Trinkaus 2002b
Qafzeh 13	Neonate	90–120 kyr BP (TL and ESR)	Fragmentary remains found just in front of cave entrance. Possibly highly disturbed burial	Vandermeersch 1981; Defleur 1993; Zilhão and Trinkaus 2002b
Qafzeh 14	Child		Fragmentary remains found just in front of cave entrance. Possibly highly disturbed burial	Vandermeersch 1981; Defleur 1993; Zilhão and Trinkaus 2002b.
Qafzeh 15	Child 8–10 yrs	90–120 kyr BP (TL and ESR)	Partial skeleton (lower elements missing). Possibly a burial; elements of the trunk and upper limbs in anatomical connection	Vandermeersch 1981; Defleur 1993; Zilhão and Trinkaus 2002b
Qafzeh 16	Isolated tooth	90–120 kyr BP (TL and ESR)	NA	Zilhão and Trinkaus 2002b
Qafzeh 17	Isolated tooth	90–120 kyr BP (TL and ESR)	NA	Zilhão and Trinkaus 2002b
Qafzeh 18	Isolated tooth	90–120 kyr BP (TL and ESR)	NA	Zilhão and Trinkaus 2002b
Qafzeh 21	Child 3 yrs	90–120 kyr BP (TL and ESR)	NA	Zilhão and Trinkaus 2002b.
Qafzeh 22	Child 4–6 yrs	90–129 kyr BP (TL and ESR)	NA	Zilhão and Trinkaus 2002b
Qafzeh 25	Adult	90–120 kyr BP (TL and ESR)	NA	Bar-Yosef Mayer et al. 2009

At least six Qafzeh individuals seem to represent formal burials; Qafzeh 8–11, 13 and 15 (Vandermeersch 1981; Belfer-Cohen and Hovers 1992; Figures 4.4, 4.5, 4.6). As Defleur (1993, 141) has noted it is conceivable that the fragmentary remains of Qafzeh 6, 7 and possibly 3, although from different individuals, were originally interred in the same grave, although as with Skhūl VII and X it is impossible today to verify this. Perhaps the clearest example of a deliberate double burial is that of the Qafzeh 9 adult and Qafzeh 10 child, the latter of which was recovered at the feet of the former, and possibly represents the burial of a child with its mother (Bar-Yosef and Vandermeersch 1993). Sedimentological conditions allowed the recognition of a distinct grave cutting, a rectangle some 1.4 × 0.5m in dimension. Intriguingly, the child's feet were missing, although no signs of post-depositional disturbance were found; both skeletons were horizontal and entirely in anatomical articulation. An abundance of ochre fragments were recovered in close proximity to the skeletons.

In addition to several ochre fragments, Qafzeh 8 seems to have been associated with a large ochre block bearing traces of scraping, and two worked flints, an ensemble unlikely to be entirely fortuitous (Vandermeersch 1969). In fact, at least 84 fragments of ochre were recovered from layers XXIX–XVII, the majority of which were clustered within $4m^2$ in the western side of the excavation irrespective of their stratigraphic layer (Hovers et al. 2003, 494). Some of these bore traces of utilisation and ochre-stained artefacts further attest the use of the pigment in the cave. It seems that there was a clearly defined area of ochre processing, perhaps for use in activities relating to the burials (ibid., 507). A degree of correlation at least is evident in the association in Layer XVII of the highest number of burials (five) and the highest frequency of the largest, heavy pieces of ochre.

The use of stone blocks to line and/or mark the position of a grave may be in evidence in the Qafzeh 11 child burial. Blocks at least 40cm in maximum dimension had been deposited in places at the edge of the burial, close to the cave wall. A large block was also placed atop the body, and a large antler and frontal bone of red deer were recovered by the hands and head, possibly as it was being clasped close to the chest (Vandermeersch 1981; Belfer-Cohen and Hovers 1992). An abundance of red ochre was also found within the grave cutting. Given the clarity of the grave cutting, deliberate placing of stone blocks as architectural elements of the grave, and lack of other items within the grave's fill, it seems likely that the red deer antler and bone and ochre fragments were deliberate grave inclusions. This is the richest known grave with a Middle Palaeolithic cultural association. Intriguingly, Defleur (1993, 148) has noted that the grave cutting – 1 × 0.5m in dimensions at least – is very generous for the size of body deposited within, which occupied less than 50 per cent of the grave, and has speculated that the grave possibly contained other deliberate inclusions that have now perished. This is an interesting possibility, although the location of the large stone blocks generally in the

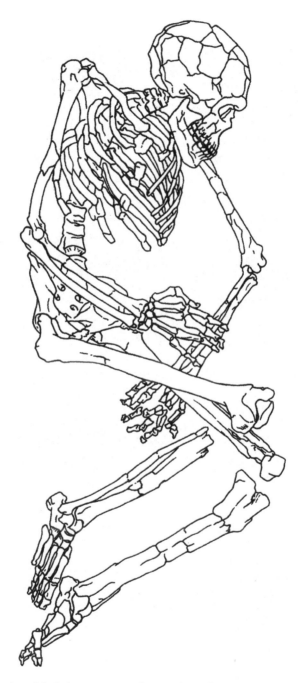

Figure 4.4 Plan of Qafzeh 9 (courtesy of Bernard Vandermeersch).

Figure 4.5 Photograph of the double grave of Qafzeh 9 and 10. The infant can be seen bottom right of the grave, at the feet of the Qafzeh 9 adult (courtesy of Bernard Vandermeersch).

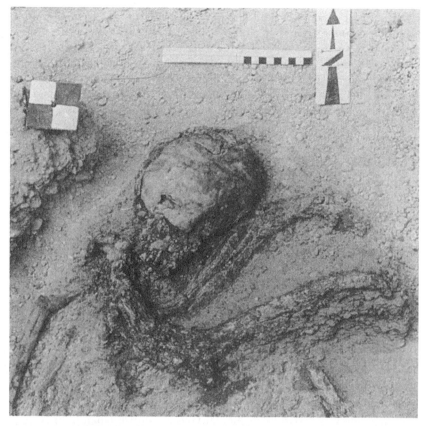

Figure 4.6 Close-up of the Qafzeh 11 burial showing antler of *Cervus elaphus* placed close to head (courtesy of Bernard Vandermeersch).

area of the burial's feet and 'lower' grave suggest to me that the grave was deliberately excavated large so as to allow for the placement of the blocks within it, at the feet of the burial. If this is correct, it seems most likely that the blocks functioned as markers.

Hovers *et al.* (2003, 507) note an association between the burials, isolated human remains, ochre, inedible marine molluscs and a possible further association with fire at Qafzeh, none of which are documented in the upper layers. It is possible that shell beads were associated with the one burial in stratum XXIV too (Bar-Yosef Meyer *et al.* 2009). As Hovers *et al.* (2003, 508) have noted, the association seems to reflect a 'structured ensemble of behaviors'. This is of interest as, if true, this could represent the introduction of patterns of use of personal ornamentation and burial that on occasion co-vary, which one finds later in Border Cave (discussed below). The relevance of these data to an emerging 'symbolic capacity' is debatable; to Hovers *et al.*

(2003, 508) 'the bones of dead kin are *at least* iconic of the living person in that they point to their referent by physical resemblance'. While this is debatable, I suggest that the further association in Qafzeh Cave with two plausible examples of grave inclusions (the engraved stone block, lithics and ochre fragments with Qafzeh 8 and the deer antler with Qafzeh 11) and the plausible double burial of an adult (female?) and infant (Qafzeh 9 and 10) strengthens the argument for a degree of symbolic underpinning of these activities. Shea (2001, 55) has noted that

> the wide variety of body positions and orientations seems to reduce the repetitive 'ritual' dimension of [the Skhūl/Qafzeh burials] to digging a shallow pit and placing a body within it. Such simplicity raises the question of whether there are other reasons why [Middle Palaeolithic] humans might have buried bodies.

Carnivore avoidance is one possible reason he cites for why corpses were 'protected' within shallow graves. But the association of other activities at the site documented by Hovers *et al.* suggest that deeper meanings underpinned these early inhumations.

The issue remains as to whether one can regard the Skhūl and Qafzeh burials as relating to relatively discrete periods of time, and, of course, whether one can regard the two sites as close in age. The chronometry of the sites, based on TL dates, does not help: at 2σ the human remains could have been buried up to 30,000 years apart. Stringer (1998) has argued on the basis of a high degree of morphological variability in the samples from both sites that they were deposited over a significant time span, perhaps even more than the age range of the TL dates suggests, although sedimentological analyses at Qafzeh suggest relatively fast burial (Farrand 1979). We should, however, be cautious about making inferences about depositional processes from anatomical characteristics: as the Skhūl/Qafzeh sample is as yet the only multiple sample we have for early *Homo sapiens* we do not know how variable these populations were: they may have been highly variable. Given the clustering of burials and other human remains in discrete areas of each cave, the similarity of depositional processes, and the lack of inter-cutting of previous interments by later, it is perhaps parsimonious to assume that the depositional processes in each cave occurred over relatively brief periods of time. Whether or not both caves received their dead close in time or widely apart is, of course, another issue. We should simply regard each as discrete samples of similar processes within a broad period of time, that is, the last interglacial *sensu lato*.

Border Cave, South Africa

The fragmentary remains of four individuals were recovered from Middle Stone Age deposits in Border Cave (Kwazulu Natal, South Africa: BC1, 2, 3 and

5: Cooke *et al.* 1945; Rightmire 1979). These take the form of a fragmentary adult cranium (BC1), a near-complete mandible (BC2) too small to articulate with BC1 and possibly female, the partial skeleton of a 4–6-month-old infant (BC3) and a complete adult mandible (BC5) (BC4 is Iron Age in date). The deposits, archaeology and human remains at the site are well dated, by a combination of ESR, U-series, radiocarbon and amino-acid racemisation which are in good agreement (Grün and Beaumont 2001). There is a degree of uncertainty about the relevance of chronometry for BC1 and 2, which are broadly unprovenanced. They have been traced to stratum 4BS on the basis of the 'soft dark earth' of this layer still adhering to them, although BC1 could derive from the underlying stratum 5BS (Grün and Beaumont 2001). This places BC2 ~82,000 ± 2,000 BP on the basis of ESR measurements for 4BS, and BC1 either around this age or significantly older (~150,000–170,000 BP for 5BS). BC3 is well stratified, cut into 4BS and sealed by the lower part of Howieson's Poort stratum 1RGBS and thus with a minimum age of ~76,000 ± 4,000 BP. This is stratigraphically near the location of BC5, stratified below stratum 3WA and thus with a minimum age of ~66,000 ± 2,000 BP. A parsimonious reading of the data would place BC1, 2, 3 and 5 between 70,000 and 80,000 BP.

It is impossible to establish the relevance of the fragmentary BC1 and 2 remains which, perhaps, should be seen as part of the occasional 'spread' of human remains on occupation sites as seen at Klasies River Mouth. BC3, however, is highly relevant, as it is derived from a grave clearly cut into stratum 4BS (Cooke *et al.* 1945). This firmly establishes the practice of formal inhumation of infants in Africa by ~76,000 BP. The grave cutting was shallow (~24cm deep), ~38cm long by ~30cm wide. As we have seen above, the practice can be extended back to ~120,000 BP in the Near East – palaeo-environmentally part of Africa at the time – which may suggest that the practice had a long antiquity among *Homo sapiens* during the first half of MIS5. The bones carry a red-brown staining, probably from ochre (de Villiers 1973). A perforated *Conus* shell was also found in association with the burial. If this association is correct, while one cannot interpret this as a 'grave goods' *sensu stricto* it does at least provide early evidence of the burial of an infant with its personal ornamentation, and possibly an indication of the symbolic interaction between the two to which I shall return below.

Taramsa, Egypt

At Taramsa Hill in Upper Egypt, systematic quarrying of chert cobbles was undertaken over the duration of the Middle Palaeolithic, resulting in a number of pits and trenches (Vermeersch *et al.* 1986, 1998). In a 5 × 4 × 1.2m deep extraction pit, the skeleton of a child was recovered, apparently originally lain against the pit's southwestern side, lying atop extraction debris and leaning against the unexploited chert cobbles at the pit's sides. Extraction debris and numerous lithic artefacts surrounded the body, which was covered with Middle Palaeolithic extraction debris (Figure 4.7). OSL dates suggest an age of ~50,000–60,000 BP, which is in accord with its Late Middle Palaeolithic attribution. The skeleton has been assigned to *Homo sapiens* and cranial similarities to the Qafzeh 9 young adult female as well as to later Epipalaeolithic North-African populations have been noted (ibid., 481).

Scholars who debate whether Border Cave remains represent a true burial have seen the Taramsa child as potentially the earliest example of intentional burial in Africa (ibid., 483). As the discoverers note, from the seated position of the skeleton and its dump environment, an intentional burial can be assumed' (ibid., 478). If, however, one defines formal burial as a three-stage process, involving 1) the excavation of a grave cutting, 2) the deposition of a body or human remains within the cutting and 3) the covering of the remains with the excavated sediment (see Chapter 1), then one cannot define Taramsa as such, as the original excavations were undertaken for the purpose of chert mining. The excavation of small, vertically sided, shallow chert extraction pits seems to have been practised widely in the area, and if the Taramsa discovery represents the use (or *exaption* to use a term coined by Gamble 1993) of such a mine trench for subsequent interment then one should formally define it as an example of funerary caching. This I prefer to do on the grounds of parsimony, and thus see Taramsa as a late example among *Homo sapiens* of the long-lasting caching tradition, which seems to have persisted as late as A37,000 BP at Nazlet Khater in Upper Egypt which is discussed in Chapter 6. It is, however, clear how formal burial could arise

Figure 4.7 The Taramsa funerary cache (photograph courtesy of Pierre Vermeersch).

from caching in pits created for other purposes and in this sense Taramsa
provides an example of the conceptual fusion of caching and burial.

Mungo, Australia *first cremation*

Evidence of funerary activity occurs in the context of domestic activity in the
sand lunette that developed at the edge of Lake Mungo in New South Wales,
one of a series of lakes (now dry) of the Willandra Creek (see Figure 7.16).
Two examples of funerary activity at the site – a burial in a pit of a cremated
adult and the interment in a shallow grave of another adult – are dated
somewhere between ~40kyr BP (based on ^{14}C and TL dating: Bowler *et al.*
2003) and ~60kyr BP (based on U-Series dating of bone, ESR dating of tooth
enamel and OSL dating of the sediments into which the burials were emplaced:
Simpson and Grün 1998; Thorne *et al.* 1999) or a little younger than 20,000
BP (based on an assessment of ^{14}C measurements: Gillespie 2002; Gillespie
and Roberts 2000). A third simple burial in the Willandra area – WLH3 –
may be of broadly similar antiquity (Habgood and Franklin 2008). Mungo I
is comprised of the cremated and smashed bones of about 25 per cent of a
skeleton of an adult, usually identified as female (Bowler *et al.* 1970; Mulvaney
and Kamminga 1999). It seems that the young adult individual was cremated
on the beach, after which the bones were smashed up and gathered into a
conical pit some 20cm deep. It may be significant that the cremation and
burial occurred in an area in which hearths and earth ovens were abundant.
While this is often the case for Eurasia Middle Palaeolithic inhumations of
both *Homo sapiens* and *Homo neanderthalensis* these are from cave sites where
the available space is relatively limited, although at Willandra these occur in
the open air where, presumably, bodies could be disposed of away from cooking
areas. Could this association be meaningful? Could the adult have been 'cooked'
in the same way that foodstuffs were?

Half a kilometre to the east of the Mungo 1 cremation burial, the body of
another adult, probably a male of advanced years, was interred, this time
without cremation or smashing (Bowler and Thorne 1976). This was named
Mungo III (Mungo II being highly fragmentary remains found close to Mungo
I). The man had been laid out in an extended position in a shallow grave,
with his knees slightly flexed. Ochre staining was abundant in the grave
cutting, suggesting that he was interred wrapped in an ochre-stained shroud
or wearing ochre-stained clothing, and may have occurred in the wider context of the use of this pigment in painting (Mulvaney and Kamminga 1999,
211). Humans were clearly in Australia (including Lake Mungo) by at least
50kyr BP, and the funerary evidence, albeit later (perhaps much later) than
the date of the first arrivals, however sparse, suggests that a variety of cremation and inhumation was on occasion practised in open locations, in the wider
context of ochre use and perhaps in part associated with the processing
of foodstuffs. The simple inhumation tradition does not differ from that

practised at Skhūl and Qafzeh, although at present Mungo I is the earliest known example of cremation.

From funerary caching to formal burial

Skhūl VIII was emplaced in a wholly natural erosional channel within the cave, and the apparent association of Skhūl III, at least in part, with an alcove may represent a similar concern for 'containment' in an otherwise natural feature. Qafzeh VIII was placed in a natural fissure in the rock of the cave, which would constitute funerary caching, although the artificial enlargement of this feature in the Middle Palaeolithic by chiseling moves it towards the category of formal burial. In a conceptual sense this is similar to the caching observed at Taramsa. In these sites, then, one not only finds a mixture of funerary caching and formal burial, but an intriguing combination of the two in one interrment. It is possible that the Skhūl and Qafzeh remains, at 90,000–120,000 BP, were interred near to the time where, in the Near East at least, funerary caching was giving way to formal burial in artificially modified contexts. This may have occurred in a wider context as part of the growing association of mortuary activities and those that required the production and use of ochre and fire. One prediction of this is that formal burials, and the association of such with ochre and fire, should not be found much earlier than the Upper Pleistocene. This discussion will be taken up in Chapter 5.

One can summarise the period from the Late Middle Pleistocene to the Mid Upper Pleistocene as follows:

- 150–60kyr BP: Mortuary defleshing and curation of crania among African early *Homo sapiens* populations, possibly as a continuation of a Middle Pleistocene tradition. Hovers and Belfer-Cohen have contrasted this with the earliest indications of Eurasian funerary activity, which takes the form of burials.
- 90–120kyr BP: Funerary caching and formal burial of children and adults, males and females, in shallow features that appear to respect the positioning of each other, possibly assisted by grave markers.
- 90–120kyr BP: Occasional deliberate inclusion of objects (well-made lithics, faunal remains, ochre fragments) into formal graves.
- 90–120kyr BP: Possible association of rituals using ochre and/or fire with interment of the dead.
- 40–60kyr BP: A tradition of simple inhumation in shallow graves continues in Africa (coincidentally preserving an infant with red ochre and personal ornamentation), and simple inhumation and cremation appears among some early *Homo sapiens* populations in Australia.

Further to this, it is probable that, by ~120,000 BP at least, funerary practice formed part of the wider cultural repertoire of *Homo sapiens* that included personal ornamentation. Ultimately, these probably relate to developing methods of symbolism. Although the notion of a symbolic capacity has been seen by archaeologists as the defining characteristic of *Homo sapiens*, the notion has not been problematised and needs further definition. This is outside the scope of this book, although I have attempted an initial problematisation elsewhere (Pettitt in press). One should remember, however, that funerary activity is not restricted only to Middle Palaeolithic *Homo sapiens*, but is at least evident among Eurasian Neanderthals (Hovers and Belfer-Cohen in press). It is of interest, however, that there is possibly a co-variation in the occurrence/ absence of burial and personal ornamentation among both Neanderthals and early modern humans (Figure 4.8).

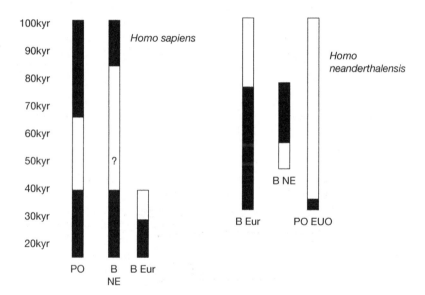

Figure 4.8 Presence/absence of personal ornamentation (PO) and burials (Near East: B NE and Europe: B Eu) for *Homo neanderthalensis* and *Homo sapiens*. Black bars indicate presence, white bars indicate absence in periods that the taxa were present in the regions. Note for *Homo sapiens* there is a correlation between personal ornamentation and burials: both co-occur in the Near East. Note also the inverse correlation between *Homo sapiens* and Neanderthals; between ~70,000 and 35,000 BP there is evidence for burial among Neanderthals but not among *Homo sapiens*.

Note: Question mark indicates apparent absence, although data are ambiguous.

5

THE NEANDERTHALS

Death in the Neander Valley, 40,000 BP

When the Neanderthals quite literally exploded onto the scientific scene in 1856, the remains – in this case of an adult male – had probably originally been buried ~40,000 years ago. The remains were thrown into the air by the dynamite of the limestone quarrymen in the Neander Thal (Neander Valley) about 13km east of Düsseldorf, Germany. How touching it is that the first remains of a fossil human to be recognised by science probably derive from a burial. The original find comprised a calotte, clavicle, scapula, five ribs, two humeri, radius, two ulnae, two femora and part pelvis, and recent excavations of the cave's spoil heap located a left zygomatic and part maxillary body and a right temporal bone that refits onto the calotte (Schmitz *et al.* 2002, 133–43). In addition to these, other remains, which do not refit onto the remains of Neanderthal 1, nevertheless probably derive from it (ibid., 13343). Overall – especially given the action of dynamite – the remains seem to have been complete enough to suggest burial. The new excavations have revealed for the first time the presence of a second individual, represented by four post-cranial specimens that duplicate elements already known for Neanderthal 1 (Schmitz and Thissen 2000; Schmitz *et al.* 2002). This shows that at least one other individual was deposited in the cave. The dimensions of one of the remains of Neanderthal 2 – a segment of a right humerus – shows that it was smaller and more gracile than Neanderthal 1, which is usually assumed to be male. Finally, a deciduous molar (NN 50) is pre-adult and therefore represents a third individual. Direct AMS radiocarbon dating of remains from both Neanderthal 1 and 2 show that they were chronometrically contemporary at ~40,000 BP.

We will, of course, never know whether these two or three individuals were the subject of mortuary rituals within the Kleine Feldhofer Grotte, although the relative completeness of the remains of Neanderthal 1 suggests that it may have been buried. If Neanderthal 2 was also buried, the type site for the Neanderthals may well have functioned as a place of multiple burial, one of the cultural achievements of the Neanderthals to which I shall return below. In this chapter, I review the relatively large and varied evidence for

78

Neanderthal funerary activity. In some respects we shall see a repeat of what has been discussed for *Homo sapiens* in the last chapter. Some interesting parallels are evident, although there is also, I shall suggest, evidence for more varied funerary activity among the Neanderthals than currently exists for their contemporary *Homo sapiens* populations.

Neanderthal remains and the development of mortuary activity

There has been little discussion among specialists of the nuanced details of Neanderthal mortuary activity. Instead, a rather straightforward debate as to whether or not the Neanderthals genuinely buried their dead occurred in the late 1980s, but fizzled out fairly quickly and can hardly be said to have dominated the literature. This is nothing new; the discovery of the La Chapelle-aux-Saints skeleton in 1908 precipitated a debate as to whether Neanderthals had the cultural capacities to bury their dead (Roche 1976). Two brave – but in my opinion flawed – critiques of the burial data were forwarded by Gargett (1989, 1999), who concluded that there was little or no convincing evidence for deliberate burial among Neanderthals. These stimulated a fairly negative response from specialists, the majority of whom seem to agree that a number of convincing examples of Neanderthal burial exist. While I deal below with the major points raised by Gargett, my main stance is not only that there is clear evidence for deliberate burial, but that there is also evidence for considerable mortuary variability at the time. My concern, therefore, is to explore and interpret, noting what I see as developments in the mortuary realm over the course of the Eurasian Middle Palaeolithic.

The Neanderthal hypodigm is the largest for all fossil hominins and is indeed far richer than that for our own species prior to the Holocene. The greater part of the hypodigm, however, is highly fragmentary, and wherever remains are recovered from most are isolated teeth and fragmentary material. Some of these fragmentary remains could, of course, derive from what were originally burials, and sites where numerous individuals are represented could represent highly disturbed sites of multiple burials, but it is now impossible to demonstrate this. By contrast, it certainly seems that carnivores were on occasion responsible for the deposition of Neanderthal skeletal material in rockshelters and caves, but such an explanation cannot account for the entire hypodigm, particularly where more complete and articulated skeletal material is concerned. It is no surprise therefore that the notion of deliberate interment of the corpse by at least some Neanderthal groups has been forwarded to explain some of the more complete Neanderthal specimens. The initial recognition that 'Neanderthals buried their dead' as the generalisation goes, can be traced back to the turn of the twentieth century with the discovery of the remains from La Chapelle-aux-Saints (Bouyssonie *et al.* 1908). In the 1960s the fact that Neanderthals expended effort in burying their dead, and especially as some burials were seen to provide evidence of care of the elderly and the inclusion of flowers in graves (Shanidar I and IV respectively: Solecki 1972) brought burial to bear as another indicator of the 'humanity' of Neanderthals in that great decade of flower-power-inspired humanisation of our evolutionary ancestors.

While it seems undeniable that at least 30 Neanderthals came to be buried by their kin over some 30,000 years or more in three regions of Eurasia, it is certainly timely to decouple simple 'estimates' of the number of 'burials'. As will be seen below, Neanderthal mortuary phenomena, while perhaps not common occurrences, were varied, and it is probably incorrect to view this as one monolithic 'burial' phenomenon. Furthermore, the issue of corpse-disposal is central to interpretations of mortuary activity. If we assume that removal of the dead from occupation sites is an important activity, not least because it minimises the risk of attracting carnivores and other unpleasant saprophages as well as minimises the unpleasantness of proximity to rotting corpses, then the apparent presence/absence of corpses on occupation or other sites may be informative. Were Neanderthals in control of the fate of their own remains? Mussi (1988, 1999, 55) has suggested that corpses were carefully removed from occupation sites when Neanderthals were in command of situations, although the implications of this is that whatever their fate, burial was probably not the main means of disposal, at least in the Italian Middle Palaeolithic.

The question of whether or not Neanderthals buried their dead has understandably played a role in the exploration of the similarities and differences between Neanderthals and early anatomically modern humans. This is particularly so in Europe, where the Middle to Upper Palaeolithic transition has been seen by many scholars as relatively abrupt (e.g. White 1982; Stringer and Gamble 1993; Mellars 1996; Gamble 1999; papers in Mellars and Stringer 1989; papers in Mellars 1990). It is probably fair to say that most scholars, except Gargett (1989, 1999) accept that *some* Neanderthals received deliberate burial after death, and that such burials appear not to have included grave goods or any other form of elaboration visible in the archaeological record. Although, however, a number of surveys over the last two decades are generally favourable to the notion of deliberate burial, reviews tend to make generalisations of the 'Neanderthals did bury their dead' variety. Such a generalisation over Upper Pleistocene time and space may not be justified, and certainly merits closer inspection. The purpose here is to examine the available data in terms of potential variability of mortuary practice among at least some Eurasian Neanderthal communities. Mortuary belief and ritual is, needless to say, remarkably complex among modern human populations (e.g. Chamberlain and Parker Pearson 2001), and there is no a priori reason why the same need not apply to the Neanderthals. The issue relates to several areas of importance, from the simple behavioural and technical to the metaphysical. Kolen, for example (1999), has made a convincing argument that Neanderthals in life ordered space from their bodies outwards, and I have argued that the nature of their bodies played an important social role (Pettitt 2000). If this is the case, did they return that organisation to centre upon the body in death?

In Chapter 4, I interpreted the hominin remains in the Skhūl and Qafzeh caves in terms of the practices of funerary caching and simple grave inhumation, in association with the use of fire and ochre. Chronologically, the subject matter of this chapter – the Neanderthals – continues on from the early *Homo sapiens* among whom these practices were first observed. Although it would be incorrect to link them – as we shall see at least 30,000 years may separate the two – this could nevertheless be meaningful: as I discuss below Neanderthals seem both to have continued the practice of funerary caching, simple inhumation (in some cases in multiple numbers) but also to add a number of practices to the record. It may be, therefore, that they do represent a degree of development in the mortuary realm.

Chronology of Neanderthal remains

The greater part of the Neanderthal hypodigm is comprised of highly fragmentary skeletal remains, which probably account for approaching 500 individuals in total. This stands in sharp contrast to the remains of the preceding hominin taxon in Europe, *Homo heidelbergensis*, which, excluding the remarkable specimens from the Sima de los Huesos discussed in Chapter 3, are represented by only a couple of dozen remains for a period of 300,000 years or more. Surprisingly (although perhaps importantly from a mortuary sense as we shall see in Chapter 6) the record of the earliest *Homo sapiens* populations who replaced the Neanderthals in Europe is also poor. In terms of physical anthropology the Neanderthals present a chronologically defined sample of skeletal material spanning in the main some 100,000 years between ~130,000 and 30,000 BP, broadly corresponding to the Upper Pleistocene (MIS5, 4 and 3).

Although Neanderthal remains are found throughout the Upper Pleistocene (and depending on how one classifies earlier hominin fossils back into the Middle Pleistocene), the more complete skeletons that are usually seen as burials have a far more restricted chronological distribution. With the possible exception of Tabun and La Ferrassie, all burials for which there is reliable chronological data post-date *c.*70,000 and run down to ~34,000 BP. Chronological data, where it exists, is noted in Table 5.1. It is questionable whether the fragmentary Neanderthal remains at La Quina were deliberately buried. It is possible that they were on the grounds of preservation and articulation and a 'horizontal' positioning; if one assumes they were they could establish the practice of burial back to MIS4 on sedimentological and archaeological grounds, although the scanty dating evidence suggests an age between *c.*48 and 75ka BP which is consistent with the main cluster of dated burials after 60,000 BP. The La Ferrassie remains are also undated, at least to anything more precise than a similar 'second stage of early Last Glacial'

Table 5.1 More complete Neanderthal remains discussed in the text. In addition to specific references, the following monographs and papers are of particular use: Oakley et al. 1971; Day 1986; Binant 1991; Defleur 1993; Riel-Salvatore and Clark 2001; Zilhão and Trinkaus 2002b; Maureille and Vandermeersch 2007; Maureille and Tillier 2008. La Ferrassie 4a and 7 are not included as they have been shown to be part of La Ferrassie 3 and Le Moustier 2 respectively, and La Ferrassie 4b is now numbered La Ferrassie 4 (B. Maureille pers. Comm.). I have also excluded Teshik-Tash as dubious, and Zaskalnaya due to a lack of information.

Specimen	Site details	Chronology	Arguments for	Preservation, sex, age, pathologies	Cultural features of the skeleton	Archaeological features	Major references
La Ferrassie 1	La Ferrassie Rockshelter, Savignac-de-Miremont, Dordogne, France	60–75,000 BP (chrono-stratigraphy)	Completeness, articulation, association with stone slabs, proximity to La Ferrassie 2, definition of shallow depression	Adult male, near-complete skeleton	Placed in natural or artificial depression close to rear wall of shelter, laid on right side and flexed. Three large, flat stones placed below head and either side of torso	Base of Bed C, Ferrassie Mousterian occupation horizon	Capitan and Peyrony 1912a, 1912b, 1921; Peyrony 1934; Delporte 1976; Heim 1976; Maureille and van Peer 1998; B. Maureille pers. comm.
La Ferrassie 2	La Ferrassie Rockshelter, Savignac-de-Miremont, Dordogne, France	60–75,000 BP (chrono-stratigraphy)	Completeness, articulation, proximity to La Ferrassie 1	Adult female, near-complete skeleton	Close to rear wall of shelter, laid on right side and flexed	Base of Bed C, Ferrassie Mousterian occupation horizon	Capitan and Peyrony 1912a. 1912b. 1921. Peyrony 1934 Delporte 1976. Heim 1976; B. Maureille pers. comm.
La Ferrassie 3	La Ferrassie Rockshelter, Savignac-de-Miremont, Dordogne, France	60–75,000 BP (chrono-stratigraphy)	Preservation, grave cutting, proximity to La Ferrassie 4 and 4b	~10-year-old child. Partial cranial and postcranial remains	Placed in small grave cutting and part of group	Ferrassie Mousterian occupation horizon	Capitan and Peyrony 1912a, 1912b, 1921; Peyrony 1934; Delporte 1976; Heim 1976; B. Maureille pers. comm.

La Ferrassie 4	La Ferrassie Rockshelter, Savignac-de-Miremont, Dordogne, France	60–75,000 BP (chrono-stratigraphy)	Preservation, grave cutting, proximity to La Ferrassie 3	Neonate, partial skeleton	Placed in grave cutting	Ferrassie Mousterian occupation horizon	Capitan and Peyrony 1912a, 1912b, 1921; Peyrony 1934; Delporte 1976; Heim 1976; B. Maureille pers. comm.
La Ferrassie 5	La Ferrassie Rockshelter, Savignac-de-Miremont, Dordogne, France	60–75,000 BP (chrono-stratigraphy)	Preservation, clear grave cutting	~6–7 month foetus, partial cranial and postcranial skeleton, found close to La Ferrassie 8	Placed in small, shallow bowl-shaped depression, possible association with three flint scrapers placed at the base of a small mound possibly constructed above	Ferrassie Mousterian occupation horizon	Capitan and Peyrony 1912a, 1912b, 1921; Peyrony 1934; Delporte 1976; Heim 1976; B. Maureille pers. comm.
La Ferrassie 6	La Ferrassie Rockshelter, Savignac-de-Miremont, Dordogne, France	60–75,000 BP (chrono-stratigraphy)	Preservation, articulation, recovered from one of six depressions	~3-year-old child. Near-complete postcranial skeleton	Placed in sub-triangular depression, three flint implements found in association (one point and two scrapers)	Ferrassie Mousterian occupation horizon	Capitan and Peyrony 1912a, 1912b, 1921; Peyrony 1934; Delporte 1976; Heim 1976; B. Maureille pers. comm.
La Ferrassie 8	La Ferrassie Rockshelter, Savignac-de-Miremont, Dordogne, France	60–75,000 BP (chrono-stratigraphy)	Clear grave cutting possibly removed by water leaching	~2-year-old child, fragmentary cranial postcranial elements found close to La Ferrassie 5		Ferrassie Mousterian occupation horizon	Delporte 1976; Heim 1976; B. Maureille pers. comm.
La Quina 1	La Quina, Charente	55–65,000 BP (chrono-stratigraphy)	Preservation, articulation	Adult, cranium and partially complete skeleton of upper body	'Placed horizontally' facing out to valley according to excavator	Found amid lithics and fauna of Quina Mousterian layer	Defleur 1993

continued . . .

Table 5.1 continued

La Chapelle-aux-Saints	La Chapelle-aux-Saints cave, near Brive, Corrèze, France	ESR measurements suggest ~40–60,000 BP (2σ)	Completeness, articulation, clear rectangular grave cutting	Male, adult. Near complete cranial and postcranial skeleton	Contracted partially on right side, within rectangular shallow grave cutting 145 × 100 × 30cm deep	Stratum 5, in context of Mousterian occupation deposit of Quina Mousterian nature	Bouyssonie et al. 1908; Roche 1976
Le Moustier 1	Le Moustier Lower Shelter	~40,000 BP (TL)	Articulation, position	14–16-year-old adolescent. Cranium, mandible and partially-complete postcranial skeleton	Laid on right side, flexed	Bed J Typical Mousterian occupation horizon	Defleur 1993
Le Moustier 2	Le Moustier Lower Shelter	~40,000 BP (TL)	Preservation, found within pit	Neonate	Found within pit but details non-existent	Bed J Typical Mousterian occupation horizon	Maureille 2002
Roc de Marsal I	Roc de Marsal cave, Dordogne, France	~70,000 BP (chrono-stratigraphy)	Preservation, articulation, found within clear grave cutting	Partial cranial and postcranial skeleton of infant ~2–3 years	Unclear, possibly laid on left side and flexed	Quina Mousterian	Turq 1989
Le Regourdou 1	La Grotte du Regourdou, Dordogne, France	55–65,000 BP (chrono-stratigraphy)	Relatively complete, articulation, apparent tomb	Adult	Laid on left side, probably flexed, covered with limestone paving and cairn and in apparent association with buried brown bear	Bed 4, lack of occupation traces other than brief pulse	Bonifay 1964; Bonifay and Vandermeersch 1965; Madelaine et al. 2009

Site	Location	Date	Condition of deposit	Skeleton	Position/articulation	Context	References
La Roche-à-Pierrot (Saint-Césaire)	La Roche-à-Pierrot rock-shelter, Saint-Césaire, Charente-Maritime, France	~36,300 ± 2,700 BP (TL on burnt flints)	Location of remains within restricted area, with articulation of some elements e.g. hand bones; lack of articulated faunal remains by contrast	Adult, fragmentary and disarticulated cranial and postcranial skeleton with most elements represented except the feet	Disarticulated remains within 70cm diameter area close to rear wall of shelter	Uppermost Level E$_{JOP}$ Châtel-perronian occupation horizon, close to combustion zone	Mercier et al. 1991; Lévêque et al. 1993; Backer 1993; Backer and Guilbaud 1993; Vandermeersch 1993

Belgium

Spy I	Spy Cave, Orneau Valley, Namur, Belgium	34–36,000 BP (chrono-stratigraphy)	Deposits seem undisturbed	Cranio-mandibular and some postcranial elements, not in articulation	Not in articulation	Layer F yellow clay, in association with Mousterian occupation deposit	Semal et al. 2008
Spy II	Spy Cave, Orneau Valley, Namur, Belgium	34–36,000 BP (chrono-stratigraphy)	Deposits seem undisturbed, articulation	Partially complete cranial and postcranial skeleton	Laid on right side with hand lying against mandible	Layer F yellow clay, in association with Mousterian occupation deposit	Semal et al. 2008
Neanderthal 1	Kleine Feldhofer Grotte, Neanderthal, Near Düsseldorf	39–41,000 ^{14}C BP (direct AMS radiocarbon measurements)	Relative completeness (given that it has been dynamited)	Partially complete cranial and postcranial skeleton	Unknown	Micoquian	Schmitz and Thissen 2000; Schmitz et al. 2002

continued . . .

Table 5.1 continued

	Location	Date	Evidence	Description	Position	Context	References
Neanderthal 2	Kleine Feldhofer Grotte, Neanderthal, Near Düsseldorf	39–41,000 ^{14}C BP (direct AMS radiocarbon measurements)	Second individual	Fragmentary postcranial elements	Unknown	Micoquian	Schmitz and Thissen 2000
Israel							
Tabun 1 ('Tabun C1')	Mugharet-et-Tabun, Mount Carmel, Israel	Stratigraphic attribution is contested but probably ~110–150,000 BP	Preservation and articulation, possibly in shallow grave, close to large limestone block	Female adult ~30 years old), near-complete cranial and postcranial skeleton		Either Layer B or Layer C, Levalloiso-Mousterian occupation	Garrod and Bate 1937; Bar-Yosef and Callander 1999
Amud 1	Amud cave, Wadi Amud, Upper Galilee, Northern Israel.	50–80,000 BP (TL)	Articulation, lack of disturbance despite location in centre of cave under drip line	Male adult, almost complete skeleton	Contracted, on left side	Formation B, deposited amidst occupation level attributable to Levalloiso-Mousterian	Suzuki and Takai 1970; Sakura 1970; Rak et al. 1994; Hovers et al. 1995; Valladas et al. 1999; Hovers et al. 2000
Amud 7		50–80,000 BP (TL)	Articulation and number of elements present; by contrast all faunal remains highly fragmentary	10-month-old infant. Cranial, mandibular and dental elements; vertebrae, ribs, longbones, fragmentary scapulae, pelvis, sternum, phalanges	Placed on right side, atop bedrock in a small niche against the cave's wall. Maxilla of red deer contacting pelvis	Occupation level attributable to Levalloiso-Mousterian	Rak et al. 1994; Hovers et al. 1995; Valladas et al. 1999; Hovers et al. 2000

Specimen	Location	Dating	Taphonomic criteria	Skeletal description	Grave/context description	Occupation level	References
Amud 9		*Terminus post quem* of 50–80,000 BP	Articulation, located in same area of cave as other hominin remains/burials	Adult, articulated bones of lower leg and foot.		Occupation level attributable to Levalloiso-Mousterian	Hovers *et al.* 1995; Valladas *et al.* 1999; Hovers *et al.* 2000
Kebara KMHI	Kebara Cave, Mount Carmel, Israel	~50–60,000 BP (^{14}C, TL, ESR)	Preservation, recovery from restricted area, association with stones	~7–9-month-old infant partial skeleton	Found close to three stones and a *Rhinoceros* tooth	Levalloiso-Mousterian occupation horizon (in dump area)	Bar-Yosef *et al.* 1992. Tillier *et al.* 2003
Kebara KMHII	Kebara Cave, Mount Carmel, Israel	~50–60,000 BP (^{14}C, TL, ESR)	Preservation, articulation	Adult male partial postcranial skeleton	Laid on its back in grave cutting	Levalloiso-Mousterian occupation horizon (in central area)	Bar-Yosef *et al.* 1992. Tillier *et al.* 2003
Syria							
Dederiyeh I	Dederiyeh Cave, Afrin, Syria	Layers dated to ~47–55,000 (^{14}C) BP	Near-complete, articulation, excellent preservation despite intense occupation activity	~2-year-old infant, articulated near-complete cranial and postcranial skeleton	Laid on back, arms extended and legs flexed. Head possibly lain on stone slab; triangular flint found near chest	Layer 11	Dodo *et al.* 1998; Akazawa and Muhesen 2002; Akazawa *et al.* 2002a, 2002b
Dederiyeh 2	Dederiyeh Cave, Afrin, Syria	Layers dated to ~47–55,000 (^{14}C) BP	Partially complete, found in pit context	~2 years old, remains isolated within pit but in anatomical position	14 Mousterian lithics, >100 waste flakes, and fauna also found in pit	Layer 3	Dodo *et al.* 1998; Akazawa and Muhesen 2002; Akazawa *et al.* 2002a, 2002b

continued . . .

Table 5.1 continued

Iraqi Kurdistan

Shanidar I (Shanidar 1 of Trinkaus 1983)	Shkaft Mazin Shanidar, Zagros Mountains	40–50,000 BP	None forwarded	Male, 30–45. Skull, postcranial skeleton	Associated with rock fall	Layer D: deposited amid occupation level attributable to Levalloiso-Mousterian. close proximity to hearths, lithics and fauna	Solecki 1963, 1972; Trinkaus 1983; Cowgill *et al.* 2007
Shanidar II (Shanidar 2)	Shkaft Mazin Shanidar, Zagros Mountains	40–50,000 BP	None forwarded	Male, 20–30. Skull, vertebrae, some limb bones	Associated with rock fall	Layer D: deposited amid occupation level attributable to Levalloiso-Mousterian. close proximity to hearths, lithics and fauna	Solecki 1963, 1972; Trinkaus 1983; Cowgill *et al.* 2007
Shanidar III (Shanidar 3)	Shkaft Mazin Shanidar, Zagros Mountains	40–50,000 BP	None forwarded	Male, 40–50. Teeth, some postcranial bones	Covered with cluster of limestone cobbles possibly not resulting from rock fall, but evidence of rock fall is also present	Layer D: deposited amidst occupation level attributable to Levalloiso-Mousterian. close proximity to hearths, lithics and fauna	Solecki 1963, 1972; Trinkaus 1983; Cowgill *et al.* 2007

Shanidar IV (Shanidar 4)	Shkaft Mazin Shanidar, Zagros Mountains	*Terminus ante quem* of 40–50,000 BP	Articulation, location, spatial association with other Shanidar hominins	Male, 30–45. Skull, postcranial skeleton	Probably a burial. Contained within niche of large rocks.	Layer D: deposited amid occupation level attributable to Levalloiso-Mousterian. close proximity to hearths, lithics and fauna	Solecki 1963, 1972; Trinkaus 1983; Cowgill *et al.* 2007; Sommer 1999
Shanidar V (Shanidar 5)	Shkaft Mazin Shanidar, Zagros Mountains	40–50,000 BP	None forwarded	Male, 35–50. Cranium, some limb bones	Associated with rock fall	Layer D: deposited amid occupation level attributable to Levalloiso-Mousterian. close proximity to hearths, lithics and fauna	Solecki 1963, 1972; Trinkaus 1983; Cowgill *et al.* 2007
Shanidar VI (Shanidar 6)	Shkaft Mazin Shanidar, Zagros Mountains	*Terminus ante quem* of 40–50,000 BP	Articulation, location, spatial association with other Shanidar hominins	Female, 20–35. Skull, postcranial skeleton	Probably a burial	Layer D: deposited amid occupation level attributable to Levalloiso-Mousterian. close proximity to hearths, lithics and fauna	Solecki 1963, 1972; Trinkaus 1983; Cowgill *et al.* 2007

continued . . . .

Table 5.1 continued

Shanidar Child (Shanidar 7)	Shkaft Mazin Shanidar, Zagros Mountains	40–50,000 BP	Articulation, location, spatial association with other Shanidar hominins	Indeterminate sex, 6–9 months	Associated with rock fall	Layer D: deposited amid occupation level attributable to Levalloiso-Mousterian. close proximity to hearths, lithics and fauna	Solecki 1963, 1972; Trinkaus 1983; Cowgill *et al.* 2007
Shanidar VII (Shanidar 8)	Shkaft Mazin Shanidar, Zagros Mountains	*Terminus ante quem* of 40–50,000 BP	Articulation, location, spatial association with other Shanidar hominins	Female, young adult. Cranium, some limb bones	Probably a burial	Layer D: deposited amid occupation level attributable to Levalloiso-Mousterian. close proximity to hearths, lithics and fauna	Solecki 1963, 1972; Trinkaus 1983; Cowgill *et al.* 2007
Shanidar VIII (Shanidar 9)	Shkaft Mazin Shanidar, Zagros Mountains	*Terminus ante quem* of 40–50,000 BP	Articulation, location, spatial association with other Shanidar hominins	Indeterminate sex, 6–12 months. Cevical and thoracic vertebrae	Probably a burial	Layer D: deposited amid occupation level attributable to Levalloiso-Mousterian. close proximity to hearths, lithics and fauna	Solecki 1963, 1972; Trinkaus 1983; Cowgill *et al.* 2007

Shanidar 10	Shkaft Mazin Shanidar, Zagros Mountains	MIS3, MIS4 or MIS5: *terminus ante quem* of 50–80,000 BP	None forwarded	Indeterminate sex, 1–2 years		Layer D:	Cowgill *et al.* 2007
Ukraine							
Kiik-Koba 1	Kiik-Koba (Ibex Cave), Crimea	50–70,000 BP (indirect chronostratigraphy)	Contained within artificially widened natural hollow, proximity to burial 2	Adult, fragmentary postcranial skeleton	Laid on right side and probably flexed, within natural fissure	Kiik-Koba lower level, Crimean Middle Palaeolithic occupation	Stepanchuk 1998
Kiik-Koba 2	Kiik-Koba (Ibex Cave), Crimea	50–70,000 BP (indirect chronostratigraphy)	Articulation and preservation; proximity to burial 1	~1-year-old infant partial postcranial skeleton	Located 30cm from burial 1, laid on left side and flexed	Kiik-Koba lower level, Crimean Middle Palaeolithic occupation	Stepanchuk 1998
Zaskalnaya VIa	Zaskalnaya VI	~39–40,000 BP (^{14}C)	Information unavailable	~1-year-old infant	Possible association with (empty) pits	In context of Eastern Micoquian occupation	Smirnov 1989
Zaskalnaya VIb	Zaskalnaya VI	~39–40,000 BP (^{14}C)	Information unavailable	~2–3-year-old infant	Possible association with (empty) pits	In context of Eastern Micoquian occupation	Smirnov 1989
Zaskalnaya VIc	Zaskalnaya VI	~39–40,000 BP (^{14}C)	Information unavailable	~5–6-year-old child	Possible association with (empty) pits	In context of Eastern Micoquian occupation	Smirnov 1989
Russia							
Mezmaiskaya	Mezmaiskaya Cave, Northern Caucasus	Directly dated by AMS ^{14}C to 29,195 ± 965 (Ovchinnikov *et al.* 2000)	Contained within pit	Some cranial remains, 7 month foetus – 2 month neonate	Found within a pit, possibly covered with limestone block	Layer 2, in context of Middle Palaeolithic occupation	Golovanova *et al.* 1999; Ovchinnikov *et al.* 2000

[handwritten annotation: An indicate new taphonomic phenomenon → cultural change]

period, although if techno-typological schemes such as those of Mellars (e.g. 1996) are correct one might expect the burials to belong broadly to MIS5, given that the association is with a Ferrassie Mousterian variant and therefore would pre-date the Quina variant of MIS4.

As currently known, therefore, burials *sensu stricto* are restricted in the main to MIS3. The Amud 1 skeleton has a *terminus post quem* of 50–80 ka BP (I incorporate here both early and late uptake models for U-Series results, reading each at two sigma. These agree well with the Thermoluminescence terminus post quem of 50,000–60,000 BP: Schwarcz and Rink 1998). The Roc de Marsal infant is indirectly dated to ~70,000 BP which is in accord with its Quina Mousterian context (Turq 1989). The Shanidar burials are fairly convincingly dated to 40,000–50,000 BP as discussed below, and the Kebara skeleton is securely dated to c.60,000 BP (Valladas *et al.* 1988; Schwarcz *et al.* 1989). At the younger end of the range the Roche-à-Pierrot (Saint-Cézaire) burial has been directly dated by thermoluminescence to 36,300 ± 2,700 BP (Mercier *et al.* 1991). Clearly a new depositional phenomenon came into play on Middle Palaeolithic sites at the start of MIS3 or late in MIS4. This should, in my opinion, be taken as evidence of *cultural* change, rather than taphonomic; given the abundance of Middle Palaeolithic sites before 60,000 BP and rich Lower Palaeolithic cave assemblages before that, it is difficult to see why it is only from this time that decently complete Neanderthal skeletons are found. If the change is, as I believe, cultural, the sensible interpretation is that it relates to the introduction of burial into whatever funerary traditions already existed. That this change in the Middle Palaeolithic record should occur *after* another similar change seen in the record of *Homo sapiens* in the Levant – which should also be taken to reflect cultural, not taphonomic, change – could be significant (Hublin 2000).

Funerary caching

While fragmentary remains of single individuals could derive from many depositional factors, funerary caching may account for the preservation of skeletal parts at sites where Neanderthal remains are fairly numerous. In the absence of indications that the relative abundance of Neanderthal remains relate solely to occupational intensity one would otherwise have to account for catastrophic events that led to the deposition of multiple Neanderthals within a few square metres of space. Caching, however, is not inconsistent with a desire to *remove* the decaying bodies of the dead from the camp sites of the living; as Mussi (1988, 99) has suggested, Neanderthals in Italy seem to have been 'clearing' their occupation sites of their dead, perhaps to minimise the dangers of carnivores that such decay might bring, and if this is so, bodies need to be taken *somewhere*. It follows that the development of specific places of funerary caching arise from an enculturation of the landscape, the concept that there are appropriate places to dispose of the dead.

·Have a appropich Places for dead

I discussed in Chapter 3 the possibility of early Neanderthal funerary caching before ~225,000 BP at Pontnewydd Cave, Wales. This is an isolated case and potentially fully taphonomic in explanation, although a number of sites with multiple fragmentary Neanderthal remains derive from the Upper Pleistocene. Notable among these are La Quina, Charente, the Caverna (Grotta) delle Fate, Italy, El Sidrón Cave, Spain, and Krapina, Croatia. The latter two sites present important evidence of carcass processing and are discussed later in this chapter. At La Quina, the remains of at least five individuals were recovered over several excavations (Verna et al. 2010). Most of these are partial, and mainly cranial elements, although one (H5) contains many bones of the upper body at least.[4] While it is unclear that H5 was intentionally buried, the recovery of many parts of the upper body and apparent lack of carnivore gnawing adds weight to a deliberate deposition of this body. The proliferation of parts, and an MNI of 5 with the probability that the actual number of individuals represented was much higher as with Pontnewydd, make La Quina a likely focus for caching of bodies or their parts, somewhere in mid MIS3 on the basis of available radiometric data. The 13 Neanderthal specimens recovered from the Caverna (Grotta) delle Fate in Liguria, Italy (Giacomo and de Lumley 1988), representing a minimum of one adult and two infants (aged 3–4 and 8–10) and a maximum of 13 individuals of which up to five infants may be represented, and dominated by cranial fragments, mandibles, teeth and a phalange may, albeit less convincingly, also relate to the deliberate deposition of body – in this case head – parts.

These four sites belong to two broad periods – MIS7 and MIS3. If the interpretation of funerary caching is correct, then their observations are most important, as they not only indicate the potential origins of mortuary deposition of the dead, but by implication also indicate the use of persistent places as foci for the deposition of *multiple* individuals. Needless to say, the database is too poor and ambiguous to make any clear statements, but the re-emergence of the tradition in two distinct regions obviously requires explanation.

Primary and secondary activity

Stone tool cut marks have been found on a number of Neanderthal bones. While the old case for 'cannibalism' and 'skull cults' at Grotta Guattari, Monte Circeo, Italy, relied on a cranium that has subsequently been shown not to bear deliberate hominin modification (White and Toth 1991), the widening of its foramen magnum probably caused by hyenas (d'Errico 1991), some clear examples do exist and need to be explained, and offer a limited indication that, at least on occasion, Neanderthals were processing the soft tissues of the dead. While claims for cannibalism have never quite gone away, these are now usually interpreted as reflecting defleshing rather than cannibalism per se. Most recently, however, cannibalism has been suggested as the cause behind modifications to a number of the 78 fragments of Neanderthal bones (MNI=6) from level XV of Moula Guercy Cave in Southeast France (Defleur et al. 1999). Here, as with many of the ungulate remains with which they are spatially associated, the Neanderthal bones bore traces of cut marks, percussion impact scars, anvil striae and internal conchoidal scars indicative of defleshing before smashing with a hammerstone and anvil. Defleur et al. (1999, 131) infer that 'qualitative and quantitative studies of modifications to the hominid and nonhominid faunal assemblages from Moula-Guercy level XV demonstrate parallels in processing', and furthermore point to cut mark evidence for 'successive strokes of the same implement in defleshing and percussing', concluding that individuals were defleshed and disarticulated. There would be no reason to use this data to separate the treatment of the Neanderthal body here from that at Krapina, but the case for cannibalism *of sorts* is presented by the subsequent smashing of bones to expose the marrow cavity. The authors conclude that 'the Moula-Guercy fossils . . . are now the best evidence that some Neanderthals practiced cannibalism' (ibid. 131). But how extensive is this? The cut marks reveal the severing of tendons and the temporalis muscle, which are consistent with defleshing. The more robust evidence for cannibalism relates to the removal of a tongue as indicated by cut marks on the lingual surface of a juvenile mandible, and some removal of thigh musculature and possible disarticulation of the shoulder on other individuals. Given the ambiguity between evidence of defleshing and cannibalism, and the lack of a comprehensive account of the data as yet, it is best to treat the Moula Guercy data as preliminary.

Peyrony suggested that the infant buried in a pit at La Ferrassie (burial 6) – see below – had been decapitated and had its face removed, on the basis of bone preservation and location (1934, 35), and the secondary processing of numerous Neanderthal remains at Krapina, Croatia, apparently for defleshing (Russell 1987) is well known. In addition, cut marks on Neanderthal bones from Engis, Belgium, Marillac and Combe Grenal, France and El Sidrón, Spain (Le Mort 1988, 1989; Defleur et al. 1993; Rosas et al. 2006) also relate to defleshing, and one cannot eliminate the possibility that incomplete remains of infants – notably those found in pits (see p. 135) reflect the inhumation of body parts originally defleshed, whether naturally or artificially, elsewhere. The Engis 2 calvarium, which bears cut marks indicative of the removal of the scalp, is that of a juvenile (Russell and Le Mort 1986). Whatever the real reason, or reasons, behind the removal of soft tissues from dead Neanderthals, the cut mark evidence at least must be taken as a very clear and unambiguous indicator of interest in the dead body among at least some Neanderthal communities. Perhaps this is not surprising: hunting communities have an intimate knowledge of the anatomy of their prey (e.g. Spiess 1979) and it is difficult to see how at least some simple knowledge of their own anatomy could escape Neanderthals. The question is, of course, whether this interest in and exploration of the body was practised primarily through a concern for subsistence (i.e. cannibalism) or other 'life-based' reason we do not understand, or a concern about the dead body. The nature of the evidence as it stands urges caution, and it is simply noted here that this *may* present some evidence for secondary processing.

Cronos compulsions and multiple processing sites: Krapina and El Sidrón

Krapina, Croatia

The relatively high number of Neanderthal remains recovered from Beds 3 and 4 of the Krapina rockshelter have attracted considerable attention and merit specific discussion here. The proliferation of highly fragmentary Neanderthal remains from the site – about 900 dating to MIS5e (with mean ESR determinations of 130 ± 10ka BP: Rink *et al.* 1995) – represents around two dozen individuals (based on the postcranial remains), with an MNI of 23 based on associated dentition (see Trinkaus 1995, 127 and Orschiedt 2008 for a discussion of this). These were associated with Middle Palaeolithic tools and fauna indicative, it would seem, of occupation of the rockshelter (Radovčic 1988). Clearly all major age ranges are present (Orschiedt notes five infants, four juveniles and 14 adults). Cut marks are relatively abundant on cranial and postcranial remains – particularly of juveniles (Patou-Mathis 1997, 76), and although estimates differ and are difficult to evaluate as the remains are covered with preservative (compare the figures of Ullrich, Russell and Patou-Mathis discussed by Orschiedt 2008 for example) even the most cautious figures of Patou-Mathis (1997) show that they are relatively abundant on crania (N=6, 3 per cent), clavicles (N=3, 18 per cent), scapulae (N=2, 11 per cent), one humerus (4 per cent), one ulna (10 per cent), one femur (11 per cent), one tibia (10 per cent), ribs (N=3, 4 per cent), one talus (8 per cent) and one metacarpal (20 per cent). From this one can at least conclude that several individuals were processed at the site. Nutritional cannibalism was dismissed as an explanation for the fragmentary and cut marked remains by Russell (1987) who interpreted them as being indicative of defleshing, probably as part of secondary burial. Although one cannot fully eliminate the possibility that a catastrophic natural event deposited the remains (Bocquet-Appel and Arsuaga 1999), the evidence of processing is clear, and Krapina provides the most compelling evidence for secondary processing of Neanderthal bodies, and potential evidence for funerary caching of the processed bones of the dead. Orschiedt (2008) has conducted a comprehensive analysis of the case for cannibalism at Krapina. He argued that it is unlikely that the remains were originally buried in anatomical position as elements of the facial skeleton, skull base, vertebrae and hand and foot bones are under-represented. He further showed that several cut marks appear more recent in origin and that the orientation of those that bear genuine antiquity does not in all but two cases

95

indicate disarticulation. The clearest signs of activity – themselves still open to question according to Orschiedt – are cut marks on the frontal bone of cranium 3 that are consistent with scalping. His results are, however, consistent with the notion of secondary burial, as discussed by Patou-Mathis (1997).

El Sidrón, Spain

At least eight individuals are represented by ~1,323 fragmentary fossils from El Sidrón Cave in Asturias, Spain. The bones seem to have been deposited outside the cave system and subsequently redeposited within a transverse gallery ~150m from the cave's current entrance (Figure 5.1), although refitting of a number of bones, representation of all skeletal parts including small elements such as hyoids and phalanges, and lithics suggest that movement has been limited (Rosas *et al.* 2006, 19266). Direct ^{14}C dating of three hominin specimens and amino-acid racemisation dates on gastropods from the thin horizon in which the fossils were found demonstrate an age of ~37,000–41,000 BP (2σ). Four young adults, one infant, one juvenile and two adolescents are so-far recognised. As with the Sima de los Huesos, faunal remains were relatively rare, and associated Mousterian lithics include Levallois points and

Figure 5.1 Excavations in the transverse gallery at El Sidrón, Asturias, Spain, have yielded a number of Neanderthal remains with marks indicative of processing (photograph courtesy of Antonio Rosas, Grupo de Paleo Antropologia MNCN-CSIC).

several flakes that refit to a core show that activity near the cave includes occupation. Evidence for human modification is abundant, in the form of cut marks, flakes, percussion pitting, conchoidal scars and adhering flakes (Rosas *et al.* 2006, 19269). Broadly these modifications relate both to disarticulation and skinning, although there is evidence that treatment of the corpse varied between individuals. Some cranio-mandibular remains, for example, show a concern with the removal and probable consumption of brains, whereas on other individuals these are unmodified. Thus while a degree of nutritional cannibalism is evident, processing seems to have had wider purposes.

The inhumation debate: burying the doubts over Neanderthal burial

Gargett (1989, 1999, see also 2000) has forwarded a literature-based critique of Neanderthal burial based on sedimentology, stratigraphy and taphonomy. He drew attention to the 'double standards'[5] applied to Palaeolithic research in that 'it is simply assumed that with [anatomically modern] human remains discovered in an archaeological context [they] were placed there purposely' (ibid. 157), given that the criteria for recognition of purposeful burial were ill-defined due to the ubiquity of burial in later prehistory, history and the ethnographic present. With Neanderthals, as he notes, the proportion of fragmentary remains is considerably higher in the Upper Pleistocene record than for modern humans, which has led to the assumption that preservation of more complete Neanderthal remains is owing to deliberate burial. While he is right to stress processes of sedimentation in enclosed sites as potential factors in the preservation of skeletal remains, his critique of possible burials at 11 sites is largely unconvincing. Recent interpretations of Neanderthal burial are certainly more conservative than previous, because a number of dubious examples have been eliminated as part of a wider critique of Neanderthal 'ritual', such as the Drachenloch and Regourdou 'bear cults' (Bonifay 1964).[6] More recent estimates, however, still vary considerably, from 36 burials spread over 16 sites (Harrold 1980); 34 (Defleur 1993, 216, who notes that 22 adults and 12 infants retain at least a degree of anatomical connection); to more inclusive counts at (60 (Smirnov 1989), and a cautious reading of the evidence by Bar-Yosef (1988) putting the number at 12–14 for Europe and about 20 in western Asia, and Otte (1996) who notes 20 burials for the European continent split into western and eastern groups and 12 for the Near East. In all, then, excluding Smirnov's optimistic account, it would seem that scholarly opinion converges on *c.*32–36 convincing indicators of burial (Maureille and Tillier 2008). While most scholars would probably agree that Neanderthals therefore at least on occasion buried their dead, even if one includes possible 'caching' of Neanderthal remains (see below) this still only amounts to well under 100 individuals for the Late Middle and Upper Pleistocene overall. On the basis of this it is certainly premature to make simple conclusions such as 'Neanderthals buried their dead'. As apparently with Upper Palaeolithic modern humans, burial may have been a very rare event for the Neanderthals and non-existent for much of the time.

My opinion that Gargett's attempt to deny any Neanderthal burials is largely unconvincing obviously requires justification. Many of his specific and literature-based readings of the data have been questioned by original excavators (see responses to Gargett 1989) and other specialists (e.g. Belfer-Cohen and Hovers 1992), and will be further explored below. In addition, the logic of Gargett's approach, particularly in his second paper (1999) can be criticised. In Levantine caves, for example, post-depositional disturbance of faunal and lithic assemblages is usually severe, yet superimposed upon this are the near-complete remains of several dozen Neanderthals and early modern humans that *must* have been protected by graves (Hovers *et al.* 1995, 52). In this, Gargett sets himself five main questions as a prelude to examining possible burials at five sites from France to the Near East. While there is no space to examine fully Gargett's methods and conclusions here, I list and discuss some salient criteria used by Gargett to 'identify' or reject burials. A comprehensive presentation of the evidence for Neanderthal burial has been made by Defleur (1993) and forms an excellent point of departure for the discussion below. Gargett's five questions are:

What constitutes evidence of purposeful protection of the corpse?

Gargett suggests that simple recognition of cuttings, pits and depressions that happen to contain Neanderthal remains is not enough to identify purposeful burial. Rather, he suggests that 'unless a new stratum can be distinguished, there is no logical way to argue that the remains were purposely protected' (ibid. 33). He derives this argument from the notion that the new (i.e. overlying) stratum is 'the key to discerning *unequivocally* that purposeful burial has occurred' (ibid. 33, his emphasis). To Gargett, 'if the overlying sediments are part of a more extensive deposit that includes the "fill" of the "pit", this greatly weakens the argument that the overlying sediments were the result of purposeful burial' (ibid. 33). It is difficult to find any logic in this statement. By their very nature – excavations into existing sediments that were eventually filled by those same sediments – there is no reason at all why one need invoke the deposition of new sediments above the grave fill. This is certainly no grounds for rejecting potential burials. There is a wider problem here, as identified by Hovers *et al.* (2000, 254), in that in caves with homogeneous sediments one simply cannot expect to identify a grave cutting, even with modern excavations methods. The excavation of a shallow grave followed by its re-filling with sediments identical to those surrounding it will by definition be impossible to identify as a sharp grave cutting millennia later. Using the lack of evidence of cuttings as evidence against burial is therefore 'raising the bar unrealistically high' (E. Hovers pers. comm.).

What is the probability of natural burial in caves and rockshelters?

Gargett's alternative explanation that Neanderthal skeletons may often be the result of rock falls or natural deaths while sleeping relies on cryoclastic depositional environments. Noting that such sites are 'inherently variable, inherently complex . . . which obviate the use of simplistic models of site formation and bone preservation' (ibid, 38), he suggests nevertheless one monolithic explanation, that materials may often accumulate favourably against cave walls or among boulders. If this is so, then delicate bones, and bones in articulation, will tend to preserve better in such protected locations. Taking into account various taphonomic factors, animal behaviour and spatial patterning, this conclusion is a gross simplification. There is no a priori reason why such locations should be 'more protected' than more central areas: streams, debris flows, mud flows, burrowers and denning carnivores are no respecters of low roofs and 'out-of-the-way places' as Gargett refers to them. In addition, the available spatial data from sites where burials do occur indicate that the density of archaeological materials *overall* does not cluster in such locations, so simple favourable preservation surely cannot be held likely. Burials can and do occur in very central locations; for example, the child at Roc de Marsal was recovered from almost the absolute centre of the cave and under 3m from the cave mouth (Figure 5.2). While sedimentological data is still ambiguous as regards deliberate burial, as Turq (1989) has noted, it certainly cannot be used to argue against burial. The Amud 1 virtually complete skeleton was also recovered 4m from the cave wall and right below the cave's over-hang line, hardly a protected position (Sakura 1970; Figure 5.3) even if it cannot be said to be central to the main occupation spread within the cave (E. Hovers pers. comm.). The Kebara 2 skeleton was emplaced in a central position where the interstratification of hearths was most intense, that is, a 'high activity' area (see below: Figure 5.4). This area, named the *décapage,* was an exceptionally rich cluster of large mammalian bones (Speth and Tchernov 1998).

Hovers *et al.* (2000, 254–5) have provided an excellent refutation of the case for the natural deposition of the Amud 7 infant in its niche (the nature of which is discussed below). Even if one took at face value the suggestion that if individuals come to lie close to cave walls they are more likely to be preserved, one might expect a far higher incidence of relatively complete animal remains, especially of denning animals, against walls. This is obviously not the case, as Bar-Yosef (2000) has noted. Despite the ubiquity of *Ursus spelaeus* in caves across Upper Pleistocene Europe, with the exception of several rich sites the greater majority of denning episodes are represented by milk teeth, claw-sharpening marks and paw prints, hardly taphonomically tough phenomena (Kurtén 1976). Neither do denning carnivores always deposit the bones of other cave users: as Aldhouse-Green (2001, 116) has noted, Neanderthal remains are extremely rare in Britain despite a profusion of caves with evidence

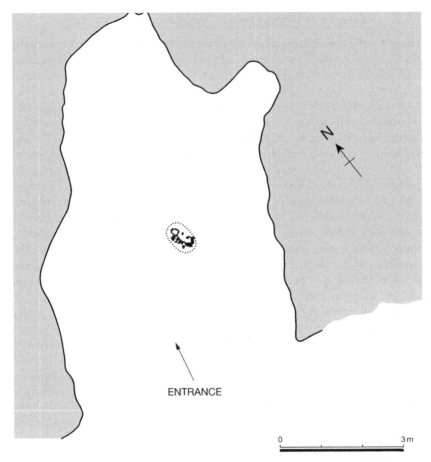

Figure 5.2 Plan of Roc de Marsal, Dordogne, showing the location of the child burial (redrawn from Turq 1989).

of carnivore activity and a respectable Middle Palaeolithic artefactual record. In fact, the same applies across Europe, that is, carnivore remains and archaeological indicators of human activity in caves are abundant from the Lower Palaeolithic onwards, despite apparent increased use of such caves from the later Middle Pleistocene (Fosse 1999). If a simple carnivore activity/ hominid bone accumulation correlation were ubiquitously in effect, one would expect a far richer Middle Pleistocene hominid fossil hypodigm. Nor need this be a depositional bias: carnivores depositing human remains cannot even be held to deposit remains mainly towards the sides of caves. For example, the fragmentary Neanderthal remains bearing traces of hyena processing found in MIS5 deposits at the Rochelot cave, Charente, were 'découvertes dispersés le long de la galerie' (Tournepiche 1994) and almost definitely represent one

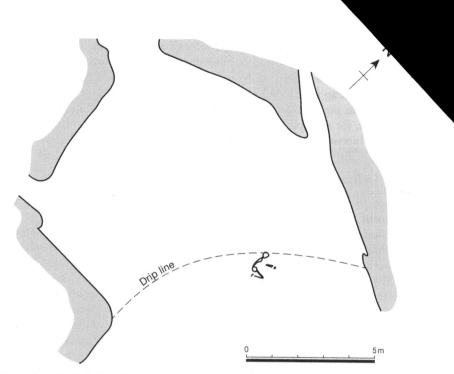

Figure 5.3 Plan of Amud Cave, Israel, showing the location of the Amud I burial under the cave's drip line (redrawn from Sakura 1970).

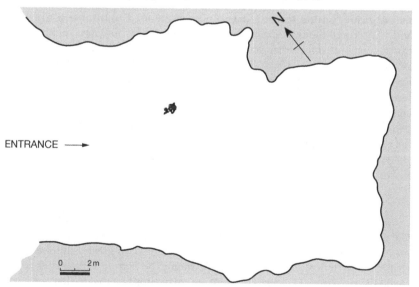

Figure 5.4 Plan of Kebara Cave, Israel, showing the location of the KMH2 burial (redrawn from Bar-Yosef *et al.* 1992).

ito the cave by hyenas (Tournepiche and Couture 1999).
ʳe in Hungary several remains pertaining (probably) to
ımature Neanderthal were discovered spread over more
ʼ.1996). Although the original excavator was unable to
ʼeason for such dispersal, enough animal modification of
le, on the manubrium of Subalyuk 1 (ibid., 244) exist
a likely cause.

What is the prior probability of preservation under any circumstances?

Noting that most Middle Palaeolithic human remains are known 'only from fragments of skeletal elements' (ibid., 38), Gargett observes that caves and rockshelters tend to preserve bone better than open air sites,[7] and that almost all Neanderthal skeletons recovered from such enclosed sites are incomplete. From this, Gargett believes that 'it is reasonable to suggest that equal weight be given to alternative explanations to account for the presence of articulated skeletal elements' (ibid., 39), that is, such locations where favourable preservation is more likely as discussed above. Thus, Gargett suggests that in 'out-of-the-way places' one not only finds greater preservation of bones per se, but greater preservation of small and articulated bones. Many such 'out-of-the-way places' are natural depressions in the floors of enclosed sites, and Gargett's reasoning that unless the depressions in which Neanderthal remains are found can be demonstrated to have been artificially excavated for the purpose of containing a body then they are not convincing indicators of burial, is tautological. Natural features may obviously be used to dispose of the dead and I interpret them as examples of my category of funerary caching, and features excavated for other original reasons such as storage may subsequently be employed for burial too. True, the issue is confused, but to use natural features to argue *against* the skeletons found within them being deliberately buried (or cached, as I would call it) is as simplistic as taking every near-complete Neanderthal skeleton as a deliberate burial. In some cases natural deposition can be eliminated as, for example, Hovers *et al.* (2000, 255–7) do for the Amud 7 infant. Most scholars seem to accept good preservation of skeletons, alongside articulation, as evidence of deliberate interment (see discussion in Smirnov 1989, 213; Maureille and Tiller 2008).

What is the importance of articulation?

Gargett suggests that 'all things being equal, the species dying in greater numbers [in enclosed sites] would naturally preserve in greater numbers' and that the dearth of skeletal preservation among the hominins of earlier times, such as *Homo erectus* (Gargett's attribution) may simply indicate that the latter spent less time in caves than Neanderthals. True, archaeological indicators of frequent use of enclosed sites only pick up from the later Middle Pleistocene.

However, archaeological assemblages from enclosed sites dating to before MIS5 are often rich in both lithics and fauna: I list several in Pettitt 2002. Logic determines, as Hayden (1993, 121) has noted, that depositional and tapho-nomic factors have remained similar in enclosed sites through the Lower, Middle and Upper Palaeolithic. One cannot therefore imply, as Gargett does, that the preservation of Neanderthal skeletons in enclosed sites relates simply to increased use of these sites, and one must remember the caution of Bar-Yosef (1988) that humans do not always bury their dead on their habitation sites. If this were so, they must surely be littered with near-complete skeletons of animals. In addition, why are they restricted to only three geographical clusters as Defleur (1993) has noted,[8] despite the occurrence of rich Middle Palaeolithic archaeology in many caves across Europe? To subscribe to Gargett's view one would also have to explain the absence of convincing Aurignacian burials (anywhere: see Chapter 6), the paucity of Gravettian burials in enclosed sites and the rarity of Solutrean and Magdalenian burials. By his own criteria, Upper Palaeolithic communities, who clearly used enclosed sites more intensively than Neanderthals, must surely have also wound up in natural features and become preserved by accident? But they are not there.

What is the variability in decomposition rates, disarticulation sequences, and the likelihood of disturbance?

Gargett points to the variable rates of destruction of anatomical elements by disarticulation, disturbance and decomposition. His conclusions that 'the vast majority of Middle Palaeolithic hominid remains succumbed to some form of physical disturbance, since there are so few skeletons' (ibid., 46) is hardly threatening to the notion of burial. It is difficult to see his point here. Further-more, his conclusion that 'postmortem disturbance, of whatever kind, need not, and I would argue did not happen in every case' seems to contradict his own view. From this it would seem that Gargett's point is that some other factor must be invoked to account for missing anatomical elements. Again, this is a separate issue from modes of deposition.

Simple inhumation

It is probably fair to say that most scholars would accept as deliberate burials a minimum of La Chapelle-aux-Saints, eight individuals at La Ferrassie, La Roche-à-Pierrot (Saint-Césaire) and Le Regourdou, in Europe; and Kebara 1 and 2, Amud 1, 7 and 9, Tabun C1, Shanidar IV, VI, VII and VIII and Dederiyeh 1 in the Near East (Figure 5.5). One might add several more to this list but this should be enough to convince us that some Neanderthals, at some times, buried some of their dead (Maureille and Vandermeersch 2007. Maureille and Tillier 2008). It would be incorrect to infer from this simply that 'Neanderthals buried their dead'; it may have been a rare event, although

Figure 5.5
Neanderthal
burials
discussed in the
text.

the repeated patterning evident at some sites where multiple individuals were buried suggests that there were at times burial 'traditions', even if these were relatively short-lived. I discuss here the major examples of simple inhumation. Others are discussed below under a consideration of multiple burial sites. I discuss first the burial of infants, as these are often described as being in 'pits' and might at first sight seem to warrant separate treatment from the burials of adults in shallow graves.

In death treated same as adults

Infants and pits

The proportion of foeti and infants in Middle Palaeolithic burials essentially mirrors their proportion in life, suggesting that in death they were accorded the same treatment as adults (Zilhão 2005). As Tillier (1995, 2008) has noted, the number of remains of infants in the Middle Palaeolithic hominin sample from the Near East is relatively large, possibly implying a taphonomic bias afforded by the protection of simple inhumation. More widely, the disposal of the dead – or parts of them – in pits must on occasion have been important, as in a number of cases the excavation of these has profoundly altered the palaeotopography of occupation sites such as at La Ferrassie and La Chapelle-aux-Saints in France and Dederiyeh, Syria. Human remains recovered from pits are usually published as burials – even an empty pit has been published as a burial (see below) – but it is worth examining the phenomenon of 'pit burial' in detail. I discuss the several infants from La Ferrassie towards the end of the chapter. The completeness of the recently rediscovered Le Moustier 2 neonate (to which belong the 'La Ferrassie 4a' isolated longbones: Maureille 2002a, 2002b), which died at four months or younger on the basis of its longbone size and concomitant stature, as well as a degree of articulation of the bones recently excavated from a sediment block (Maureille 2002b) suggest that it was intentionally buried in the site's Lower Shelter. The partial skeleton of a Neanderthal foetus or <2 month newborn[9] recovered from the lowest Mousterian level (Layer 3) at Mezmaiskaya Cave, northern Caucasus, is thought to represent an intentional burial despite the lack of sedimentological indications of a clear burial cutting (Golovanova et al. 1999). It would seem that the body was laid on its right side: the left scapula, humerus and radius and much of the vertebal column and ribs were in anatomical position, although the skull was damaged in the facial area and displaced and the legs had been severely displaced. The remains of an infant interred in the centre of the cave of Roc de Marsal, France (see above) also seems a convincing case of burial (Turq 1989). The partial skeleton was recovered from a clearly defined grave cutting 90 × 70cm in dimensions cut into Bed I. Although a degree of post-depositional disturbance seems evident, the plan of the burial suggests that the infant was laid on its left side.

Neanderthal pit burial has on occasion been suggested on the flimsiest of evidence. One unlikely example is an irregular subcircular pit 80 × 70cm in plan from Locus 1 of recent excavations at La Quina, Charente. Two lacteal human teeth were recovered on the periphery of this pit, which has therefore been viewed as 'la possibilité d'une sépulture' (Debénath and Jelínek 1998, 37). As the excavators suggest, the function of the pit may not have been primarily funerary, and while they are correct in that there is no a priori reason to discount a burial, two lacteal teeth on the periphery of a small pit is hardly a convincing indicator of mortuary behaviour, particularly on a site where fragmentary human remains are relatively numerous. Similarly, Bordes (1972, 135) suggested that a pit dug into Level 50 at Combe Grenal had a funerary function, even though no human remains were recovered from it. He reasoned that this must have been the burial of a child, the bones of which are more susceptible to decay, thus explaining their absence. One might, however, wonder why teeth or more robust bones didn't survive here and it is sensible to discount this pit as mortuary evidence. Other infant remains may represent burials but existing contextual evidence renders it impossible to establish this, such as the cranial and fragmentary postcranial remains of the child from Pech de l'Azé I, Dordogne associated with an MTA B assemblage and dating to ~40,000 BP (Soressi et al. 2007).

In addition to a possible adolescent burial discovered by Hauser and for which surviving data is ambiguous (Le Moustier I; see below), the Lower Shelter at Le Moustier, Dordogne, yielded the near-complete remains of an infant within a small pit in stratum I (Le Moustier 2: Peyrony 1930). Although lost for a time, the remains recently came to light and were reunited with their phalanges, which had been classified as 'La Ferrassie 4a' (Maureille 2002b). This pit (actually one of two, the other of which was empty apart from three limestone blocks near its surface), was roughly circular in plan, about 50cm in diameter and c.40cm deep, as opposed to 70–80 × 60cm for the 'empty' pit. Even Gargett (1989, 164) is forced to conclude that 'the evidence constrains us to accept that this pit was purposely dug'. He questioned, rather, whether the pit was deliberately dug to contain a burial. As Gargett notes, it is impossible to distinguish between various hypotheses due to insufficient data, although it has to be said that if the pits were excavated well after the deposition in the cave of the 'cranium, mandible and post cranial bone' of an infant (Oakley et al. 1971, 150) the chances of one of two pits being dug down directly onto the only surviving infant remains are necessarily slim. If, on the other hand, infant remains were placed in the pit in the later Middle Palaeolithic, then the issue of why only partial remains were recovered must be addressed. This can be seen elsewhere, notably at La Ferrassie, Dordogne and Dederiyeh, both discussed below.

The Amud 7 infant was laid on its right side within a niche against the cave wall, a clear case of funerary caching (Figure 5.6). Despite its fragile nature the skeleton is remarkably complete, which, in addition to a lack of gnawing marks, can be taken as a convincing indication that it was deliberately buried (Hovers et al. 1995). The recovery of a complete maxilla of red deer (Cervus elaphus)

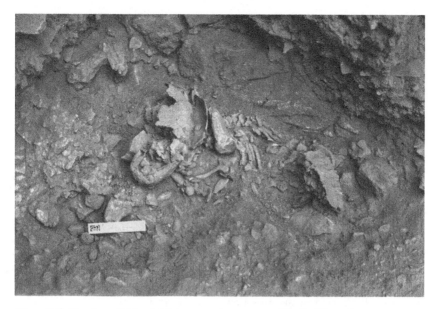

Figure 5.6 The Amud 7 burial (photograph courtesy of Erella Hovers).

adjacent to Amud 7's pelvis, at a site where this taxon is otherwise represented only by isolated teeth (Rak *et al.* 1994, 314) further supports a case for burial. In this sense Amud 7 is similar to the modern human burials of Skhūl V and Qafzeh II both of which were also associated with a single faunal item that does not appear to be simply intrusive from occupation deposits surrounding the burials. In cases such as the latter one might expect a relatively random representation of faunal remains (and probably more of them, as noted by Hovers *et al.* 2000, 258). Obviously one would not want to make too much of three examples but the fact that two are mandibles and another element also relating to the head might suggest that there is some meaning behind these. Further burials from Amud are discussed below.

The Middle Palaeolithic layers of the Dederiyeh cave, Syria, situated 450m above sea level, have yielded the remains of 15 hominins, several of which are intrusive but which include two *in situ* burials, Dederiyeh 1 and 2 (Akazawa and Muhesen 2002; Akazawa *et al.* 2002a, 2002b). These have not been directly dated although AMS ^{14}C dates on charcoal samples from Layer 3 which contained Burial 2 varied between 48,100 ± 1,200 BP and 53,600 ± 1,800 BP (Akazawa *et al.* 2002b). Burial 1, a child estimated at ~2 years at death on the basis of dental formation, was found towards the rear of the cave in Layer 11. The skeleton was near-complete, including small bones such as phalanges, and in a high degree of articulation; this, and its excellent state of preservation supports the notion that this was a deliberate burial (Dodo *et al.* 1998). The child was laid on its back, with arms extended and legs

107

flexed. The sediment around the skeleton was sterile apart from a roughly rectangular stone slab located next to the cranium on which the head was possibly laid, and a small, triangular piece of flint atop its chest. As Akazawa *et al.* (2002a, 75) have noted, the preservation of the skeleton in an area of the cave that shows considerable occupational activity at the time it was deposited, strongly argues in favour of the protection that deliberate burial would afford.

Burial 2 was found *in situ* in Layer 3, in the context of intermittent occupations during which time numerous hearths were utilised preserving plant remains in which hackberry (*Celtis* sp.) was dominant (Akazawa *et al.* 1999, 2002a; Figure 5.7). The depositional context therefore seems to have been occupational use of the cave. This partial skeleton of a ~2-year-old (estimated on the basis of cranial and postcranial fusion and dental traits) was recovered from a 70 × 50 × 25cm deep pit dug into the lowest part of Layer 3, filled with a fine-grained brown sediment and associated with 14 Mousterian flint implements, >100 pieces of lithic debitage, and numerous animal bone fragments including a large piece of tortoise shell. Skeletal parts are attributable to one individual, and the excavators believe that the body was intentionally buried in the pit (Akazawa *et al.* 2002a, 76).

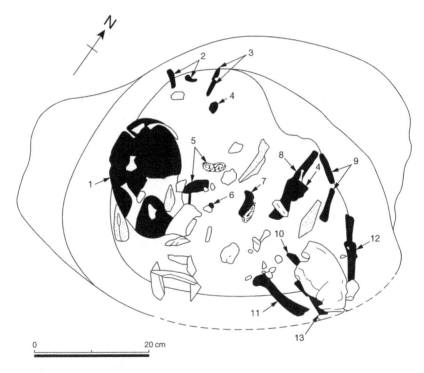

Figure 5.7 Plan of the Dederiyeh 2 infant burial (courtesy of Takeru Akazawa).

It is interesting to speculate why skeletal representation of Dederiyeh 2 is partial. Neonate and infant Neanderthal remains are usually partial, and one has to consider that this may relate to the differential conservation of fragile body parts. Certainly, the recovery of a complete or near-complete infant skeleton would amply support a burial interpretation as with Dederiyeh 1, but one may not be justified in eliminating cases of burial because of such factors. Nor may one be justified interpreting all cases of partial skeletal element survival as reflecting later disturbance, particularly in cases where sedimentological evidence of such disturbance is not forthcoming. This seems to be the case for the Dederiyeh infant, as the fill of the grave pit appears to be relatively homogeneous. If post-depositional disturbance did occur, then it left no visible sedimentary evidence. Given the general sedimentary context of the site as a whole one might expect the pit to be filled with the black, white and brown ashy deposits typical of Layer 3 if it were disturbed within the occupational 'life time' of this layer. Alternatively, if it were disturbed during a later geological phase then one would surely see stratigraphic evidence of this rather than the clear indication that the feature was dug from the lower part of Layer 3. On the basis of the available evidence it seems logical to conclude that the pit was probably not subject to post-depositional disturbance after it was dug and filled some time during a relatively early stage of the formation of Layer 3.

The remains of the infant within the pit feature were not in articulation, and have been described by the excavators as 'isolated' (Dodo et al. 1998, 130), that is, found in isolation within the feature. Assuming, as suggested above, that the infant's remains were not subject to post-depositional sorting, scrutiny of exactly which parts of the infant's body were deposited in the feature may be informative. The parts deposited in the feature were much (but not all) of the head, the mandible (retaining only some teeth), some finger parts and much of the legs and feet. With the exception of a few vertebral parts and four rib fragments most of the axial body is missing. Assuming first that a complete infant corpse was laid in the shallow pit, disturbance would have selectively removed the axial body, much of the arms and selective parts of other represented body portions in addition to removing the epiphyses of the lower limbs. While this cannot be ruled out on the grounds of anatomical representation, I find it most unlikely that an entire thorax could be removed by water or carnivore activity leaving behind only four rib fragments and a handful of vertebral parts. In addition, one must explain the presence of a great amount of lithic waste as well as formal tools and animal remains. For these reasons it is unlikely that one is dealing here with the deliberate burial of an entire corpse with subsequent disturbance responsible for the destruction or removal (and deposition off site) of select skeletal parts. I have suggested elsewhere (Pettitt 2002) that the infant may have originally been deposited and probably defleshed elsewhere, after which his/her remaining parts were scooped up and deposited in the pit before erosional processes had been too destructive. It may well have been that, during one brief occupation of the cave, the remains of an infant – its head, fingers, legs and feet and little else – was deposited in a shallow pit with some concern for articulation, along with discarded tools, knapping waste and animal parts. The abundance of lithics and animal remains in the fill of the feature suggests either that litter was also incorporated into the feature as a general clearance, or that no concern was given to remove such waste from the sediment removed to form the scoop or pit. In either case, the infant came to be associated with the rubbish that comprised much of the feature's fill.

Twenty-four fragments of a Neanderthal between one and two years old at death were recovered from a small pit of 40 × 20cm and 50cm deep in layer 2 at Mezmaiskaya Cave, northern Caucasus (Golovanova et al. 1999). The pit was overlain by a limestone block, but it is unclear as to whether the pit itself was excavated by Neanderthals and/or deliberately covered with the block (sensu La Ferrassie, see below) or whether the pit was caused by a natural process such as the deposition of the block from above. The latter might account for the great degree of fragmentation (the pieces represent only the frontal and left and right adjoining parietal bones) and a degree of post-depositional deformation of the curvature of the fragments, although it is hard to see how a rock fall could create a relatively well-defined pit containing skull parts. It seems, therefore, that this is another example of the deliberate deposition of body parts – possibly originally a complete skull – in a naturally occurring or deliberately excavated subsurface feature.

Perhaps the relatively high frequency of Neanderthal infant remains recovered from pits is not surprising. A small subcircular pit is the most economical feature to excavate to contain a small body. That pits and scoops were, in all probability, excavated by Neanderthals for other purposes such as for setting hearths and possibly for storage, the pit 'template' could presumably be exapted easily for mortuary use. The 'hearth scoops' that most readily come to mind are the second of two numerous hearth forms from the Mousterian levels at Kebara Cave, Israel, which are bowl-shaped, 30–90cm in diameter and about 10cm thick. The abundance of these hearths – they were superimposed for more than 4m in the deep soundings (Bar-Yosef et al. 1992) suggest that 'scooping' at Kebara was an habitual activity. This said, the KHM1 infant burial seems instead to have been associated with large stones (see p. 115).

Adult burials

La Chapelle-aux-Saints, France

At La Chapelle-aux-Saints, southwest France, the near-complete skeleton of an adult Neanderthal was recovered from a roughly rectangular depression 145 × 100cm in plan and c.30cm deep, within stratum 5 (Bouyssonie et al. 1908; Figure 5.8). It was emplaced immediately at the entrance to the cave, and contracted partially on its right side and partially on its back. The head rested against the side of the grave, apparently wedged in with several stone blocks. Three or four large longbone fragments were found below the head, and a large number of flakes of quartz and flint, and other bones, some in articulation, against the edges of the grave. Evidence of fire was also found in its vicinity. Although it is impossible today to establish whether or not these are grave goods, the nature of the burial itself seems clear enough. Gargett (1989), however, rejected this as a burial, on the basis of stratigraphic data and the fact that the ceiling of the cave at the time of burial was not high and would therefore have required crawling, a situation Gargett believes 'sounds more like a [carnivore] den' (ibid., 163). This latter point is dubious: if we were to discount burial because 'access to his grave might have required a crawl of some metres' then by the same argument we would have to discount many examples of Upper Palaeolithic parietal art, or for that matter Neolithic collective burial in megalithic tombs. In any case, the ubiquitous archaeology in stratum 5, which Gargett cites as evidence against burial, indicates that Neanderthal activity of other forms certainly occurred at this broad time, and that a low ceiling was no obstruction to this. Other sites, in fact, exist where rich Mousterian accumulations occurred under ceilings too low to allow standing, such as Les Canalettes, France (Meignen 1993). Gargett suggests that the depression in which the skeleton was found could have occurred through stream action, pointing to other depression features discovered by Peyrony that probably formed in this way. One of these contained fragmentary remains of a Neanderthal infant, now lost. These are, however, found in stratum 1, not 5, and are of different shape and size to the 'burial' depression (they are circular, 50–80cm in diameter and 40–50cm deep), and I see no a priori reason to invoke the same causative process. The likelihood that this represents a true burial is emphasised by Frayer and Montet-White who question Gargett's reconstruction of the stratigraphy and note that they

> know of no example of a naturally produced rectangular, straight-walled, flat-bottomed pit in the middle of a karstic shelter. That such a natural phenomenon would have occurred and a skeleton would have found its way into it is so unlikely as to make it impossible to consider seriously that the pit sunk into the marl was not the result of deliberate human activity.
>
> (comment to Gargett 1989, 180)

It is difficult to disagree with their opinion, that this represents a 'strong indication of intentional burial'.

There are no clear reasons for concluding that the La Chapelle-aux-Saints individual is not a simple inhumation, and represents the burial of an adult Neanderthal in a low-ceilinged cave that at other times at least saw intense occupation.

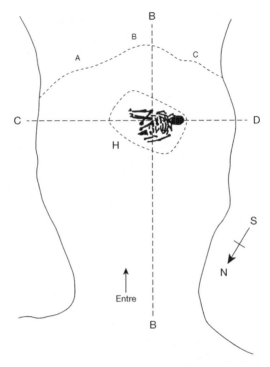

Figure 5.8 Plan of the La-Chapelle-aux-Saints cave showing the location of the adult burial (redrawn from Bouyssonie *et al.* 1908).

La Grotte du Régourdou, Dordogne, France

The burial of a Neanderthal was discovered during excavations in the Régourdou Cave in 1957, and excavated between that year and 1962. Regourdou 1 comprises the partially complete postcranial skeleton of an adult Neanderthal, with a degree of anatomical articulation, deposited in the context of a poor Mousterian assemblage in Bed 4. This, and the grave cutting in which it was placed, occurred in close proximity to the possible burial of brown bear crania and longbones, to a tumulus of small stones and to two low walls of small stones (Bonifay 1964, 2008; Bonifay and Vandermeersch 1965; Madelaine *et al.* 2009). A section drawing of the ensemble of materials is shown in Figure 5.9. The Neanderthal burial itself was covered with a tumulus of large stones, and in this sense strikes a parallel with the practice in Shanidar Cave discussed below. As the majority of stones comprising the tumulus are large (30–60cm in maximum dimension) it is difficult to see how these could have accumulated naturally and, in fact, they clearly derive from outside the cave (E. Bonifay pers. comm.). A description of the 'assemblage' of structures was given by Bonifay to Defleur (1993, 100). The base was formed by a bed

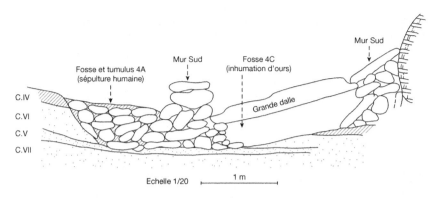

Figure 5.9 Section drawing of the Neanderthal and brown bear burials in Regourdou Cave, Dordogne. 'Fosse 4A' is the Neanderthal burial covered with the tumulus of stones and 'Fosse 4C' is the brown bear burial covered with the large stone ('grande dalle') (reproduced from Bonifay 1964 courtesy of E. Bonifay).

of flat stones, onto which the skeleton was laid resting on its left side and probably highly flexed. Two brown bear tibiae were recovered with the corpse and may represent deliberate grave goods. The corpse was covered with limestone 'paving', apparently without covering it with sediments. Next, a tumulus of large stones ('Tumulus 4A') was constructed atop the burial. Finally, a layer of burnt sand and a number of artefacts and bones of brown bear were found atop this. If this reconstruction is correct, this is the only example of an actual constructed *tomb* for the Middle Palaeolithic. The context of the 'Tumulus 4A burial' is of further interest. Several intentional structures occur in its vicinity, including ditches cut into the sandy sediment that were filled or covered with blocks or 'pavements' of stone, low dry stone 'walls', piles of stones and stone slabs. It is unclear what the function of these structures was; one ditch contained the near-complete skeleton of a young brown bear and was covered by a block of limestone measuring 2 × 2m. Although the block had probably fallen from the vault of the cave it had clearly been placed carefully atop the ditch and skeleton (E. Bonifay pers. comm.). Furthermore, as this was further covered with a tumulus ('Tumulus 4b') it is difficult to see how this could be a natural accumulation (Bonifay 2008). The two walls that delineated the grave of the brown bear were neatly constructed and clearly not natural accumulations; both reached around one metre in height and were 2 and 3m in length (E. Bonifay pers. comm.). One must remember that the associated archaeological remains are poor; as Bonifay (1965) noted, the archaeology seems to correspond to a brief period of activity, and it is certainly difficult to see this as the remains of prosaic occupation. The recovery of a bone of another individual – Regourdou 2 – may indicate that further funerary activity was practised in the cave (Madelaine *et al.* 2009).

Regourdou provides a compelling case for complex activity associated with the burial of a Neanderthal. As Bonifay (2008, 28) has noted, one observes the following:

- excavation of several ditches;
- positioning of the corpse;
- association of artefacts and bones with the corpse;
- covering of the corpse by a tumulus and in the case of a brown bear a slab;
- association of burnt sediments and artefacts with the top of the tomb;
- association close by of the burial of bear remains.

All this from a site with impeccable, finely bedded stratigraphy. It is difficult to disagree with Bonifay's (ibid., 30) conclusion that this is a monumental 'ensemble sepulcral'.

La Roche à Pierrot, St Césaire, Charente-Maritime, France

The near-complete Neanderthal skeleton from the rockshelter site of La Roche à Pierott was recovered from an upper Châtelperronian level in 1979. Although water action had disturbed some of the remains, the preservation of small bones such as those of the hands, articulation of some parts and the location of the skeleton one metre from the cliff face in an area probably protected by a rockshelter overhang suggests that it was deliberately buried (Backer 1993; Vandermeersch 1993). No grave cutting was apparent, although the remains were recovered from a small, sub-circular area 70cm in diameter, which was free of the limestone blocks and cultural debris otherwise common to the level (ibid., 130). How else could one explain this clearance in an otherwise homogeneous rubbly and implementiferous sedimentary matrix? If this clearance were erosional in nature then there would be no skeleton preserved in the cleared area.

Spy Cave, Namur, Belgium

If the recovery of relatively complete Neanderthal skeletons indicates deliberate burial then one might accept material excavated in 1886 from Spy Cave, Belgium, as burials (Harrold 1980; Defleur 1993). Spy I is an incomplete skeleton consisting of cranio-mandibular remains, and several postcranial elements that were not recovered in articulation. Spy II was also incomplete (although somewhat more elements are present) but seems to have been recovered in a degree of articulation and lying on its right side with a hand lying against its mandible. Its position certainly recalls that of a number of single inhumations, for example, La Ferrassie, Amud and Shanidar. These remains were found in the lowest of three Middle Palaeolithic levels in the cave, apparently in the midst of occupation traces in the form of Mousterian lithics and fauna (see Semal *et al.* 2008 for an excellent summary). Although the excavators dismissed the notion of burial the remains were found atop bedrock and covered by a discrete layer of yellow clay immediately below a brecciated fauna-bearing level, evidence, it would seem, of undisturbed deposits. Recent direct AMS ^{14}C measurements on Spy I and II are in very good agreement and fit well into the dating of faunal remains from above and below, and have established an age of ~34,000–36,000 BP for the two (Semal *et al.* 2008).

Kebara Cave, Israel

Various hominin remains relating to several individuals were recovered from the Middle Palaeolithic levels of Kebara Cave on Mount Carmel (for a review see Tillier *et al.* 2003). All of these were found inside the cave, and five individuals, including KMH2, were found in its central area. Others, such as the KMH1 infant skeleton, were recovered from the cave's northern section, close to the northern wall, which seemed to act as a dump at the time (Bar-Yosef *et al.* 1992). Most of the remains come from the cave's oldest Mousterian layers, approaching ~60,000 BP. The remains of the KMH1 infant were well preserved and recovered from a very small area, in close association with three stones and a *Rhinoceros* tooth (Schick and Stekelis 1977, 103), all suggesting that it was deliberately buried.

The excavation of a grave cutting and deliberate interment of an adult Neanderthal (KHM2) is beyond doubt. It was placed in a deliberately excavated pit, the lower limit of which had clearly cut obliquely through two hearths in the underlying level. The eastern and northeastern limits of the pit were easily observable, the pit sediments (yellow-brown) were easily distinguished from those of Unit XII (black) into which the grave was cut, and most anatomical connections – including its hyoid bone – were still intact and there was no displacement of the bones beyond the initial volume of the body (Bar-Yosef *et al.* 1988; Bar-Yosef *et al.* 1992, 527–8). The body was placed on its back, with the head (now missing) probably at a slightly higher level than the rest of the body. The preservation and orientation of the intact bones suggests that the right side of the body was lying against a wall of the pit (Figures 5.10 and 5.11). The position of the upper limbs suggested that the body was deposited before rigor mortis set in, that is, rapidly. Even the looser ligamentous connecting parts such as hand bones were still in articulation. Based on these clear observations, the excavators concluded that 'the body decomposed in a filled grave' (Bar-Yosef *et al.* 1992, 528). The absence of the cranium was originally thought to represent the deliberate removal of the head after the decay of the atlanto-occipital ligaments, although is now thought to have occurred through natural taphonomic processes

Figure 5.10 The Kebara KMH2 burial *in situ* (photograph courtesy of Ofer Bar-
Yosef).

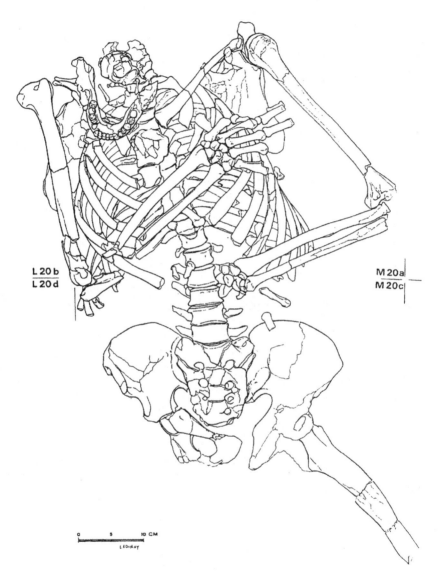

L 20 b
L 20 d

M 20a
M 20c

0   5   10 CM

LADIRAY

Figure 5.11 Plan of the Kebara KMH2 burial (from Bar-Yosef *et al.* 1992 and courtesy of Ofer Bar-Yosef).

(E. Hovers pers. comm.). The morphology of the grave pit indicates also that the head lay at a higher level than the rest of the body against a steep side of the pit, and the positioning of the atlas between the branches of the mandible, tilted towards the vertebral column, suggests that the head originally leaned forward. This relatively high position and posture indicates that the head may well have been easily exposed on the surface and thus susceptible to erosion.

Amud Cave, Israel

The remains of up to 16 Neanderthal individuals were recovered from the Middle Palaeolithic occupation deposits in the Amud Cave, northern Israel during excavations in the 1960s (Suzuki and Takai 1970) and later (Rak et al. 1994; Hovers et al. 1995). Most of these are highly fragmentary and typically represented by only one skeletal element, but three individuals – Amud I, 7 and 9 – are complete enough to provide strong evidence that they were buried. Most of the remains are of immature individuals (see Table 5.1). It is impossible to establish whether or not these derive from burials, although as most are small and fragile it is not inconceivable that they represent burials that have been preferably disturbed by taphonomic processes.

The Amud 7 infant burial has been discussed above. Amud 9 comprises the articulated foot and lower leg of an adult. The accumulation of (10cm of sediment between the burial and a rock fall above it demonstrate that it was not killed by the rock fall (Hovers et al. 1995, 52). The rock fall does, however, seem to have been responsible for fragmenting the rest of the burial beyond recognition.

As has been noted above, Amud I was found 4m from the cave's wall, lying on its left side in a contracted position (Sakura 1970). The skeleton was interred immediately below the drip line of the cave, and given this and its location in a cave that saw frequent animal and hominin use including the apparent excavation of numerous pits, it is difficult to view this as anything but a deliberate burial. It is interesting that Amud I and 7 were oriented in the same direction. A further observation made by Hovers et al. (ibid., 54) is the clustering of hominin remains close to the cave's wall in the northwest part of the site. As one can reject taphonomic explanations for this non-random patterning it seems that an element of choice was in operation at the site.

Tabun Cave, Israel

Tabun could be instrumental in demonstrating an older antiquity for Neanderthal burials than is generally considered, but it should not be regarded as a problematic burial site. At least one Neanderthal – an adult female (Tabun C1) – was interred in the cave (Garrod and Bate 1937; Defleur 1993; Figure 5.12) although the possible association of the female with a neonate – which

Figure 5.12 The Tabun C1 burial (from Garrod and Bate 1937).

if true might represent a double burial perhaps following death in childbirth – remains open to debate (Bar-Yosef and Callander 1999). The remains of a third individual – a mandible of an adult, possibly male, *Homo sapiens* shows that, overall, at least three individuals came to be deposited in the cave. Indirect evidence of a grave cutting may come from the location of the mandible of Tabun I underneath its cranium, suggesting that it was lying against its wall, and the location of the burial close to a large block may have afforded additional protection (Defleur 1993, 121). The corpse seems to have been laid partially on its left side, with a slight flexion to the legs.

Kiik-Koba, Crimea

The partial remains of two adolescent and three juvenile Neanderthals from Layers III and IIIa of the Zaskalnaya VI cave in Crimea may represent burials, but it is today impossible to establish this as they were disturbed by the excavation of a pit probably shortly after their deposition (Kolosov 1996). A more convincing Crimean Neanderthal burial is that of an adult, probably male, buried in an artificially widened natural hollow in the floor of the lower layer at Kiik-Koba, in a fairly central position (Stepanchuk 1998). Although only the bones of the lower limbs and feet survive, their articulated and bent position indicates that the individual was lain on its right-hand side and was probably flexed. At face value this is a case of funerary caching, although if the hollow was widened deliberately in order to facilitate burial this is an intriguing example of a mortuary deposit that is transitional between caching and burial. Only 30cm from the head of Kiik-Koba an infant was laid on its left side, facing towards the adult, the articulation of which suggests that it too was an inhumation. The early date of this excavation (1920s) renders it impossible to evaluate this further, but it seems likely that the burials were emplaced in the context of occupation of the cave.

More questionable cases: Le Moustier and La Quina (France) and Teshik Tash (Uzbekistan)

Where information on the spatial configuration of Neanderthal remains is available, the case for burial, on occasion, may appear questionable, especially if the remains of a single individual are distributed in an unnaturally tight cluster. One might include in the inventory of burial that of an adolescent in the Lower shelter at Le Moustier, although the excavator, Hauser's apparent re-burial and 're-excavation' of the skeleton in front of an invited 'tribunal' of academics (Trinkaus and Shipman 1993, 176–7) does not inspire confidence and one has to treat this with caution. Taking Hauser's description at face value it is plausible that Le Moustier 1 represents a deliberate burial laid partially contracted on its side (Hauser 1909), although the relatively confined space, as with Teshik Task and St Césaire does make it open to question. As

Gargett (1989) notes, the skeleton of an 8–10-year-old boy at Teshik Tash, in Uzbekistan near the Afghan border, is an unconvincing indicator of burial. The boy's remains, partial as they are, were recovered from a restricted spatial area and formed along with small limestone *eboulis,* the well-known ibex horns and a hyena coprolite, a circular spread with little vertical definition. In addition, erosion was noted in the area of the burial (Defleur 1993). Similarly dubious are the partial remains of at least 22 individuals at La Quina, only four teeth of which are in articulation, although the possibility of caching of the dead at La Quina has been discussed above.

Places of multiple burial of the Middle Palaeolithic

It seems sensible to consider sites where multiple individuals were buried after I have already discussed sites where the processed body parts of several individuals came to rest. I refer to sites at which more than two individuals were buried as multiple burial locales. I use this term specifically to avoid use of the term 'cemetery' which is often used but hardly ever defined. As I use the term 'cemetery' only to refer to multiple burial sites at which a degree of spatial organisation, a redundancy of practice and a lack of settlement debris is evident, I do not use the term for the few Middle Palaeolithic sites at which more than two individuals received simple inhumation, as there is no evidence of organisation on these, for example in terms of uniform orientation of burials (Riel-Salvatore and Clark 2001). A small number of sites are exceptional in preserving multiple inhumations. One must include in this category the early anatomically modern human burials at Skhūl and Qafzeh discussed in Chapter 4. In fact, three categories of multiple individual recovery can be identified. First, it is a plausible, although at present untestable, hypothesis, that human bodies were being cached in or by entrances to caves as early as MIS7. Second, from MIS5 (or probably later) a small number of sites preserve the highly fragmentary remains of several Neanderthal individuals that clearly stand apart from other sites that have yielded fragmentary Neanderthal remains. It is tempting to view these as sites where bodies were processed in mortuary ritual: as cut marked Neanderthal bones are not common overall in a hypodigm of *c.*500, one might plausibly conclude that cut marked Neanderthal bones, where found, do not simply reflect the mundane defleshing of their bodies in the context of cave habitation. The rarity of this activity suggests a more exclusive activity. Third, from MIS5 (again probably later) a small number of sites stand out as they preserve the fairly complete remains of several Neanderthal individuals that have been convincingly *interred.* At the fissure site of L'Hortus an MNI of 20 individuals are represented, among whom young adults feature significantly (de Lumley 1972); at least 25 individuals are represented by the highly fragmentary remains at Krapina (Trinkaus 1995), and at least 22 fragmentary individuals at La Quina, Charente (Defleur 1993). The seven individuals represented at La Ferrassie form a particularly interesting case in that two of these are foeti/neonates, three are children and only two are adults. At least nine individuals are represented at Shanidar Cave, and while old notions of 'flower burials' have now been discounted it seems that at least five individuals were buried in the cave over a period of time of 10,000 years or more (see below). It is tempting to interpret limestone blocks found in apparent association with burials as grave markers, although this of course remains speculative. Whatever the case, clearly a mortuary function was given to these caves, and this function extended beyond the life and death of single individuals. At Shanidar this function appears to have been extended considerably over time, and indeed it is difficult to imagine that the great number of individuals recovered from la Quina, L'Hortus and Krapina died in a very close period. It is therefore tempting to conclude that at least some transmission of mortuary tradition occurred among some Neanderthal groups, centred around a fixed point in the landscape that could be used, if not exclusively, to hide, process and bury the dead. Whether or not such use of a node in the landscape reflects social reference to group–land relationships even bordering on concepts of 'land tenure' (Belfer-Cohen and Hovers 1992, 469) is debatable, although such an hypothesis is worth consideration, as the relatively small and repetitive nature of Neanderthal landscape use, at least as reflected by lithic raw material movement (e.g. Geneste 1989), could well have engendered a sense of territoriality among at least some Neanderthal groups, as has been suggested by Hovers (2001). As with other categories of Middle Palaeolithic mortuary activity, however, such cases should not be exaggerated, but do contribute towards an emerging picture of variability in Neanderthal mortuary practice and even potentially interaction between the spheres of life and of death.

Shkaft Mazin Shanidar, Iraqi Kurdistan

The Shkaft Mazin Shanidar ('Big Shanidar Cave') was excavated by a team led by Ralph Solecki between 1951 and 1960 (Solecki 1972). From a trench some 7 × 13m in extent that was excavated by arbitrary spits, the remains of nine Neanderthal individuals were recovered, some of whom seem to have lain where they died as a result of the natural rock falls to which the cave was prone, whereas others seem to have been deliberately buried. Although the physical preservation of bone was generally good, rock falls had considerably broken up crania and longbones, which required considerable consolidation and reconstruction, and while some skeletons were decently complete, others were partial. The distal leg and pedal bones of a tenth individual – a 1–2-year-old infant – were found during analysis of the cave's faunal remains in 2000 (Cowgill et al. 2007). All of the hominin remains were found in close spatial association with Levalloiso-Mousterian lithics, faunal remains, ash and hearths, showing quite clearly that they died, or were buried, in the context of occupation of the cave (Solecki 1972).

Rock falls seem to have been regular occurrences within the Shanidar cave in the Pleistocene. Solecki (1972) established that the cave's Middle Palaeolithic record indicated a series of Neanderthal occupations that were on repeated occasions interrupted by rock falls, of which at least four main episodes were evidence (ibid., 152; Figure 5.13). All of the Neanderthal remains were found in close proximity to fallen rocks – in some cases the rocks lay directly atop them – and many were fragmented by the same. The best evidence for deliberate burial in the cave is provided by the near-complete skeletons of adults Shanidar IV, VI and VII and the partial child remains of Shanidar VIII. These were found in a tight cluster within the middle part of Layer D, and were excavated carefully within the space of one week (Solecki 1972, 156). The upper parts of Layer D in the cave – and thus the uppermost Neanderthal remains (Shanidar I and V) – date to ~40,000–50,000 BP (Cowgill

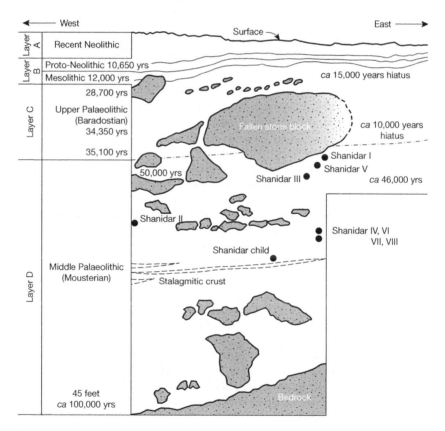

Figure 5.13 Section of the Shanidar cave showing the location of Neanderthal remains. Large rocks result from periods of rock fall (courtesy of Ralph Solecki).

et al. 2007), and thus, given the stratigraphic position of Shanidar IV, VI, VII and VIII ~2m below the uppermost part of Layer D, these must certainly pre-date 50,000 BP although need not date to earlier than MIS3. Exactly how old the lowermost parts of Layer D are (and thus the oldest Neanderthal remains) remains debatable. The lowermost hominin remains (Shanidar 10) were found 3.5m below Shanidar IV, VI, VII and VIII, and could be significantly older. Although Solecki's (1963) estimate of ~100,000 BP for the base of Layer D on the now-discredited basis of sedimentation rates is possibly an overestimate, the lowermost remains may indeed date to early MIS3, MIS4 or even MIS5 (Cowgill *et al.* 2007), although modern radiocarbon dates are sorely needed for the site and the existing chronology could be highly misleading. This having been said, the lowermost (and uppermost) hominins in the cave do not, it seems, represent burials, and while the deposition of Neanderthal remains in the cave could span 50,000 years or considerably more, the actual practice of burial in the cave could span only part of that, perhaps as little as ~10,000–20,000 years or less.

It is Shanidar IV, VI, VII and VIII that form the most convincing evidence for burial in the cave (Figures 5.14, 5.15 and 5.16). They form a tight spatial cluster; the remains seem to respect the position of each other and appear to form a deliberate sequential group; they seem not to have been killed or deposited by natural agents such as rock fall, and there is a good case that at least one of them was placed within a natural 'niche', the fill of which differed from that outside. The debate about whether Shanidar IV represented a 'flower burial', however, detracted attention from this burial group. One should not underestimate the effect on palaeoanthropology that the perceived deliberate placement of flowers with Shanidar IV subsequently had. Solecki (1972, 194) saw this and the 'care' of Shanidar I as evidence of the 'first stirrings of social and religious sense and feeling'. Palynological analysis of samples from the vicinity of Shanidar IV contained the pollen of seven flowering plant species, which the pollen analyst interpreted as representing brightly coloured wild plants that were woven into the branches of a pine-like shrub (Solecki 1972, 175). This has now been convincingly eliminated. A recent examination of the microfauna of Layer D strongly suggests that the pollen was deposited by the burrowing rodent *Meriones tersicus*, which is common in the Shanidar microfauna and whose burrowing activity can be observed today (Sommer 1999). In fact, Solecki (1972, 169) noted that rodent burrows were common throughout Layer D and had disturbed all of the hominin remains, significantly in the case of Shanidar V (ibid., 171). There is also the issue of how representative the samples are: according to Solecki's account (1972, 174) soil samples from which the palynological work derived were taken only from the adjacent Shanidar IV and VI burials and 'some . . . from outside the area of the skeletal remains'. This is not a comprehensive sample, especially when one takes the size of the excavation trench relative to the size of the cave into account. As to my knowledge no details of the palynological contents of the other samples

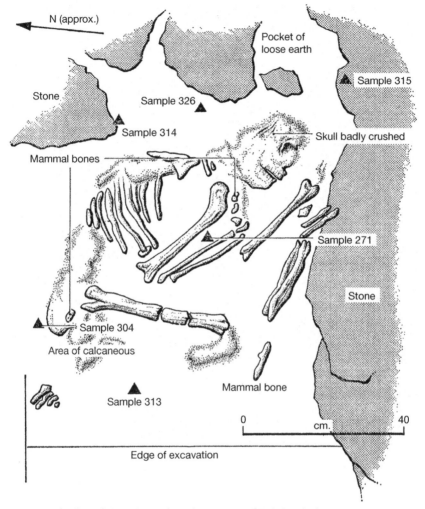

N (approx.)

Pocket of
loose earth

Sample 315

Stone

Sample 326

Sample 314

Skull badly crushed

Mammal bones

Sample 271

Stone

Sample 304

Area of calcaneous

Mammal bone

Sample 313

0   40
                    cm.

Edge of excavation

Figure 5.14 Plan of Shanidar IV burial (courtesy of Ralph Solecki).

have been published one simply cannot substantiate the claim that the pollen
is restricted to a discrete space around Shanidar IV.

It is the apparently sequential nature of (in stratigraphic order from bottom
to top) the Shanidar VIII, VI, VII and IV burials that is significant. The child
(Shanidar VIII) was interred first, followed by the two female adults (Shanidar
VI and VII), and finally the adult male (Shanidar IV). The close proximity
of all of these burials – Shanidar VI lay only ~10cm below Shanidar IV (ibid.,
167) and Shanidar IV and VII were adjacent for example – suggests that they
were interred relatively close in time. Shanidar VI was disturbed, possibly

125

Figure 5.15 The Shanidar IV burial, with bones of Shanidar VI visible top centre (courtesy of Ralph Solecki).

when the adult male Shanidar IV was interred last in the group. Although it is impossible to evaluate Solecki's suggestion that the male 'received the main attention of the burial [group], and the Shanidar females were given subordinate burial next to him' (ibid., 169), there is a clear focus on a very restricted area of the cave for four burials within a relatively short period of time. Whether or not burial was widely practised by this group clearly it was felt that four adults should receive burial in a certain part of the cave, which suggests a degree of burial tradition, however long- or short-lived, and in this sense the site can be regarded as a place of multiple interment.

There is no unambiguous evidence of any other form of funerary activity other than simple inhumation without accompanying grave goods. It is pos-

Figure 5.16 Shanidar V (courtesy of Ralph Solecki).

sible that Shanidar III was deliberately placed within a crevice within large rocks. This would represent a case of funerary caching and the occurrence of this with inhumation would lend a degree of similarity with Skhūl as discussed in Chapter 4. It should be noted, however, that this individual seems to have been killed by rock fall, and its position with those body parts that survive 'jammed into a crevice' (Solecki 1972, 151) could simply be due to the rock fall itself. A more probable example of caching is the recovery of Shanidar IV – itself part of a sequence of burials it should be remembered – within a niche of large stone blocks that clearly pre-dated the burial and that did not, therefore, relate to a rock fall that killed this individual. Solecki believed that 'a crypt had been scooped out among the rocks, and that the individual had been interred and covered over with earth from the living floor of the cave' (ibid., 168–9). In support of this he noted that the sediment surrounding the skeleton and within the 'niche' was soft.

On the basis of published data, the question of whether some of the Neanderthal burials at Shanidar were covered with 'cairns' of small rocks must, in my opinion, remain open. Solecki – who was very familiar with natural rock fall formations in caves – felt that the clusters of small, portable stones over Shanidar I (Solecki 1972, 139) and II (ibid., 162) were deliberately placed over the corpses, as the nature of these clusters differed considerably from those clusters that resulted from natural rock falls in the cave. It is of interest that Shanidar I and II were not buried; they died from rock falls, probably *in situ*. By contrast, the burials from the cave are not associated with rock cairns. Perhaps this is to be expected: there would be no reason to cover corpses with cairns if they were buried, so perhaps there is a degree of variability in practice observable in the cave, with burial occurring early in the occupational sequence and 'cairn covering' later in time. In this sense, cairns could be seen as somewhat intermediate between funerary caching (whereby corpses are brought to and placed within natural features) and burial (whereby a feature is created and into which they are inserted); cairns are formed by bringing natural objects to the corpse and a part-natural, part-artificial space is created around it. It could be that they were rapid and ad hoc solutions to the problem of caching or burying the remains of individuals killed by rock fall. But this remains pure speculation; only further excavation will allow us to investigate this possibility.

Mortuary space

I have noted above the restricted spatial distribution of the burials at Amud, for which taphonomic explanations can be eliminated. The deposition of burials occurred over a relatively short period of time and, clearly, in a restricted area of the cave. Analysis of faunal remains suggests that the area did not function as a dumping area, and unlike Kebara, the fragmentary hominin remains also occur in the same area as the burials, suggesting that this restricted area was meaningfully associated with both sets of remains (Hovers *et al.* 1995, 56). As Hovers *et al.* note, this can only be indicative of a behavioural tradition – a purposeful association of an area of the cave with the dead, as with Shanidar. As noted above, the Kebara KMH2 burial occurred in a central space where activity seems to have been intensive, although isolated parts of infants were found towards the cave's wall in an area interpreted as a dump (Bar-Yosef *et al.* 1992, 533). Although the position of remains in Kebara Cave became more central over time, this is an intriguing spatial dichotomy, and however one interprets the specific meaning of it further supports the notion that Neanderthals were associating certain areas of caves with the dead. Hovers *et al.* 1995, 56) have also noted how the few isolated hominin remains from Tabun were recovered from the cave's inner chamber, whereas the C1 burial was placed at its entrance. Most importantly they have noted how this patterning differs from that of the early modern human burials at Skhūl and Qafzeh, which occur at each cave's entrance or on its terrace, a potentially important difference in the mortuary traditions of the two species.

Grave offerings and mortuary variability

A number of examples of apparent grave goods in Neanderthal burials have been forwarded, although most scholars would now agree that these are not convincing, as the objects recovered from within grave cuts never differ in form from those recovered from the sediments into which graves themselves were cut (e.g. Klein 1999, 467-70). For example, Peyrony (1934, 31–2) notes the apparent placement of three flints with the La Ferrassie 5 burial, although given the ubiquity of lithic artefacts in the level concerned it is difficult to accept these as deliberate grave offerings. Bouyssonie *et al.* (1908) drew attention to several bovid remains associated with the adult burial at La Chapelle-aux-Saints, some long bones of which were recovered above the head; several flint artefacts within the grave, two of which were found near the nasal aperture, and articulated reindeer vertebrae found in the grave's proximity, suggest that these were deliberate grave goods emplaced with the corpse. As with La Ferrassie, given the ubiquity of faunal and lithic remains in stratum 5 this should be taken with caution and, as Gargett (1989, 162) has observed, as most of these were found at a level above the head of the interred Neanderthal, the notion that grave goods were deliberately emplaced here is doubtful. Lithic items and a few animal bones were recovered from the burial pit of Kebara KMH2, although in the excavators' opinion their distribution 'would not indicate any explanation other than that they were part of the refill of the pit, which was dug into layers rich in artefacts and bone' (Bar-Yosef *et al.* 1992, 529). The confined spatial extent and circular shape of the teshik Tash 'burial' render the deliberate inclusion of a goat horn highly doubtful, like the burial itself (see above). The convincing rejection by Sommer (1999) of flowers in the grave of Shanidar IV has been discussed above.

Some examples seem a little more convincing, such as the red deer maxilla associated with Amud 7 and possibly the bear tibiae associated with Le Regourdou 1. In addition to these one must also note the longbone fragment incised with numerous parallel lines found in the grave cutting of La Ferrassie 1 (Peyrony 1934; Maureille and Vandermeersch 2007). It is possible that the limestone block engraved with cupules above the grave cutting of La Ferrassie 6 was associated with the burial, although this is unclear and may be a fortuitous association (B. Maureille pers. comm.). Overall, however, convincing indications of grave good emplacement are rare indeed. Given the apparent degree of variability in treatment of the Neanderthal body in death, should we be surprised at this lack? Not necessarily so. The treatment and exploration of the corpse *post mortem* is a logical extension of the social role of the body in life, and a number of behavioural templates already existed in the Middle Palaeolithic to incorporate into an emerging mortuary ritual. The emplacement of anthropogenic objects in grave cuts need not relate at all to this dialogue between the living and the dead body. Grave goods may or may not relate to metaphysical notions of an afterlife or bodily extension; they probably speak more of self-expression and concepts of ownership. It may well be that neither existed in Neanderthal societies. As suggested elsewhere, perhaps society hinged upon the body as its main focus. If objects played a role in social negotiation, as suggested by Gamble (1999), perhaps one might be entitled to expect grave goods. The lack of convincing examples of them suggests to

me that they played no role beyond the immediate kinetic tasks for which
they were made.

Inhumation patterns

Given that the number of burials for which extensive information is available
is low, it is probably premature to make much of apparent patterning in the
position of the corpse and its associations. Some broad patterns are evident,
however. Burials cluster in several regions separated by vast areas for which
there is no mortuary evidence. Noticeable clusters are western Europe (France,
Belgium and Germany), eastern Europe (Ukraine and Russia), southwest Asia
(Israel, Syria, Iraqi Kurdistan) and central Asia (Uzbekistan) (Delfeur 1993;
Bonifay 2008; Maureille and Tillier 2008). These occur in the context of
well-understood Middle Palaeolithic occupation of each region, although in
relation to Mousterian occupation sites burials are remarkably rare. In addition, there are vast areas of Europe and Asia for which a respectable Middle
Palaeolithic is known but for which no burials have yet been found (Maureille
and Vandermeersch 2007). As Bonifay (2008, 26) has noted, this regionalisation probably reflects 'l'existence des comportements différents des populations
Néandertaliennes face au problem au mort'. Aquitaine and the Levant contain
relatively large numbers of burials as well as places of multiple burial, which
might suggest that burial was practised more widely in these areas, and that,
by contrast, Neanderthals in other regions either did not bury their dead, or
did not practise it frequently. These are regions where Mousterian archaeology
suggests that Neanderthals were particularly numerous, and it is tempting
to suggest that the practice of burial may have been connected to population
size, and perhaps to a sense of territoriality.

All ages are represented among burials, although the relatively high proportion of juveniles is of interest, particularly given the fragility of these remains.
Although there is little evident patterning along the lines of sex, Defleur
(1993, 236) suggested that there is a tendency for males to be tightly flexed
more than females, among whom more lateral positions are noticeable, and
infants tend to be contracted, although it must be said, contracted positions
are most common (Smirnov 1989). Given that some Neanderthals were placed
within natural depressions and fissures, this position could simply relate to
the constraints of space available for burial, rather than to any symbolic meaning of this position. Although patterns of orientation vary, a majority (13/20
according to Defleur's figures) are oriented east–west. Grave cuttings have
been observed for around 50 per cent of assumed burials, and can be inferred
for several others, in addition to a few for which a tumulus is observable and
five for which both tumuli and graves are known (Defleur 1993, 246).

Taylor (2002, 212) has suggested that the function of burials within
Neanderthal societies was to isolate the dead: 'caves, with no dawn or dusk,
are a symbolic limbo. Their [Neanderthals] location after death in the timeless

space of caves echoes and emphasises their exclusion from the normal cycle of life and death,' although as noted above burials are overwhelmingly placed amidst occupation traces in high-activity areas with natural light, and one might equally interpret them as being interred with the living. Furthermore, as Bonifay (2008) has noted, there is no predominance of burial in caves; rockshelters were used just as commonly. Thus, if anything, I suggest that the rare burials that Neanderthals created were contextualised within the prosaic, daily life, although one need not invoke any complex symbolism underlying this. If anything it probably suggests that, with single burials at least, burial could occur wherever the group were camping at a given time, rather than with rule-bound associations of specific places with the dead and not with the living. Even with places of multiple interment, which may well indicate the origins of an association of place with the dead, prosaic occupation traces are still present, suggesting that the presence of the dead, if known, did not preclude 'normal' activity.

La Ferrassie: the zenith of Neanderthal funerary activity?

The La Ferrassie rockshelter in the Dordogne, yielded seven Neanderthal skeletons; two adults, two foeti/neonates, and three infants (Capitan and Peyrony 1912a, 1912b, 1921; Delporte 1976; Maureille and Vandermeersch 2007). The deposition of these, and other constructed features apparently associated with them, significantly altered the topography of the site during its occupation by Neanderthals, and for this reason, and the simple abundance of burials, I have left attention to this site until last. Spatially, the hominin remains fall into four groups: burials 1 and 2 close to the rear wall of the shelter; burials 3, 4 and 4b in a more central position; burials 5 and 8 close to the rear wall and at the edge of a group of possible sediment mounds; and easternmost burial 6 in a central position within one of several bowl-shaped pits (Figure 5.17).

The first group, the westernmost, comprises two near-complete adult skeletons (La Ferrassie 1 and 2), present in overall quantity and preservational circumstances that might be 'too extraordinary to accept as accidental' (Ossa, comment to Gargett 1989, 183). One of these – La Ferrassie 1 – an adult male between 40 and 55 years old at death (Fennell and Trinkaus 1997) – was located towards the back of the shelter, on its right side and partially flexed. The excavators observed that it lay within a depression – probably a deliberately excavated grave (Maureille and van Peer 1998) and that it was associated with three large stone slabs, one underneath the head, and the other two flanking its torso (Figure 5.18). A recent re-evaluation of the site's burials based on correspondence of the excavators has provided further evidence that the body was placed in a grave cutting (Maureille and van Peer 1998; B. Maureille pers. comm.). Given this, and the spread of faunal and archaeological remains at the site, the morphology of the shelter and known activities of

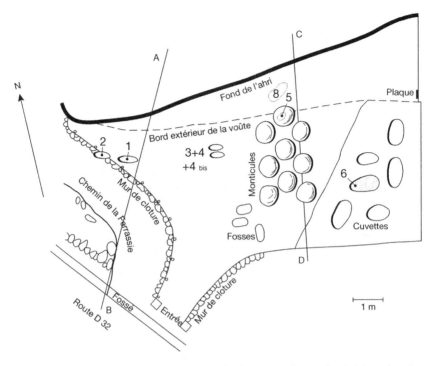

Figure 5.17 Plan of La Ferrassie showing the location of Neanderthal burials. The groups of La Ferrassie 1 and 2, 3 and 4 (marked 3, 4, +4 bis on plan: see text), 5 and 8 and 6, plus the sediment mounds are clearly shown (from Capitan and Peyrony 1912a).

small carnivores it is difficult to agree with Gargett's conclusion simply that 'the location of the skeleton, on a sloped surface near the back wall of the shelter, may have contributed to its preservation' (ibid., 166), and his argument that it is not *tightly* flexed as the excavators suggested is irrelevant to the issue of burial. Given that all of the hominin remains at La Ferrassie were deposited in rich occupation horizons one can assume that its preservation was due to deliberate placement within the natural depression. A number of highly fragmentary faunal remains – one of which bore a number of parallel engraved lines – were found just above the skeleton, although it is today impossible to eliminate the possibility that these derive from the occupation deposit. The La Ferrassie 2 skeleton – of an adult female – was found only 0.5m from the first (head to head in Capitan and Peyrony's view), and similarly flexed on its right side. Unlike La Ferrassie 1, however, no evidence of a depression or stone slabs was found despite careful excavation. The association between the two – and their separation from the other burials at the site – is intriguing, and as one cannot interpret them as a double burial *sensu stricto*

132

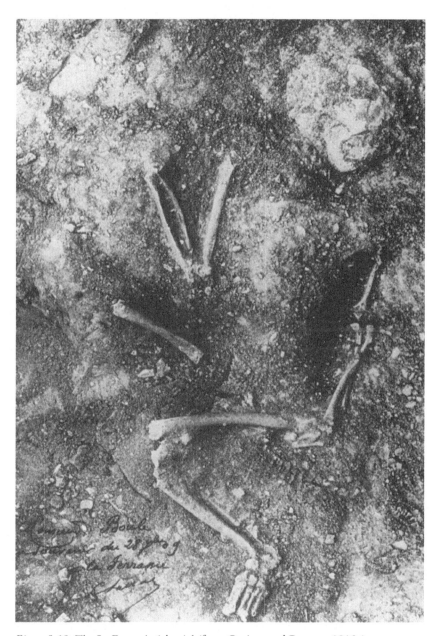

Figure 5.18 The La Ferrassie 1 burial (from Capitan and Peyrony 1912a).

(as they were not interred in the same grave cutting) it is difficult to see how this 'group' could have formed naturally.

The second group comprises the La Ferrassie 3 ~10-year-old child and La Ferrassie 4 neonate (Confusingly, 4a, which appears on the original plan, has now been shown to be part of La Ferrassie 3, and 4b subsumed into 4: B. Maureille pers. comm.). These were found 4m to the east of the first group, and were placed within two artificial graves of elongated oval shape, each 0.7 × 0.3m in dimension, and separated by 40cm – the child alone, and the two neonates together. The two graves were oriented parallel to each other – another argument for intention – and their contents thus oriented east–west. The graves were filled with stony rubble. I have dealt with Gargett's objections to these burials elsewhere (Pettitt 2002) and shall not repeat the reasons for my rejection of his argument here. As with the two adult inhumations of the first group, it is the similarity and 'group' integrity of this second group that argues for intentionality. What are the chances of a natural event that caused a child and two foeti to be deposited in parallel artificial cuttings together, isolated from other groups in the shelter?

The third group comprises La Ferrassie 5 (the partial skeleton of a foetus) and La Ferrassie 8 (a partial skeleton of a ~2-year-old child). Again close to the rear wall of the shelter, the foetus was placed within a small oval depression 0.4 × 0.3m in dimensions, close to three flint scrapers that were found at the base of one of several mounds in this central part of the cave, which covered the grave. The child was placed within another depression, roughly rectangular in shape, 0.8 × 0.3m in dimensions and in an area of the cave particularly disturbed by solifluxion, which probably explains its highly fragmentary state. The most controversial aspect of this area of the rockshelter is the presence of nine sediment 'mounds', typically circular in shape, one of which apparently overlay the pit containing La Ferrassie 5. As it was only one such mound that yielded a burial underneath, one would have to explain the function of the remaining eight if these were truly artifical. It would be pushing interpretation to suggest that they are funerary markers, and to invoke isolated taphonomic factors destroying eight further burials or to a possible 'cenotaph' function. Gargett (ibid. 167) pointed to the numerous natural agencies – not least of which are periglacial – that may produce such mounds, although in this case it remains to be seen why such periglacial features should be so localised on a site otherwise unaffected by the processes. Thus, while one cannot argue for their deliberate construction by Neanderthals, their explanation by natural factors does not, of course, weaken the argument that La Ferrassie 5 underneath was a deliberate burial. If, on the other hand, they were deliberate, this would add further complexity to the modification of space in a campsite used to bury a number of individuals.

The final group contained only La Ferrassie 6, albeit like the previous group in the context of a localised area of modification of the topography of the shelter. This comprises the partial skeleton of a ~3-year-old child.

It was placed within one of six wide and irregularly spaced bowl-shaped depressions, scattered over several metres with no apparent patterning. The depression that contained the child was sub-triangular in plan and 1.4 × 0.3m in maximum dimensions (Figure 5.19). The skeleton was discovered in articulation, oriented east–west like La Ferrassie 1, 2, 3 and 4/4b, although with its calotte located 1.25m from the rest of the skeleton. Three well-made Mousterian tools were recovered from the depression – an interesting parallel with the three tools associated with La Ferrassie 5. The depression and burial was covered with a large limestone block of sub-triangular planform 0.8m in length, the face of which was covered by one large and several small 'cupules' which are seen as artificially produced. If this is indeed the case this would be the only example of the association of deliberate marking of an object associated with a Neanderthal burial.

Sadly, so many questions arise from this fascinating site that cannot be answered with the excavation data that have come down to us. The excavations were meticulous, although too scanty information exists to allow us to eliminate natural causes for the 'mounds' and bowl-shaped depressions. The quality of the excavations should lend us some confidence that these features

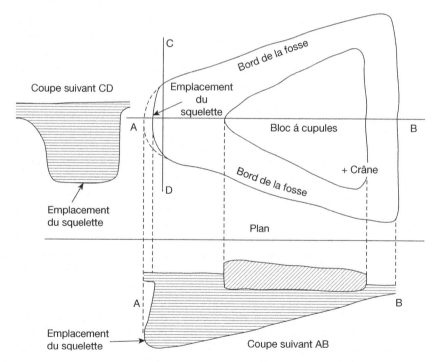

Figure 5.19 Plan and section of the La Ferrassie 6 infant burial. Note the well-defined triangular shape of the pit and the triangular-shaped stone with cupules under which the skeleton was found (from Capitan and Peyrony 1912a).

did exist, so why are mounds and bowls so rare on modern excavations? Might they be deliberate features? If so, it remains to be seen whether they are associated with the burials. What one can say about La Ferrassie is that eight individuals were associated spatially, in burials that share general characters and that appear to respect the same orientation. As Delporte (1976, 10) has noted, further organisation is present in the restriction of the adult burials to the western part of the site and of the infants and foeti to the centre and east. It is difficult to interpret this in any way other than intentional planning of a site of multiple burial.

Implications and conclusion

The possibility that pre MIS5 humans used certain areas of the landscape to dispose of the dead without involving artificial modification has been suggested by certain scholars, although it is difficult to evaluate these hypotheses with the data available currently. Logically perhaps it may be expected, and it takes only a small conceptual step from such behaviour to the excavation of features specifically to contain a corpse. As with the Dederiyeh 'scoops', such a template might have existed in at least certain Neanderthal groups, such as for the simple construction of hearths, sleeping scoops or even storage pits. Up to 30 indications of simple unaccompanied inhumation exist for the Eurasian Neanderthals. It is unclear whether the burial context was always excavated deliberately for burial, although in a few cases it seems likely that natural features or those excavated to serve other functions in the first instance could be employed for burial. As all possible examples of the inclusion of grave goods in Neanderthal burials (and those of modern humans prior to ~29,000 BP) are always open to other, simpler explanations, it must be acknowledged that no convincing example of grave goods is known from Neanderthals. On the other hand, the occasional secondary processing of body parts, for example at Krapina, and the presence of a number of infants in places of multiple burials, indicates that more complex mortuary 'rules' than simply 'burying the dead' were in operation at least on occasion and in some regions. They cannot be said to have been common, however. What this does demonstrate, though, is that at least some inter- and even intra-regional differences can be found in the treatment of the dead in Neanderthal societies. Clearly then, we cannot treat the Neanderthals as one monolithic, behaviourally redundant archaic species.

Gamble and Roebroeks (1999, 11) have suggested that 'the creation of place and the embodiment of this quality can be traced through [Late Mousterian] burials'. True, it would certainly seem that certain sites, such as Shanidar and La Ferrassie may at least have retained some persistent meaning for mortuary behaviour – in the case of Shanidar possibly for several millennia. But it seems to me that the focus of Neanderthal social life was the body: it was the body that created individual relations in life (Pettitt 2000) and it is therefore no surprise that it is the body that was explored and treated, at least on occasion, in death. True, we may not agree with broad-brush attempts to deny Neanderthal burial, but likewise we must not make simple conclusions that 'Neanderthals buried their dead'. Given the large amounts of space and time one is sampling here, it is wholly possible that Neanderthal burials were a brief epiphenomenon in their behavioural repertoires of dealing with the living and the dead. If there was any general means of disposal of the dead in Neanderthal society we shall never recapture it as it is obviously archaeologically invisible.

A good degree of variability can be observed in Neanderthal mortuary activity, which certainly matches that for early *Homo sapiens* populations discussed in the previous chapter. They can be summarised as follows:

- Cronos compulsions continue to manifest themselves, either as nutritional cannibalism, or defleshing for other purposes. On occasion, disarticulated remains were the subject of funerary caching or burial.
- Funerary caching continues from earlier beginnings, using natural fissures, depressions and niches within caves. On occasion this occurs alongside burials in deliberately excavated graves. In places, such natural features were widened, and at others stone slabs or cairns were used to cover burials.
- Infant burials are relatively common in the accepted sample (Riel-Salvatore and Clark 2001).
- Within formal inhumations, bodies were buried in a wide variety of positions (Smirnov 1989, 223) – on their backs, sides, flexed and extended – possibly with more emphasis on the right side (Riel-Salvatore and Clark 2001).
- Where information exists, graves were often oriented on an east–west axis, although sites with multiple inhumations fail to show consistent orientations (Riel-Salvatore and Clark 2001).
- Almost all are associated with occupations (Smirnov 1989, 220), and situated well within the caves.
- Pits, shallow graves and large stones (in the case of Regourdou a tomb comprised of a large slab and a cairn) were employed to contain the corpse.
- While none can be regarded as 'double, triple or multiple' graves as we will see in Chapter 6, some do seem to be associated.
- Whole bodies were buried, as were parts of bodies.
- Faunal remains and lithic artefacts were recovered in association with over 5 per cent of accepted burials, although it is unclear as to whether or not these are deliberate grave goods.
- Some places saw the burial of multiple individuals. In some cases these burials probably occurred within a short period of time and were relatively unstructured (e.g. Shanidar) but at others a degree of organisation is evident (e.g. La Ferrassie). The latter suggests at times complex interactions between the living and the dead and their remains.

These patterns occur until the latest Neanderthal populations, such as the Le Moustier and Saint-Césaire burials around 40,000 and 36,000 BP respectively. By this time it appears that Upper Palaeolithic *Homo sapiens* populations had established themselves in some regions of Europe. Although some funerary activities are observable in these earliest European modern human populations, it seems that several thousand years were to pass before some individuals came to be afforded burial, and possibly for very different reasons than the Neanderthals and Levantine modern humans.

6

THE FIRST *HOMO SAPIENS* POPULATIONS IN EUROPE

Early and Mid Upper Palaeolithic funerary activities ~35,000–21,000 BP

1823: a discovery in the dark

I discovered beneath a shallow covering of six inches of earth nearly the entire left side of a human female skeleton. [all the bones were] ... stained superficially with a dark brick-red colour, and enveloped by a coating of ruddle. The entire body must have been entirely surrounded or covered over at the time of its interment with this red substance. Close to the part of the thigh bone where the pocket is usually worn, I found laid together, and surrounded also by ruddle, about two handsfull of small shells of the nerita littoralis ... at another part of the skeleton, viz. in contact with the ribs, I found forty or fifty fragments of small ivory rods nearly cyclindrical, and varying in diameter from a quarter to three quarters of an inch, and from one to four inches in length. Rings made of the same ivory [were] ... found with the rods. Both rods and rings were stained superficially with red and lay in the same red substance that enveloped the bones; they had evidently been buried at the same time with the woman.

(Buckland 1823, 87–9)

One of the first recorded excavations of what is now known to be a Pleistocene archaeological and palaeontological cave site occurred in 1823 in the Goat's Hole cave, Paviland, on the Gower Peninsula, Wales. The cave is small, dark, wet, and reeks of the excretia of sea birds, yet commands a spectacular view over the Severn estuary that in the Upper Pleistocene formed a vast plain that would ultimately link the British hunting grounds eastwards to the continent. Excavations in the cave by local amateurs attracted the interest of the Oxford geologist William Buckland, whose participation in the clearance of the cave's sediment and publication at the end of the year ensured its lasting fame (Buckland 1823). Little did Buckland know, however, that he has described the first known Mid Upper Palaeolithic burial. Among scant traces of what is now known to be Gravettian occupation of the cave, the excavations revealed the partial skeleton of an adult, stained with 'ruddle' (ochre), and associated with items of personal ornamentation and enigmatic objects of bone and ivory. Buckland was happy that the fauna recovered from the cave derived from 'antediluvian' deposits relating to floods, but his progressivism prohibited him from countenancing the fact that the human remains also belonged to this remote period (White and Pettitt 2009). Buckland therefore assigned the remains to the later prehistoric or Roman period, and despite originally identifying them as a male, reclassified them as a female. The resulting 'Red Lady of Paviland' was published in the 1823 monograph and thus entered the history of archaeology.

Today, it is clear that the 'Red Lady' was a young adult male of Gravettian cultural attribution (Aldhouse-Green 2000a; Trinkaus and Holliday 2000), who was buried (28,000–29,000 BP on the basis of recent ultrafiltered AMS ^{14}C measurements on the skeleton itself (Jacobi and Higham 2008).[10] From Buckland's description of the find, and from a partly idealised plan and section of the cave (Figure 6.1) one can reconstruct the general details of the burial. The body seems to have been placed in extended position, probably on its left side, given that almost all of its right side is missing, presumably due to erosion. Limestone slabs may have been placed on or around the body, perhaps to delineate or weigh down its head and feet (Aldhouse-Green 2000c). It seems that the area of the burial – the body and the associated grave goods – was stained with ochre. On the skeleton itself the staining is strongest on the bones of the pelvis and lower body, suggesting that the Red Lady was wearing two-piece clothing, probably a parka and leggings, rather than a funeral shroud. The small amount of ornaments recovered with the body probably reflect items sewn onto this clothing; the clustering of perforated and ochre-stained periwinkle shells 'close to the part of the thigh bone where the pocket is usually worn' suggests that they were sewn onto a loincloth (Pettitt 2006, 296). The 'forty or fifty small ivory rods', many of which apparently 'crumbled to dust' upon excavation and of which most are now lost, seem to have originally formed short, tapering batons or rods. The surviving examples are ochre-stained, and have been interpreted as magical wands or other items of power (Aldhouse-Green and Pettitt 1999, 766; Aldhouse-Green 2000b) and it is interesting that they were deliberately broken before being placed on and around the chest of the Red Lady. Fragments of two rings of mammoth ivory, often described as bracelets but in fact of small diameter and perhaps sewn onto the clothing, seem also associated with the burial. The bones of large herbivores seem to have been buried with or around the young man, and the recovery of a complete mammoth skull with tusks in close proximity to the burial and within the same alcove in the cave's left wall, seems also to have formed part of the burial.

SECTION OF THE CAVE CALLED GOAT HOLE.
In the Sea Cliffs 15 Miles West of Swansea.

Figure 6.1
Plan and section of Goat's
Hole cave at Paviland, Wales.
Note position of 'the Red
Lady' and proximity of the
mammoth cranium and tusks.
The plan does not do the
cave's morphology justice: the
burial was placed in a small
alcove. Buckland has drawn a
complete skeleton yet half of
it was missing (from
Buckland 1823).

The burials known from the European Mid Upper Palaeolithic (the Gravettian *sensu lato*, ~29,000–21,000 BP) represent a major watershed in human mortuary activity (Figure 6.2). Unlike the preceding burials among Levantine early *Homo sapiens* groups and Eurasian Neanderthals they are richly furnished and correspond to traditions that were not localised regionally but widespread on the continental scale. It seems fair to assume, too, that widespread shared belief systems underpinned funerary practices of this period. Many of the elements observable in the burial of the Red Lady could pertain to most of these. The young man was laid on one side in a shallow grave, wearing elaborate clothing stained with ochre and ornamented with perforated teeth, shells and enigmatic objects of mammoth ivory. The bones of large, dangerous animals – including a mammoth skull complete with tusks – were associated with the burial. By Mid Upper Palaeolithic standards the grave's inclusions were relatively poor, although by the standards of the burials discussed in Chapters 4 and 5 this is rich indeed and a new, continent-wide

Figure 6.2 Mid Upper Palaeolithic burials discussed in the text.

burial tradition had clearly emerged among *Homo sapiens* populations by ~29,000 BP. Whether this tradition will eventually be demonstrated to extend back to the earliest *Homo sapiens* arrivals in Europe and their Early Upper Palaeolithic context remains to be seen, although in this pioneer period new traditions of funerary caching seem to have emerged at least in some regions. These traditions were at first focused on the dark regions of caves, and only later did funerary rituals extend to the sophisticated and semi-sedentary camp sites in the open air. The traditions of body processing arising from Cronos compulsions continued, and reached their greatest development after 29,000 BP when it can be seen that in some centres of civilisation human relics are circulating within complex ritual and mortuary contexts.

Funerary caching and body processing in the European Early Upper Palaeolithic

Early Upper Palaeolithic open-air sites with large and well preserved bones are rare. Instead, caves and rockshelters have provided the majority of sites that can be ascribed to the Aurignacian. A number of these sites have yielded major assemblages, with well preserved faunal assemblages, yet despite this human remains are remarkably rare for the period. While it must therefore remain open to question as to whether Aurignacians buried their dead on open sites, enough information derives from caves and rockshelters to make some generalisations.

Caves of the dead

Caves in two regions – the Czech Republic and Romania – have yielded relatively large numbers of Early Upper Palaeolithic human remains, enough to suggest the practice of traditions of funerary caching among the earliest populations of *Homo sapiens* in Europe. Remains of a human mandible and cranium were recovered from a displaced bone bed (the Panta Strămoșilor – 'slope of the ancestors') in the Peştera cu Oase ('Cave with Bones'), in the Carpathians, Romania (Trinkaus *et al.* 2003; Rougier *et al.* 2007). The bones seem to derive from the cave's upper galleries, and were recovered in the context of abundant evidence of denning in the cave by the cave bear *Ursus spelaeus*, although with no associated archaeology. It is possible that some of the bear remains were intentionally displaced, which if correct might suggest an association of deposition of the human remains with the interaction with those of bears, although it is impossible to establish this with confidence. A series of AMS ^{14}C measurements on bones from the deposits including a direct measurement on the Oase 1 mandible indicate an age of ~33,000–36,000 BP for the human remains (Trinkaus *et al.* 2003), which is in accord with a minimum age on the Oase 2 cranium of ~29,000 BP (Rougier *et al.* 2007). There are no signs of human or carnivore modifications of the bones; it seems that they were washed down the Panta Strămoşilor when at least partially decomposed. The different ages at death of Oase 1 and 2 show that at least two individuals – an adult and an adolescent – derive from the cave's upper galleries.

Several fragmentary remains of one individual and a cranial fragment probably of a second were recovered from a surface depression at the back of a gallery in the Peştera Muierii ('Cave of the Old Woman'), Baia de Fier, Romania (Soficaru *et al.* 2006). Direct AMS ^{14}C measurements indicate an age of 29,000–31,000 BP (Table 6.1) for these *Homo sapiens* individuals, rendering it unlikely that they are meaningfully associated with the cave's Middle Palaeolithic artefacts. As the fossils were found in the 1950s and assumed to be Late Upper Palaeolithic (or later) it is now impossible to establish whether they were deliberately deposited in the cave. Of similarly questionable origin, a human cranium was found in the Peştera Cioclovina Uscată gallery, part of the Ponorici Cioclovina karstic system in the southern Carpathians, which has been dated directly to ~28,000–30,000 BP (Table 6.1) (Soficaru *et al.* 2007). This was found with cave bear remains – apparently found in close proximity to a cave bear cranium – although it is impossible today to establish whether this is a meaningful link or whether the human remains were deposited during activities that left Aurignacian artefacts in the cave.

Over 100 specimens classified as *Homo sapiens* have been recovered from debris cones that accumulated under chimneys in the Mladeč cave system in the Třesín Hill, Moravia (Svoboda *et al.* 2002). The largest of these – the Dome of the dead – accumulated in Site I. The human remains were found in the upper parts of the cones, most of which accumulated in the Middle Pleistocene and therefore would have been pronounced features by the time that modern humans arrived in the region. Direct AMS ^{14}C dates on four specimens reveal an age of ~30,000–32,000 BP and of carbonate deposits sealing the remains a minimum age of 34,000–35,000 BP (Table 6.1) for the deposition of the bones, perhaps best interpreted as an age of ~34,000–36,000 BP at 2σ. The dates are consistent with an Aurignacian cultural attribution, and diagnostic bone Mladeč points are present in the cone although their direct association with the human remains is unclear and they also lack enough collagen for direct dating. It should be remembered, however, that the remains are chronometrically contemporary with the latest Bohunician in the region, and one cannot rule out a cultural attribution to this 'transitional' technocomplex. The remains include those of adult males and females, as well as immature individuals, and the recovery of multiple specimens of cranial and postcranial elements suggests that entire bodies were deposited at the sites.

Fragmentation and curation of the dead

Cranio-dental and postcranial remains of at least four individuals were recovered from Initial Upper Palaeolithic (Baradostian) levels in the Eshkaft-e Gavi cave, Iran (Scott and Marean 2009). Although only one of these is

Table 6.1 Early Upper Palaeolithic human remains discussed in the text. Two ^{14}C measurements on Mladeč fossils have been excluded as they are probably underestimates – see Wild et al. 2005. Similarly, the Vogelherd human remains have been omitted as they are demonstrably post-Palaeolithic (Conard et al. 2004).

Site	Sample	Chronology	References
Peştera cu Oase, Caraş-Severin, Romania	Oase 1 mandible, adult	~34,950 +990/–890 BP (direct AMS ^{14}C measurement)	Trinkaus et al. 2003 Rougier et al. 2007
Peştera cu Oase, Caraş-Severin, Romania	Oase 2 cranium, adolescent	~34,950 +990/–890 BP (minimum age of ~29,000 BP)	Rougier et al. 2007
Peştera Muierii, Baia de Fier, Romania	Muierii 1 cranial and postcranial elements	LuA-5228, 30,150 ± 800 BP; OxA-15529, 29,930 ± 170 BP (direct AMS ^{14}C measurements)	Soficaru et al. 2006
Peştera Muierii, Baia de Fier, Romania	Muierii 2 temporal fragment	OxA-16252, 29,110 ± 190 BP (direct AMS ^{14}C measurement)	Soficaru et al. 2006
Peştera Cioclovina Uscată, Hunedoara, Romania	Cioclovina 1 cranium, possibly female	LuA-5229, 29,000 ± 700 BP (direct AMS ^{14}C measurement on temporal); OxA-15227, 28,510 ± 170 BP (direct AMS ^{14}C measurement on occipital)	Soficaru et al. 2007. See also Harvati et al. 2005 for the question of whether this is a hybrid
Mladeč, Moravia, Czech Republic	Mladeč 1, female	VERA-3073, 31,190 +400/–390 BP (direct ^{14}C measurement on tooth)	Wild et al. 2005
Mladeč, Moravia, Czech Republic	Mladeč 2	VERA-3074, 31,320 +410/–390 BP (direct ^{14}C measurement on tooth)	Wild et al. 2005
Mladeč, Moravia, Czech Republic	Mladeč 8	VERA-3075, 30,680 +380/–360 BP (direct ^{14}C measurement on tooth)	Wild et al. 2005
Mladeč, Moravia, Czech Republic	Mladeč 9	VERA-3076A, 31,500 +420/–400 BP (direct ^{14}C measurement on tooth)	Wild et al. 2005
Mladeč, Moravia, Czech Republic	Mladeč I-1	GrN-26333 34,160 +520/–490 BP (AMS ^{14}C on calcite: minimum age)	Svoboda et al. 2002
Mladeč, Moravia, Czech Republic	Mladeč I-2	GrN-26334, 34,930 +520/–490 BP (^{14}C on calcite: minimum age)	Svoboda et al. 2002
La Crouzade, Aude, France	La Crouzade V (frontal bone) and VI (maxilla), one adult	ERL 9415, 30,640 ± 640 BP (direct AMS ^{14}C measurement on Crouzade VI)	Henry-Gambier and Sacchi 2008

demonstrably associated with the Baradostian, the other three bear cut marks, demonstrating that they were processed no later than the Epipalaeolithic. Fragmentary human remains from Russia suggests that curation began in the Early Upper Palaeolithic of the region as discussed below. Fragmentary human remains have been found in early Aurignacian contexts in three interlinked caves at Brassempouy, Landes, the Grotte du Pape, Galerie Dubalen and Grotte des Hyènes (Henry-Gambier *et al.* 2004; Henry-Gambier and White 2006). Single items were found in the first two of these, but the Grotte des Hyènes yielded 16 cranio-dental fragments and two phalanges representing at least two infants and two adults. These were recovered from a sediment rich in ochre, which had impregnated two teeth, probably resulting from occupation of the cave rather than from deliberate deposition (Henry-Gambier and White 2006, 77). Four teeth bear modifications consistent with their use as personal ornamentation (and for this reason they are discussed below), and a cranial fragment bears traces of intense fracturing while fresh.

A human frontal bone and mandible belonging to the same individual were recovered from Aurignacian levels at La Crouzade cave in Aude, France (Henry-Gambier and Sacchi 2008; Table 6.1). Direct AMS ^{14}C dating places the remains ~29,000–31,000 BP, in accord with the late Aurignacian archaeology in the cave. Striations on the surface of the frontal bone are indicative of processing, possibly scalping. At Les Rois cave, Charente, France, two mandibles and 37 isolated teeth of *Homo sapiens* were found amidst occupation deposits including Aurignacian artefacts, butchery waste and hearths (Gambier 1989; Ramirez Rozzi *et al.* 2009). It is one of the few sites on which human remains can be demonstrably associated with the Aurignacian. AMS ^{14}C measurements on five humanly modified faunal remains associated with the human remains indicate an age of ~27–31,000 BP (Ramirez Rozzi *et al.* 2009, 166). Cut marks on juvenile Mandible B take the form of parallel striations on the lingual aspect, of a form and location similar to those on mandibles of reindeer from the site and probably indicative of the removal of the tongue (ibid., 174). This is of interest, as the mandible was originally found within a hearth, possibly indicating that it was processed in the same way as other food refuse, although one cannot exclude defleshing and a non-nutritional purpose behind the processing. The possibility that mandible B is 'neanderthal like' or actually of a Neanderthal in a deposit otherwise of the remains of modern humans, on an archaeological site left (one assumes) by modern humans, is fascinating (ibid., 174), although it must be said that support for this notion comes only from dental size and perykymata packing rather than any autapomorphic traits, so it is not particularly convincing.

A new development visible in the Early Upper Palaeolithic record of Europe is the use of human remains as personal ornamentation. It is, in fact, interesting that, although personal ornamentation has an antiquity paralleling that of *Homo sapiens,* despite the processing of bodies as discussed in Chapter 4, no curation of human remains in the form of personal ornaments is known before

Human or dementation

the European Upper Palaeolithic, which may suggest that the development occurred in the context of wider developments in belief and ritual systems of which the circulation of human remains and, later, origins of elaborate burials were part. Human teeth perforated through the root for suspension are known from several French Aurignacian sites, notably: La Combe, Dordogne (Le Mort 1985, 191); Isturitz (Pyrénées-Atlantiques); the Grotte des Hyènes at Brassempouy (Landes) (Henry-Gambier *et al.* 2004; Henry-Gambier and Sacchi 2008); Les Rois in the context of the defleshed remains discussed above (Henry-Gambier *et al.* 2004); and Tarté (Haute-Garonne) (White *et al.* 2003). The four perforated teeth from the Grotte des Hyènes occurred in the context of an occupation deposit with ornaments of wolf and fox canines and, occasionally, those of red deer. Clearly, the human teeth from the site (two premolars and two molars) were part of a small subset of teeth that had symbolic meaning to its Aurignacian occupants. It is interesting that canines were overwhelmingly chosen from the restricted number of animal taxa, whereas premolars and molars are only found among the human remains.

One cannot, of course, demonstrate that the curation of human teeth as personal ornamentation resulted from the disarticulation of carcasses. Modifications such as striations relate to the process of piercing, rather than to the deliberate removal of an otherwise healthy tooth. It remains possible, therefore, that teeth were retained as they fell out naturally. Given the clear demonstration of defleshing of head parts, however, it is plausible that teeth were removed from the mouth during processing of carcasses, as part of an organised (and, one assumes, symbolically mediated) acquisition of body parts.

The European Mid Upper Palaeolithic

No convincing burials are known from the European Early Upper Palaeolithic. The supposed Aurignacian grave 'pseudomorphs' of Cueva Morin, Spain (Freeman and González-Echegaray 1970) are unconvincing; nothing like the information required for assessment of these claims has been published, and as Straus (1991) has noted, no human remains were recovered from the supposed graves despite good faunal preservation across the site. The human skeleton from the Grotte du Bouil Bleu in Charente-Maritime, long supposed to be an Aurignacian burial, was shown by direct AMS ^{14}C dating to be an intrusive burial of the Roman period (Foucher *et al.* 1995); fragmentary remains from La Rochette, Dordogne, similarly thought to be Aurignacian have been shown to be Gravettian on the basis of an AMS ^{14}C measurement on a fragmentary right ulna of 23,630 ± 130 BP (Orschiedt 2002) and several claimed Early Upper Palaeolithic human remains from Germany such as Stetten I have been shown to be much later by direct dating (Street *et al.* 2006). No other claims exist. As Henry-Gambier (2008, 12) has noted, 'entre 35,000 BP et 27,000 BP,[11] le seule intervention démontré sure le cadavre est le façonnage des dents isolées'. By contrast, burial seems to have been practised in Africa by ~37,000 BP, as three individuals were recovered from two burial pits at Nazlet Khater in Upper Egypt (Vermeersch 2002). These comprise an adult (Nazlet Khater 1a) and foetus/neonate (1b) interred within the same grave, for which an AMS ^{14}C measurement on charcoal found at the feet of 1a provides an age of 37,570 +350/–310 BP (GrA-20145), and an adult buried separately (Nazlet Khater 2; Figures 6.3 and 6.4). The recovery of the 1b foetus/neonate in the pelvic area of individual 1a suggests that that this was a death during pregnancy or childbirth. The robust adult 2 was buried with a bifacial axe identical to those recovered from chert mining at the site, and the sedimentary fill of the burial pit was identical to that in mining pits. In this sense, pits were already in existence at Nazlet Khater and provided ready graves for burial, and it is unclear as to whether these were excavated deliberately for burial. In view of this, it is perhaps sensible to see these burials as representing a continuation of the tradition of funerary caching witnessed earlier at Taramsa as discussed in Chapter 4. The partial skeleton of an elderly adult of indeterminate sex from Tianyuan Cave at Zhoukoudian, China, has been classified as *Homo sapiens* and directly dated by AMS ^{14}C to 34,430

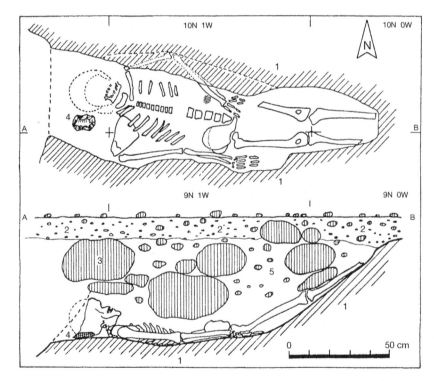

Figure 6.3 Plan and section of Burial 2 at Nazlet Khater, Egypt (courtesy of Pierre Vermeersch).

Figure 6.4 The Nazlet Khater 2 burial (photograph courtesy of Pierre Vermeersch).

± 510 BP (Shang *et al.* 2007) although no grave cutting or cultural associations were demonstrated for this and it is impossible to establish whether it was deliberately buried.

In Europe, by contrast, a little over 50 examples of burial are known from the European Mid Upper Palaeolithic, much of which reflect the repeated burial use of the same location (Zilhão and Trinkaus 2002b). Evidence for primary inhumation – the burial of an intact, fresh corpse – and secondary inhumation of body parts exists (Henry-Gambier 2008). This is clearly a new phenomenon. Similarities between graves are observable across Europe that link the earliest examples of these (~29,000 BP) to the latest (~23,000–22,000 BP) in general terms, although there is some argument for an earlier period in which graves are not well furnished, and a later that contains all of the richer burials. As Henry-Gambier (2008, 15) has observed, at the European scale,

> l'image qui se dessine est celle de groups partageant une même logique de gestion des morts . . . mai qui l'expériment selon des modalities propres adaptées pour les matières premiers du mobilier, de la parure et du dispositive funéraire aux stratégies d'exploitation du milieu naturelet au mode de vie.

Within some regions strong local traditions are observed that suggest that strong social grammars underlay these burials, and that probably reflect relatively short periods of time. As with the Neanderthals, however, one should certainly not infer that 'Mid Upper Palaeolithic societies buried their dead'. Some regions that provide a rich record of Gravettian settlement have yielded only a few fragmentary human remains and no evidence of mortuary ritual, such as southern Germany (Street *et al.* 2006, 567), suggesting that burial at least was not ubiquitous across Gravettian space. Furthermore, there are a number of reasons to assume that many or all of the individuals for which we have burials were odd, and that the circumstances of their detachment rituals stood out from the norm. These appear in the context of the processing and circulation of body parts, and a continuation of the use of perforated human teeth as personal ornamentation can be observed even where no formal burials are known such as in the French Gravettian; for example, a perforated canine from Abri Pataud (Dordogne) (Vercoutère *et al.* 2008; Figure 6.5) and a scored root from Les Vachons (Charente) (Ferembach 1956). A perforated tooth root is also known from Dolní Věstonice, Moravia (Vercoutère *et al.* 2008). The humerus of an adult male from the 'bone cave' of Eel Point, Caldey Island, Wales, which has been dated to 24,470 ± 110 BP (Schulting *et al.* 2005) appears not to have been associated with occupation of the area and may derive from curation of human remains, as with several human remains from La Rochette, Dordogne, the Gravettian attribution of which has been noted above.

150

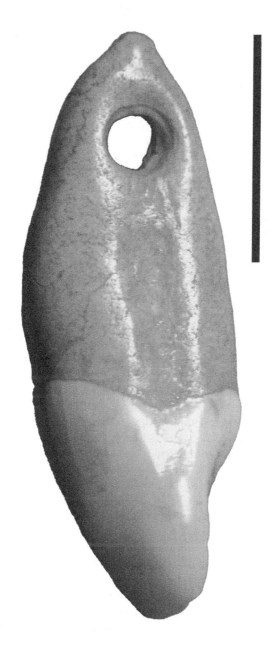

Figure 6.5 Perforated human tooth from the Gravettian of Abri Pataud, Dordogne (photograph courtesy of Carole Vercoutère, Giacomo Giacobini, Marylène Patou-Mathis and Laurent Chiotti, Muséum National d'Histoire Naturel, Paris, and Elsevier Publishing).
Note: Black bar = 1cm.

Funerary caching in the French caves

Given the relative abundance of burials for the European Mid Upper Palae-olithic overall the lack of Gravettian burials in France is of interest.[12] Isolated and fragmentary human remains on Gravettian sites such as Abri Pataud (fragmentary remains of six individuals: Movius 1975; Nespoulet *et al.* 2008) may have originally constituted burials, and seem to have been associated with mammoth ivory beads, although it is now impossible to establish whether deliberate graves were cut for these individuals. Despite this, partial and near-complete human skeletons have been recovered elsewhere in France from contexts suggestive of funerary caching, which would indicate that this practice persisted in the region and formal burial was not practised.

The remains from Cro-Magnon, Les Eyzies, Dordogne, may provide evi-dence of funerary caching under the same rockshelter as Abri Pataud. Although originally thought to be Aurignacian on the basis of apparent stratigraphic associations, an AMS ^{14}C measurement of 27680 ± 270 BP on a *Littorina* sp. shell associated with the skeletal material indicates that they are of Gravettian age (Henry-Gambier 2002; see Table 6.2). Remains of the near-complete Cro-Magnon 1 (the 'old man') and fragmentary remains of four other individuals were found together in March 1868, along with a number of isolated elements that may represent further individuals (Oakley *et al.* 1971). The bones were stained with ochre (Henry-Gambier 2000); ~300 perforated shells (mostly *Littorina* sp.) were recovered from the area of the human remains although it is, of course, unclear today whether this is a deliberate association or because of the fact that the human remains were found in the context of occupation of the rockshelter (May 1986). Although it is impossible today to establish whether these individuals were deliberately interred, authorities generally assume on the basis of completeness and archaeological association that they were (e.g. Binant 1991, 50 and Henry-Gambier 2002, 203, for whom it is a 'sépulture multiple'). However one interprets the material, it is interesting that it represents two adult males, an adult female and a neonate, calling to mind the Mid Upper Palaeolithic triple burials of Barma Grande and Dolní Věstonice and the female/neonate burial from Ostuni, all discussed below.

Human remains were recovered from three separate locations in the Grotte de Cussac, Dordogne, dating to ~25,000 BP (Aujoulat *et al.* 2001, 2002). This takes the form of a long, narrow gallery, and the skeletons were in each case placed in depressions – at least two of which are bear 'wallows' (hibernation hollows) ~75m (Locus 1 and 2) and ~100m (Locus 3) into the cave. At Locus 1 the remains of an adolescent was placed within a clear hibernation hollow; at Locus 2 the near-complete and partially articulated skeleton of an adult was placed within a hollow close to the foot of the cave's wall and was apparently covered with a film of silt; and at Locus 3 the remains of three adults were placed within a depression atop a 'seat' of limestone over which stalactite later formed as well as close by against the cave's wall (Aujoulat *et al.* 2001, 2002; see Table 6.2). These were disarticulated, and no traces of crania were found, although the recovery of many parts of the postcranial skeleton as well as small elements such as phalanges suggests that post-depositional processes are not the cause. The lack of gnawing and other processing, furthermore, suggests that the cave may have been inaccessible to carnivores (Henry-Gambier 2008, 9). It is possible that the heads had already been removed from the bodies, or that they were removed subsequent to their deposition. Four adults and an adolescent clearly came to be deposited carefully within the cave's depths, in an area in which figurative engravings were also produced, as discussed below. As there is little evidence of disturbance in the cave this must indicate that the remains were deliberately placed within the depressions, and given that one of these is clearly a hibernation hollow and that the others resemble it, it is probably not pushing interpretation too far to invoke a connection between the dead and hibernating bears. Bears often die in hibernation and their bodies would have been a relatively common site within deep caves, which may have prompted a connection with death, or perhaps a symbolism of the cyclical nature of life and death: bears hibernate (thus symbollically die) in winter, and return to life in spring (A. Verpoorte pers. comm.).

In the Les Garennes cave system near the village of Vilhonneur (Charente) the partial skeleton of a young adult male was found in the deepest chamber, in close proximity to a Gravettian hand stencil (Henry-Gambier *et al.* 2007). Although his postcranial remains had become dispersed across a scree, his cranium was recovered from a low gallery, and the overall context of the remains suggested that they derive from a primary deposition, although not an inhumation but possibly an 'above ground interment' (ibid., 749). If the position of the head is indicative of the original position of the corpse, this is consistent with funerary caching, in this case against the wall of a small niche, which saw at some point the production of a hand stencil.

The presence of parietal art in both Cussac and Villhonneur caves strongly suggests that the caching of human remains occurred in a wider context of which art was part. In Cussac, the art is not directly dated but strong thematic and stylistic similarities with the Gravettian art of Pech-Merle (Lot) and Gargas (Hautes-Pyrénées) (Lorblanchet 2001) indicate that it has the same cultural context as the burials, which for Locus 1 has been dated to 25,120 ± 120 BP (see Table 6.2). Almost all of the art is grouped into panels in the same area of the cave as the human remains (Aujoulat *et al.*, 2002, 136), the latter 'encapsulated' by the art panels that one encounters first and last when progressing into the cave's interior. The recovery of the Vihonneur 1 adult male from the same gallery as a hand stencil suggests further deliberate associations between the dead and art. This may be an important indication that the symbolic associations of places of funerary caching had by now become more widely contextualised into the artistic and ritual space of caves. As

Table 6.2 Mid Upper Palaeolithic human remains discussed in the text. Unless stated, dates are AMS ^{14}C BP

Specimen	Site	Chronology and cultural context	Site details	Age, sex, pathologies	Context	Archaeological associations	References
Egypt							
NK 1a and 1b	Nazlet Khater, Upper Egypt	AMS ^{14}C measurement of 37,570 +350/-310 BP (GrA-20145) on charcoal found at feet of NK1a	Occupation and stone extraction site	Adult (NK1a) and foetus/neonate (NK1b) interred in same grave	Buried in shallow grave, foetus/neonate in vicinity of adult's pelvis	Chert mining	Vermeersch 2002
NK2	Nazlet Khater, Upper Egypt	Probably the same as for NK1a and 1b	Occupation and chert extraction site	Adult	Laid in shallow 'pit' in extended position	Bifacial axe similar to forms from nearby chert mining pits	Vermeersch 2002
United Kingdom							
Paviland 1 ('The Red Lady' of Paviland')	Goat's Hole (cave), Paviland, Gower Peninsula, Wales	Gravettian occupation. Direct AMS ^{14}C measurements on bones of the Red Lady of 28,870 ± 180 BP (OxA-16412) and 29,490 ± 210 BP (OxA-16413)	Occupation horizon	Partial skeleton (lacking cranium and right side) of young adult male, no observed pathologies	Body placed in alcove to side of cave. Area stained with red ochre, fragmented ivory rods laid on chest, head and feet possibly covered with stone slabs, body wearing clothing onto which were sewn periwinkle shells and probably elaborated with ivory rings and perforated shells. Probable association with mammoth skull and bones of other large mammals	Derives from Gravettian occupation	Buckland 1823; Aldhouse-Green and Pettitt 1998; Aldhouse-Green 2000a, b; Pettitt 2006; Jacobi and Higham 2008

Specimen	Date	Context	Description	Horizon	Associations	Reference
Eel Point	OxA-14164, 24,470 ± 110 BP (direct AMS ^{14}C measurement on humerus)	Cave shows evidence of hyena denning, no archaeological association	Isolated humerus of adult male	Not from occupation horizon, possibly (but not demonstrably) associated with hyena denning	No archaeological associations	Schulting et al. 2005
France						
Cro-Magnon 1	Gravettian. Associated with *Littorina* sp. shells, one directly dated by AMS ^{14}C to 27,680 ± 270 BP (Beta-157439)	Early excavations by Lartet: Gravettian (and earlier Aurignacian) occupation	Near-complete cranial and postcranial skeleton of adult male. Histiocytosis X	Gravettian occupation horizon	Found in location with ~300 shells and stained with ochre	May 1986; Henry-Gambier 2002
Cro-Magnon 2	As Cro-Magnon 1	As Cro-Magnon 1	Partial cranial and postcranial skeleton of adult female	As Cro-Magnon 1	As Cro-Magnon 1	May 1986; Henry-Gambier 2002
Cro-Magnon 3	As Cro-Magnon 1	As Cro-Magnon 1	Partial cranial and postcranial skeleton of adult male	As Cro-Magnon 1	As Cro-Magnon 1	May 1986; Henry-Gambier 2002
Cro-Magnon 4	As Cro-Magnon 1	As Cro-Magnon 1	Cranial fragments of adult, possibly male	As Cro-Magnon 1	As Cro-Magnon 1	May 1986; Henry-Gambier 2002
Cro-Magnon 5	As Cro-Magnon 1	As Cro-Magnon 1	Fragmentary cranial and postcranial skeleton of neonate	As Cro-Magnon 1	As Cro-Magnon 1	May 1986; Henry-Gambier 2002

continued . . .

Table 6.2 continued

Cussac 1	Grotte de Cussac, Le-Buisson-de-Cadouin, Dordogne	Beta 156643, 25,120 ± 120 BP (direct AMS ^{14}C measurement on rib)	Includes Gravettian engravings including rhino, bison, horse and human females similar to Pech-Merle and Gargas	Partial postcranial skeleton, adolescent, found within bear hibernation hollow	Locus 1, ~75m into cave	Possible association with red staining adjacent to hibernation hollow	Lorblanchet 2001; Aujoulat et al. 2001, 2002
Cussac 2	As Cussac 1	Problematic date (too young)	As Cussac 1	Near-complete adult cranial and postcranial skeleton, found within oval depression and with silt coating at the foot of the cave wall; a degree of articulation was evident	Locus 2 ~75m into cave, at foot of cave wall	None obvious	Lorblanchet 2001; Aujoulat et al. 2001, 2002
Cussac 3	As Cussac 1	Lack of collagen prevented dating	As Cussac 1	Near-complete, disarticulated postcranial skeletons of three adults	Placed within depression atop limestone 'seat', later covered with flowstone, and longbones close-by against cave wall	Red ochre traces found atop silt cone and possibly connected to deposition of human remains	Lorblanchet 2001; Aujoulat et al. 2001, 2002

Vilhonneur 1	Les Garennes cave, Vilhonneur, Charente, France	Beta 216141, 27,010 ± 210 BP (direct AMS ^{14}C measurement on rib 18). Beta 216142, 26,690 ± 190 BP (direct AMS ^{14}C measurement on rib 19). Agree with Gravettian attribution of hand stencil	Deep cave with hyena denning, human remains, and Gravettian parietal art	Cranium and partial postcranial skeleton of a young adult male	Postcranial remains dispersed across scree. Cranium within low gallery below hand stencil	No associated archaeology	Henry-Gambier et al. 2007
Pataud 1–6	Abri Pataud, Dordogne	Late Gravettian (Protomagdalenian) occupation horizon ~22,000 BP	Rich occupation deposit	250 fragmentary remains pertaining to MNI of 6. At least one probably disturbed primary inhumation	Disturbed, unclear	Mammoth ivory beads apparently associated with some remains	Nespoulet et al. 2008
Portugal							
Lagar Velho 1	Abrigo do Lagar Velho, Lapedo Valley, Portugal.	~24–25,000 BP (AMS ^{14}C measurements on grave associations)	Appears not to have been occupied at the time of burial	Minor traumatic injury to left radius. Non-pathological hyper-arctic body proportions	4–5-year-old child laid extended in shallow pit	Ochre staining, one (probably two) perforated *Littorina* shells, four red deer canines, rabbit	Duarte et al. 1999; Zilhão and Trinkaus 2002a and papers therein; Zilhão 2005
Czech Republic							
Brno I	Brno, Moravia	Unknown (remains now lost). Possibly not of Pavlovian age	Fluvial terrace, otherwise unknown	Cranium and several postcranial remains	Unknown	Unknown	Oliva 2005

continued . . .

continued . . .

Table 6.2 continued

Brno II	Francouzská Street, Brno, Moravia	OxA-8293, 23,680 ± 200 BP (direct date), Willendorfian-Kostienkian-Pavlovian	Apparently not an occupation site.	Skull and partial postcranial skeleton of adult male. Periostitis on femora and ulna, possible cranial trauma	Secondary interment, covered with mammoth scapula and tusk, stained with ochre, dentalium shells, stone, bone and ivory roundels, ivory marionette, reindeer antler rod	No apparent culturally diagnostic material	Pettitt and Trinkaus 2000; Svoboda et al. 2002; Oliva 1996, 2000a, 2000b, 2005
Brno III	Sušilova Street, Brno-Žabovesky, Moravia	Undated (no datable grave goods and bones destroyed)	Unknown.	Adult woman	Body covered with ochre	No associations	Oliva 2005
Pavlov I	Pavlov Northwest, Moravia	~27–26,000 BP (AMS ^{14}C measurements on associated charcoal)	Occupation site	Partial skeleton of adult. Neurocranial trauma evident	Secondary burial, covered by mammoth scapula	Pavlovian occupation horizon	
DV 3	Dolní Věstonice I, Moravia	~30–26,000 BP (AMS ^{14}C measurements on associated charcoal from occupation horizon)	Occupation site	Adult female cranial and postcranial skeleton. Pathologies to cranium evident: e.g. traumatic loss of left mandibular condyle), subchonral pits in articular regions	Laid on right side and highly flexed within shallow depression, covered by two engraved mammoth scapulae, 5 fox teeth in its right hand, several lithics near the head and covered with ochre	Pavlovian occupation horizon	Trinkaus and Jelínek 1997; Oliva 2000a, 2005

DV 4		~30–26,000 BP (AMS ^{14}C measurements on associated charcoal from occupation horizon)	Occupation site	Fragmentary remains of child	Covered by mammoth scapula	Pavlovian occupation horizon	Trinkaus and Jelínek 1997; Oliva 2000a, 2005
DV 13, 14, 15 (triple burial)	Dolní Věstonice II, Moravia	GrN-14831, 26,640 ± 110 BP (associated charcoal); ISGS-1616, 24,000 ± 900 BP (associated charcoal); ISGS-1617, 24,970 ± 920 BP (associated charcoal), Pavlovian	Occupation site	Three late adolescent or young adult complete skeletons: two males (DV13, 15) and one indeterminate sex (DV14) often identified as female, the latter with abnormalities on femur, humerus, radius and ulna; pathologically short left forearm, curved spine (possibly scoliosis), abnormalities of dental number and positioning, traumatic injuries possibly resulting in several soft-tissue pathologies	Left and central individuals laid on backs with arm of left placed over pubic region of central. Right individual placed face down and facing away from the others. Ochre staining to heads, upper torsos, and public area of DV14. Pendants of mammoth ivory, fox and wolf teeth worn on headgear, some lithics. Burnt branches represent fire or structure	Pavlovian occupation horizon	Klíma 1988, 1995; Trinkaus and Jelínek 1997; Alt et al. 1997; Formicola et al. 2001; Trinkaus et al. 2001; Svoboda et al. 2002

continued . . .

Table 6.2 continued

DV 16	Dolní Věstonice II Western Slope, Moravia	GrN-15276, 25,570 ± 280 BP (associated charcoal): GrN-15277, 25,740 ± 210 BP (associated hearth): ISGS-1744, 26,390 ± 270 BP (associated charcoal), Pavlovian	Occupation site	Complete skeleton of adult male laid crouched on right side. Scoliosis of spine, deformed right femur, cranial fracture during infancy resulted in asymmetrical face	Laid at southern end of depression with central hearth and ritual deposits of faunal and cultural material in piles and pits. Fox canines, ochre staining and worked lithics found in close association with body. Complete animal bodies laid next to burial	In the centre of first settlement complex, Pavlovian occupation	Svoboda 1988, 1991; Svoboda *et al.* 2002
Předmostí	24,340 ± 120 BP (AMS ^{14}C measurement on bones from Pavlovian cultural level at site)	Occupation site	Partial skeletons of ~20 generally young individuals	Remains placed within large shallow pit close to 'skalka' rock, lined with mammoth bones and associated with fauna, lithics and organic items. Fox skulls above and below skeletons. Mammoth paw and burnt bones beneath them. Near-complete wolf skeletons found with burials	At the periphery of a Pavlovian settlement complex	Svoboda 2008; Oliva 2000a, 2005

Austria

Krems-Wachtberg Burial 1	Krems-Wachtberg, Lower Austria	~26–27,000 BP (date for layer from which grave pit was cut)	Occupation site	Complete, well-preserved skeletons of two ~9–10-month-old babies	Both laid strongly flexed side-by-side in flat bottomed pit, covered by mammoth scapula propped up by portion of mammoth tusk. Both embedded in considerable amounts of ochre. Western individual had string of mammoth ivory beads wrapped around its pelvis	At the periphery of a Willendorfian settlement, close to Burial 2	Einwögerer *et al.* 2006, 2008
Krems-Wachtberg Burial 2	Krems-Wachtberg, Lower Austria	~26–27,000 BP (date for layer from which grave pit was cut)	Occupation site	Complete skeleton of 0–2-month-old baby	Laid in flexed position in flat-bottomed pit 1m from Burial 1, head towards them. Embedded in ochre, probably wrapped in ochre-stained shroud fastened at the head with a mammoth ivory pin. No mammoth scapula covering	At the periphery of a Willendorfian settlement, close to Burial 1	Einwögerer *et al.* 2008

continued . . .

Table 6.2 continued

Italy

Arene Candide I ('Il Principe')	Grotta delle Arene Candide cave, Near Finale Ligure, Savona	OxA-10700, 23,440 ± 190 BP (direct AMS ^{14}C measurement on bone)	Occupation site	Complete skeleton of adolescent male Traumatic loss of left mandibular ramus and part of left clavicle	Laid in shallow grave, ochre stained, rich headgear of perforated shells and deer canines, others found with mammoth ivory pendants around body, four elk antler *batons percées*, yellow ochre to wound in jaw. Possible association with hearth lit above the burial	Late Gravettian occupation horizon	Bietti and Molari 1994; Mussi 2001; Pettitt *et al.* 2003
Barma Grande 1	Barma Grande Cave, Balzi Rossi, Grimaldi	~24–25,000 BP (comparison with age of BG6)	Occupation site	Complete skeleton of adult male. Skeleton destroyed in 1884	Clear grave cutting and lack of occupation debris around the grave, aligned with cave wall	Found closest to cave's entrance, probably from Gravettian occupation horizon	Mussi 1986, 1995, 2001; Formicola 1989
Barma Grande 2,3,4 ('Triple burial')	Barma Grande Cave, Balzi Rossi, Grimaldi	~24–25,000 BP (comparison with age of BG6)	Occupation site	Adult male (Barma Grande 2), adolescent, probably female in central position (Barma Grande 3), adolescent, probably male (Barma Grande 4). Frontal grooves on the squama of all	Triple burial in clear grave cutting, stained with ochre, perpendicular to cave wall. Adult male had long flint blade in his left hand, bone pendants on upper body and two *Cypraea* shells on his left tibia. Male adolescent had	Probably from Gravettian occupation horizon	Mussi 1986; Formicola 1988, 1989

	Location	Date	Site type	Skeletal description	Grave details / position	Context	References
(continued)				three may indicate genetic relatedness. Considerable osteophytosis on vertebrae of all three individuals caused by degeneration of vertebral discs. Humeral asymmetry on BG2. Many parts were destroyed in the Second World War and are replaced in plaster in the modern reconstruction of the burial	an endscraper under his head and bone pendants on his head. Young female had a flint blade in her left hand and one bone pendant on her head		
Barma Grande 5	Barma Grande Cave, Balzi Rossi, Grimaldi	~24–25,000 BP (comparison with age of BG6)	Occupation site	Adult female, placed on left side but with rotation of the trunk towards the right	Aligned with cave wall.	Found close to BG6, probably from Gravettian occupation horizon	Mussi 1986; Formicola 1989
Barma Grande 6 (the 'burnt skeleton')	Barma Grande Cave, Balzi Rossi, Grimaldi	OxA-10093, 24,800 ± 800 BP (direct AMS ^{14}C measurement on BG6 bone)	Occupation site	Partial skeleton (lower limbs) of adult male.	Found above the remains of a hearth and described as intentionally burnt, but bones are not burnt. Some perforated *Cyclope* shells were found in the area of the burial	Found deepest into cave, close to BG5, probably from Gravettian occupation horizon	Formicola 1989; Formicola *et al.* 2004

continued . . .

Table 6.2 continued

Grotta dei Fanciulli (Grotte des Enfants) 4 and 5 (double burial)	~26–22,000 BP (general site stratigraphy)	Occupation site	Complete skeletons of adult female and adolescent male. The burial has often been referred to as a 'negroid' burial, now known to be incorrect. Asymmetrical hypertrophy on Fanciulli 4 possibly caused by nerve injury to upper limb	Adolescent male buried first, laid on left side. Numerous perforated marine shells around head area and also disturbed, suggesting that the grave had been opened up to facilitate burial of the adult female. Female placed head down and in highly contracted position	Burial excavated into Level I, from bottom of Level H, the earliest Gravettian horizon in the cave	Mussi 2001; Formicola 1988
Grotta dei Fanciulli (Grotte des Enfants) 6	~26–22,000 BP (general site stratigraphy)	Occupation site	Adult male	Unclear	Burial excavated probably from Level G, with a Perigordian Vc assemblage including noailles burins	Mussi et al. 1989; Mussi 1986, 2001; Formicola 1988
Baousso da Torre 1	No absolute chronology, ~26–22,000 BP based on age of Italian Gravettian	Occupation site	Robust adult male	Flint blade under left shoulder, perforated shells and deer canines around the neck, wrist and knees	Possibly excavated into underlying Aurignacian horizon	Mussi 1986, 2001; Formicola 1988; Vilotte and Henry-Gambier 2010
Baousso da Torre 2	No absolute chronology, ~26–22,000 BP based on age of Italian Gravettian	Occupation site	Adult male	Numerous perforated marine shells and deer canines around head, neck, elbows, wrist and thighs.	Possibly excavated into underlying Aurignacian horizon	Mussi 1986; Formicola 1988

Site	Chronology	Site type	Skeleton	Burial / grave	Context	References
Baousso da Torre 3	No absolute chronology, ~26–22,000 BP based on age of Italian Gravettian	Occupation site	Adolescent ~12 years at death, unsexed, possibly male (skeleton missing)	Lying face down, no grave goods	Possibly excavated into underlying Aurignacian horizon	Mussi 1986; Formicola 1988; Vilotte and Henry-Gambier 2010
Grotta del Caviglione ('L'Homme de Menton')	No absolute chronology, ~26–22,000 BP based on age of Italian Gravettian	Occupation site	Complete skeleton of adult male. Fractured right radius	Numerous perforated shells and deer canines on the head and close to left knee. Bone point at chest. Two flint blades under the head	Unclear	Mussi 1986, 2001
Paglicci 2, Apulia	Radiocarbon measurement of 24,720 ± 420 (F-55) for Level 21 cultural horizon.	Occupation site	~13 years old male	Aligned with the wall of the cave	From Level 21 Gravettian horizon including Font Robert points	Palma di Cesnola 1974; Mussi 2001
Paglicci 3, Apulia	~26–24,000 BP (associated ^{14}C measurements)	Occupation site.	Fragmentary remains of adult	Unclear	Unclear	Palma di Cesnola 1974; Mussi 2001
Ostuni 1 (Grotta di Santa Maria di Agnano, Ostuni, Brindisi)	Gif-9247, 24,410 ± 320 BP	Occupation site	Near complete cranial and postcranial skeleton of young adult (~20 years) female with foetus/neonate	Laid flexed on left side in ochre stained shallow grave. Rich shell and deer canine ornamentation. Horse and bovid bones and teeth within grave. Foetus/neonate close to her pelvic cavity	From upper Gravettian level	Vacca and Coppola 1993; Coppola and Vacca 1995; Mussi 2001

continued . . . .

Table 6.2 continued

Ostuni 2	Grotta di Santa Maria di Agnano, Ostuni, Brindisi	The same as Ostuni 1, based on spatial and stratigraphic association	Occupation site	Partial cranial and postcranial skeleton of adult	Placed close and parallel to Ostuni 1 but on right side, flexed, and facing away	From upper Gravettian level.	Vacca and Coppola 1993; Coppola and Vacca 1995
Veneri Parabita 1 and 2 (double burial)	Grotta della Veneri a Parabita	Dates from occupation of Formation B correlated with Level 20c of Paglicci dated to 22,220 ± 360 BP and 22,110 ± 330 BP	Gravettian occupation horizon	Two adults. Ankylosing spondylitis on Parabita 1	Unclear	From upper part of Formation B containing small Gravettian assemblage	Mussi 1986, 2001

Russia

Kostenki 12 burial	Kostenki 12 (Volkov)	~23–29,000 BP (radiocarbon measurements on items from cultural horizon	Occupation site.	Neonate partial skeleton.	Extended skeleton, no evidence of grave cutting	From cultural horizon attributed to the Gorodtsovskayan culture	Sinitsyn 2004
Kostenki 14 burial	Kostenki 14 (Markina Gora)	At least 28,000 BP based on radiocarbon measurements from the overlying Layer 2. Dates for Layer 3 are problematic	Occupation site	Complete skeleton of adult male	Laid tightly flexed on left side in pit, the face turned downwards. Hands clenched into fists and placed by head. All bones had thick covering of ochre. No ornamentation, grave goods only mammoth phalange and two hare bones	Probably relates to the base of Cultural Layer 3, attributed to the Gorodtsovskayan culture	Sinitsyn 1996, 2004; Sinitsyn et al. 1996
Kostenki 15 burial	Kostenki 15 (Gorodtsovs-kaya)	~21–26,000 BP (radiocarbon measurements on	Occupation site	Juvenile	Pit burial of 6–7-year-old child, seated on clay, with flakes,	From Gorodtsovskayan settlement	Sinitsyn 2004

	Location	Date/Culture	Site type	Remains	Grave description / goods	Stratigraphy	References
		items from the settlement horizon)			needles, burnisher and (150 fox canine pendants around the head. Grave pit covered with mammoth scapula	horizon	
Sungir 1	Sungir, near Vladimir, Russia	Kostenki-Streletskayan culture. AMS ^{14}C measurements vary between ~27,000 and 23,000 BP; most probably at older end	Occupation site	Complete skeleton of adult male	Laid in shallow grave in extended position. At least 2,936 mammoth ivory beads in clusters on clothing, 25 mammoth ivory bracelets, schist pendant, ochre. Sungir 5 female cranium placed atop burial in ochred area and in association with stone slab	Cut into Kostenki-Streletskayan occupation horizon	Bader and Mikhajlova 1998; Pettitt and Bader 2000; Sulerzhitski et al. 2000; Kuzmin et al. 2004; Formicola 2007
Sungir 2 and 3 (Double burial)	Sungir, near Vladimir, Russia	Kostenki-Streletskayan culture. AMS ^{14}C measurements vary between ~27,000 and 23,000 BP; most probably at older end	Occupation site	Adolescent (Sungir 2) and child (Sungir 3). Suite of developmental deformities on Sungir 3	Laid head-to-head in extended position in shallow grave. At least 10,100 mammoth ivory beads adorned the clothing of both individuals, 250 fox canines around waist of Sungir 2, mammoth ivory sculptures, pins, 'lances' some associated with openwork ivory discs, a perforated bâton, femur of adult human, ochre	Cut into Kostenki-Streletskayan occupation horizon	Bader and Mikhajlova 1998; Pettitt and Bader 2000; Sulerzhitski et al. 2000; Kuzmin et al. 2004; Formicola 2007

considerable patterning of cave art can be demonstrated in situations where human remains are not found (most cases), it would be parsimonious to suggest that the rare act of funerary caching obeyed the grammar of cave art and ritual, rather than the other way around.

European Mid Upper Palaeolithic burials

The relative abundance of burials dating to ~29,000–21,000 BP, their broad similarities across Europe, often rich grave goods and other associations, association with settlements and occasional glimpses of extraordinary individuals in single, double and triple graves, show quite remarkably that a new phenomenon – the ritual burial – emerged at the start of the Mid Upper Palaeolithic, alongside the emergence of regional expressions of the continent-wide Gravettian (Table 6.2 and Figure 6.2). Although the number of burials for this period of ~8,000 radiocarbon years is not huge – Henry-Gambier (2008) notes 45 for example – there are no known burials for *Homo sapiens* in Europe before this, and no burials with rich grave inclusions including personal ornamentation at all. Many Mid Upper Palaeolithic examples have clear grave cuttings, and are otherwise identified by the delineation of the grave area by colourant or other architectural associations (Henry-Gambier 2008, 3). Most burials were interred in open locations within or on the periphery of settlements; most are singular, although double and triple examples exist that raise the possibility of intriguing relationships between individuals. Although general similarities exist – the elaborate ornamentation of the dead, for example – regional traditions exist and many individual burials possess unique traits as to warrant separate consideration, which will be undertaken here on an arbitrary west-to-east basis.

The Lagar Velho child, Portugal

A 4/5-year-old child was buried under the overhang of the Lagar Velho rockshelter in the Lapedo Valley, Portugal (Duarte *et al.* 1999; Zilhão and Trinkaus 2002a; Figure 6.6), apparently when the site was not occupied (Zilhão and Trinkaus 2002b, 519).[13] Although insufficient collagen remained in the child's bones to allow direct AMS radiocarbon dating, measurements were obtained from four samples associated with the grave that established its age ~24–25,000 BP (Pettitt *et al.* 2002). The burial was probably isolated, and although much of the site had been destroyed prior to excavation there are several reasons to believe that no other burials had been emplaced in the rockshelter (Zilhão and Almeida 2002, 40–1). Given the excellent state preservation of the skeleton (only the cranium, some cervical vertebrae and the right clavicle and scapula had been damaged or destroyed by recent disturbance), and meticulous excavation and recording, the details of the burial are clear (Duarte 2002; Zilhão and Almeida 2002). A shallow grave was

Figure 6.6 The Lagar Velho child burial *in situ*. The cranium has already been removed (photograph courtesy of Joao Zilhão and with thanks to Jose Paulo Ruas).

excavated, and a small branch of scots pine burnt in place in the bottom of the grave, before the child, probably wrapped in an ochre-stained shroud, was laid in it in extended position, its head lying on its left side, legs slightly flexed and the right hand resting on the hip. A perforated shell pendant of *Littorina obtusata* was recovered in the neck region – probably a necklace to which belonged a second such shell found in a disturbed context above the burial – and four ochre-stained red deer canines were found in the head area, probably representing head gear. A juvenile rabbit was placed atop the child's legs. Two pelves of male red deer were probably placed at the child's shoulder and feet, reminiscent of the limestone slabs at Paviland. The burial is not spectacularly rich, particularly in the context of later burials from Italy and Russia, but in the sense of the personal ornamentation and ochre fits with other burials dating to the earlier parts of the Mid Upper Palaeolithic, for example Paviland and those of the Pavlovian. Vanhaeren and d'Errico (2002) have studied the child's personal ornamentation, establishing that each of the four deer teeth pendants came from separate animals, two hinds and two stags. The stags' teeth are similar in size, deriving from very large animals, and they appear to have been made by the same person. By contrast, the hinds' teeth differ from each other and appear to have been made by separate people, demonstrating a complex derivation of the child's ornamentation probably through exchange systems based on multiple kinship systems.

169

Krems-Wachtberg, Austria

Fragmentary human remains are known from several sites in Hungary belonging to the Pilisszántó Culture or 'Cave Gravettian', although a partially complete skeleton of a child recovered from Balla Cave in the northeast of the country thought to belong to this period was recently shown to be Neolithic on the basis of AMS ^{14}C dating (Tillier *et al.* 2009). Clearer data come from Lower Austria, where a rich series of Mid Upper Palaeolithic sites of broad Gravettian tradition are known, which form the regional Willendorfian tradition, a name reserved for the late Gravettian of the region (Neugebauer-Maresch 2003). The similarities between this and the Pavlovian of Moravia are widely known, and burials from the latter are discussed below. Isolated human remains are known from several sites (Teschler-Nicola and Trinkaus 2001; Teschler-Nicola *et al.* 2004) and suggest that the processing and use of human remains such as seen in the Pavlovian extended to this region, which is no surprise given the cultural similarities and geographical proximity of the two regions. Although no adult burials are known – the partial skeleton of an adult assumed to be a Gravettian burial from Krems-Hundssteig has been shown by direct AMS radiocarbon dating to be Holocene (Trinkaus and Pettitt 2000) – the discovery in 2006 of the burials of three infants at the nearby Krems-Wachtberg has demonstrated that the Willendorfian groups of the region practised similar burial traditions to their Pavlovian and Italian neighbours. The burials were removed as blocks and have been published in excellent detail (Einwögerer *et al.* 2006, 2008).

A single and a double burial of infants were found at the periphery of the main concentration of settlement in 2006 (Figures 6.7 and 6.8). These derive from the lowermost parts of the occupation at the site, which has been dated to ~26,000–27,000 BP, that is, broadly contemporary with the Pavlovian to which the Willendorfian is usually linked. Burial 1 was placed within a flat-bottomed pit. The complete skeletons of two neonates, embedded in red ochre, were covered by a mammoth scapula supported by a fragment of mammoth tusk, a clear link with Pavlovian practices. The scapula showed traces of burning and part of it had been deliberately flaked off. Both neonates were strongly flexed and placed side-to-side, their heads to the north. A line of mammoth ivory beads, probably indicative of a string, was placed around the pelvis of the western neonate. The developmental age of the second individual suggests an age of ~9–10 months at death and the similar lengths of the femora of both burials suggest that they were approximately the same age. The distribution of ochre suggests that both had been smeared with it as well as having been laid in it. The placement together in death of two neonates of the same age raises the possibility that they were twins, and the lack of an adult female in the grave, *sensu* Ostuni 1 (discussed below) might suggest that if the babies died during or shortly after childbirth the mother survived.

Burial 2 was located only 1m north of the double burial, and at the same stratigraphic height. The pit contained a single individual 0–2 months old,

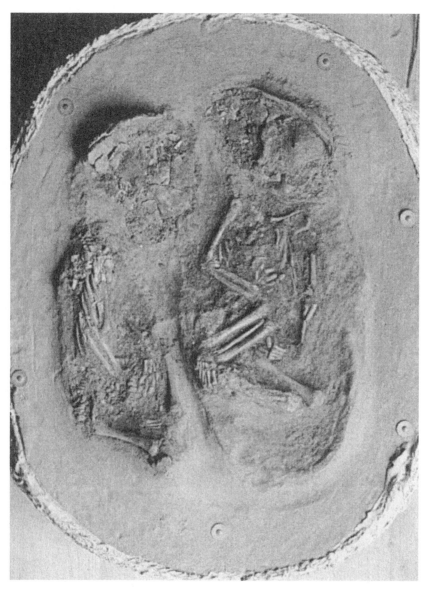

Figure 6.7 The double infant burial from Krems-Wachtberg, Austria (photograph courtesy of Maria Teschler-Nicola, Christine Neugebauer-Maresch and Thomas Einwögerer and Natural History Museum Vienna).

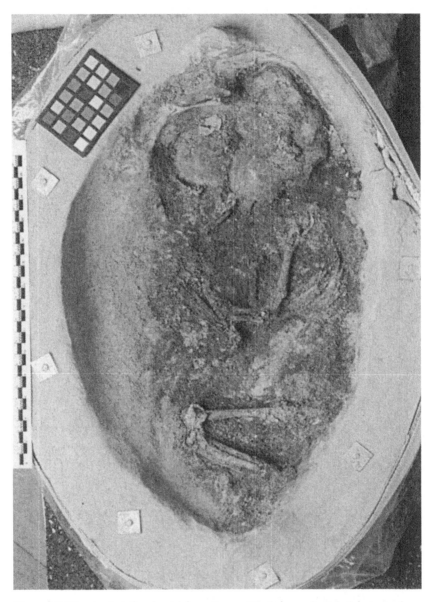

Figure 6.8 The single infant burial from Krems-Wachtberg, Austria (photograph courtesy of Maria Teschler-Nicola, Christine Neugebauer-Maresch and Thomas Einwögerer and Natural History Museum Vienna).

once again highly flexed but with its head towards the south. Viewed as a group, which may or may not be correct, the head-to-head placing recalls that of the children in the double burial at Sungir discussed below. This individual was also embedded in considerable amounts of red ochre, the sharp boundaries of which indicated that the colourant had been applied to an organic shroud, and the recovery of a mammoth ivory pin 2cm above its head suggests that the shroud was wound and pinned closed. Unlike Burial 1, no mammoth shoulder blade protected this burial. The length of the femur and degree of mineralisation of the incisors suggests an age of 0–3 months after birth.

It may be stretching things to interpret the Krems-Wachtberg burials as suggesting that even the newly born (or stillborn) possessed status. Other than the string of beads with one individual in Burial 1 and the mammoth ivory pin in Burial 2, there are no rich grave goods. The lack of a mammoth scapula covering over the single individual is of interest. Was the scapula in burial 1 intended as a 'lid' to allow subsequent burial? Did one of the neonates die first, followed by an expectation that its twin may also die, and thus provision was made for its interment alongside? This we will never know, although future genetic analyses should allow the testing of the hypothesis that the two individuals of Burial 1 are related, but unrelated to that of Burial 2.

Italy

Seventeen Mid Upper Palaeolithic burials are known from Italy, containing a total of 15 adults, five adolescents and a single foetus/neonate associated with its presumed mother. These occur in two clusters; the northwest (Liguria) and southeast (Apulia) (Mussi 1986, 1995, 2001a; Formicola 1988a, 1988b, 1989; Mussi *et al.* 1989). No burials are known from the oldest Gravettian phase in Italy (Mussi *et al.* 1989): where dates are available these cluster between ~25,000 and 22,000 BP (Mussi 1986, 2001a, 2003) and burials without dates clearly derive from later Gravettian occupation horizons and contain similar grave goods as those of the dated cluster. The sample is dominated by single burials of males (mainly adult, MNI=10), and it is of interest that, with the exception of an adult female buried with a foetus/neonate at Santa Maria di Agnano, females, where they exist, are buried with males, for example, in the 'double burial' of the Grotta dei Fanciulli and the 'triple burial' of Barma Grande.

No burials are known from open sites. They were typically placed in the deeper parts of caves, close to a wall or other marker such as a large boulder, and most were placed in extended position and aligned with the axis of the cave. Large stones were associated with a number of burials, usually placed over the head and/or feet. Grave goods are ubiquitous in the Italian Gravettian burials, and include items of exotic flint, ochre, personal ornamentation of marine shells, cervid canines, pendants of bone and mammoth ivory and, occasionally, fish vertebrae. Mussi (1986, 2001a) has noted how personal ornamentation is usually found in restricted areas of the body, notably the head, upper torso, wrist and knees, and has also noted that younger burials seem to be more elaborated.

A cluster of similarly positioned and accompanied graves occurs in Liguria, amounting to 13 individuals in ten burials (including one double and one triple burial) at Grimaldi, in addition to a single burial (100km to the east at Arene Candide. The sample is dominated by males, and with one exception, burials were accompanied by rich personal ornamentation and grave goods, typically of personal ornamentation of perforated marine shells and deer canines and occasionally of mammoth ivory (Mussi 1986, 1995, 2001a). The caves in the cliffs of Balzi Rossi under the village of Grimaldi were excavated when the caves were being cleared of their deposits during the infancy of prehistoric archaeology; some of their burials have been subsequently lost or destroyed in part, and the cave of Baousso de Torre has been destroyed by quarrying (Figures 6.9 and 6.10). Among the rich Gravettian archaeology from the caves and neighbouring rockshelters, a number of Mid Upper Palaeolithic 'venus' figurines have been found (Mussi *et al.* 2000) and I have elsewhere drawn out the similarities between Mid Upper Palaelithic burials and figurines and noted that, at Grimaldi, there seems to have been a distinction between the caves in which burials were found and figurines were apparently not (Caviglione, Baousso da Torre, Grotta dei Fanciulli)[14] – Barma Grande, which yielded two figurines and the largest number of burials, and the Grotta del Principe

Figure 6.9 The caves of Balzi Rossi, Grimaldi, Italy, looking towards France (photo: author).

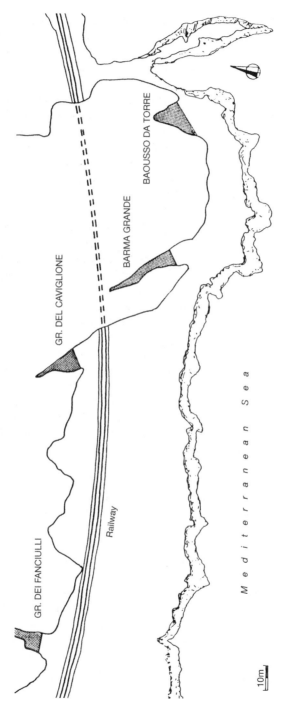

GR. DEI FANCIULLI

Railway

GR. DEI FANCIULLI

GR. DEL CAVIGLIONE

BARMA GRANDE

BAOUSSO DA TORRE

M e d i t e r r a n e a n   S e a

10m

Figure 6.10 The caves of Balzi Rossi (courtesy of Margherita Mussi).

in which a number of figurines but no burials were found (Pettitt 2006). Furthermore, the 'zonated' lines engraved onto female figurines is reminiscent of the zonated decoration of 'real' burials (Pettitt 2006). This suggests a complex cosmological relationship between the two, and in this light it is of interest that almost all burials are male, identifiable figurines are female, a pattern that holds true at the European scale (Pettitt 2006).

In the Grotta del Caviglione a young adult male was laid flexed on his left side, both hands close to his face (Figures 6.11 and 6.12). His head was ornamented with perforated marine shells and deer canines, representing some form of headdress. A clearly defined area of ochre staining containing ~8,000 small shells, ~50 fish vertebrae, many of them ochre stained and pierced, was found stratified beneath the burial (Mussi 1986, 102). Interestingly, isolated human remains were also found below the level of the inhumation (ibid., 102), although it is unclear as to whether these are Gravettian in attribution and whether they represent the circulation of human remains as one finds in the Pavlovian (see pp. 188–9) or whether they represent disturbed burials. The recovery of such a rich area of ochre and personal ornamentation beneath the burial is of interest. Although surviving records of this early excavation are not precise enough as to allow us to examine this further, it is conceivable that these represent clothing, either deposited before the burial, or onto which the burial was laid.

Before the cave of Baousso da Torre was destroyed in 1901, excavations yielded three burials, two of adult males and one of an adolescent, all from a similar depth and a restricted spatial area (Mussi 1986, 102). The first adult, Baousso da Torre 1, had a flint blade placed under his left shoulder, perforated marine shells and deer canines in the head and neck area, the wrist and knees. Baousso da Torre 2 had a large number of shells and canines around the head, elbows and left wrist and a *Cypraea* shell at the upper end of each femur, perhaps sewn onto the bottom of a parka or onto a loincloth. The total lack of ornamentation of the adolescent is in striking contrast to the two adults, more so when one considers the unusual positioning of the body in this grave.

An adult male seems to have been buried in the Grotta dei Fanciulli,[15] although no report of a grave cutting exists (Mussi 1986, 95). This was found stratigraphically higher than the famous double burial. This contains an adolescent, probably male, and a female adult, who seem to have been placed in the grave sequentially. The excavators noticed that the original grave had contained the adolescent laid carefully on his side, but that the distribution of perforated marine shells that formed part of the decoration of his head gear dispersed around the surrounding soil indicated that the grave had been subsequently opened and the female's body placed within. The grave cutting seems to have been enlarged to provide for this addition, and the apparently forced position of the woman in head down and highly contracted supports this notion (Figure 6.13).[16]

Figure 6.11 The Grotta del Caviglione (photo: author).

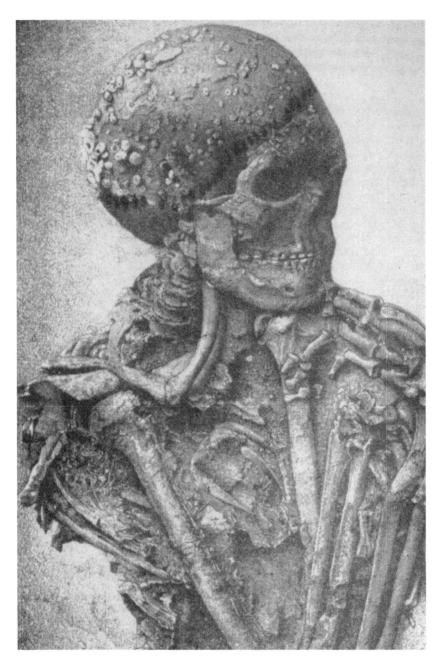

Figure 6.12 The Caviglione burial (from Rivière 1887).

Figure 6.13 The double burial of the Grotta dei Fanciulli. Note the face down position of the female (reconstruction photograph courtesy of the Soprintentenza ai Beni Archeologici della Liguria and with thanks to Angiolo Del Lucchese).

Six burials are known from Barma Grande, in the form of three single inhumations and one triple inhumation. Information about these is relatively poor for some of the burials, although enough exists to allow some generalisations. The practice of aligning the burials with the axis of the cave walls observable in all single inhumations and the concern with placing the heads of all three individuals in the triple burial close to the wall, the similarity of grave goods from all of the burials, and the proximity of BG5 and 6, suggests that they are at least broadly contemporary (Mussi 1986; Figure 6.14). A direct AMS ^{14}C measurement of 24,800 ± 800 BP (OxA-10093) dates BG6, yet attempts to date BG2 and 5 failed due to insufficient collagen (Formicola *et al.* 2004).[17] Three of the burials are single inhumations, two of adult males (BG1 and 6) and one of an adult female (BG5). BG1 was laid in a clear grave cutting closest to the cave's mouth, whereas BG5 and 6 were found close to each other against the cave's east wall and deepest into the cave. BG6, represented only by the bones of the lower limbs, had been laid on a black soil rich in charcoal. This seems to have been a hearth, and from which the notion that the skeleton had been burnt arose, although Formicola (1989) has noted that no traces of burning can be seen on the bones. It is plausible that the hearth was lit and extinguished before the inhumation, although it is now impossible to eliminate the possibility that it simply derives from an underlying occupation deposit. The male probably wore clothing ornamented with shells of *Cyclope neritea* as several were found in the vicinity of the burial (Formicola *et al.* 2004, 116).

The triple burial comprises three individuals laid side by side within a shallow grave, the posterior wall of which was clearly discernible (Barma Grande 2, 3 and 4: Formicola 1988a, b). All were stained with red ochre (Figure 6.15). Sadly no photograph exists of the burial *in situ*, although the excavators sketched the skeletons and provide a description of their orientation and associations. Barma Grande 2 was on the far right of the group, laid on its back in extended position, its head turned to the left, a position that recalls that of Baousso da Torre 3. The other two were placed on their left

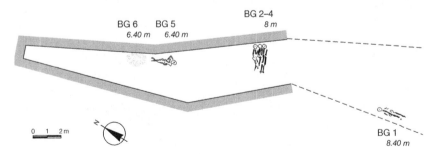

Figure 6.14 Plan of the Barma Grande cave showing the location of its burials (courtesy of Margherita Mussi).

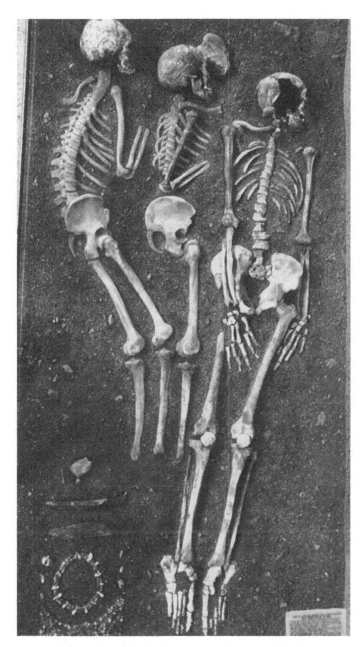

Figure 6.15 The Barma Grande triple burial, as reconstructed in the Museo
Nazionale Preistorico dei Balzi Rossi (courtesy of the Soprintentenza ai
Beni Archeologici della Liguria and with thanks to Angiolo Del
Lucchese).

sides in flexed positions, facing into the grave. A bovid femur was placed under the head of the central individual (Barma Grande 3) and a large flint scraper was placed under the head of the outer individual (Barma Grande 4) in flexed position. The excavation geologist noted that the central skeleton was partly covered by the other two, indicating that it had been placed first. All three were elaborated, ornamented with perforated shells of *Cyclope neritea* and incised deer canines, fish vertebrae, and plano-convex bone pendants, and 'double olive' bone pendants on the chest. Barma Grande 2 had a long flint blade in its left hand, a clear similarity with Arene Candide 1. The triple burial is the only example from Balzi Rossi that is not aligned along the axis of the cave but perpendicular to it. As Mussi (2001a) has suggested, this could reflect a concern for all three individuals to have close proximity to the cave's wall, as their head are oriented towards it. The staining of all three individuals and the clear distinction between the ochre staining of the grave cutting and surrounding area suggest that all three individuals were interred at the same time (Formicola 1989).

In the Arene Candide cave near to Finale Ligure, the skeleton of an adolescent male was found amid a bed of ochre, laid in extended position with its head turned to the left (Figures 6.16 and 6.17). The edge of the shallow grave seems to have been defined by large stone blocks in a way reminiscent of the use of block 'linings' in the Epipalaeolithic burials within the cave (see Chapter 7). The young male came to be known as 'Il Principe', given the richness of his burial. His head was surrounded by hundreds of perforated shells and deer canines deriving from a hat or mask. Pendants of mammoth ivory, perforated *Cypraea* shells, four perforated batons of elk antler were found about the torso and a long blade of exotic flint was held in his right hand. A direct AMS ^{14}C measurement of 23,440 ± 190 BP (OxA-10700: Pettitt *et al.* 2003) provides a late Gravettian age for the burial that is in accord with a date on charcoal of 19,630 ± 250 BP (Beta-48684: Bietti and Molari 1994) from a hearth – 'Hearth V' – that was placed above the burial, although it is unclear whether the hearth relates to activity connected with the burial or to subsequent occupation. It is interesting that part of the left mandible of Il Principe is missing, and a mass of yellow ochre was found at exactly the same area. Although the wound had begun to heal by the time of his death, it is plausible that the ochre was placed there to 'amend' for the wound (Mussi 2001a, 257).

The single inhumation of an adolescent male in the Grotta Paglicci (Foggia, Apulia) was laid extended and aligned with the wall of the cave, with the cranium turned to the right (Palma di Cesnola 1974; Figure 6.18). It was found in a superficial depression cut into the Gravettian layer 21. No traces of a grave cutting were visible, and it seems that the body was simply placed directly onto the ground within the depression. A faint trace of ochre staining was visible around the body, particularly around the head and upper body. The left forearm was laid obliquely across the trunk. Three stone slabs lay

Figure 6.16 'Il Principe', Arene Candide, Liguria. Note flint blade held in right hand, elk antler bâtons and shell cap (courtesy of the Soprintentenza ai Beni Archeologici della Liguria and with thanks to Angiolo Del Lucchese).

Figure 6.17 'Il Principe' *in situ* (from Cardini 1942).

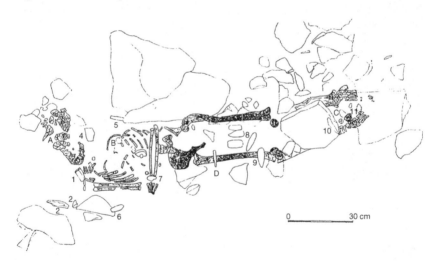

Figure 6.18 Plan of the Grotta Paglicci burial (from Palma di Cesnola 1974).

over its lower legs, head and feet. A suite of grave goods consisting of ~30 perforated deer canines were found around the head area – a hat again – and two further pierced teeth were found close to the left wrist and presumably indicative of a bracelet, and another near the right ankle. A pierced *Cypraea* shell was found on the chest, probably deriving from a necklace. A fragmentary bone awl was found above the right femur, and a series of flint tools were scattered around the grave.

Ostuni 1, the burial of a young adult female and her foetus/neonate was laid flexed on her left side in a roughly rectangular shallow grave cut into breccia and defined by ochre staining and a rich scatter of bones and charcoal (Coppola and Vacca 1995; Figure 6.19). Her right forearm was placed over her abdomen and her left arm highly flexed and lying under her head. A number of pierced shells of the genera *Cyclope, Cypraea, Trivia* and *Columbella* were found close to the right wrist, obviously representing a bracelet or personal ornamentation found amidst a crust of ochre around the head and particularly the frontal area, and a perforated deer canine and shell (probably *Columbella rustica*) were found at the level of the parietal area, all presumably representing a highly ornamented hat or mask. A fragment of horse cranium lay to the left of the head, and around the entire skeleton horse and bovid teeth, worked flint and fragments of bone with traces of engraving or other working were found. The recovery of a foetus close to the pelvic cavity suggest that the woman died either while pregnant, during birth or shortly thereafter. A second adult burial, Ostuni 2, was found under one metre from Ostuni 1, similarly flexed and in the same orientation and with a hand beneath its head, but on its right side and facing away from Ostuni 1. Another double burial is known from Veneri a Parabita cave in Apulia, although specific details of the burial have yet to be published.

The cave burials of Liguria and Apulia provide a window onto the symbolism of the body. Personal ornamentation, especially around the area of the head, emphasised the marine realm (shells), deer canines and on occasion the ivory of mammoths, a rare species in the region (Mussi 2001a; Figure 6.20) – a symbolism of both coast and land. The blades of flint clasped in the hands of BG2, BG3 and Il Principe must have held specific meaning relating to distance, especially as their source was in the Vaucluse in southern France (Negrino and Starnini 2003). But it is the nature of the burials themselves that is striking; as I shall discuss below, several traits link them to the burial practices of the Preceding Pavlovian 500km or more across the Alps, and enough information survives to suggest that these were not 'normal' burial events.

Pavlov Hills, Moravia

Human remains are relatively well known from Mid Upper Palaeolithic sites in Moravia ascribed to the Pavlovian, typically dating to ~27,000–25,000 BP. Remains of some three dozen individuals are known. Most of these are fragmentary and isolated remains, although 20 partial skeletons are known that probably derive from disturbed burials as well as six essentially complete skeletons from clear burial contexts (Trinkaus and Jelínek 1997; Oliva 2000a; Svoboda 2008). The more complete remains have been altered by various taphonomic processes (Svoboda 2008), whereas the fragmentary remains attest

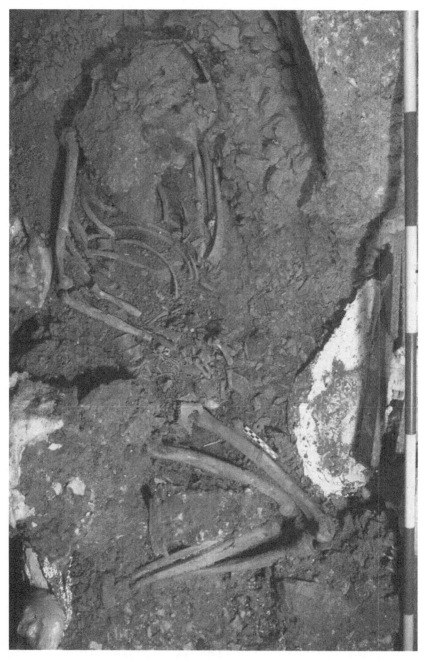

Figure 6.19 The Ostuni 1 burial (courtesy of the Museo di Civiltà Preclassiche – Ostuni, D. Coppola and E. Vacca).

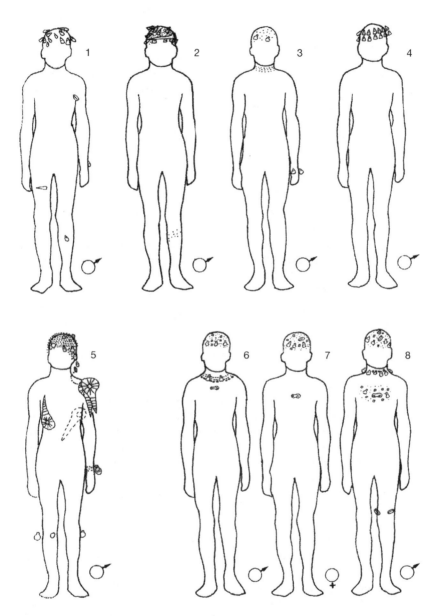

Figure 6.20 Location of personal ornamentation as revealed by the Italian Mid Upper Palaeolithic burials. Key: 1 Grotta Paglicci; 2 Grotta del Caviglione; 3 Barma Grande 5; 4 Veneri; 5 Il Principe; 6–8 Barma Grande triple burial (courtesy of Margherita Mussi).

to the complex processing and circulation of human remains on occupation sites and elsewhere. Bodies, or parts of them, could be deposited under covers of mammoth scapulae or of wood, or be placed in shallow graves.

Shallow pits excavated into the permafrost are known (albeit rare) in Pavlovian sites, containing carcasses, bones and artefacts. Most of these are small and probably functioned as cooking pits or small caches, and may have formed a precedent – or an adaptable feature – for the deposition of human bodies below ground. One pit at Pavlov I, for example, contained the partial remains of at least three mammoths, a reindeer cranium, over 500 stone artefacts, objects of worked mammoth ivory, and sculpted lumps of loess, all deposited on the ashy remains of a hearth set in the pit's bottom (Oliva 2005, 69). This is, as yet, unique.

The Pavlovian settlement traces around the Pavlov hills at Dolní Věstonice can be divided into two main localities, each characterised by large faunal accumulations dominated by mammoth but among which hare and reindeer were important resources and to which wolves and foxes were drawn, the former possibly part-domesticated. Pits for storage and possibly ritual and dwelling structures part dug into the ground and occasionally utilising mammoth bones occur but are rare. Cultural artefacts include stone tools on high quality flints and radiolarites, personal ornamentation of fox teeth, and abundant examples of worked bone and ivory tools decorated with a distinct Pavlovian artistic style, which form a readily identifiable archaeological signature, dating to ~29,000–27,000 BP (Oliva 2005; Svoboda 2008). Two localities – Dolní Věstonice 1 and 2 (the latter with a separate component on its western slope) – are known, each with several dense clusters of cultural debris or settlement units, with Dolní Věstonice 1 restricted to the earlier chronological range of the Pavlovian (28,000–26,000 BP) and Dolní Věstonice 2 taking the form of a number of clusters of occupational traces spanning its duration (~28,000–23,000 BP). One single burial is known from Dolní Věstonice 1, and two burials containing four individuals from Dolní Věstonice 2, although given the frequency of fragmentary human remains on the sites it is probable that a number of secondary burials of singular or fragmentary body parts were made (Oliva 2005, 73) and that other burials were subsequently disturbed, perhaps by wolves, or simply decomposed, as in the case of an infant skeleton – probably a burial – reduced to articulated teeth from Dolní Věstonice 2 (DV36: Trinkaus *et al.* 2000). As traces of burning are visible on some human (and wolf) remains, complex processing rites seem apparent.

Fragmentary human remains are common at Dolní Věstonice 1 and 2; 19 separate infant and adult remains derived from the main part of Dolní Věstonice 1, among which was a tooth pierced for suspension (DV8); Dolní Věstonice 2 yielded the remains of at least seven individuals in addition to the four individuals who were buried complete (Trinkaus *et al.* 2000, 2009); and Pavlov I yielded some two dozen remains of infants and adults (Oliva 2000a, 207) including the bones of a pair of hands from the same individual

(Trinkaus *et al.* 2009). Although postcranial elements (typically phalanges and longbones) are known, the dominance of cranio-dental elements and phalanges is striking, and it is possible that in some cases at least these represent the deliberate curation and/or deposition of the head and hands. Recognisable grave cuttings were shallow, and bodies were covered with thin layers of earth and usually 'protected' with mammoth scapulae or, possibly, wooden structures. Fox teeth pendants accompany all Pavlovian burials (Oliva 2005, 59).

At the Dolní Věstonice 1 settlement, the burial of an adult female (DV3) was laid within a shallow grave cutting, and covered with two mammoth scapulae. It was positioned on its right side, ventral side down with the head turned to the left and both arms flexed at the elbow, and the exceptional flexing of the legs at both hips and knees may suggest that it was tightly bound (Trinkaus and Jelínek 1997, 37–8). The woman held in her right hand five fox incisors (not perforated, suggesting a function for these items beyond that of personal ornamentation), and arctic fox bones were found near her left hand. The tight clustering of her bones may indicate that the corpse was at least partially defleshed by the time of burial, and Oliva (2005, 77) has speculated whether the burial of the woman was delayed, perhaps for the snow to melt and soil to thaw. A thin layer of ochre on the dorsal surfaces of most bones and under several of the longbone diaphyses, however (Trinkaus and Jelínek 1997, 35), is suggestive of either clothing or funerary wrapping.

At Dolní Věstonice 2, a triple burial of three young adults and a single burial of an elderly male were recovered from within the settlement accumulations. Within the first of three settlement units of the western slope accumulation, a single inhumation of an adult male (DV16) was placed near to a stone-lined hearth within a shallow depression (4.5m in maximum extent (Svoboda 1991, 17; Figure 6.21). The depression seems to have been surrounded by smaller fires and pits filled with cultural objects (Svoboda 1988, 829). The hearth seems to have been a central focus, and bones and a handful of worked stone artefacts were found within and around it. Radiocarbon measurements on charcoal from the hearth establish the age of the whole feature ~27,000–26,000 BP, that is, contemporary with Pavlovian occupation of the site. The male was laid flexed on his right side in the southern part of the depression. Three perforated fox canines were found by his legs, ochre stained his head and pelvis, and 123 worked lithics were found in his proximity. A radiocarbon measurement on charcoal from the vicinity of the corpse is statistically the same age as those from the hearth. Two shallow pits excavated within the depression (depressions A and E) contained the bones of small animals, charcoal, ochre, *Dentalium* shells, pellets of fired loess (which were distributed widely around the site – Soffer *et al.* 1993) and lithics and singular items in depression E included a bone spatula, bone awl, pierced tooth and fragment of a fired loess animal figurine (ibid., 17–18, which have a far more restricted distribution to the pellets and seem exclusively to be of a ritual nature – Soffer *et al.* 1993). The base of the main depression is undisturbed

Figure 6.21 The DV16 burial, Dolní Věstonice (courtesy of Jiří Svoboda).

and these pits are not later disturbances; they must surely represent associated ritual deposits. Other clusters of lithics and bones, an area of fired sediment, and a grinding stone stained with ochre complete the feature, and the faunal remains suggest that the complete carcasses of several animals were laid next to the male (Svoboda 2008, 28).

Some 55m east of the adult male, three individuals (left to right DV13, 14 and 15) were laid within a shallow grave ~1.5m in width (Klima 1988). A row of hearths stretched away from the triple burial, which may be significant (Oliva 2005, 68).

All of the individuals were young adults, and were laid side by side in a shallow pit (Figure 6.22). The left most and central individuals were laid on their backs, while the third was laid on his chest with his head facing away from the others, a striking similarity with the Barma Grande triple burial (although the third individual there was laid on its back it still looks away from the other two). The right arm of DV13 – which faces DV14 – was stretched towards it, with a hand resting on its pubic area, and in this sense it may be said to be 'engaging' with the central DV14. By contrast, DV15 may be said to be 'disengaged' from the other two as it is facing away. This positioning bears a striking similarity to the triple burial from Barma Grande discussed above, and surely cannot be coincidental. The outside individuals (DV13 and 15) are robust and usually identified as male, whereas the central individual (DV14), is of uncertain sex due to the blurring effect of its considerable pathologies, but it does bear several female traits and the nature

190

Figure 6.22 The Dolní Věstonice triple burial (courtesy of Jiří Svoboda).

of its pathologies strongly suggest that it is female (see discussion in Formicola *et al.* 2001 and Trinkaus *et al.* 2001). DV14 suffered serious developmental abnormalities including defects of the dental enamel, asymmetrical curvature, deformities and shortening of the femur, a deformity of the diaphysis of the right humerus, length asymmetries of the forearms, abnormalities in tooth number and positions, and a healed fracture of the left ulna with associated deformity of the radius (Formicola *et al.* 2001; Trinkaus *et al.* 2001). Formicola *et al.* (ibid., 375) have suggested that a number of the pathologies could relate to maternal diabetes and to an inherited dysplasia, both of which can cause considerable abnormalities in a foetus, in addition to trauma suffered early in life. Associated soft-tissue pathologies suggested by these conditions could include cataracts and alopecia among others, and it is difficult not to have sympathy for this individual which, nevertheless, survived until adulthood despite considerable deformities that would have been apparent since infancy. It is possible that the abnormal nature of DV14 conferred some kind of social importance or difference to this individual, and in this light it is interesting that it was placed centrally within the grave, the bones of DV13 and 15 laying over it and suggesting that it was laid first, and with DV13 'engaging' with it and DV15 disengaged from it. The clear fit of the three individuals and relationship to each other in the pit indicate that they were interred at the same time. Ochre staining was found on the upper torsos and particularly heads of all three individuals, and formed a matted crust on the head of DV13, suggesting that it was matted onto an elaborate mask or other headgear. The

191

heads of the two external males were further elaborated by pendants of perforated mammoth ivory and arctic fox and wolf teeth. A flint knife and several flakes lay around the central individual. The grave was surrounded by fragments of burnt branches, suggesting that after the bodies were laid in place, they were covered either by a wooden structure or by branches, which were set on fire yet soon extinguished by throwing soil over the grave (Klima 1988, 835). The carbonised remains of a thick branch or 'pole' embedded deep into the hip of DV13 suggests either his forced death (ibid., 835) or perhaps that he had been staked down. Svoboda (2008, 30) suggested that the carbonised branches/pole possibly represent the remains of a wooden structure deliberately constructed over the grave, possibly in replacement of mammoth scapulae.

Alt *et al.* (1997) employed systematic kinship analysis to various traits on the skeletons and concluded that the occurrence of several rare traits on the teeth and mandible such as aplasia on the right frontal sinus, exostoses in the region of the auditory opening, and impaction of the wisdom teeth, were unlikely to co-occur randomly, and suggest that the three individuals were genetically related and probably belonged to the same family. Although the analyses preclude the establishment of the actual degree of relatedness, Alt *et al.* (ibid., 130) suggest that 'as circumstances indicate that the three individuals died at the same time, the close range of their ages at death suggests that the individuals were not only genetically related, but they may have been siblings'. One should of course be cautious about interpreting the results of such data on genetic relatedness in the light of modern concerns about social organisation, and in the remarkably small-scale societies of the harsh and isolated conditions of the European Mid Upper Palaeolithic one might expect a degree of relatedness between individuals within a social group. Furthermore, the death at the same time of three adolescents or young adults does not necessarily make it likely that they were siblings, even in the small populations of the European Gravettian.

The Dolní Věstonice triple burial adds several dimensions to the phenomenon of triple burial that complements the Barma Grande example; violence is evident on two of the individuals. The male on the right bore evidence of a blow to the rear of his head, and the pelvis of the male on the left of the grave was pierced by one such wooden stake or spear. The central individual – probably a female – bore considerable pathologies in life and must have been marked out as 'special' in a similar way to the Romito dwarf, which will be discussed in Chapter 7. I shall return to these oddities below.

The extensive settlement at Pavlov I was excavated by B. Klima from 1952 to 1972 and represents a settlement of 13 units of the same broad period a little smaller in size than Dolní Věstonice 2. Other activities at Pavlov I include scorched wolf skeletons, apparently with their legs tied (Oliva 2005, 68). At Pavlov the secondary deposition of an adult male's skeleton was placed under mammoth remains (Pavlov 1 burial: Oliva 2005, 68). Although the burial was considerably disturbed by solifluction, it is clear that a scapula covered his longbones, and a molar his cranium, and a structure, probably a dwelling, was constructed last (Svoboda 2008, 30). Fragmentary human facial bones were apparently associated with this, and other isolated human remains were scattered across this intensively reused site (Trinkaus *et al.* 2009). The Pavlov 31 hand bones comprise 16 carpals, metacarpals and phalanges, all in far more eroded condition than the other human remains on the site, and represent both hands of the same individual.

At Brno Francouzská Street, the cranium and partial postcranial skeleton of an adult male was found covered by a mammoth scapula and tusk and possibly by rhinoceros ribs, in ochre-stained sediment within the sandy sediments of a river terrace, a similar situation to the Dolní Věstonice and Pavlov settlements. A direct AMS ^{14}C date of 23,680 ± 200 BP (Pettitt and Trinkaus 2000) established without doubt the Pavlovian context of the burial. Approximately 600 Miocene *Dentalium* shells (probably more originally) were recovered in the vicinity of the skull (probably part of headgear), and other finds associated with the burial include 14 carved roundels of mammoth ivory probably lying close to the head, tooth, bone, marl and haematite, some bearing fine engravings around their edges; a large ring of slate split horizontally into two in antiquity; a reindeer antler worn or polished at the tips, a mammoth ivory marionette, and a worked cylindrical fragment of ivory, probably from another object (Oliva 2000a, b). The 2m surrounding the burial was excavated, yet no trace of prosaic objects or charcoal was found, although this was in 1880 and the 'search' was relatively limited (A. Verpoorte pers. comm.). The bones were stained red with ochre. Oliva (1996, 2005, 79) has suggested that this should be treated as the deposition of ritual objects, among which were the bones of the adult male. If this is correct, it reorients our view of Mid Upper Palaeolithic burials: they become 'ritual deposits' similar in nature to deposits of other materials on Pavlovian sites, notably the remains of mammoths, reindeer, foxes and wolves, in association with cultural items. Oliva (1996, 2005, 79) has likened the roundels to the discs worn about the body by Siberian shamans, the marionette to witch doctors' puppets for catching ghosts, and the reindeer antler with a worn tip to a drum stick, in short, the accoutrements of shamanism. It is not the place here to discuss whether this is an appropriate interpretation, although the non-prosaic and ritual nature of the deposit and objects is without question. Oliva (2000b, 149) has discussed the 'odd' nature of the burial. Unlike other known Pavlovian burials it was not interred in or on the periphery of an occupation site but apparently alone on the floodplain of a river and away from the main concentration of Pavlovian settlement in Moravia, and the skeleton bears considerable evidence of pathology (periostitis) which has been taken to mean that the man 'must have been in considerable pain for years' (ibid., 149), although there is no reason why this condition need cause any pain and such inferences may be premature (A. Chamberlain pers. comm.). This question, however, does not detract from the apparent isolation of the deposit.

One of the most fascinating examples of Mid Upper Palaeolithic funerary activity is the 'mass burial pit' at Předmostí. In 1894 the partial remains of ~20 humans were found in a large pit within a typical Pavlovian settlement above the Bečva River in the southern part of the Moravian Gate. Abundant remains of mammoths in particular drew early attention to the site, and several occupation layers were excavated from the 1880s onwards. Although finds from the site were moved to Mikulov in the latter weeks of the Second World War and most were subsequently destroyed in a fire, the excavator, K. J. Maška, left detailed diaries of the excavations, and several casts of the skeletal material. Later excavators such as M. Kříž and K. Absolon left fuller records, and when Absolon took stock in the 1920s of the discoveries to date the mass grave was hailed as 'a discovery as wonderful as that of Tutankhamen's tomb' (Keith 1925). Recent excavations directed by J. Svoboda have contextualised the entire site, and from the combination of data old and new now available, Svoboda (2008) has conducted a detailed review of the ritual and taphonomy of the burial area (Figure 6.23).

At Předmostí, three sites clustered around two limestone formations in this important migrational route, and yielded abundant remains of mammoths, lithic and organic artefacts of the Pavlovian culture, and a number of human remains. As with other Pavlovian settlements the site is littered with deposits of mammoth, fox and wolf piled up in heaps across the site (Svoboda 2008). Radiocarbon dates reveal the oldest (and richest) settlement at Předmostí to date to ~27,000–26,000 BP. All of the human remains were recovered from Předmostí I, most of which were fragmentary, a situation that pertains on all of the Pavlovian sites discussed above. Some of the fragmentary human remains were clearly buried or cached in association with bones, such as an adult mandible covered by a mammoth scapula found by J. Wankel in 1884 and of an adult and child found in association with mammoth bones just outside of the main burial area by Maška in 1894 (Svoboda 2008, 18). Maška, however, found a large concentration of partial skeletons concentrated in an area 4 × 3.5m in size, close to a large rock ('Skalka'). This comprised mainly young individuals including three females and three males, all younger than 30 years, two adolescents (probably female), seven juveniles younger than 10 and three infants in their first year of life. In addition to these, two males, one 35–40 and the other 40–50 stand out as the oldest in the sample (Svoboda 2008). No formal plan of the burial area exists, although Svoboda was able to reconstruct it from sketches and verbal descriptions. Vertically set mammoth scapulae and long bones, and two mandibles found in the vicinity of the burial area seem to have been deliberately associated with it, and it is of interest that fragmentary remains of an adult and child were found below these (Svoboda 2008, 20). A pierced human pelvis and a cranium covered by two mammoth scapulae were found on the southern periphery of the pit. The pit seems to have been lined with mammoth scapulae – no surprise given the constant association of this element with Pavlovian human remains and those

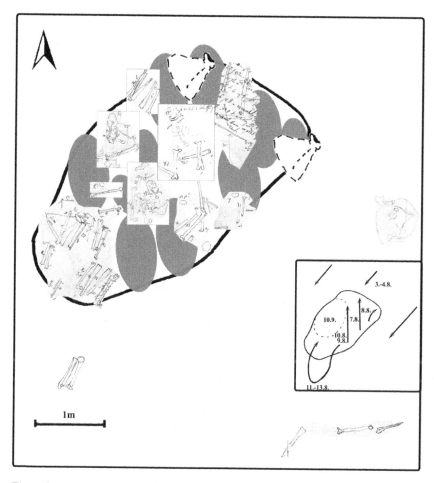

Figure 6.23 Reconstruction of the Předmostí mass grave, from Svoboda 2008 (courtesy of Jiří Svoboda).

in the Willendorfian (discussed above). Here, however, these did not 'cover' the entire burial area, but perhaps covered three of the individuals lain within. In addition to mammoth (also represented by crania, tusks and molars), the remains of animals including reindeer, fox, horse, wolf, bear, wolverine and hare were recovered from the pit, and loose canines of carnivores appear not to have been pierced for suspension. This recalls the unmodified fox canines held in the hand of the DV3 female. The burials came to be covered with limestone cobbles and, although one cannot rule out their deliberate placement, are more likely to have formed by downslope movement from the Skalka rock (Svoboda 2008, 32). The human remains, although partial and disarticulated, largely occur as isolated groups each pertaining to one individual, that is, the bones are not mixed into one overall jumble. Ashy patches were found in several places, as were isolated lithics, shells, rods of mammoth ivory, and the famous mammoth ivory 'fork'. Interestingly, the marl disc from the pit recalls those from Pavlov I and from the Brno II burial.

One must view the 'mass grave' in the context of the distribution of isolated human remains at the site. A human mandible, for example, was found near a fireplace in one area; fragments of human hands were found besides a concentration of fauna, a juvenile cranium was found under two mammoth scapulae and some heaps of mammoth bones seem to have been deliberately placed and do not relate to prosaic butchery, suggesting that they were treated in similar ways to human remains. K. Absolon recovered isolated human remains from the site that include a left femur bearing numerous incisions similar to cut marks on faunal remains recovered from recent excavations (Svoboda 2008, 25).

Several points can be made about the Předmostí mass grave:

- The Skalka, located on the periphery of the settlement, seems to have acted as a focus for repeated burial in the same location beneath it.
- A shallow pit 4m in maximum extent was excavated through the Pavlovian cultural horizon. The edges of the pit seem to have been 'lined' with mammoth scapulae and, perhaps, numerous fox bones. One of the mammoth scapulae bore traces of incision. Further mammoth remains, probably deliberately placed (in some cases vertically) were found on the edge of the pit, as were deposits of fragmentary human remains and other cultural items.
- The bones were not complete, nor found in articulation. In some cases individuals were represented only by cranial fragments. Small bones such as ribs were absent. The bones of each individual were, however, discrete, rather than mixed into a collective whole, with heads oriented to the north.
- Some of the remains bore traces of burning, and lenses of ash were recovered from the pit indicative of burning events; the two are possibly connected.
- Most of the remains were found beneath the bottom of the cultural layer, covered by a layer of limestone debris.
- Conspicuous 'grave goods' are rare, probably restricted to the marl disc. There is no evidence of ochre.

Opinion has divided as to whether the remains were interred in one event, which is suggested by the dominance of young individuals (Zilhão and Trinkaus 2002), or gradually, as suggested by the contextual and taphonomic analysis of Svoboda (2008). It does seem that the skeletons, although partial, were originally more complete than later accounts would allow, some of the smaller bones being lost since excavation (ibid., 29). The lack of cut marks rules out processing and cannibalism. Svoboda's careful assessment has shown convincingly that bodies were probably complete when deposited, and were subsequently disturbed to some degree by various taphonomic processes operating on the shallow pit, including slope movement of limestone debris and soil, as well as a small contribution from carnivores such as hyenas and wolves.[18] Svoboda suggests that in a cumulative depositional scenario, each interment of a new individual will to some extent disturb one or more previous interments, and in this respect it is perhaps no coincidence that the best preserved skeleton, Předmostí 3, is uppermost in the excavated area. One cannot, however, rule out the possibility that part-carcasses and 'bundles' of disarticulated human remains were interred in the grave, as indicated in the plans of the excavator Maška's sketches.

For the Pavlovian, a complex mix of the processing, circulation and deposition of body parts, burial of partial skeletons and burial of complete individuals singularly and, in one case, as a group of three, suggests the complex role of the dead in the cosmologies of the living that also occasioned the ritual burial of animals such as wolves. Compared to the Isolated human remains, burials of complete bodies are rare, and may not reflect 'normal' funerary activity. A concern with fire in association with the processing and/or burial of bodies is strong, and perhaps held some transformational symbolism. Verpoorte (n.d.) has speculated on the role of fragmentary human remains in Pavlovian society. Drawing on analogies from Medieval Europe and twentieth-century Papua New Guinea he notes the importance of disarticulated bones in the veneration of saints and the perpetuation of ancestor cults respectively, and suggests from this that some of the Mid Upper Palaeolithic examples represent a cultural involvement with disarticulated human bones and a large variety of secondary burial rites. Burials, where they exist, were placed into shallow graves, probably because permafrost precluded deeper excavation, although these were sufficient to preserve a number of complete skeletons, and post-depositional disturbance seems minimal (Svoboda 2008, 30).

Complete burials and partial body parts were often covered with mammoth scapulae, and in the case of Předmostí buried in a collective pit lined with them. Where these are missing, for example in the DV13–15 triple burial, a wooden structure may have replaced them. There therefore seems to have been a concern with containment, under earth, and under stronger structures, although it is quite possible that such 'lids' facilitated later access to the space of the dead, as is implied by the sequential burials in the pit at Předmostí.

The recovery of pellets and a fragmentary figurine of fired loess from the grave of DV16 is of interest. As Soffer *et al.* (1993) have noted, these objects have different contexts on the settlement. The pellets form a major part of the ceramic inventory of the site; they are intact (not broken) and are associated with hearths, ash lenses and kilns across the site. Given that they are too small (4–10mm) for utilitarian contexts such as cooking, they presumably derive from rituals that were contextualised in routine places such as dwellings and the external spaces between them. By contrast, the figurines were famously fractured by thermal shock, and the lack of intact examples suggests that this was deliberate (and that they are not 'kiln wasters'); and their distribution is restricted to hearths and ash lenses at the periphery of the settlement such as the 'wizard's hut'. It is probably fair to assume that both pellets and figurines relate in some way to ritual acts, and the inclusion of both in the DV16 grave demonstrate an association with these 'visible' and 'hidden' rituals in death. These practices, however, may have varied from settlement to settlement: at Pavlov I they are found in large numbers in the main accumulations of settlement debris (A. Verpoorte pers. comm.).

Russia: Kostenki and Sungir

As with the Pavlov hills, the Kostenki-Borshchevo region on the Don river is characterised by a number of rich settlement locales, many of which are multi-stratified, and demonstrate a degree of cultural stability for the duration of the Upper Palaeolithic ~35,000–10,000 BP (Anikovich 2005; Valoch 2007). Isolated human remains are known from these sites, although not in the number found in the Pavlovian. A human tibia from an Aurignacian context dated directly by an AMS radiocarbon measurement to 32,600 ± 1,100 BP (OxA-7073; Richards *et al.* 2001) suggests that the curation of human remains began in the Early Upper Palaeolithic of the region, and the fractured and smashed cranial remains of an adult located close to a hearth within a habitation structure at Kostenki 8 (Telmanskaya), suggests that such curation continued into the Mid Upper Palaeolithic Gorodtsovskayan culture. Several burials are known, from the Gorodtsovskayan (discussed here) and Late Upper Palaeolithic Spitsynian and Streletskian cultures (discussed in Chapter 7). Three sites have yielded Mid Upper Palaeolithic burials, Kostenki 12, 14 and 15.

At Kostenki 12 (Volkov) a neonate was laid extended on its back. A degree of postdepositional disturbance had occurred and no evidence of a grave cutting was evident (Sinitsyn 2004, 240). Radiocarbon measurements for the cultural layer in which it was found vary between ~23,000 and 29,000 BP, which are in agreement with dates for other Gorodtsovskayan layers elsewhere. At Kostenki 15 (Gorodtsov), within a Gorodtsovskayan settlement horizon dated to ~21,000–26,000 BP, a child of 6–7 years was interred within a small pit 124 × 80cm in diameter and some 40cm deep, apparently in a sitting position (Sinitsyn 2004, 239; Figures 6.24 and 6.25). A 'seat' comprised of yellow and grey clays – neither of which are known from the region – was constructed to facilitate the seated position. The tomb was covered with a fragment of mammoth scapula. The grave contained 70 worked lithics including endscrapers, piercers and blades as well as knapping waste, a lissoir (burnisher) and a needle of bone, and over 150 perforated arctic fox canines around the head. The headdress implied and the mammoth scapula covering show a clear link with the Pavolovian and Willendorfian traditions to the west.

Figure 6.24 Plan of the Kostenki 15 burial (courtesy of Andrei Sinitsyn).

Figure 6.25 The Kostenki 14 burial (photograph courtesy of Andrei Sinitsyn).

At Kostenki 14 (Markina Gora) a 20–25-year-old male was placed into a small pit ~80cm in length (Sinitsyn 1996, 2004; Figures 6.26 and 6.27). He was apparently interred in the midst of the settlement, his grave pit cut from the lowermost part of Cultural Layer 3, which probably belongs to the Gorodtsovskayan tradition, and dates of ~26,000–28,000 BP for the overlying Cultural Layer 2 suggest that Layer 3, and the burial, date to at least ~29,000 BP[19] (Sinitsyn *et al.* 1996). His legs were tightly drawn up to the chest, probably indicating that they were bound; his head facing downwards and his hands clenched into fists and lying by the head. A considerable covering of red ochre was apparent, although the only grave inclusions were three small flint flakes, the scapula and vertebra of a hare, and a mammoth phalange. The binding and face-down position is of interest (and recalls to some extent the female in the Grotta dei Fanciulli double burial), and the clenched fists may suggest that the man experienced considerable pain before – or during – his death. His low cranial capacity (1160–70cc, Sinitsyn 1996, 285) may have marked him out.

The Mid Upper Palaeolithic settlement of Sungir, on the outskirts of the city of Vladimir ~190km east of Moscow has provided the burials of three individuals that since their discovery in the 1950s have remained the richest burials of the period. The settlement overlooks the Klyasma River, and was occupied relatively intensively for a long period; over 4,500m² have been excavated, which can be ascribed to the Kostenki-Streletskaya culture (Alexeeva and Bader 2000). A number of human remains are known from the site, pertaining at least to nine individuals, of which four were clearly buried (ibid., 28). Two partial skeletons (Sungir 8 and 9) were recovered from outside of the main settlement and without cultural remains, and it is as yet unclear whether these were buried. The other fragmentary remains (Sungir 4–7) are associated with the famous single and double burials (Sungir 1, and Sungir 2 and 3 respectively). As with the Pavlovian and Gorodtsovskayan, a complex history of human remains seems to have pertained at the site.

The Sungir burials clearly belong to the Kostenki-Streletskaya Culture and thus broadly between ~29,000 and 21,000 BP, although there is as yet a discrepancy between direct AMS ^{14}C measurements on all three individuals from the burials of ~23,000–25,000 BP from Oxford (Pettit and Bader 2000; Sulerzhitski *et al.* 2000) and of ~26,000–27,000 BP from Arizona (Kuzmin *et al.* 2004). The latter are in greater agreement with measurements on samples from the cultural horizons into which the graves are cut (~27,000–28,000 BP – Sulerzhitski *et al.* 2000), and as the Oxford measurements were undertaken before the introduction of ultrafiltration pretreatment, it is best to assume provisionally that the older age range is most likely to be correct. Whichever is the case, it seems that the single burial of an adult male (Sungir 1) is youngest, succeeding the famous double child burial (Sungir 2 and 3, although at present it is unclear how much time separates the two burial events.

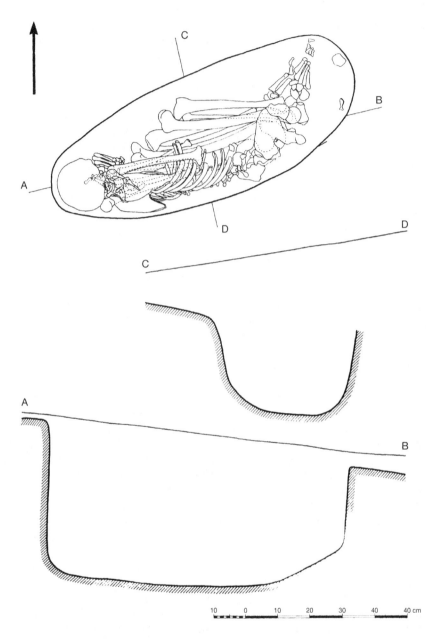

Figure 6.26 Plan of the Kostenki 14 burial. Note the close 'fit' of the burial to the grave pit (photograph courtesy of Andrei Sinitsyn).

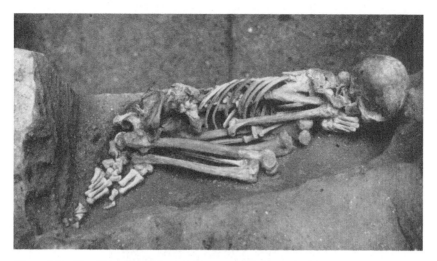

Figure 6.27 The Kostenki 14 burial (photograph courtesy of Andrei Sinitsyn).

Sungir 1, an adult male, was buried in a shallow grave excavated into the permafrost beneath the settlement (Figure 6.28). He was laid on his back in extended position, his hands folded across his pelvic region. At least 2,936 mammoth ivory beads were arranged into bands, probably strung onto his clothing, a 'stratigraphy' of which suggests in separate layers (Bader and Mikhajlova 1998). His head area is also adorned with a number of perforated fox teeth (White 1993); 25 mammoth ivory bracelets adorned his arms, some showing evidence of black colouring, and a flat pendant of schist was found about his neck, painted red and with a black dot on one side, a similar decoration to a sculpture of a horse on mammoth ivory from the settlement. Sungir 5, the cranium of a female, was found on the surface of the burial of Sungir 1, and appears to have been placed atop it deliberately. It was associated with a stone slab in an area rich in ochre, characteristics that make it appear like a ritual deposit, perhaps a term that should be used for Mid Upper Palaeolithic burials as a whole. Between Sungir 1 and the Sungir 2/3 burial a fragment of human femur (Sungir 7) was recovered.

The second burial is richer by far (Figure 6.29). Two children, usually interpreted as an ~11–13-year-old boy (Sungir 2) and a ~9–10-year-old girl (Sungir 3)[20] on the basis of femoral morphology and DNA, were laid head to head in a long shallow grave cutting ~3m from Sungir 1, their hands across their pelvic regions in the same way as Sungir 1. Their rich assemblage of grave goods includes thousands of mammoth ivory beads suspended from head gear and clothing, hundreds of perforated arctic fox canines similarly worn, mammoth ivory pins presumably securing clothing, disc-shaped pendants, mammoth ivory carvings, and long 'spears' of straightened

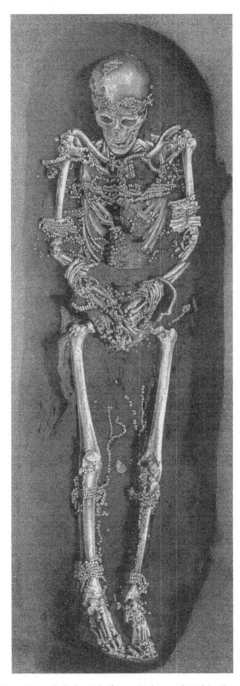

Figure 6.28 The Sungir 1 adult burial (from Bader and Mikhajlova 1998).

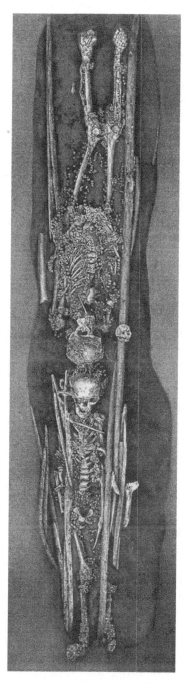

Figure 6.29 The Sungir 2/3 double burial (from Bader and Mikhajlova 1998).

mammoth tusk (e.g. Formicola 2007, 446). Sungir 2 was ornamented by at least 4,903 mammoth ivory beads, all of the same form as those on Sungir 1 but ~30 per cent smaller (White 1993, 1995), suggesting that strict rules governed the production of the personal ornamentation in a way observed some 10,000 years later in time in the Magdalenian (discussed in Chapter 7). Unlike the adult male, however, Sungir 2 had over 250 arctic fox canines around his waist, presumably representing some kind of decorated belt, as well as an ivory animal figurine (possibly a horse) on his chest and a large ivory sculpture of a mammoth beneath his left shoulder. An ivory pin at his throat probably secured an item of clothing, perhaps a cloak. Alongside his right upper arm was placed a human femur lacking epiphyses from a large individual, the medullary cavity packed with ochre (Sungir 4: Alexeeva and Bader 2000, 28), a clear example of the circulation of human relics. At Sungir 2's right side, partially overlapping with Sungir 3, lay a 2m 40cm long 'lance' usually described as made from straightened mammoth ivory. As White (1993, 292) has noted, the weight of this item probably precludes use as a weapon, and a function related more to display or ritual seems most likely. Next to it was a disk of ivory carved with open work and akin to a spoked wheel, perhaps originally mounted on a wooden 'lance' as White (ibid., 292) has suggested. Two further 'sticks' of ivory were found alongside his legs.

Sungir 3 was ornamented with even more ivory beads – at least 5,274 – again arranged in bands from head to feet, and an ivory pin at her throat similar to Sungir 2. No fox teeth were associated with her, however, nor did she possess a pendant on her chest. A number of small 'lances' of mammoth ivory akin to the smaller examples with Sungir 2 – at least 10 – were laid at her sides (Bader and Mikhajlova 1998), as White (ibid., 292) has noted 'more appropriate to her body size than that accompanying the boy' [Sungir 2], and the largest – approximately the same height as Sungir 3 – was also associated with a line of lithic microarmatures. Two pierced batons, one decorated with rows of incised dots, were also laid at her side. Three open-work ivory discs akin to that alongside Sungir 2 were found at the left side of her head (the smallest, only (2cm in diameter) and the larger two at her sides by the ivory 'lances'. One of the ivory 'lances' was inserted into the central hole of one of the discs like the basket of a ski pole, although a line of lithic microflakes extended from the disc away from the lance, suggestive of a flint-barbed weapon (Bader 1978). Sungir 2 is without any obvious pathology, and is normal in size and shape. Formicola and Buzhilova (2004), however, have noted the pathological condition of Sungir 3 – a marked bowing of the femora – and suggest that this is indicative of a congenital disease perhaps connected with a diabetic mother.

Both context and content of the Sungir burials are exceptional. The place-ment of a female cranium in an apparently ritual deposit above the grave of Sungir 1, and the femur of a large individual packed with ochre within the grave of the Sungir children, and possibly of a fragment of femur between the two graves, cannot be accidental and must indicate that meaning was attached to the remains of some individuals, which remained in circulation, were ornamented at least with ochre, and which on occasion came to be associated with primary burials. Although most of the grave goods on the Sungir individuals (and on all Mid Upper Palaeolithic burials for that matter) seem to relate to clothing rather than specific grave goods, their richness at Sungir is remarkable. Soffer (1985, 456) has suggested that the mammoth ivory beads from the burials alone represent over 2,500 person-hours of labour. It is difficult to disagree with the numerous scholars who see the richness of the double burial as indicative of status differences from early in life, and the nature of the burial suggested to Soffer (ibid., 457) that 'social differences marked in the burials were associated with some sort of ritual control'. She has also suggested (ibid., 444) that the richness of the Sungir burials might reflect the deliberate removal of goods from circulation, a 'dumping' behavior akin to potlatch that acts as a control on 'inflation'. It is, however, more likely that the children were buried in the clothing they possessed during life, and, although deliberate removal of goods may be an anachronistic concept, it is easy to see how such a conspicuous deposition – thousands of person hours – may have had social effect among those left living. This 'status' interpretation is often favoured, although one cannot rule out the possibility that *everyone* wore elaborately ornamented clothing (J. Orschiedt pers. comm.).

Interpreting Early and Mid Upper Palaeolithic funerary practice

Origins and regional patterns

At present, there is no evidence for burial during the Early Upper Palaeolithic. Evidence of the curation of human body parts in the form of personal ornamentation is clear for this period, however, as are regional traditions of funerary caching. The picture is strongly regionalised; there are no continent-wide similarities in practice, which may suggest that the belief systems underpinning funerary traditions were also regionalised. The contrast with the succeeding Mid Upper Palaeolithic is clear, from which time one can talk of a continent-wide shared practice. This may be relevant to the debate over the origins of 'modern' human behaviour. A strongly regionalised set of practices is, I suggest, more reminiscent of the preceding Middle Palaeolithic record, and not a reflection of widespread symbolic systems.

As radiocarbon chronology stands, the earliest known Mid Upper Palaeolithic burials occur in the northwest of Europe (Paviland (29,000 BP), Kostenki 14 (~28,000–29,000 BP) and in the Pavlovian (~28,000 BP) although in terms of radiocarbon imprecision and possible inaccuracy one should not read anything further into the data.[21] A parsimonious reading would see the practice of single and triple inhumation arising ~29,000 BP, spreading rapidly across Gravettian space, probably as a result of the high levels of group mobility across the continent as a response to climatic downturn (Roebroeks *et al.* 2000). Those few individuals for whom we have burials at this time appear not to have been buried in richly ornamented graves, although they were associated with grave goods and other indications of non-prosaic activity probably connected with funerary rituals (e.g. the binding of Kostenki 14, broken ivory rods at Paviland and the wooden stakes or structure in the Dolní Věstonice triple burial). The two examples of western European burials appear to have been isolated (e.g. Lagar Velho, Paviland) and without the context of curation of fragmentary remains, whereas those from the more intensively settled Pavlovian and Kostenki-Borschevian sites are more numerous and more richly contextualised.

Svoboda (2008, 29) has observed that rich burials, that is, those accompanied by elaborate personal ornamentation, ochre-stained clothing and/or burial shrouds and other cultural items, such as Sungir, Arene Candide and Brno 2, belong to the younger phases of the Gravettian, whereas earlier examples (~30,000–26,000 BP) such as those from Paviland, Dolní Věstonice, Pavlov and Předmostí are relatively poor, and has suggested that a degree of temporal development can be seen in Mid Upper Palaeolithic burials. Perhaps traditions of burial either became more elaborated as they spread and were incorporated into the behavioural repertoires of other regions, or, more probably, became elaborated as regional societies themselves developed, perhaps along the lines of increasing social stratification. Similarities between general practices – and specific, as we shall see below – are perhaps remarkable given the distances involved and given that the Alps do not appear to have been a barrier between the Italian and Moravian examples nor were the high mountains between Balzi Rossi/Grimaldi and Arene Candide (Mussi 2001a, 258).

Difference within similarity: Moravia and Italy compared

By contrast to the Pavlovian burials, those of Italy are relatively richly furnished, placed in caves and not in the open, and extended or only slightly flexed, differences possibly owing to the Italian examples postdating those of Moravia; the former date to ~27,000–26,000 BP and the latter to ~25,000–24,000 BP (Mussi 2003). Despite this, similarities exist: the relatively high number of burials relative to other regions of Europe where excavations have been intense; their excavation into shallow graves within settlement contexts; the setting of hearths in grave cuttings prior to the placement of the bodies; rich personal ornamentation including ochre, and, of course, the two triple burials as yet known to science. One must be cautious about invoking similarities between the triple burials of Dolní Věstonice and Barma Grande. Although the Dolní Věstonice example was exceptionally well excavated and is well documented, the Barma Grande example was excavated in 1892 and for which only a sketch and some descriptions survive. The reconstruction of this burial in the Museo dei Balzi Rossi di Ventimiglia involves a degree of interpretation (see Formicola 1991, 79 for a photograph of the reconstruction and a critical discussion of it), although it may be said to be correct in general. This said, the demonstrable similarities between the two triple burials are striking, and must point to a common tradition underlying the practice of triple burial, and possibly underlying the deaths of the individuals themselves. It is clear that each:

• contains three individuals placed extended side-by-side in a common shallow grave;
• contains ochre staining, personal ornamentation probably sewn onto headgear and clothing;
• probably comprised one female and two males;
• contained one individual on the extreme right of the group facing outwards as if 'disengaged' from the group;
• contained the left most and central individuals facing inwards as if 'engaged' with the group.

The recovery of three individuals in a single grave is odd at the outset. A triple burial cannot be described as a 'mass burial' as there is obvious evidence of planning and order to the phenomenon. That the general structure of this order is shared between burials separated by ~500km and at least 1,000 radiocarbon years is remarkable and must be of significance. There are several issues to consider that may be critical to the interpretation of this phenomenon. First, three young adults apparently died at the same time, or at least close enough in time to warrant burial in the same grave at the same time and without the later addition of individuals as with the double burial in the Grotta dei Fanciulli. Taylor (2002, 213) has suggested that they may have been 'scapegoated' – deliberately killed to contain social contagion – and buried in the middle of the settlement and therefore in front of a large audience, although in the dangerous lifestyle of hunter–gatherers during the cold climates of the period multiple deaths could occur simultaneously, perhaps through fighting among the young during periods of stress when 'walk away' options are not viable (A. Verpoorte pers. comm.). Evidence of violence is present on two individuals in the Dolní Věstonice triple burial. Second, it has been suggested on the basis of shared (but uncommon) physical traits such as grooves on the frontal squama, that all individuals in the double burial of the Grotta dei Fanciulli may have been related and that the same relationship may be observed at Barma Grande (Formicola 1989, 484–5). Third, and perhaps most pertinently, is the clear association of all three individuals in death, and *with a grammar of engagement and disengagement with the group*. Two of the three 'engage' with the others, or with each other, while a third – in the same position in both graves – disengages. This *must* reflect a connection between the three individuals in life, the third individual disengaged from the others. Closer connections between the other two – probably a male and female in both graves – is demonstrated by the similar orientation of Barma Grande 3 and 4 and by DV13's hand placed over the pubic region of DV14. This latter requires full extension of the arm and cannot have been accidental; this must be a deliberate connection of DV13 with the pubic region of DV14, and this may have been emphasised by the ochre in the region, which has not been found on any other Mid Upper Palaeolithic burials. It should not be pushing interpretation to assume that the connection between the two was intimate, and that the underlying 'story' behind the two graves (or possibly motivation behind their murder) involved two individuals who were intimately connected in some way and a third 'interloper' who must originally have shared a connection with the other two (as it is buried with them) but whose detachment ritual emphasised a disconnection with them. I do not want to invoke a 'love triangle' explanation here, although one cannot rule this out, and it should be remembered that most small-scale societies have strict taboos about this sort of thing. Perhaps more complex factors were at play. Several clues may come from the nature of the central female in the Dolní Věstonice burial. She bears signs of numerous pathologies including scoliosis of the spine, deformities of the limbs, and traumatic injuries that may well have led to several soft-tissue pathologies such as alopecia. Given that a number of individuals buried in the Mid Upper Palaeolithic are pathological (see pp. 211–12) this probably indicates some particular significance or role for this individual in society. This is not a case of a happy couple disrupted by an affair, and given the similarities with Barma Grande we might assume the same for both graves. Further clues might come from both the Dolní Věstonice triple burial and the Baousso da Torre 3 adolescent burial, both of which were placed face down. As noted above, no personal ornamentation accompanied Baousso da Torre 3, unlike the two richly ornamented and provisioned adults buried in the cave. This alone separates the adolescent from the others, a disengagement from the phenomena afforded the others. Was he stripped of his clothing before burial? If some of the carbonised branches from the Dolní Věstonice burial do represent staking of at least one body this further adds to the odd nature of the interments. While one cannot speculate further, it seems fairly clear that these represent an odd circumstance, linking three probably related individuals, two of whom appear to have been intimately connected and a third who is disconnected at least in death, and further factors and parallels in other graves suggest this third individual was for some reason treated 'more poorly' than the others. Circumstances dictated that they must be buried – or contained – together. This is not normal burial.

Infants and male adults

Zilhão (2005) has noted that, unlike the preceding Middle Palaeolithic wherein infants are represented in burials in approximately the same proportion as in life, with the Mid Upper Palaeolithic sample their number drops to less than 10 per cent of known burials. Given this, as he notes, the burial of the Lagar Velho child must indicate that social standing was accorded to the child. Considering the implications of his finds, Zilhão hypothesises that the lack of burials of children under ~5 years relates to the social significance of weaning, before which infants were not regarded as independent and thus not afforded burial, but after which they were. He furthermore suggests that the spatial data for infant burials where they exist suggests a policy of avoidance; all multiple burials of the period associate adults with adults or adolescents, but not with children (with the exception of Ostuni 1). Children, on the other hand, are only associated with adolescents. Indeed, child burials do seem to be isolated phenomena, suggesting that 'a special place [was] required for the ritual disposal of the body of such a young child' (ibid., 235). Zilhão's conclusion is that it is only after ~35,000 BP (at present one might say after ~29,000 BP) that age-related social distinctions were in operation.

One striking pattern is the apparent dominance of males, although whether this is a real phenomenon or a factor of taphonomy and identification is unclear and a re-evaluation of the sexing of these burials is desirable (Henry-Gambier 2008, 13). For the Pavlovian, only the DV3 burial is clearly female, although if one includes the indeterminate and highly pathological DV14 from the middle of the Dolní Věstonice triple burial the number is only two from complete burials, and perhaps five from the multiple interment pit at Předmostí. Both Mussi (2001a) and Formicola (1988b) have noted the dominance of males in Italy, and the latter (ibid., 47) has noted that the rare appearance of females in the Ligurian burials only in association with males 'seem[s] to relegate the female to the role of marginal member in a male burial'. This, perhaps, pertains only to the Grotta dei Fanciulli double burial, and it must be remembered that both triple burials are single phenomena, and in the case of the Barma Grande example the female was buried first, thus at the very least she played an integral (and literally central) role in the burial's 'story'. A further anomaly is the lack of the elderly in the sample.

The sample: society, pathology and social standing

Henry-Gambier (2008, 13) has raised the question as to whether the individuals buried possessed social privilege in life. Zilhão (2005) has made a convincing case that the rare burial of non-adults such as the Lagar Velho child indicates that age-related social status had come into being by the Mid Upper Palaeolithic, and if this were so then one might expect other forms of status differentiation to have been in operation too. Although the practice of burial may have been determined by odd events rather than by the status of the individuals of concern – deaths during childbirth and whatever is represented by the triple burials for example – the nature of the individuals buried suggests that social distinction may have been given to those 'odd' individuals who stood out from the norm, visually and, in some cases perhaps, behaviourally. The association of a pathological individual with otherwise 'normal' individuals in the Dolní Věstonice triple burial and in the Sungir double burial has been stressed by Formicola *et al.* (2001) and Formicola and Buzhilova (2004, 196), who note that these associations 'reassert the possibility of ideological connections between "abnormality" and extraordinary funerary patterns'. In Italy, this association seems to have continued into the Late Glacial (Formicola 2007) as I shall discuss in Chapter 7.

Perhaps such social differences also determined exactly how corpses were treated in the wider sense. The frequency of isolated and fragmentary human remains on Pavlovian settlements is striking, and their differing contexts, associations and preservational states suggest that several factors were involved in their deposition. It certainly seems that these individuals were left to decompose and be scavenged, and certainly that they were treated separately to those individuals who received the protection of burial. Spatially, the Pavlov 31 hand bones were found on the periphery of dwellings, and were possibly eroded out of a small pit near to which they were found, and the levels of erosion visible on them is consistent with the microbial activity that would be expected had they been buried intact (Trinkaus *et al.* 2009). It is therefore conceivable that a pair of hands were buried in a pit, further support for the notion that human relics were in circulation in the Pavlovian and, for that matter, for the hand symbolism that emerges in the form of hand stencils and prints in cave art in the Mid Upper Palaeolithic.

Complete burial does stand out from this pattern, and it is difficult to see the partial human remains from settlements as the remnants of highly disturbed graves. These could, however, reflect the remnants of bodies laid exposed on the ground (perhaps as settlements were abandoned) or on platforms (J. Orschiedt pers. comm.), for which, of course, no archaeological evidence would survive. Whatever the case, these hypothetical 'exposures' are still distinguishable from burials. As Formicola *et al.* (2001, 378, my emphases) have suggested, 'a few Upper Palaeolithic burials included *selected* individuals and that *physical diversity* may have played a role in selective patterns from that period'. Perhaps human relics reflected 'good' deaths, and burials 'bad'.

Face down and forgotten: burials or ritual deposits?

Perhaps 'bad deaths' explain the deposition of complete corpses in what we define from our modern standpoint as 'burials'. It is undeniable that the context and associations of several Mid Upper Palaeolithic burials reveal odd 'back stories' and activities that can safely be regarded as ritual in nature, adding more complexity to the burial phenomenon than one might expect if these were simple inhumations akin to those practised in the Holocene. We might realistically assume that burial was rare in all Mid Upper Palaeolithic societies, and therefore cannot be taken to be the funerary 'norm'. Whether or not excarnation of corpses and the circulation of body parts was closer to the norm is unclear, although both seem to have played a role in cosmological and ritual life in the heart of settlements, as did 'venus' figurines (Verpoorte 2001). A comparison of burials with venuses allows us to defocus from a head-on approach to the burials as burials and approach them side-on as another phenomenon. Although contextual information about a number of the venuses discovered in the infancy of archaeology is lacking, enough information survives as to facilitate a general comparison of the two, which I have undertaken elsewhere (Pettitt 2006, 300–6). While I shall not repeat this in detail here, several points are worth making. Given that most burials are male, the prevalence of female figurines is of interest. Where contextual information does survive (ibid., table 19.2) the deposition of venuses parallels that of human remains, that is, they are tucked away in caves in France and otherwise 'buried' in pits across the continent. More specific parallels are apparent among figurines and burials, notably:

- a concern with fire, either preceding the interment (body or figurine), atop it, or in its close proximity;
- an association with the bones of large, dangerous resource animals, possibly representing 'offerings' of meat;
- an association with enigmatic items of bone and mammoth ivory;
- occasional placement of stone blocks over the interment;
- a complex 'use life' often involving fragmentation and circulation in parts during life;
- use of ochre on the body and/or in the grave;
- elaboration of the body, often as lines or 'zones' of ornamentation;
- elaboration of the head area with head gear;
- occasional reference to the pubic area.

Viewed in this way, that is, not from the point of view that they are 'burials' but from the assumption that burials were similar to venuses, may be a more instructive approach to the phenomenon of Mid Upper Palaeolithic burials. While semantically we must, of course, call them burials, and while also they must be seen as ritual acts, they may not have functioned in any way like we in the modern world view burials. It may be better to consider them to be examples of ritual *containment*, especially where a concern is evident to cover them with mammoth scapulae (Předmostí, Krems-Wachtberg), pin them down with wood (Dolní Věstonice), tightly bind them (Kostenki 14), or weigh them down with stone (Sungir 1, possibly Paviland). The detachment rituals associated with some, such as the setting of hearths in grave pits or in proximity to them (Lagar Velho, Barma Grande, Dolní Věstonice) and their wider associations with fire, the peculiar panoply of objects deposited with Brno II, and the broken ivory rods with Paviland suggest non-ordinary acts at the graveside before, during and after the deposition of the bodies, suggesting that the burial per se formed part of a wider set of ritual acts, themselves blending into the wider ritual world with which they were united by the cosmological beliefs that underpinned them. Such a view accommodates the odd individuals and circumstances reflected in several of the burials. In this interpretation there are no burials *as we understand them* in the Mid Upper Palaeolithic, but a rich and complex set of ritual acts no different to the 'burials' of single (and at Avdeevo double and triple: see discussion in Pettitt 2006) venuses in 'pit graves'.

Missed this class discussion

- Maybe didn't dig holes for burial (repurpose)

- buried in occupational areas

- infant burials common

- Lots of variation

7

FROM FRAGMENTATION TO COLLECTIVITY

Human relics, burials and the origins
of cemeteries in the Late Upper Palaeolithic and
Epipalaeolithic

Murder and cannibalism in the
Middle Magdalenian?

The Maszycka Cave in southern Poland is an exceptionally well preserved camp site attributed to a single occupation of the Magdalenian III with Navettes (Allain *et al.* 1985), with ^{14}C measurements between ~14,000 and 15,000 BP. The high proportion of artefacts on bone and antler relative to stone, and a good degree of spatial resolution have lead to this being called a 'Palaeolithic Pompeii' (Kosłowski and Sachse-Kosłowska 1993). Groups of processed faunal remains, lithics, organic artefacts and human remains defined several functional areas within the cave's outer chamber, and the homogeneity of all finds and their recovery from a thin layer indicate that a single occupational episode is represented at the site. At the interpretational heart of the site is the observation that, at least in terms of non-perishable material it is 'complete', that is, those artefacts that took considerable time to make and that were usually removed from sites when they were abandoned, are still present at Maszycka Cave. Whereas complete artefacts on bone and antler typically represent ~10–15 per cent of single assemblages they represent 54 per cent at Maszycka and include a 'rack' of sagaies. Clearly, the site was abandoned rapidly, and it has been hypothesised that 'the inhabitants of Maszycka Cave were annihilated by enemies' (ibid., 121). The lithic assemblage fits well into both Magdalenian and Molodovan types, although the organic assemblage fits more closely with the former. Raw materials represented on the site, other than local flints, include several German flints linking the site to the Magdalenian to the west, as well as Dneistr and Wolhynian flints from the area of the Molodovan to the east. A number of scenarios could account for this; the mobility of these 'generic' Magdalenian/Molodovan group could have accessed all of these sources; the occupants could have been culturally

Magdalenian and acquired Dneistr flints through exchange with Molodovans, or the Magdalenian occupants could have been murdered by Molodovan or Eastern Gravettian raiders 'who may not have looked too kindly on the newcomers from the far west' (ibid., 170).

Whatever the case, a whole group seem to have been killed at the site. Fifty fragmentary human remains – all cranial – represent at least 16 individuals, and given that a great degree of selection has occurred the actual number is likely to be higher.[22] At least five adults, three juveniles, and eight infants are represented, essentially a catastrophic profile possibly representing a band of two or three 'families'. Their bones were scattered randomly over the terrace in front of the cave, and clustered with faunal remains in the cave's entrance. Traces of scalping, cutting, scraping and biting are visible on the outer surfaces of the cranial remains, indicative of 'cannibalism, clearly focussed on brain consumption' (ibid., 170). Clearly, Cronos compulsions were at the core of the annihilation of the occupants of this site. It seems that it was not enough simply to kill them; their bodies had to be disposed of and their brains consumed too. That this should occur in the Middle Magdalenian, during which time there is ample evidence for the processing of heads, suggests that the fragmentation of the body, whether for 'good' or for 'bad' was at the heart of belief systems at the time.

This is part of wider traditions. The mortuary processes identified in the European Mid Upper Palaeolithic – processing of bodies and curation of relics as well as the formal burial of the dead often with rich grave inclusions – continued into the Late Upper Palaeolithic. Despite a remarkably high number of excavations, however, the number of burials remain remarkably low and it should not, therefore, be regarded as an habitual mortuary activity. The developments seen during the Late Upper Palaeolithic and Epipalaeolithic, between ~20,000 BP and the end of the Pleistocene ~10,000 BP, in a sense witness the elaboration of the two extremes of mortuary treatment of the body. On the one hand the traditions of disarticulation of the corpse and circulation of body parts represent a fragmentation of the body that, I shall argue below, occurs alongside the artistic use of the fragmented body in symbolic systems. By contrast, a collective concern is witnessed by the growth of cemeteries *sensu stricto*, which have appeared in several regions by the end of the period but may have emerged sporadically around the Last Glacial Maximum. Thus, by the end of the Palaeolithic the two extremes of human mortuary activity had been realised.

The fragmented person: human relics and art

Most Late Upper Palaeolithic human remains are fragmentary. In France, for example, of the remains of some 232 individuals known for the Magdalenian, only 5 per cent comprise decently complete skeletons and probably derive from burials, whereas 95 per cent are highly fragmentary, and 40 per cent bear cut and scrape marks indicative of defleshing (Gambier 1992; Le Mort and Gambier 1992). As with preceding periods, one clearly cannot conclude from this that burial was the primary mortuary activity. If anything, it seems that the long tradition of Cronos compulsions came to the fore in the period, with an escalation in the frequency of body processing. The resulting fragmentation of the body, I argue below, can be seen in the context of a concern with fragmented bodies in the parietal and portable art of the period. Bodies – in art, in death and, one assumes, in life – functioned as symbols in the period.

If, as suggested in the last chapter, fragmentary human remains began to function as relics in the European Mid Upper Palaeolithic, the practice of reducing the body to parts by processing seems to have become more common and variable in the succeeding Late Upper Palaeolithic, notably the Magdalenian of western and central Europe. A relatively high number of remains of bones – cranial in particular – bearing striations and other marks of defleshing are found in western Europe, notably France, Germany and the United Kingdom. Such marks are found from the Early to Late Magdalenian and are, at times, associated with the practice of inhumation. The variety of practices reflected by these marks reveals the diversity of funerary practice in the Magdalenian world. Most numerous are marks indicative of defleshing, and almost all marks are found on cranio-dental elements, whether adult, adolescent or infant of both sexes.

A noticeable feature of Magdalenian parietal art and *art mobilier* is the depiction of isolated body parts or bodies lacking extremities, particularly heads. Of 79 representations of human heads among the engraved plaquettes from La Marche, 58 are isolated (without bodies), and of 51 bodies, 14 are acephalous (Pales and Saint Péruse 1976). Isolated heads occur among the humanoid engravings at Les Combarelles (Archambeau and Archambeau 1991). Headless females occur on the Lalinde engraved stone blocks (Roussot 1965) and among the engravings of humanoids in the Cantabrian Middle Magdalenian (Corchón Rodríguez 1998). Overall, a trend towards high degrees of stylisation of the human form can be found among the 'spindleform' humanoid carvings, for example, from Kesslerloch in Switzerland (Braun 2005) and, most clearly, among the widespread engravings and carvings of females of Gönnersdorf type from Poland, Germany, Czech Republic, Ukraine, Belgium, France, Spain, Italy, and possibly the United Kingdom, from which heads, feet and arms are missing (Bayle des Hermens 1972; Delluc and Delluc 1981; Ripoll López 1988/9; Höck 1993; Welté and Cook 1993; Lorblanchet 1995; Bosinski and Schiller 1998; Bosinski *et al.* 2001; Mussi 2001a, fig. 7.30; Valoch 2001; Pettitt 2007). In the German Magdalenian, for example at Oelknitz and Nebra (Feustel 1970) this stylistic 'fragmentation' reaches its greatest extent, with females represented solely by sculpted buttocks. A further theme is the 'vulva' – usually interpreted as a female pubic triangle (cf. Bahn 1986) – which can occur in association with Gönnersdorf-style females, for example at Gouy (Martin 2007, fig. 9.23). This artistic concern

217

with body parts and incomplete bodies possibly derived from the same motives that underpinned the disarticulation of the real body in Magdalenian funerary activity.

Fragmentary remains and Cronos compulsions in the Late Upper Palaeolithic

Human remains from the Last Glacial Maximum or shortly thereafter are remarkably rare in Europe. A small amount of human remains from France date to Solutrean and Badegoulian contexts but these are very rare (D. Henry-Gambier pers. comm.). Direct AMS ^{14}C dating demonstrated that a human mandible from a Solutrean level at Solutré is actually a Holocene intrusion (Pestle *et al.* 2006). Fragments of a child's cranium were recovered from the Badegoulian levels at Badegoule itself (Rosendahl *et al.* 2003). In France, human remains are more numerous in the Magdalenian than in any other Upper Palaeolithic technocomplex, although are rare before ~16,000 BP. They were, for example, found scattered throughout the 14 Magdalenian levels at La Madeleine itself, and throughout the Magdalenian II and III levels at Saint-Germain-la-Rivière (Gambier and Lenoir 1991). In a review Gambier (1992) has estimated that of the remains of 232 individuals that can be assigned to the French Magdalenian, ~54 per cent are highly fragmentary and retain no details of post-mortem treatment, ~9 per cent were buried, and ~40 per cent show evidence of processing, a pattern that is witness to the 'diversité et de la complexité des practiques et des comportements des Magdaléniens face à la mort' (Le Mort and Gambier 1992). The number of individuals grows as the Magdalenian progresses, from 5 per cent in the Lower Magdalenian, 19 per cent in the Middle Magdalenian and with the majority – 46 per cent in the Late Magdalenian[23], and this broadly correlates with the growth in number of examples of 'fragmentation' visible in art as the Magdalenian progressed. At the younger end of the period the cranium of an adolescent was recovered from a Final Magdalenian/Azilian context in the front of the rockshelter of Roc-de-Cave, Lot, France. This has been dated to 11,210 ± 140 BP (Gif-A 95048: Bresson 2000), although it is unclear as to whether it was deposited in disarticulated state or whether it derives from a burial. A proximal fragment of femur bearing probable traces of deliberate percussion and transverse striations was recovered from a Younger Dryas context at the Grotte Rochefort, Mayenne, dated to ~10,300–10,900 BP (Colleter and Hinguant 2006).

The fragmentary remains of at least 24 individuals were recovered from an early Magdalenian level in Le Placard Cave, Charente, France (Le Mort and Gambier 1992). These are mainly cranio-dental, and represent adults and children over the age of two. Traces of defleshing particularly reveal the removal of the occipito-frontal, masseter and temporal muscles, and the location of the cut marks and clustering of several closely parallel marks suggests that the organisation of the defleshing seems to have been systematic (Figure 7.1).

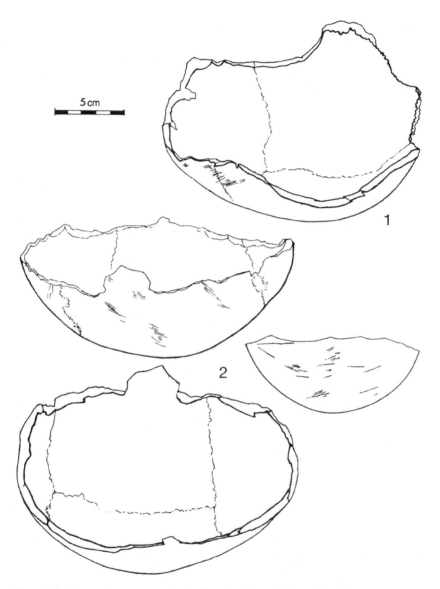

5 cm

1

2

Figure 7.1 Cut marks on two calvaria from le Placard, Charente (from Le Mort and Gambier 1992 and courtesy of Dominique Henry-Gambier).

Furthermore, certain fragments of calvaria that resulted from the butchery bear traces of subsequent breaks indicating that they were deliberately worked, perhaps for use as containers (ibid., 39). The number of individuals processed at Le Placard is exceptional, and it may be that the site had some significance as a place of multiple processing, possibly over a relatively short period of time if the similar weathering on all the bones is anything to go by (Le Mort and Gambier 1992, 32).

Cranial fragments representing three adults and an infant were recovered from the Solutrean levels at Nerja Cave, Málaga, Spain (Lalueza Fox 1995), although they bear no evidence of processing. The same can be said for examples from the Spanish Magdalenian, which are relatively rare and fragmentary. The earliest examples cluster in Cantabria (El Castillo and La Pasiega) where they are associated with the Lower Magdalenian, although persist in the region until the Late Magdalenian (El Pendo, Grotte d'Erralla), at which time they are also found in the Spanish Levantine coast (Garralda 1992). Unlike French examples, however, no modifications are reported for any of the Spanish remains, although one cannot rule out that some of these represent secondary burials as cut marks are not inevitable on the remains of all secondary burials (J. Orschiedt pers. comm.). Even at the rich Magdalenian site of La Garma and its neighbouring sites no human remains have been found and the earliest burial in the area is Mesolithic (P. Arias Cabal pers. comm.).

Several German sites have yielded fragementary human remains from Magdalenian contexts, some of which bear evidence of processing.[24] A cut marked cranial fragment from the Magdalenian of Burghöhle Dietfurt seems to relate to scalping (Gietz 2001); teeth and bones from several individuals including children from the Magdalenian of Petersfels, and postcranial elements from Hohler Fels also attest to processing (Street et al. 2006, 571).

The dominance of cranio-dental remains among modified human remains of the Magdalenian is clear, and given the good preservation of numerous faunal elements on most of the sites on which they are found cannot be ascribed simply to taphonomic factors. An element of deliberate selection is evident, and perhaps in this sense the Magdalenian stands out from the preceding Mid Upper Palaeolithic in which postcranial elements were curated also.

Secondary burial

A degree of funerary caching may still be evident in the Late Upper Palaeolithic, although it seems to have declined in the face of disarticulation and secondary burial and formal burial. The skeletal remains of a female were recovered from a deep cavity in the complex Koněprusy cave system under the Zlaty Kůň Hill, Bohemia, Czech Republic. It was found on the surface of a debris cone that had accumulated under a vertical chimney, and in this sense is reminiscent of the deposition of human remains at Mladeč in the Early Upper Palaeolithic. Direct AMS ^{14}C dating of the remains, however, established that they were deposited around 12,870 ± 70 BP (GrA-13696: Svoboda et al. 2002), which accords well with a rich Magdalenian settlement in the region. Culturally and chronologically, therefore, this suggests that regional Magdalenians were using caves for funerary caching, a regional tradition with a deep antiquity (ibid., 959). The recovery of two teeth of an adult male and fragments of a mandible from Late Magdalenian contexts in Kůlna Cave, Moravia (Svoboda et al. 1996) may result from the same practice.

In contrast to funerary caching, the evidence for disarticulation and in some cases secondary burial is arguably clearest in the Magdalenian than in any period of the Upper Palaeolithic. A secondary burial of Lower Magdalenian age is evident in the cave of Le-Rond-du-Barry, Haute-Loire, France (Heim 1992), where the cranium of an adult male lacking an associated mandible was placed upside down within a small rectangular enclosure of breccia blocks, within an Early Magdalenian (Magdalenian I) horizon with an associated ^{14}C date of 17,100 ± 450 BP (Gif-3038). A few items were also recovered from within the rectangle – a flint core and flake, a retouched blade, a fragment of a basalt cobble, a fragment of reindeer antler, numerous small bone flakes, teeth and a number of microfaunal remains. As Heim (ibid., 54) has noted, it is difficult to interpret this in any way other than ritual, and the group of objects suggests that this should be viewed as a ritual deposit similar to those of the Mid Upper Palaeolithic discussed in Chapter 6. Fragmentary cranial remains of a ~10-year-old child and a young female from the Mas d'Azil (Bayle des Hermens 1972) suggest that wider curation of human relics may have occurred during the Magdalenian at the site.

Disarticulated human remains from Mittlere Klause near Neuessing in the Altmühl Valley, Germany, represent a secondary burial. The remains have been dated directly by AMS ^{14}C to 18,590 ± 260 BP, placing them within a Badegoulian/Epigravettian cultural context (OxA-9856; Street et al. 2006, 567). Although the initial recognition of cut marks (Gieseler 1977; Narr 1977) has now been shown to be incorrect (they are modern: J. Orschiedt pers. com.) the deposit at least is convincing enough. The skeleton was deposited within a patch of ochre, supine from the waist down and with the upper body twisted onto its left side. Several fragments of mammoth ivory found in close proximity to the remains may have formed part of the deposit.

Thirty-eight cranial and postcranial remains from a Magdalenian context in the Brillenhöhle in the Swabian Alb, Germany, reflect the process of secondary burial (Orschiedt 1997, 2002). The remains pertain to at least three individuals, two adults and a child, and probably a third adult. A direct AMS ^{14}C measurement on a cranial fragment of 12,470 ± 65 BP (OxA-11054) confirms the Magdalenian attribution. The remains were recovered from a hearth positioned centrally within the cave, and one can eliminate taphonomic or other factors for their positioning (Orschiedt 2002, 247). Although the original excavators considered the bones to have been burnt, discolouration on the bone is from ash and no traces of burning are present, and they seem to have been placed atop the hearth while it was still visible, probably shortly after it had been extinguished (J. Orschiedt pers. comm.). Orschiedt's careful study of the modifications has revealed evidence of dismemberment, defleshing, and careful 'cleansing' of the soft tissue from the bones probably shortly after death and prior to this deposition. Orschiedt found significant differences in the location and type of cut marks on the bones compared with processed faunal remains from the site and from other Magdalenian sites, revealing that the majority of cut marks on the human remains did not result from 'normal' butchery but from defleshing that was considerably more intense and careful. 'The aim was evidently to free the skeletal remains as far as possible from their tissue' (ibid., 247). Cut marks on phalanges, which are very rare among faunal assemblages, indicate careful skinning of the individuals, and marks on the crania indicate detachment from the cervical vertebra and scalping. The lack of longbones and dominance of cranial parts indicates that deliberate selection has taken place, that is, the removal of all but the smallest anatomical elements and fragments. Orschiedt demonstrated that all of the recovered bones fit into the better preserved calotte (Figure 7.2), suggesting that it may have functioned as a container in which the retained remains were taken to the hearth. This is strikingly similar to the suggested 'calotte containers' from Le Placard discussed above. The importance of Orchiedt's study is that this is a clear case of secondary burial, rather than one of cannibalism. There is some ambiguity, however, as to what the primary focus of activity was. Although a clear concern with cleaning the bones prior to deposition is in evidence, one cannot rule out another possibility, that human skin was a desired

Figure 7.2 The cut marked human remains from Brillenhöhle, Germany, contained within the calotte (photograph courtesy of Jörg Orschiedt).

222

product, possibly as a trophy or talisman, a phenomenon clearly demonstrated in numerous ethnographic contexts.

The recovery of the cranial and postcranial remains of at least four adults and one juvenile from the Late Magdalenian ('Creswellian') of Gough's Cave, Cheddar Gorge, United Kingdom attests to remarkably similar activity to that in Brillenhöhle, as Orschiedt (ibid., 251) recognised. Direct AMS ^{14}C measurements on several of the bones indicate an age of ~12,600–12,500 BP (Jacobi and Higham 2009), that is, broadly contemporary with the Brillenhöhle remains. The remains were recovered from a restricted spatial area close to the cave's wall (C. B. Stringer pers. comm.) generally where the traces of activity were greatest (Currant *et al.* 1989). Cut marks are restricted to the cranial vault, mandible and ribs, and reveal *careful* defleshing and dismembering. Cook (1991, 127) lamented in relation to the Gough's Cave remains that 'modern excavations do not necessarily make the identification of death rituals or mortuary practice any easier' and that 'on the basis of such evidence it is only possible to say that the inhabitants of the site dismembered the corpses of five individuals'. Andrews and Fernández-Jalvo (2003) thought the marks indicative of cannibalism, although the similarity with Brillenhöhle (a high cut mark frequency indicative of the careful defleshing of the same body parts) and Maszycka Cave (clustering of the remains with those of animals) is remarkable and may well attest similar concerns that ultimately resulted in secondary burial (Orschiedt 2002, 251).

Human jewellery and amulets

The dominance of cranio-dental elements in modified and curated human remains is apparent from the discussion above, and on a number of Magdalenian sites clearly relates to deliberate selection of these parts. In places, human skin may have been carefully removed and possibly curated, perhaps as 'trophies' or as talismans, and crania may have been used as containers at Le Placard and Brillenhöhle, at the latter as part of funerary activity. In addition to this, a number of examples of the curation of human remains as personal ornamentation are known. As discussed in Chapter 6, this practice seems to have arisen in the earliest European Upper Palaeolithic, although does not seem to have been particularly common. By contrast, the practice seems to have been more widespread after the Last Glacial Maximum, which is perhaps not surprising given the concern with fragmenting and curating human relics in general.

Although animal teeth perforated for suspension are common in Magdalenian contexts, perforated human teeth are much rarer. Two incisors, three canines and a premolar with perforations were recovered from the Late or Final Magdalenian of Bédeilhac Cave, Ariège, France (Le Mort 1985, 191), and others, poorly reported, may exist for the Magdalenian of Le Placard (Charente, France) and Chaffaud (Vienne, France).

In addition to a burial discussed below, the Magdalenian of Saint-Germaine-la-Rivière rockshelter (Gironde, France) produced an upper second premolar that was perforated at the extremity of its root for suspension, probably dating to ~16,000 BP (Le Mort 1985). Considerable traces of wear on the tooth – the enamel was completely worn away on the occlusal surface for example – suggests that it had been curated for some time.

Other examples show the fashioning of pendants (one might call them amulets) from cranial fragments. A regularly shaped circular fragment of infant parietal was recovered amidst various animal bones from the Magdalenian occupation site of Veyrier Cave, Haute-Savoie, France (Vallois 1971, 493). This bore a small hole created by careful rotation of a lithic tool, apparently to facilitate suspension. Begouen *et al.* (1936) reported a pendant formed by a fragment of human mandible from the Magdalenian of Enlène (Ariège, France). The fragment – part of the right front of the mandible – was coloured with ochre and pierced with a circular hole below the second premolar. The hole is certainly artificial (D. Henry-Gambier pers. comm.). It also bore straight striations indicative of scraping. The ochre staining on this piece is of interest given the Magdalenian *art mobilier* of the cave and the importance of the connected caves of Le Tuc d'Audoubert and Les Trois Frères in the Magdalenian. The staining is visible on the external and internal faces of the mandible, demonstrating that it was coloured after disarticulation, and the location of the piece amidst a concentration of Magdalenian hearths may suggest an association with fire (ibid., 559). One might view in this light the cranium of a two-year-old with evidence of post-mortem trepanation from Late Magdalenian (Magdalenian VI) deposits in the Rochereil Cave, Dordogne, France (Rochereil III: Vallois 1971). Fragmentary remains of a second individual (Rochereil II) and a burial (Rochereil I, discussed below) were also found in this level. The Rochereil III cranium was found close to the cave's west wall, in close proximity to a hearth, although as superimposed hearths were common in the cave it is impossible to link this example specifically with the skull. The trepanation is 41 to 45mm in diameter and almost circular, placed medially in the frontal region. Vallois (ibid., 491) pointed to the regularity of the removal and its carefully bevelled edges, and suggested that the object of the trepanation was to obtain a circular amulet or *rondelle*, similar to numerous examples known from the French Early Neolithic. If this is correct, the parallel with engraved rondelles of animal bone of the Middle Magdalenian (e.g. Sieveking 1971) is striking.

Further evidence of the possible use of amulets of cranial remains comes from the Grande Salle at Isturitz (Pyrénées-Atlantiques) France. Around 100 fragmentary human remains were recovered from the Magdalenian levels of the cave. Among these, four bear traces of modification (Buisson and Gambier 1991). Groups of elongated parallel striations resulting from scraping are visible at the edge of the parietal area on the specimens. Defleshing is clearly evident, and a degree of shaping of the cranial fragments is also clear. Beyond this, however, two of the cranial fragments bear engravings. One of these is clearly of a stylised animal (possibly an ibex), and the other a sub-circular motif. This is rare indeed; a human tooth from La Combe is the only other example of engraving on human remains from the period (ibid., 177). Although it is unclear whether the engravers simply used materials that were at hand as supports for engraving, the careful defleshing and shaping of these human remains,viewed from the wider context of Magdalenian treatment of body parts, makes it probable that the engravings were intentionally placed onto these relics. In this sense they are similar to bone rondelles and engraved stone plaquettes from the Magdalenian that, interestingly, display complex use-lives on the sites at which they are found (Tosello 2003). Is this a shadowy glimpse of a link between Magdalenian *art mobilier* and human relics?

Continuing containment: single inhumations of the Late Upper Palaeolithic

At least 26 single or double burials containing 31 individuals are known from Late Upper Palaeolithic contexts in Europe and the Near East (Table 7.1 and Figure 7.3). Including ambiguous examples in the count would raise this count by 50 per cent or so, and in addition to this, from ~15,000 BP in Australia, at least ~12,000 BP in Africa and ~11,000 BP in regions of Europe the number significantly increased due to the origin of what one can formally refer to as cemeteries. Many of the burials for which good data exist reveal the preservation of items of personal ornamentation with the dead, although few examples of 'rich' graves exist, and in this sense the period stands in contrast to several burials of the Mid Upper Palaeolithic discussed in the last chapter. Unlike the preceding period, however, burials in the Near East suggest that it formed part of the Eurasian Upper Palaeolithic world in the Late Upper Palaeolithic, at least in terms of funerary ritual. The existence of burials towards the end of the Pleistocene in most regions of the Old World and in places in the New World suggest that far-flung hunter–gatherer societies were independently practising this form of disposal, although the general rarity of burial wherever it appears again suggests that it may not have been the 'norm'. Thus at the end of the Pleistocene the two extreme forms of funerary practice – fragmentation and 'dissolution' of the body and burial in collective locations, as discussed in Chapter 1 – were both in place.

Burials of the Near Eastern and European Late Upper Palaeolithic

Human remains from the Levantine Upper Palaeolithic are remarkably rare, amounting to six articulated skeletons from five sites (Nadel 1994). One of these is the skeleton of an adult female from Nahal Ein Gev I of Early Upper Palaeolithic antiquity, which was laid in a highly flexed position and probably relates to the site's Aurignacian occupation. The most comprehensive example

Table 7.1 Late Upper Palaeolithic burials and probable burials discussed in the text. Highly questionable examples have been omitted, such as the fragmentary remains of two individuals from Solutrean/Early Magdalenian levels at Le Roc-de-Sers (Charente), partial remains of an infant found in a fissure between rocks in Middle Magdalenian levels at Le Figuier (Ardèche), and fragmentary remains from early excavations in Veyrier (Haute-Savoie), La Rochette, Abri Lachaud and Labattut (Dordogne)

Burial	Site details	Chronology	Age, sex, pathologies	Position and associations	References
Africa					
Wadi Kubbaniya, Egypt	Upper Palaeolithic occupation site	~20–25,000 BP (not directly dated)	Robust young adult male	Buried face down in extended position. Two chalcedony bladelets found within abdomen	Wendorf and Schild 1986
Dar-es-Soltane 2, Morocco	Dar-es-Soltane occupation site, probably Aterian	UQ-1558, 16,500 ± 250 BP (radiocarbon measurement on shell from same level)	Adult female burial and fragmentary remains of secondary burial	Female laid on large stone on left side and highly flexed, covered with cairn of small stones. Possible association with ochre-stained cobble	Débénath 2000
Israel					
Ohalo II H2	Early Kebaran settlement	~19,000 BP based on numerous ^{14}C measurements on charcoal from settlement	Adult male	Laid supine, legs highly flexed in grave cutting. No grave goods	Hershkovitz *et al.* 1995
Germany					
Bonn-Oberkassel	Burial seems to have been isolatd, i.e. away from occupation sites	OxA-4790, 11,570 ± 100 BP (male) and OxA-4792, 12,180 ± 100 BP (female) consistent with backed point ('bipoint') cultural context	Adult female and adult male	One individual apparently laid atop the first. Both found in ochred patch and possibly associated with skeleton of domesticated wolf, bone or antler cervid carving and bone pin of Terminal Upper Palaeolithic form	Baales and Street 1998; Street *et al.* 2006

Neuwied-Irlich	Burial seems to have been isolated, i.e. away from occupation sites	Direct AMS ^{14}C measurements on adult: OxA-9847, 11,910 ± 70 BP; on foetus/neonate OxA-9848, 11,965 ± 65 BP and UtC-9221, 12,110 ± 90 BP	Adult (probably female) and foetus/neonate	Unclear, although probably an isolated double burial, possibly of mother and child	Street et al. 2006

Poland

Wilczyce	Late Magdalenian hunting camp	OxA-16729, 12,870 ± 60 BP (direct AMS ^{14}C measurement on bone) and Contemporary with the camp (~13,000 BP) based on numerous ^{14}C measurements on bone and charcoal from the camp	~60% complete skeleton of foetus/neonate	Stratified beneath dwelling structure	Irish et al. 2008

France

Les Hoteaux (Ain)	Cave occupation site	Lower Level, possibly attributable to the Late Magdalenian (VI)	Skeleton of young adult male extended on back in shallow grave cutting	Ochre staining. Perforated bâton found alongside right femur. Some flint artefacts possibly associated. One perforated reindeer tooth	May 1986
Saint-Germain-la-Rivière 1, Gironde	Rockshelter occupation site	Probably Middle Magdalenian	Calotte and mandible of adult male	Unknown	Gambier et al. 2000; Henry-Gambier et al. 2002; Vanhaeren and d'Errico 2003
Saint-Germain-la-Rivière 2, Gironde ('La Dame de Saint-Germain-la-Rivière')	Rockshelter occupation site	GifA 95456, 15,780 ± 200 BP (direct AMS ^{14}C measurement on bone), consistent with Magdalenian III attribution	Complete skeleton of young adult female	Laid in shallow grave and covered with stone slabs. Possible association with hearths	Gambier et al. 2000; Henry-Gambier et al. 2002; Vanhaeren and d'Errico 2003

continued . . .

Table 7.1 continued

Site	Type	Dating	Skeleton	Context/grave goods	References
La Madeleine infant, Dordogne	Rockshelter occupation site	GifA 95457, 10,190 ± 100 BP (direct AMS ^{14}C measurement on bone) indicates post-Magdalenian VI date, possibly Azilian	Complete skeleton of 2–4-year-old infant	Laid in a large grave cutting apparently banked with sediment from the layer above. Covered in ochre, rich suite of perforated shell pendants, two deer canine and two fox canine pendants	Gambier et al. 2000; Taborin 1993; Vanhaeren and d'Errico 2001
Roc de Cave, Lot	Occupation site	GifA 95048, 11,210 ± 140 BP (direct AMS ^{14}C measurement on bone) corresponding to the Final Magdalenian or Azilian at the site	Near-complete skeleton of adolescent	Context and actual associations unclear: possible burial. Perforated deer teeth necklace possible associated with burial	Gambier et al. 2000
Le Cap Blanc, Dordogne	Rockshelter occupation site with Magdalenian sculpted frieze	Unclear; found at base of Magdalenian deposit possibly attributable to Magdalenian III	Complete skeleton of adult, probably female, laid flexed on left side and covered by three large stones at head and feet	No apparent grave goods	May 1986
Laugerie-Basse 'l'Homme écrasé de Laugerie-Basse'	Rockshelter occupation site	Stratigraphically post-dating Magdalenian IV occupation, direct AMS ^{14}C measurement of 15,700 ± 150 BP (Gif A 94204)	Complete skeleton of adult male, laid flexed on left side apparently under large rock	~20 Cypraea shells found at the chest, arm, knees and feet	May 1986; Gambier et al. 2000
Abri Lafaye, Bruniquel, Tarn-et-Garonne	Rockshelter occupation site	GifA 95047, 15,290 ± 150 BP (direct AMS ^{14}C measurement on adult female), confirms Middle Magdalenian attribution	Near-complete skeletons of adult female and ~3-year-old child, probably from double burial	Unclear	Gambier 1990; Gambier et al. 2000

Site	Site type	Dating	Remains	Associations	References
Sorde 1 (Sorde-l'Abbaye, Duruthy, Landes)	Rockshelter occupation site	Late Magdalenian ~11–12,000 BP (dates for cultural levels between which remains were found)	Cranium and femur of adult male	Canines of lion and bear, some perforated, found in close proximity to the burial. Other details unclear	Chauvière 2001; Henry-Gambier 2006
Sorde 3 (Sorde-l'Abbaye, Duruthy, Landes)	Rockshelter occupation site	Late Magdalenian ~11–12,000 BP (dates for cultural levels between which remains were found)	Partial cranial and postcranial skeleton of adult female	No associations	Chauvière 2001; Henry-Gambier 2006
L'Homme de Chancelade (Raymonden-Chancelade, Dordogne)	Middle Magdalenian occupation site	Possibly Magdalenian III or IV	Complete skeleton of adult male, laid on left side and highly flexed	Ochre staining in area of skeleton	May 1986
Aven des Iboussières (Drôme)	Talus cone accumulation in small cave	OxA-5682, 10,210 ± 80 BP (AMS ^{14}C measurement on faunal remains from horizon containing human remains)	Fragmentary remains of several individuals	Ochre staining, faunal remains, and engraved bones found in homogeneous horizon within talus cone	Gély and Morand 1998; D'Errico and Vanhaeren 2000
Italy					
Riparo di Villabruna	Final Epigravettian occupation site	Final Epigravettian layer dated to 12,040 ± 120 BP (R-2022). Direct AMS ^{14}C measurement on skeleton 12,140 ± 70 BP (KIA-27004)	Complete skeleton of adult male ~25 years old, laid extended on its back in rectangular grave cutting	Burial covered by stone blocks, decorated with red painted geometric motifs	Broglio 1995; Mussi 2001; Vercellotti *et al.* 2008
Maritza 1 (Grotta Maritza, Abruzzo)	Final Epigravettian occupation site	Probably ~13–10,000 BP	Partial skeleton (disturbed) of adult male	Partially articulated, otherwise unclear	Fabbri 1992; Mussi 2001; Henry-Gambier 2003

continued . . .

Table 7.1 continued

Maritza 2 (Grotta Maritza, Abruzzo)	Final Epigravettian occupation site	Probably ~14,000 BP	Partial skeleton of ~7–8-year-old child	Found close to the cave's wall, laid extended on its back. Flint tools and perforated shells associated with the burial	Fabbri 1992; Mussi 2001; Henry-Gambier 2003
Riparo Tagliente, Veneto	Final Epigravettian occupation site	Final Epigravettian, 13,070 ± 70 BP (OxA-3531) and 13,270 ± 170 BP (OxA-3532)	Adult male and child burials, probably interred separately	Burial covered by stone blocks, one of which bore an engraving of a lion and others with ochre	Bartolomei *et al.* 1974; Broglio 1995; Mussi 2001; Henry-Gambier 2003
Riparo del Romito, Calabria	Epigravettian occupation site	Upper layer 10,250 ± 450 BP (R-298); lower layer 11,150 ± 150 BP (R-300). Latter dates the Romito 1 and 2 double burial	Six individuals in four graves (two single, two double)	Details scanty: double burial of adult female and adolescent male dwarf; latter apparently resting on and cradled by former. Both placed next to engraved stone block	Graziosi 1963; Frayer *et al.* 1987, 1988; Mussi *et al.* 1989; Mussi 2001
Grotta Vado All' Arancio, Tuscany	Epigravettian occupation site	Epigravettian: probably ~13,400 BP	Adult male and 1–2-year-old infant buried close to each other in extended position	A clear oval-shaped grave cutting was obvious. Both associated with flint tools and perforated shells	Fabbri 1992; Henry-Gambier 2001, 2003
Grotta dei Fanciulli 1 and 2	Epigravettian occupation site	Level C Epigravettian occupation level. 11,130 ± 100 BP (GifA-94197, direct AMS ^{14}C measurement on cranial fragment)	Two infants ~2 and 3 ±1 years old at death and probably of the same (indeterminate) sex, laid extended side-by-side on their backs in a clear grave cutting	Several hundred perforated shells around the waist and pelvic region of both individuals	Mussi 2001; Henry-Gambier 2001, 2003

Grotta dei Fanciulli 3	Epigravettian occupation site	Level B (interred later than the infants); shell midden in layer dated to 12,200 ± 400 BP (MC-499) although probably an over-estimate (date on shell); recent work suggests age younger than 11,000 BP	Poorly preserved skeleton of adult female, laid on back in extended position in clear grave cutting	Level rich in perforated shells, although association with burial is unclear	Mussi 2001; Henry-Gambier 2001, 2003, 2005
Grotta di San Teodoro 1–5, Sicily	Epigravettian occupation site	Burials derive from the lower Epipalaeolithic level; minimum age of 12,200 ± 400 BP (AMS ^{14}C measurement on charcoal from overlying hearth) and probably ~14–13,000 BP on basis of dates for other Sicilian Epigravettian sites	Five adults, four male and one probably female. ST4 bore sclerosis of bone following damage caused by arrowhead. Details of other burials unclear	All appear to have been associated with ochre. ST4: laid in extended position. Associations include an antler and several small cobbles. Small flint flake embedded in pelvis, probably part of an arrowhead	Mussi et al. 1989; Fabbri 1992; Bachechi et al. 1997; D'Amore et al. 2009

Russia

Kostenki 2 (Zamiatnin)	Late Upper Palaeolithic mammoth bone construction site of unclear cultural affiliation	Unclear: dates on mammoth bones from the site vary greatly between ~11,000 BP and 37,000 BP. Unclear cultural association precludes culture-chronological dating.	Partial, disarticulated and disturbed remains of adult male found inside structure of mammoth bone and tusk	No associated cultural items	Sinitsyn 2004
Kostenki 18 (Khvoiko)	Occupation site of Kostenki-Avdeevo attribution	Probably younger than ~19,000 BP on the basis of oldest ages for the Kostenki-Avdeevo occupation of the site	Skeleton of 9–10-year-old child buried on its left side, in triangular grave	Skeleton covered by levels of mammoth bones (partially disturbed by recent activity). No associations	Sinitsyn 2004

Figure 7.3 European Late Upper Palaeolithic burials discussed in the text.

of Levantine burial is the complete skeleton of an adult male recovered from a shallow grave cutting at Ohalo II on the shore of the Sea of Galilee, Israel (Hershkovitz *et al.* 1995; Figure 7.4). The site is a large Epipalaeolithic settlement assigned to an early phase of the Kebaran complex and is dated to ~19,000 BP. The body (Burial H2) had been laid supine, hands crossed over its chest, and the legs highly flexed, with the bones of the heel close to the pelvis (Figure 7.4). The head was raised on three large stones. Despite careful excavation in the laboratory of the skeleton from its hard sedimentary context, no evidence of any personal ornamentation or grave inclusions beyond the lithics and fauna common to the occupation level was apparent, although several gazelle mandibles were found in close proximity.

In Europe, the richest data by far derives from France and Italy, and in both countries the data cluster into certain periods suggesting that burial traditions were not transmitted continuously over the Late Upper Palaeolithic. Although most French burials of the period were excavated during the infancy

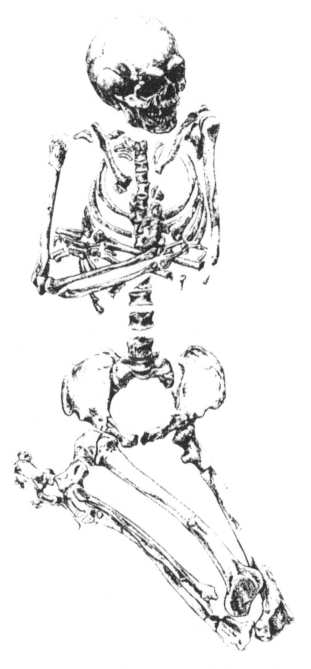

Figure 7.4 Plan of the Ohalo II burial, Israel (courtesy of Israel Hershkovitz and Dani Nadel).

of archaeology, direct AMS ^{14}C dating of known burials has revealed that elaborate burial was practised in the Middle Magdalenian in particular (Gambier *et al.* 2000). The dating of the La Madeleine infant to the Terminal Pleistocene shows either that burials belong to two distinct phases or that the practice persisted, on occasion, beyond the Magdalenian *sensu stricto* and into the Azilian and beyond. Gambier *et al.* (2000, 208) favour the former, suggesting that the clear and unambiguous examples of primary burials belong in the main to the earlier, Middle Magdalenian, phase (St Germain la Rivière, Bruniquel, Duruthy, Cap Blanc, Chancelade), whereas the La Madaleine child, the burials of the Aven des Iboussières and, probably, Les Hoteaux, belong to the younger phase.

Fragmentary human remains pertaining to at least to six adults and six infants were scattered throughout the Early and Middle Magdalenian levels at St Germain la Rivière on the banks of the Dordogne (Gambier and Lenoir 1991; Gambier *et al.* 2000, 206–7; Henry-Gambier *et al.* 2002). At least two of these relate to burials that were emplaced on the terrace below the smaller of two rockshelters at the site during the Middle Magdalenian (III) ~17,000–14,000 BP (Gambier *et al.* 2000; Henry-Gambier *et al.* 2002; Figure 7.5). One of these is poorly understood, but the second – the 'Dame de Saint-Germain-la-Rivère' – is well documented (Blanchard *et al.* 1972). A young adult female was buried in a grave cut into the limestone substrate, within which ochre stained everything (Figure 7.6). She was laid on her left side in a highly flexed position, and was protected by four large stone slabs, two of which effectively covered the entire corpse. A direct date of 15,780 ± 200 BP (GifA 95456) confirms her Middle Magdalenian attribution (Gambier *et al.* 2000). Grave goods comprised two red deer antler 'daggers' and a perforated rod made from a red deer rib, various flint tools including blades, endscrapers and burins and a large core. The body was ornamented by at least 71 perforated red deer canines, ten of which bear engraved decoration, one *Trivia europea* shell pendant and a steatite bead, although the exact position of the finds relative to the burial is unclear (Vanhaeren and d'Errico 2003). It is possible that a hearth and faunal remains found in close proximity to the grave represent a funerary ritual. Vanhaeren and d'Errico (ibid.) have conducted an analysis of the ornamentation associated with the burial, demonstrating that a preference for the teeth of young deer stags is evident. As with the personal ornamentation on the La Madeleine infant discussed below, the considerable time required for the manufacture of these ornaments presumably suggests a degree of status for the 'Dame'. The relevance of the personal ornamentation for social distinction is even more relevant when one considers that the nearest contemporary sites that demonstrate red deer exploitation (and thus availability) are in Spanish Pays Basque ~300km distant – at the upper limit of the range of hunter–gatherer groups. To Vanhaeren and d'Errico the pendants must have been obtained through prestige exchange of items with complex social meaning, and the exotic derivation of the red deer teeth is supported by stable isotope analysis of the female's bones that indicates

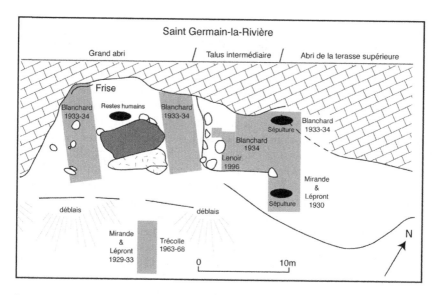

Figure 7.5 Plan of the rockshelter at Saint-Germain-la-Rivère showing the location of burials and human remains (from Vanhaeren and d'Errico 2003, and courtesy of Francesco d'Errico and Marian Vanhaeren).

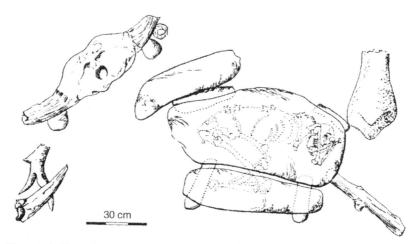

Figure 7.6 Plan of the Saint-Germain-la-Rivère burial showing location of human remains under large stone blocks (from Vanhaeren and d'Errico 2003, and courtesy of Francesco d'Errico and Marian Vanhaeren).

that red deer contributed no more than 20 per cent to her dietary protein (Drucker and Henry-Gambier 2005).

The Abri Lafaye at Bruniquel, on the bank of the Aveyron River in Tarn et Garonne, contained a number of Magdalenian levels rich in art and bone-work. The remains of at least three individuals were recovered here apparently from the same level; a near-complete skeleton of an adult female, a complete skeleton of an infant ~3 years at death and an adult cranium (Gambier et al. 2000). The near-complete remains of the adult female and child appear to have derived from a double burial, and the isolated cranium was found several metres away against the shelter's wall, although it is possible that this is intrusive as ceramics were also recovered from the area (Gambier 1990). A direct date of 15,290 ± 150 BP on the adult female, however, confirms a Middle Magdalenian attribution of the double burial (probably Magdalenian IV rather than V, as harpoons are absent; Gambier et al. 2000).

The recovery of the skeleton of a young adult male from a shallow grave in the cave of Les Hoteaux (Ain) seems to represent a burial probably associated with the Late Magdalenian (Magdalenian VI: May 1986). This was apparently placed atop a hearth ~3m from the cave's wall, and associated with other fragmentary human remains and a perforated bâton laid alongside its right thigh (Figure 7.7). A large stone lay under the head, and the whole area was ochre-stained, and a perforated reindeer tooth was found close to the head. Unfortunately, excavation standards were poor, although notes suggest that the bones of the skeleton had been displaced and were not fully in articulation. Given this, and the staining of all parts of the bones with ochre, the excavator, Abbé Tournier, concluded that the remains probably represented a secondary burial (discussed in May 1986, 52 and Wüller 1999, 55–76). No cut marks were observed on the bones, however, thus it was felt that the disarticulation must have occurred naturally. Overall, the context and general articulation of the skeleton, and its associations, suggest that this was a burial.

The great rockshelter at La Madeleine, on the banks of the Vézère River close to Les-Eyzies-de-Tayac, contained three major Magdalenian beds corre-sponding to the Middle and Late Magdalenian that form the type assemblages of the Magdalenian IV, V and VI. These are subdivided into 14 rich Magdalenian levels with overlying Azilian levels, demonstrating the long-term importance of this major habitation site from ~15,000 to the end of the Pleistocene. A number of fragmentary human remains were found throughout these levels, although attention has understandably focussed on a single inhumation cut from its upper levels. An infant ~2–4 years at death was laid extended on its back in a large grave cut into Magdalenian IV levels and 2.6m from the cave's rear wall (Figure 7.8). The grave was banked up with sediment excavated from the levels above. The whole area was richly stained with ochre. A direct date of 10,190 ± 100 BP indicates a Terminal Pleistocene age (and probably Azilian context) for the burial (Gambier et al. 2000).[25] Three stones were placed at the infant's head, and numerous perforated teeth

Figure 7.7 The Les Hoteux remains laid out (from Tournier 1898).

and shells were found at the head, elbows, wrists, knees and ankles. According to the excavators, these include at least 900 *Dentalium*, 160 *Neritina*, 36 *Turritella* and 20 *Cyclope* shells (Taborin 1993), and in view of this Gambier *et al.* (2000, 206) have remarked on the similarities of this child's burial with those of the Epipalaeolithic of Italy. Vanhaeren and d'Errico (2001) have undertaken an exhaustive study of the personal ornamentation associated with the infant. Today, a minimum of 1,275 *Dentalium*, 99 *Neritina*, 25 *Turritella*, 13 *Cyclope* shells and pendants of two deer canines and two fox canines can be clearly associated with the burial, and the manufacturing time required for the production of the ornaments must suggest social standing on the part of the infant. The shell pendants of the burial show a clear selection bias; the dimensions of the shells is not that found among natural populations of the four species nor among the shells found in the occupation levels, but falls into the lower size range of these classes, as is also found with the child burials in the Grotta dei Fanciulli (see pp. 243–4). Clearly, smaller shells were collected for the ornamentation of an infant, whereas larger shells were appropriate for adults. This 'miniturisation' of infants' personal ornamentation seems to have been widespread in the Mid and Late Upper Palaeolithic, and presumably reflects the symbolic differences of adult and pre-adult age classes and the integration of children into hierarchic social systems (ibid., 228).

Several other French Magdalenian sites have yielded human remains from contexts suggestive of burial, although the early excavations at these sites and available information render it impossible today to establish this beyond doubt. These should, however, be regarded as *likely* burials. In this category one might include the skeleton of an adult male from Laugerie-Basse (Dordogne), which was found underneath a large stone block in a Middle Magdalenian level, laid on its left side in flexed position and associated with ~20 *Cypraea* shell pendants at various parts of the body (May 1986). Originally termed the 'crushed man (homme écrassé) of Laugerie-Basse' as it was thought that he was a victim of a rock fall, the position and preservation of the skeleton in a thick and rich occupation horizon suggests that it was a deliberate burial (Figure 7.9). An adult female was found in a similar position under the shelter at Cap Blanc (Dordogne) in deposits containing a Magdalenian assemblage overlooked by a sculpted frieze of horses on the shelter's rear wall. Large stone blocks were found over her head and feet, although no cultural items were recovered with the skeleton (May 1986, 39; Sacchi 1993). The virtually complete skeleton of an adult male found within Middle Magdalenian levels at the Raymonden-Chancelade rockshelter (Dordogne) was found in a highly flexed position, its knees actually in contact with its mandible (Figure 7.10). Ochre staining was found around the skeleton, although it is unclear whether other items found close to the skeleton such as a flint endscraper and an antler *sagaie* were deliberate grave inclusions. It is almost certainly a burial (Billy 1992).

At least two adults seem to have been buried under the Duruthy rockshelter at Sorde-l'Abbaye, Landes, during the Middle Magdalenian (Henry-Gambier

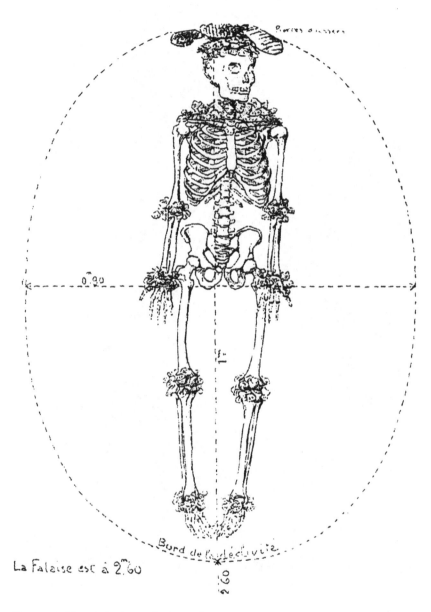

Figure 7.8 Plan of the La Madeleine infant burial (from Capitan and Peyrony 1928).

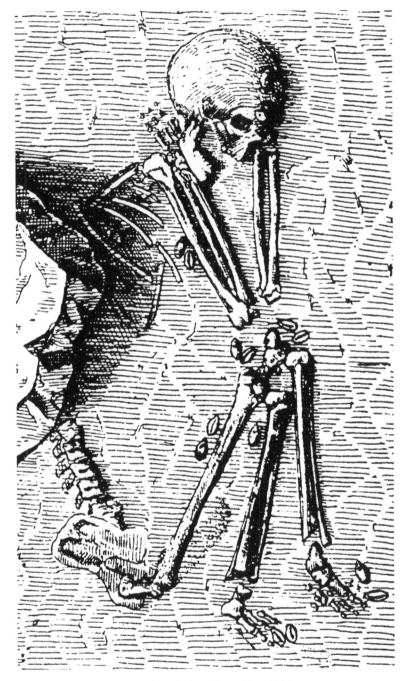

Figure 7.9 The Laugerie-Basse burial (from Cartailhac 1889).

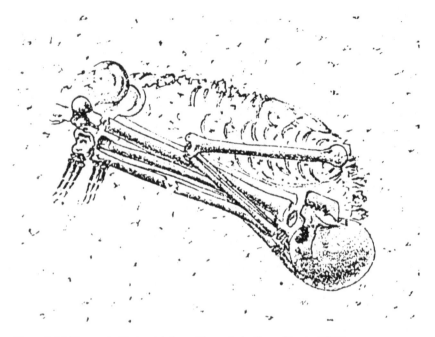

Figure 7.10 The probable burial from Chancelade (from Hardy 1891).

2006). Sorde 1 comprises only the upper part of a cranium and partial femur, apparently buried towards the rear of the rockshelter. A number of canines of lion and bear were found in close proximity to the burial. Sorde 3 comprises the partial skeleton of an adult female, apparently interred close to Sorde 1 and without any obvious associations other than fragmentary bones. Stratigraphically the two appear to have been contemporary, and lay between Magdalenian levels 3 and 4 with dates of 11,150 ± 220 BP (Ly 858) and 13,510 ± 220 BP (Ly 859) respectively (ibid., 70). Large stone blocks were found around the crania of both individuals, which may account for the preservation of these parts, whereas much of the postcrania were missing, although it is still unclear as to whether the blocks were deliberately placed or simply fortuitous. As Henry-Gambier (ibid., 73) has noted, Sorde 1 and 2 are exceptional among Magdalenian burials as they contain no grave goods. An analysis by Chauvière (2001) of 49 available lion and bear teeth found with Sorde 1 has revealed that 16 of the teeth were perforated and engraved; a further 14 were perforated and undecorated, and 19 were unmodified. The collection is remarkably heterogeneous and possibly accumulated over several events, bringing into question the generally held notion that this was one set of personal ornamentation buried with Sorde 1.

Towards the end of the Pleistocene around eight individuals were buried in the small cave of the Aven des Iboussières, Drôme, southeast France (Gély

241

and Morand 1998). Here, numerous burials were recovered from a talus cone, along with fragments of charcoal, ochre, and a number of art objects, and a direct AMS ^{14}C measurement of 10,210 ± 80 BP (OxA-5682) provides an age for what is probably a homogeneous deposit (d'Errico and Vanhaeren 2000). A large amount of shell and teeth ornaments and pendants of bone, as well as engraved stone pebbles, worked flints and tools of bone and faunal remains, derive from the deposit (ibid., 332–3). The shell ornaments include *Dentalium* sp., *Cardium* sp., *Trivia europea* and *Cyclope neritea*, and deer canines ('*Croches de Cerf*') dominated the perforated teeth, indicating that these species retained their symbolic importance to the end of the Pleistocene and were common to both the Late Magdalenian and Azilian (ibid., 336).

It is clear, then, that most French Late Upper Palaeolithic burials date to the Middle Magdalenian, with one, possibly two, examples from the Late Pleistocene in Late Magdalenian and post-Magdalenian contexts. The dominance of rockshelters is striking, and suggests that the dead were contextualised in the centre of domestic space, rather than being interred in caves of the dead. This pattern holds for the few burials known for the period elsewhere.

A rich set of examples of Late Upper Palaeolithic burial exist for Italy, and all belong to Epigravettian cultural contexts (Fabbri 1992). Where these have been dated they belong to the last 3,000 years of the Pleistocene, none apparently older than ~13,000 BP (Mussi 2001a). These Italian Late Upper Palaeolithic burials, while generally similar to those of the Mid Upper Palaeolithic, differ in several details: corpses were laid in extended position rather than flexed on the side, they contain different grave goods, and they are often present in greater numbers at sites, at least towards the end of the period (Henry-Gambier 2003). The sample can be divided into two chronological groups (Henry-Gambier 2003), one dating to ~13,000–12,000 BP (i.e. the first half of the Lateglacial Interstadial) and another to ~11,000–10,000 BP (i.e. the Younger Dryas), which includes the cemetery of Arene Candide discussed below. Burials are found over the entire peninsula from Liguria in the northwest to Sicily, and a number of features unite the burials, suggesting that the practice had by now become general tradition shared over Epigravettian space. Unlike in the Italian Mid Upper Palaeolithic, infants and females are represented more commonly, and a degree of regionalisation in grave goods has been noted by Mussi (2001a, 349). Five examples derive from the earlier period; Riparo Tagliente, Riparo di Villabruna, Grotta Maritza, San Teodoro and probably Grotta Vado All'Arancio.

In the Riparo Tagliente (Veneto) an adult male was buried supine in extended position in a grave cutting 60cm deep in its centre. The grave was surrounded and covered by stone blocks, two of which were engraved and one of which was placed between the male's feet; the bones were stained with ochre, and a fragment of bison horn and a pierced *Cyclope* shell were recovered from the grave (Bartolomei *et al.* 1974; Broglio 1995). A similar single burial of an adult male was placed in a grave cutting in the Riparo di Villabruna, also from a Final Epigravettian context, clearly associated with several flint artefacts (ibid.). AMS ^{14}C measurements from each burial indicate ages of ~13,000 and ~12,000 BP respectively. In the Grotta Maritza (Abruzzo) an infant (Maritza 2) was laid extended on its back in a shallow grave close to the cave's wall, and the partial remains of an adult (Maritza 1), although disturbed (probably by carnivores) seems also to have been a primary burial (Henry-Gambier 2003). Flint artefacts and perforated shells were associated with Maritza 2. A similar burial of an adult male and a child close by in the Grotta Vado All'Arancio (Tuscany), although undated, may belong to the same tradition, and were also associated with flint tools and perforated shells. These examples reveal a tradition of simple inhumation with little grave goods except basic personal ornamentation and flint tools.

The remains of seven individuals – including five adults (four male and one probably female) – were apparently buried in the San Teodoro cave on Sicily, probably between ~14,000 and 13,000 BP (Mussi *et al.* 1989). Of these, five are highly fragmentary (ST2, 3, 5–7: d'Amore *et al.* 2009). Little contextual information is available for these, although at least some seem to have been buried in a restricted area of the cave and stained with ochre. ST1 and 4, however, are near-complete. ST1 was inhumed in extended position, and ST5 seems to have been a secondary burial. San Teodoro 4, the probable female, was buried with a cervid antler and with several stone cobbles, and a flint flake – probably the distal part of a geometric microlith – was embedded in her pelvis (Bachechi *et al.* 1997).

Several burials are known from the end of the period in Italy, of which perhaps the most famous child burials are those of the eponymous Grotta dei Fanciulli/Grotte des Enfants. In fact three individuals – an adult female and two infants were buried on separate occasions within a century either side of ~11,000 BP in the cave. Little information is available for the adult female, although the double child burial is well recorded. Two infants, both probably of the same sex and ~2 and 3±1 years old at death, were laid side-by-side, supine and in extended position in a shallow grave cutting (Figure 7.11). The hands of each were placed at their sides, and their heads were turned to the right. Several hundred perforated *Cyclope neritea* and *Trivia europea* shells adorned the waist and pelvic regions of both arranged in linear rows. It seems sensible to interpret these as having been sewn onto items of clothing such as loincloths, although Henry-Gambier (2001, 118) has suggested that they may have adorned 'une structure de protection périssable posée sur les corps après leur dépôt'. No evidence of colouring such as ochre was found in the grave, nor any clear evidence of the deliberate inclusion of flint artefacts or faunal remains, with the possible exception of two rear leg phalanges of a cervid found by the ischium and sacrum of the first infant. A fragment of a triangular flint point was embedded in a thoracic vertebra of the second individual. Henry-Gambier's careful analysis (2001, 105–6) has shown that this was a perimortem phenomenon, and thus probably the cause of death of

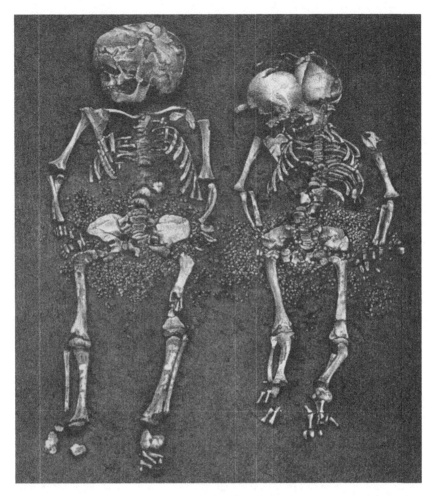

Figure 7.11 The Grotta dei Fanciulli double burial (Rivière, E. 1887. *De l'Antiquité de l'Homme dans les Alpes-Maritimes*. Paris: Ballière).

this individual. Both infants show evidence of periostitis, and the first individual (for whom a cause of death is unknown) bore rachitic lesions.

The complete skeletons of six individuals were recovered from four graves in the large rockshelter of the Riparo del Romito, Calabria, Italy (Graziosi 1963). Of these, four derive from the shelter's Epigravettian levels and comprise two single burials and one double burial, although details of these have not been published. Beneath these, an elderly adult female (Romito 1) and late-adolescent male (Romito 2) were placed together in a double burial, dated to 11,150 ± 150 BP. The two had been buried in a shallow grave of oval shape stratified below Final Epigravettian layers, lying parallel to a large stone bearing an engraving of three aurochs bulls. It is unclear whether the two were buried side-by-side at the same time, or whether one was inserted into the grave later in the style of the Grotta dei Fanciulli double burial; the excavator, P. Graziosi, noted that while they were buried 'one above the other' the female appeared to 'clasp' the adolescent, whose neck appeared to rest on her cheek (quoted in Frayer *et al.* 1988, 550). No further information is available about the burial, although the adolescent has achieved fame as being the earliest known example of an acromesomelic[26] dwarf (Frayer *et al.* 1987, 1988). This is of interest as the condition is hereditary and the individual would have clearly been marked out as 'different' from birth and, as Frayer *et al.* (1988, 564) have noted, his survival to late adolescence and subsequent burial among only six individuals at a rockshelter with intensive occupation presumably indicates a degree of status in life, for whatever reason. Formicola (2007) has compared Romito 2 with the pathological individuals buried at Dolní Věstonice and Sungir in the preceding Mid Upper Palaeolithic; all belong to multiple burials, and probably include individuals of both sexes. Noting that the dwarf's survival need not indicate high status (but that it could instead relate to fear, dislike or other reasons for grudging 'respect', and one must remember that he still died – or was killed – at a relatively young age) he notes the relative frequency of multiple burials and thus the possibility that sacrifice was practised.

The occurrence of double burials, in which at least one of the dead may have been killed following the death of the first, and the recovery of flint points embedded in the bones of one infant from the Grotta dei Fanciulli double burial and the San Teodoro burial suggest that some of the burials at least do not pertain to 'natural' or 'normal' deaths. Although one cannot rule these out, it may be that Italian Epigravettian burial practice followed the process of containment of the 'bad deaths' that seem to define the Mid Upper Palaeolithic burials discussed in Chapter 6. Once again, 'normal' definitions of burial may not apply to these examples.

Elsewhere, the picture is less clear. Fragmentary human remains from the open site of Neuwied-Irlich in the Rhineland represent an adult, child and a neonate, with possibly a mother and her infant buried together (Street *et al.* 2006). Other details of this burial are unknown, although the material is currently under re-analysis (J. Orschiedt pers. comm). Two adults – a female and a male – seem to have been buried close to each other at Bonn-Oberkassel, Germany (Verworn *et al.* 1919; Street *et al.* 2006; Figure 7.12). Although the skeletons were discovered by quarrymen, they seem to have been laid side-by-side, enough to suggest that this was a genuine double burial (Ralf Schmitz pers. comm.). Direct dating of the skeletons to 11,570 ±100 BP (male, OxA-4790) and 12,180 ±100 BP (female, OxA-4792) indicate an age of (11,800–12,000 BP for the burial, suggesting a 'bipointe' phase cultural association (Baales and Street 1998, 83–4). Although details are lacking for this early excavation, the remains of the two seem to have been found together

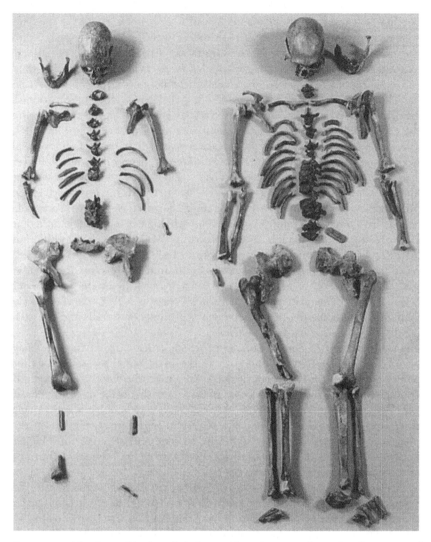

Figure 7.12 The Bonn-Oberkassel skeletons (from Street *et al.* 2006 and courtesy of Ralf Schmitz and LVR-LandesMuseum Bonn).

in an area intensely stained with ochre. The cranium and upper body of the female were particularly stained on the outer surfaces, indicating that the colourant was applied to clothing or to an intact body, rather than to disarticulated bones. Associations comprise the skeleton of a domesticated wolf, a bone pin with carved animal head, a flat carving of a cervid (probably on antler) and a cut marked red deer incisor stained with ochre (R. Schmitz pers. comm.). Alongside La Madeleine, Bonn-Oberkassel shows that the occasional practice of single and double burials occurred down to the end of the Palaeolithic, and can rightly be seen as the antecessor of Mesolithic inhumation traditions. Street *et al.* (2006, 568) have noted how both Neuwied-Irlich and Bonn-Oberkassel burials seem to have been isolated, placed away from settlements, which may suggest a regional tradition of separation of the dead from the world of the living.

A burial of a fœtus/neonate has been recovered from the Magdalenian open-air site of Wilczyce in southeast Poland (Irish *et al.* 2008). The site represents a seasonal hunting camp, probably relating to the exploitation of woolly rhinoceros, horse and other prey during late autumn or early winter, and is dated to 12,870 ± 60 BP (OxA-16729). As with much of the cultural material the infant remains were recovered from an ice-wedge cast, albeit from a restricted area ~1m^2 within it. A necklace of over 80 perforated teeth of arctic fox was recovered from the same restricted area and it is assumed that this was associated with the infant. The broader context of the burial within the site is of interest. Irish *et al.* (ibid., 739) note that it was found under a dwelling structure (a possible parallel with Pavlov I), amidst faunal waste, suggesting that it was disposed of rather than buried, although further details of its context and associations are necessary before this can be substantiated.

Mid Upper Palaeolithic burials from the Kostenki localities in Russia were discussed in Chapter 6. Two examples show that single inhumation of infants and adults continued on into the Late Upper Palaeolithic of the area, although the precise ages of the burials is unclear and they may relate to the earliest part of the period. No clear examples of burials are known for the region for the last few thousand years of the Pleistocene and in this the region differs from the European examples discussed above. At Kostenki 18 (Khvoiko) a 9–10-year-old child was laid on its left side at the bottom of a triangular-shaped grave 120cm in maximum dimension and 40cm deep (Sinitsyn 2004; Figure 7.13). No grave goods or ochre staining were apparent. Interestingly, two similarly sized and shaped pits were found at the site. These contained no burial, although they have been interpreted as 'cenotaph' burials. A further possibility is that pits that had been excavated for other purposes were on occasion adapted for funerary use, in a manner seen for the burial of infant Neanderthals discussed in Chapter 5.

The remains of a complex structure of mammoth bones and tusks at Kostenki 2 (Zamiatnin) formed an elongated construction (2.2 × 0.5m in size, inside which the partial skeleton of an adult male of great age was found (Sinitsyn 2004). The skeleton was poorly preserved in parts and disturbed, and further remains found outside the structure 1.5m to the north-west probably derive from the same individual. No cultural items were found with the skeleton and none exist for the site, and as radiocarbon measurements on mammoth bones from the site range considerably (from ~11,000 to ~37,000 BP) the site must be considered to be undated at present. Little can be said about these later Russian burials. Soffer (1985, 455) noted that they are less

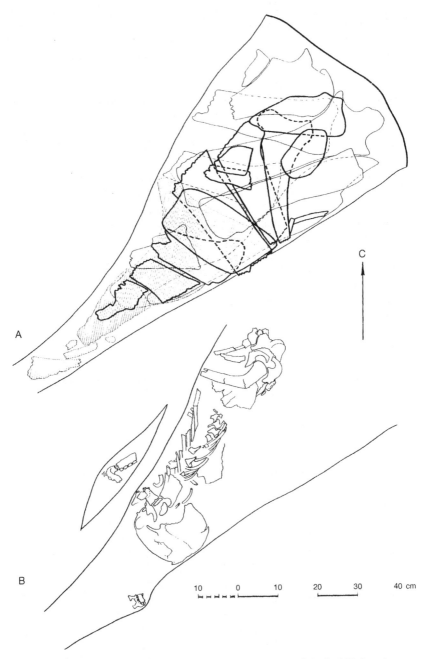

A

B

C

10   0   10   20   30   40 cm

Figure 7.13 Plan of the Kostenki 18 child burial (courtesy of Andrei Sinitsyn).

elaborate than the Mid Upper Palaeolithic examples from Kostenki XV and Sungir that were discussed in Chapter 6, and in this sense they parallel those of the European Upper Palaeolithic, although with such a small sample it is impossible to generalise about these.

Collectivity: the Late Pleistocene origins of cemeteries

It is clear from the discussion above that burials seem to have been largely a phenomenon of the millennia around 15,000–12,000 BP, although they reappear after 11,000 BP. Clearly the practice of single inhumation persisted down to the end of the Pleistocene in several regions of Europe and the Near East. During this time, however, indications appear of the formal burial of large numbers of individuals in specific sites set aside for the disposal of the dead. These traditions continue on into the Holocene, where a number of Mesolithic sites of collective burial are known. The formal term *cemetery* can be used for these sites (Table 7.2). As I defined it in Chapter 1, a cemetery *sensu stricto* is a place given over in the main or entirely to the dead, with little or no evidence of settlement. Strict cemeteries tend to be larger than places of multiple burial, and a degree of spatial organisation is often in evidence. The most striking difference with preceding burials, however, is the level of *collectivity* expressed in these places of the dead.

There are, I believe, reasons why the appearance of cemeteries towards the end of the Palaeolithic herald new beliefs and practices about the dead. It is tempting to link the greater numbers of burials and growing evidence of organisation to rising group sizes and longer sedentism (Chapman 1981; Coward and Gamble 2008) arising from a 'critical mass' of resource availability (Larsson 2004), and those factors could indeed explain the greater visibility of the dead in the archaeological record from this time. As Terberger (2006) and Brinch Petersen (2006) have noted, a number of individuals from Terminal Palaeolithic, Early Mesolithic and Late Mesolithic cemeteries show evidence of violence, itself possibly linked to demographic increase. The fact remains, however, that prior to this time, as I have suggested, burial was a remarkably rare phenomenon, and certainly cannot be taken to have been the funerary 'norm'. If this pertained for the Late Pleistocene, then there would be no a priori reason why more burials should be found on specific sites of Late Pleistocene age, as funerary practice – whatever it was – would still be archaeologically invisible. The fact that a new phenomenon appears in the archaeological record suggests that burial had taken on new meaning by this time. It is conceivable that in this period of human behavioural development burial became a 'normal' funerary practice, rather than an 'odd' practice perhaps associated with 'bad deaths' and other cosmological imbalances. Individuals become part of a wider 'cemetery site', which itself is a new phenomenon in the landscape: at such locations burials were no longer hidden away or subsumed within the settlement context, but instead combine to make large

Table 7.2 Epipalaeolithic cemeteries discussed in the text

Site	Chronology and context	Sample	Architectural and organisational features	Archaeological associations	References
Australia Kow Swamp	Discrepant dating: either ~19–21,000 BP or 15,000–9,000 BP	>40 individuals interred at the edge of the Kow Swamp palaeolake	Simple inhumations and at least one cremation	Grave goods include personal ornaments of shell and teeth, ochre, and quartz artefacts	Thorne and Macumber 1972
Italy Arene Candide 'Necropolis', Liguria	Epigravettian burials, probably deposited in two periods ~10,700 and ~10,000 BP	~20 individuals, young infants to elderly and of both sexes	Clear grave cuttings, both single and double inhumations. Graves lined by stones. Some burials disturbed by subsequent burials, some possible secondary burials	Ochre ubiquitous. Rich grave goods includes perforated red deer canines and shells. Two pairs of elk antlers found in the layer possibly functioned as markers	Cardini 1980; Fabbri 1992; Formicola *et al.* 2005
Grotta Romanelli (Apulia)	Epipalaeolithic Romanellian occupation site. Several ^{14}C measurements of levels range from ~12,000 to ~10,000 BP	Several burials of adults and children	Unclear	Unclear	Fabbri 1992; Mussi 2001
Grotta Polesini (Latium)	Epipalaeolithic occupation site with some Sauveterrian elements. One ^{14}C measurement of 10,090 ± 80 BP (R-1265)	MNI = 14 individuals including four children	Some bones ochre stained, otherwise unclear	Personal ornamentation of deer canines, shells and fish vertebrae	Mussi 2001
Morocco Taforalt (Tafoughalt) Cave	Late Pleistocene Epipalaeolithic Iberomaurusian cemetery and occupation site. Youngest burials probably ~11,000 BP	MNI of 40 individuals in 28 graves, some bearing cut marks and secondarily buried	Single, double and multiple inhumations, primary and secondary burials	Ochre staining	Mariotti *et al.* 2009

statements about the dead of society in the midst of the living (Cullen 1995). If there is any point in prehistory when an essentially 'modern' way of thinking about putting people into the ground emerged, then this is arguably it. It is impossible to establish what the specific dynamics of this new relationship with the dead were; the circumstances differ from region to region. Cemeteries appeared in Australia among hunter–gatherer adaptations that would persist for millennia before immigrants brought agriculture to the continent, whereas they appeared in the Near East among communities who had already become preconditioned for agriculture with their intensive hunter–gatherer interactions with the environment and with each other. Perhaps cemeteries – formally defined, recognisable and visible places of the dead – emerged alongside increasingly territorial notions of land and social space, at least where these accompanied growing population numbers and levels of sedentism and growing perceptions of investment in land, and in this sense it seems plausible to suggest that the emergence of formal cemeteries is part of what in broad terms may be regarded as 'agricultural thinking' (Gamble *et al.* 2005). This is not to say that single burials disappear. Far from it: as discussed above, these continue in Europe and the Near East into the Holocene, and, in fact, define the earliest examples of burial in the Americas.

The European Epipalaeolithic

At the end of the Pleistocene, at least 20 individuals were buried in the large Arene Candide cave, Liguria, in which ~14,000 radiocarbon years beforehand 'Il Principe' had been buried. These burials relate to a Late Epigravettian 'necropolis' in the words of the excavator, and herald in the cemetery (Figure 7.14). In many respects the Arene Candide 'necropolis' fits in with other terminal Pleistocene burials of Italy in terms of each of the individual burials, although given the number of burials at the site it is more appropriate to discuss it as an example of an early formal cemetery. The cave contains at least six single inhumations laid supine and extended (Burials II, VII, VIII, IX, XI, and a disturbed burial X); two double burials each containing an adult and child (V and VI) as several partial skeletons that were either probably burials themselves but had been disturbed by subsequent interments, or that represented secondary burials (burials I, III, IV, XII–XIII). Both sexes are represented although females are rare, and age classes range from early infancy to the elderly (Cardini 1980). Direct AMS ^{14}C measurements on burials III, Vb, Vib, VIII, XII and XIV show that the burials relate to two periods, around 10,700–10,600 BP and around 10,000 BP (Formicola *et al.* 2005). One of the 'disturbed' burials (III) dates to the younger period, that is, after which there were no subsequent inhumations, suggesting that it is a genuine example of secondary burial as suggested by Mussi *et al.* (1989). If this is so, clearly the practice of gathering together in one place the bones of a disarticulated individual would not be done to faciliate further burials, suggesting that the

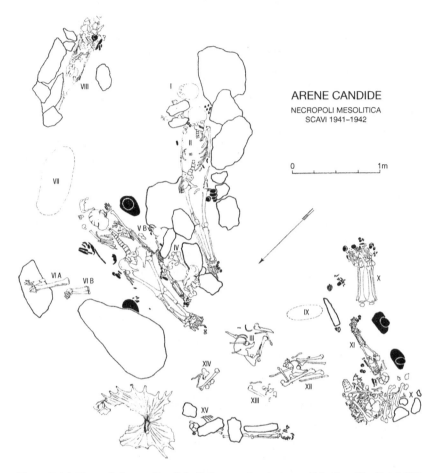

ARENE CANDIDE

NECROPOLI MESOLITICA
SCAVI 1941–1942

0 ⌐_____ 1m

Figure 7.14 Plan of Arene Candide Epigravettian 'necropolis' after Cardini 1980,
showing the position of burials. I adult male; II adult male; III adult
female; IV adult male; Va adult male with Vb 2–4 year-old-infant; Via
adult of indeterminate sex with Vb 6–7-year-old infant; VII neonate;
VIII 8-year-old child; IX neonate; X adult male; XI 2–4-year-old child;
XII adult male; XIII adult female; XIV adult female, XV adolescent of
indeterminate sex; XVb adult of indeterminate sex; XVI infant; XVII
adolescent female; XVIII adult male (identifications quoted in Henry-
Gambier 2001).

practice was important in its own right (Formicola *et al.* 2005, 1602). The
double burials in the cave stress a bond between males and children, whereas
female burials are rare and are accompanied by poor grave goods, possibly
pointing to patrilineal status and succession (Mussi 2001b). Ochre was
abundant in the cave, and the burials were accompanied by rich and varied
grave goods. These included the ubiquitous red deer canines, perforated *Patella*,

Pectunculus and *Nassa* shells, and the mandibles and limb bones of small animals, particularly *Castor* sp. and *Erinaceus europaeus*. Articulated sets of the caudal vertebrae of squirrels were found in the chest area exclusively of non-adults, indicating that squirrel tails were worn on their clothing. Two pairs of elk antlers (a rare animal in Late Pleistocene Italy) were recovered from the stratum, again ochre-stained and one bearing punctiform decoration infilled with ochre. Neither pair were associated with any specific burial, although they may have functioned as visible markers inside the cave (Formicola *et al.* 2005, 1600). Clearly, the cave was used repeatedly for formal burial in at least two periods, possibly with the marking of the graves with stone blocks, and with the marking of the cemetery itself with decorated elk antlers. The later burials in the cave straddle the Pleistocene–Holocene transition and herald the Mesolithic, and the existence of cemeteries in the Italian Mesolithic (Mussi 2001a, 349) suggests that the tradition continued on from its Pleistocene origins. A similar phenomenon probably obtained ~10,000 BP in the Grotta Polesini in Latium, although details of the burials went largely unrecorded. At least 14 individuals were buried in the cave, including males, females and four infants, and many of the bones were ochre-stained. A large number of items of personal ornamentation of perforated deer canines and shells including *Columbella rustica*, *Cyclope neritea*, *Pectunculus*, *Dentalium* and *Pecten* reveal a similarity to Arene Candide, in addition to which at least 260 fish vertebrae pendants were found (Mussi 2001a, 293). Less clear, although conceivably similar, are the apparent burials of adults and children recovered in the Grotta Romanelli, Apulia, for which little information is available (ibid., 298). Overall, enough information exists to reveal a strong tradition of emerging cave cemeteries in the peninsula.

The Natufian

Over 400 burials are known from the Near Eastern Natufian ~13,000–10,300 BP (D. Nadel pers. comm.). Complex mortuary ritual is in evidence; Natufian funerary activity included single burials, secondary burial, the use of cairns, stone circles and tumuli, decoration of the dead, disarticulation and treatment of skulls, and the association of grave goods, and burials contain plentiful evidence for symbolic activity in connection with funerary activity (Nadel 1994). Graves have been found on base camps and small settlement sites, in contexts suggestive of their placement outside dwelling structures or within abandoned ones, but not underneath existing houses (Bar-Yosef 1998). Graves could be shallow or deep, and were occasionally defined by 'architectural' elements such as stone or plaster paving. Considerable variability is evident; bodies could be supine or flexed, and both single and multiple inhumations are known. Several examples are known where skulls have been removed from burials, a practice that continued into the Neolithic of the region. Among at least 18 burials in Raqefet Cave, for example, one, possibly two bear evidence of the part-disarticulation of the head before burial (Nadel *et al.* 2008a, 2008b). Secondary burials are often found mixed with primary burials (as in Raqefet Cave), a number of which appear to have been disturbed. Dogs are well known from Natufian settlements and were included with at least two burials; a grave containing three humans and two dogs was cut into one of two semi-subterranean dwellings at Hayonim Terrace during the late Natufian, a complex sequence of deposits in which the relationship between humans and dogs was explicitly symbolised (Tchernov and Valla 1997). Clear grave goods, as opposed to accidental inclusions from the settlement deposits, typically comprise a variety of items of personal ornamentation. The variability of funerary practice, such as primary single burials, collective secondary burials, ochre-staining of bones and burnt human remains recovered from settlement contexts can be seen from the earliest Natufian period, for example at Wadi Hammeh 27, Jordan (Webb and Edwards 2002). A violent death is attested at Kebara Cave, where the fragment of a lunate point was embedded into the vertebra of an adult buried in a multiple burial pit dated to 11,150 ± 400 BP (Bocquentin and Bar-Yosef 2004).

Africa

Several sites on the African continent attest the development of burial traditions during the Late Stone Age and beyond (Figure 7.15). Between 20,000 and 25,000 BP a young adult male was buried on an Upper Palaeolithic settlement site at Wadi Kubbaniya near Aswan in southern Egypt (Wendorf and Schild 1986). He was buried face down and in extended position. Two chalcedony bladelets were found within his abdominal area, probably the cause of his death. Given this, the face-down position is of interest. The remains of two individuals, one near-complete and the other fragmentary, were recovered from Upper Palaeolithic levels at Dar-es-Soltane 2, Morocco (Debénath 2000, 137). A radiocarbon measurement on a shell from the same level indicates an age of 16,500 ± 250 BP (UQ-1558). The near-complete skeleton was that of a young adult female, laid atop a large stone in a grave cutting on her left side in a highly flexed position and covered with a cairn of small stones. No obvious grave goods accompanied the burial with the possible exception of an ochre-stained cobble. The fragmentary remains bear traces of post-mortem smashing, and seem to indicate the reburial of remains originally buried elsewhere (ibid., 138). Although this does not seem to represent a cemetery, it provides a precedent for complex primary and secondary burials that are found in cemetery contexts later in North Africa.

At least 28 multiple burials containing at least 40 individuals[27] were recovered from Taforalt cave in eastern Morocco, deriving from an Iberomaurusian context dated to ~11,000–10,000 BP. Although excavation details of the burials are scanty – no plans or detailed descriptions are available – an admirable reconstruction of the funerary activity of the cave has been undertaken by

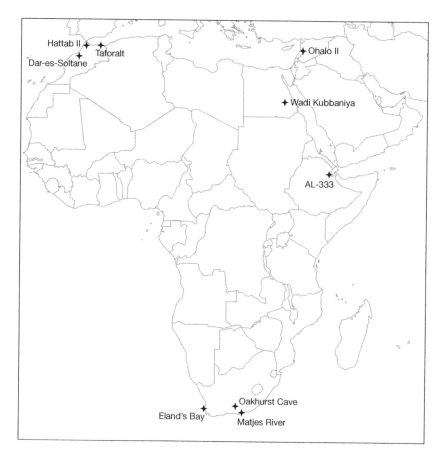

Figure 7.15 African Late Pleistocene burial and cemetery sites. The AL-333 site (discussed in Chapter 3) and Ohalo II burial (see pp. 232–3) are also marked.

Mariotti *et al.* (2009). The cemetery seems to have been restricted to the darkest area at the deepest part of the cave, isolated from the settlement area of the site by a large boulder. It seems to have comprised two 'necropoli', each comprising a cavity 7m and 10m long respectively, each containing the remains of multiple individuals 'emboîtées les unes dans les autres' (the excavator, quoted in Mariotti *et al.* 2009, 342). In this sense they seem to be reminiscent of the Mid Upper Palaeolithic Předmostí mass grave discussed in Chapter 6. It is unclear whether the burials relate to a relatively discrete period of time or whether they accumulated over a long period; informal references by the excavator to a 'stratigraphy' of each necropolis and the sheer number of individuals suggest the latter is more likely. If that is the case, the necropoli point to a long-standing tradition of burial in the same 'cemeteries'.

The 'graves' contained single, double and multiple individuals, in the latter case typically 3–7 individuals of both sexes. Both primary and secondary burials are in evidence in all graves, attesting to complex funerary traditions at the site. Ochre-stained bones were found in 13 graves as well as isolated pieces, and staining was typically resticted to the head area, pelvis, hands and chest. New excavations in the cave have uncovered infant burials placed under stones deliberately selected for their blue colour (N. Barton pers. comm.). The distribution of ochre on the stained bones suggests that it was applied after the soft tissues had been removed from the bones, confirming that bones were removed from graves for secondary treatment and reburial (Mariotti *et al.* 2009, 347). This seems to have been a long-practised tradition as even bones from the lowest 'strata' of the cemetery bear evidence of this treatment. Cut marks were found on several cranial and postcranial elements from five graves – all male – most seemingly relating to processing before ochre-staining.

Defleshing may have been a wider Epipalaeolithic tradition in North Africa. Cut marked human remains have been recovered from several early and Mid Holocene sites in the Maghreb, and were recovered from the Capsian[28] of Site 12 in Algeria (~8000 BP). At Site 12, the remains of at least six individuals – an adult female, adult (probable female), adolescent and three adult males – were recovered from separate stratigraphic levels, suggesting once again a long tradition (Haverkort and Lubell 1999), and there are several indications of a continuation of traditions from the Iberomaurusian to the Capsian (ibid., 166). These burials were associated with hearths and ochre, and show evidence of decapitation and partial dismemberment, and missing skeletal elements suggest that parts – particularly skulls – have been deliberately removed. Following Kuijt (1996), Haverkort and Lubell link this practice to nomadism, whereupon the bodies of recently deceased individuals are 'prepared' on the move by the removal of internal organs and a degree of decomposition but only finally interred when the group reaches the appropriate place.

Thus, four points in time – 20,000–25,000 BP at Wadi Kubbaniya, ~16,000 BP at Dar-es-Soltane 2, a period of perhaps one to two millennia down to ~10,000 BP at Taforalt, and as late as ~8,000 BP in the Magreb – attest to complex traditions of primary burials, defleshing and dismemberment, secondary burial and an emphasis on skulls – enough to suggest that this was a long-standing tradition – 'a certain continuity' (Mariotti *et al.* 2009, 352) – that was ultimately linked to the late hunter–gatherer and early agricultural traditions of the Near East (Kuijt 1996). This persistence in the region down to the origins of agriculture is further supported by a TL date of 8,900 ± 1,100 BP on a burnt flint associated with the burial of a young adult male in an Iberomaurusian context at Hattab II Cave in northwest Morocco (Barton *et al.* 2008).

In South Africa, although a number of sites were poorly excavated and recorded, enough data exist to show that cemeteries had come into existence by the Late Pleistocene (Wadley 1997). Several examples originated around 10,000 BP, including Matjes River and Oakhurst Cave, and several burials at these sites were deposited in the same graves (L. Wadley pers. comm.). Most Stone Age burial sites are located on the coast, and were placed within caves and rockshelters and on open sites that were also used for settlement. A number of these sites were repeatedly used for burial, some sites yielding over 100 burials. Grave goods are common at some sites, and absent from others, suggestive of local tradition. Most examples are Holocene in age, although ^{14}C measurements of 10,860 ± 180 BP (OxA-478), 9,800 ± 160 BP (OxA-456) and 8,000 ± 95 BP (Pta-3729) on burials from Elands Bay suggest that the cemetery originated in the Late Pleistocene and continued in use into the Early Holocene. The older date derives from the skeleton of an adult male buried in an oval pit covered by four stones. Intriguingly, most burials in South Africa are located in the Cape and it is these that have the richest burials, the few from the interior being poorer (L. Wadley pers. comm.).

Curiously, no evidence for Pleistocene cemeteries is known for the interior of Africa, the few burials and places of multiple burial that are known being Mid Holocene and younger in age (L. Barham pers. comm.). The pattern seems to be genuine, and could, perhaps, relate to the developments among complex hunter–gatherer societies among whom agriculture spread (in the north) and those with coastal adaptations (in the south).

Australia

A number of Late Pleistocene burials are known from Australia, appearing ~16,000 BP and continuing into the Holocene (Pardoe 1988; Habgood and Franklin 2008; Figure 7.16). These are mainly isolated burials or those in small numbers, but a striking factor is the number of individuals recovered from individual site locations: 33 at Coobool Creek in New South Wales (spanning ~14,500–9,000 BP) and over 40 at Kow Swamp (discussed below). At Lake Victoria in New South Wales a cemetery 'estimated to contain at least 10,000 burials . . . dated some time after 10,000 BP' (Habgood and Franklin 2008) and by the Early–Mid Holocene 120 to 140 individuals in over 100 burials were recovered from Roonka near the mouth of the Murray River. A degree of variability is evident in the Late Pleistocene burials, from simple inhumations with grave goods (Kow Swamp and Keilor in Northern Victoria, Coobool Creek and Nacurrie in New South Wales), and a kneeling burial dated to 15,210 ± 160 BP (SUA-1805) and a cremation dated to 12,530 +1,630/−1,350 (ANU-705) both from Lake Tandou, New South Wales. A secondary burial of the disarticulated corpse of an adult female was placed in a small grave and partially covered with a flat stone at Liang Lemdubu on the Aru Islands for which stratigraphic information and ESR dating suggest an age of ~16,000–18,000 BP, and further evidence of dismemberment and secondary burial are known from Liang Nebulei Lisa nearby. Clearly, variable funerary traditions arose widely in Australia after the Last Glacial Maximum and continued on into the Holocene.

Figure 7.16 Australian cemetery sites discussed in the text. The Willandra Lakes (location of the Lake Mungo burials discussed in Chapter 4) are also shown.

Among this emerging Lateglacial variability is the development of the cemetery *sensu stricto*. The remains of over 40 individuals have been recovered from silts on the northwestern and eastern shores of the lake now represented by Kow Swamp at the edge of the Murray River floodplain in northern Victoria, Australia (Thorne and Macumber 1972). Although remains were recovered from several locations, most came from one area, the Spark Site, and had been interred into lake silts apparently soon after the silts had been deposited. [14]C measurements of ~9,000–15,000 BP are probably under-estimates, and a combination of OSL measurements and shoreline estimates suggest that the burials date to ~19,000–21,000 BP, that is, the height of the Last Glacial Maximum (Stone and Cupper 2003). A number of grave cuttings were clearly delineated by carbonate or manganese linings. One cremation is evident, and a number of the inhumations were accompanied by grave goods including shell and teeth ornaments, ochre, and quartz artefacts. Given the number of burials and their clustering in the main at one location, it is sensible to assume that this was a clearly defined cemetery location. The clustering of early cemeteries in the southeast of the continent is noticeable, and Pardoe (1988) has suggested that these functioned as territorial markers in the context of increasingly regionalised concentrations of groups at particular locales that began in the Late Pleistocene and intensified further in the Late Holocene. Favourable environmental factors that could account for increasingly territorial behaviour in the southeast include a temperate climate, pronounced primary growth and numerous water sources, areas of which may have permitted semi-sedentism (Lourandos 1997).

North America

Cemeteries also began to appear towards the end of the Pleistocene in the Americas, where they continue intermittently into the Holocene (Chatters in press). The secondary burials of at least ten cremated individuals were recovered in the Marmes rockshelter in Washington State dated by radiocarbon to ~10,100 BP, and sand dunes at Sloan in Arkansas state contained at least 30 secondary burials – also of cremated individuals – and cached projectile points and knives dating to the Dalton phase (Jim Chatters pers. comm.). Primary burials are also known from Anzik 1, Montana (10,705 ± 35 BP), Fishbone Cave, Nevada (11,535 ± 500/10,900 ± 300 BP), Arch Lake, New Mexico (10,020 ± 50 BP) and Dalton contexts at Arnold Cave, Missouri (9,300–10,500 BP) (Chatters in press). Although the sample is small, the importance of rockshelters and the relative frequency of cremations is noticeable, and a degree of regionalisation of practice is evident (ibid.).

The European Mesolithic

The concept of collectivity clearly continued into the Holocene in several regions of the Old World. It is very evident in the European Mesolithic, for example, whether in the cemeteries of Scandinavia (Larsson 2004) or the shell middens of Téviec and Hoëdic in Brittany (Schulting 1996). The practice of using cave cemeteries also continued. Between 15 and 34 individuals were afforded funerary treatment in the Mesolithic of the Franchthi Cave, Greece (Cullen 1995). The sample includes several single inhumations in shallow pits from the earliest Mesolithic levels in the cave, at least two cremations and probable secondary burials. The site was the focus of habitation, and Cullen (ibid., 285) stressed the proximity of the dead to the living in Mesolithic Europe and the Near East. Here, 'the circumscription of the dead's own space apart from that of the living is lost'. A similar blurring of the worlds of the living and the dead is found in the cave cemetery of Aveline's Hole (Somerset, United Kingdom) where at least 21 individuals ranging from neonates to the elderly were interred between 10,000 and 8,500 BP (Schulting 2005) along-side Early Mesolithic uses of the cave that included flint knapping and hearths (Jacobi 2005).

Collectivity and fragmentation: the culmination of Palaeolithic funerary practice

As Palaeolithic groups responded to the amelioration of conditions of the Last Glacial Maximum and re-colonised areas previously abandoned, they continued the funerary traditions inherited from their Mid Upper Palaeolithic sources, notably Cronos compulsions and single inhumations. Between 15,000 and 11,000 BP, however, depending upon geographical region, the practice of formally defining cemeteries as places of collective disposal arose, and was never to disappear. That this innovation should continue alongside earlier traditions of single burial and curation of body parts suggests that considerable variability in custom pertained, and this variability can be observed on single cemetery sites. The achievement of the Late Upper Palaeolithic was therefore to embrace the extremes of funerary behaviour, from the symbolic frag-mentation of the body, probably contextualised in the wider symbolism of fragmentation, and the collective burial of the dead in cemeteries, a new innovation that, I have suggested, heralds a new and essentially 'agricultural' way of thinking. The Late Upper Palaeolithic burial record is relatively respect-able – approaching 30 burials – and is not far off that for the Mid Upper Palaeolithic, the burials that usually attract more scholarly attention. In addition to these practices, the circulation of human relics continued to the end of the period (and beyond). These are major human innovations in the funerary realm. And they are Palaeolithic.

8

THE DEAD AS SYMBOLS

The evolution of human mortuary activity

> We see life vanish but we express this fact by the use of a special
> language: it is the soul, we say, which departs for another world
> where it will join its forefathers. The body of the deceased is
> not regarded like the carcass of some animal: specific care must
> be given to it and a correct burial; not merely for reasons of
> hygiene but out of moral obligation. Finally, with the occurrence
> of death a dismal period begins for the living during which
> special duties are imposed upon them. Whatever their personal
> feelings may be, they have to show sorrow for a certain period,
> change the colour of their clothes and modify the pattern of
> their usual life. Thus death has a specific meaning for the social
> consciousness; it is the object of a collective representation. This
> representation is neither simple nor unchangeable: it calls for
> an analysis of its elements as well as a search for its origin.
>
> (Hertz 1960)

This passage was written in 1907, in Hertz' celebrated *Contribution to the Study of the Collective Representation of Death* to use the title of the 1960 English translation. Here, encapsulated in this passage, we find the familiar elements of human mortuary activity that seem familiar to us and that separate us from the rest of the animal world. There are a number of elements to this: a *soul*; a *special language* with which we refer to death and its social context; the concept of *another world* that we cannot see or do not experience directly; *forefathers* who still possess social agency despite being biologically dead; *care* and concerns for the *correct burial* of the dead; *obligations* of a *moral* nature that require and define action; and *special duties* that modify the usual patterns of life as formal responses to death, held for *certain periods*, all pertaining to a *collective representation*. There should be no doubt that several of these elements are symbolic in nature, that is, they refer to and express shared concepts. In this case these concepts straddle the real and imaginary world, and reflect the perpetuation of complex cosmological beliefs mediated through society and its social agents.

The archaeological record pertaining to human mortuary activity should allow us to evaluate exactly when and how the dead came to be embodied in symbolic systems. In Chapters 2 to 7 I have tried to take a holistic approach to the development of mortuary activity. Archaeologists often regard burial as the developmental summit of human mortuary ritual. It does indeed represent a significant behavioural innovation that separates at least two hominin taxa – Neanderthals and modern humans – from their hominin predecessors and from their contemporaries in the animal world. Although burial can be non-symbolic, it can also be held to be both a deliberate act and a symbol as it involves both the living and the dead. At its most simplistic it requires the concept that a specific form of activity is associated with the dead. A problematisation of the concept is necessary, however. How does one recognise the truly symbolic motivations for burial? The 'trait list' approach treats burial of the dead as one of several expressions of 'modern' human behaviour, although proponents of the importance of burial in the debate about modern human origins do not define why it deserves to be on the list. How, for example, does placing a corpse in a shallow grave *really* differ from a female chimpanzee carrying around the body of her dead child for several days or months (e.g. Goodall 1986, Matsuzawa 2003)? Why should the inclusion of a piece of flint or bone in a grave necessarily reflect symbolic behaviour? As with personal ornamentation, there is no reason why the treatment of the dead could not have differed in its symbolic function over the course of hominin evolution, and it serves no purpose to make overarching generalisations.

The evolutionary development of human mortuary practice

In the preceding chapters I have tried to outline a picture of the long-term development of mortuary activity in its widest sense. I outlined some caveats in Chapter 1. The record is patchy to say the least, and what we recognise as mortuary activity in the archaeological record may not only reflect a small part of an otherwise archaeologically invisible behavioural repertoire but it may also reflect only those aspects of behaviour that were in some way 'exceptional'. The 'odd' nature of burials in the European Mid Upper Palaeolithic – which arguably form the most robust dataset we have for the Palaeolithic – suggests that they stood out as exceptional and therefore that burial was not the most commonly practised detachment ritual. While some of the behaviours I have explored in an inclusive approach may be distasteful to modern eyes – Cronos compulsions for example – burial is seen by many modern societies as 'normal', although ironically such notions of 'normal' burial may have only come about with the increased sedentism, aggregation and investment in land of 'agricultural' ways of thinking. In the main I have not attempted to link funerary activity together in some kind of set of evolutionary relationships. As with other aspects of behaviour, there is no reason to believe that mortuary activity evolved in a linear fashion, and the cumulative nature of its development and increasing regional variability noticeable over time suggest that it certainly did not. Some aspects, I suggest, do link together, such as burial arising as a deliberate creation of spaces for funerary caching.

In places, however, the data are robust enough to allow a degree of interpretation, the generalisations from which should be relevant irrespective of how characteristic or not archaeologically visible mortuary activity is of hominins' total mortuary repertoires. I have argued that the social interaction of the living with the dead has a very long evolutionary history, beginning with the intellectual interest in the corpse (*morbidity*) and consumption of body parts under certain social conditions that can be observed among extant primates (Chapter 2). At some point – possibly within australopithecine groups or early *Homo* these core responses to death were elaborated, mainly through the deliberate deposition of the dead at certain parts of the natural landscape (*structured deposition*), essentially marking a conceptual link between the dead and the landscape (Chapter 3). Eventually, enclosed features, specifically caves, were repeatedly used for *funerary caching* by Neanderthals and early *Homo sapiens*, who took the next step and deliberately *created* caches for burial (simple 'graves') and on occasion gave certain locales specific meaning as places for the dead, which became *places of multiple burial* (Chapters 4 and 5). Only with the Old World dispersal of *Homo sapiens* did further innovations appear, in particular the circulation of human remains as personal ornamentation and relics from the Early Upper Palaeolithic and richly accompanied formal burials from the Mid Upper Palaeolithic (Chapter 6). One might infer from this that *commemoration* – the active remembrance of individuals, in this case through the circulation of their relics – was practised at least from this time, and thus that individuals had become frozen in the 'history' of cosmological systems. These patterns continued into the Late Upper Palaeolithic, during which time the two extreme expressions of mortuary activity – fragmentation and collection – appeared, and by the end of the period formal *cemeteries*, often containing large numbers of the dead, were in place in several regions of the Old World and herald in Mesolithic and Neolithic communities (Chapter 7).

In this view of the development of hominin mortuary activity one might recognise five main developmental periods, which might be termed in order of development the core, developing, modernising, modern and advanced phases. These phases were not specific to particular taxa; while behaviour indicative of the core mortuary phase was presumably variably expressed among Miocene hominoid groups onwards, 'modernising' mortuary behaviour can be recognised among Neanderthals as well as Middle Stone Age *Homo sapiens* groups in the Levant. Only the modern and advanced phases appear to be unique to one species, *Homo sapiens*. The phases were cumulative in nature; while developments grew out of existing practices, such as formal burial out of funerary caching, places of multiple burial out of single and cemeteries out of places of multiple burial, for much of the period these did not replace previous practices, some of which, such as Cronos compulsions and disarticulation, continued over the entire period and actually became more elaborate in the later developmental phases. New innovations increased the observable variability of practice, which from the Mid Upper Palaeolithic both corresponded to widespread practices at the continental scale and expressed regional variations within that. The developmental periods can be defined as follows.

Core mortuary phase (Miocene hominoids and Pliocene hominins onwards):

- *Cronos compulsions* of infanticide and cannibalism;
- socially mediated *morbidity* of the corpse;
- manifestations of *mourning* including signs of depression, calls and carrying of corpses as an act of detachment;
- *funerary gatherings:* social theatre around the corpse, including controlled access to the corpse and display and involved behaviour not witnessed in other circumstances (i.e. in the presence only of the living). Corpses may be used socially, e.g. as adjuncts to display.

Archaic mortuary phase (australopithecine grade hominins and early *Homo* to the origins of *Homo sapiens*):

- continuation of Cronos compulsions, morbidity, mourning. Possibly developing social theatre around the corpse as group size and neurological capacity increased;
- incorporation of places in the landscape into mortuary activity, that is, funerary caching.

Modernising mortuary phase (Middle Palaeolithic/Middle Stone Age *Homo neanderthalensis* and *Homo sapiens* and possibly European Early Upper Palaeolithic):

- continuation of Cronos compulsions, morbidity, mourning, funerary caching and developing social theatre around the corpse. Clear association of places in the landscape with the dead;
- development of formal burial from funerary caching (often association of the two);
- development of places of multiple burial;
- some use of material culture as adjuncts to burials, e.g. rare examples of grave goods, stone markers/covers and ochre.

Modern mortuary phase (European Mid Upper Palaeolithic, possibly from Early Upper Palaeolithic):

- continuation of Cronos compulsions, morbidity, mourning, funerary caching and elaboration of social theatre around the corpse. Clear association of places in the landscape with the dead and places of multiple burial. Clear use of material culture as adjuncts to burial;

• elaboration of uses of human relics and thus commemoration;
• elaboration of types of burial (single, double, multiple)
• association of new phenomena with burials, e.g. fire, symbolism (art);
• elaborate rules for burial as *containment*;
• recognition of the status of the dead in mortuary ritual;
• first signs of continent-scale general practices; funerary activity now recognisably regional variations on more widespread themes.

Advanced mortuary development (Late Upper Palaeolithic/Epipalaeolithic onwards):

• persistence of elements of the modern mortuary phase, their spread to new areas of the world (e.g. New World) and increasing regional and cultural variability;
• origin of formal cemeteries, that is, recognition of exclusive areas of the dead and the collective representation of death.

Several scales of change can be observed in this development. *Core* mortuary activities occur face-to-face in the here-and-now, reflecting the expression of emotional responses to death, morbidity and social theatre for relatively brief periods of time, although strong bonds such as mother–infant may provoke longer detachment processes. A degree of expansion is visible in the *archaic* mortuary phase, in which the caching of bodies at recognised points of the landscape brings new (albeit modest) spatial and, possibly, temporal scales into the process. Although early activity in this phase, such as that I have argued for AL-333, may still reflect very brief periods of time and little or no expansion of the conceptual horizons, later expressions such as the funerary caching at the Sima de los Huesos imply somewhat stronger conceptions of a place of the dead. The increasing variability of practice observable in the *modernising* phase – in which formal burial arose – *must* be suggestive of deliberate concepts about the dead and how they should be treated, at least from time to time. The appearance of burial per se provides an indication that deliberate reasons must have been in place among Neanderthals and early modern humans, otherwise why artificially create graves when numerous niches, fissures, caves and rockshelters provided ample opportunity for funerary caching? If disposal of the body is desirable, whether for reasons of hygiene, distaste, health, safety or other, this is a remarkably labour-intensive solution. If this were the reason for early burial, one might expect it to have been practised more frequently and in more geographical regions where late archaic and early modern humans were operating. But it was not; its distribution is remarkably patchy and cannot be explained simply on taphonomic grounds. When such patchy expressions of other behaviours are found in the

Palaeolithic (and for that matter primatological) record they are interpreted as cultural variation. That the earliest burials are already associated with a degree of materiality such as rare grave goods, ochre use, and even 'architectural' adjuncts such as the 'tombs' of Regourdou further indicates, in my opinion, that mortuary activity during the modernising period was stimulated by reasons beyond the prosaic. Clearly, some individuals were recognised as being afforded burial, whereas most were not. Although there are no convincing indications of differing social status in the period, it may be that the prime distinction was between those individuals who would be accorded burial at death and those who were not. Whether or not this arose from social distinction cannot be answered, but at the very least this indicates that some individuals were specifically associated with a particular (and new) mortuary activity. Thus a connection would have to be made, between the social persona of the deceased and the act of burial. This is not fully symbolic in the sense that archaeologists usually assume for the term, although it is easy to see how the increasing elaboration of such 'connections' between social persona and mortuary practice could result in symbolically mediated detachment rituals.

Mortuary practice and symbolic systems

Symbolism or a 'symbolic capacity' has come to be seen as a major defining characteristic of *Homo sapiens* (e.g. Bar-Yosef 2002, 378; Hovers *et al.* 2003, and see discussion in Henshilwood and Marean 2003). In all modern human groups cultural behaviour is mediated by symbolism (Chase and Dibble 1987), and Henshilwood and Marean (ibid.) define 'modern behaviour' as that which is organised symbolically. Wadley (2001) has suggested that one may only infer 'full' symbolism from the archaeological record if it displays unambiguous evidence for external storage of information. In recent years a degree of symbolic capacity has been recognised for the Neanderthals (d'Errico *et al.* 2003).

Hominin mortuary activity corresponds to several ways of interacting with the dead, which at their simplest are straightforward and non-symbolic, and at the other extreme are symbolically mediated in time and space in complex ways. As Henshilwood and Marean (2003, 644) have observed, the capacity for fully symbolic behaviour 'may have developed over tens or even hundreds of millennia' and this should apply as much to symbolically structured mortuary practice as to art and language. Although the development of symbolic aspects of mortuary activity will blur boundaries between different stages, the following major interactions may be observed:

- Simple (non-symbolic) observation: little activity occurs beyond expressions of emotion, morbidity and social theatre at funerary gatherings. Cognitively this could amount to little more than the concept 'it is dead, I am confused'.

- Emotive (non-symbolic) interaction: the living now begin to engage further with the dead, and their emotional response affects certain simple behaviours of disposal. 'It is dead, I am mourning; hide the corpse away as it is distasteful.'
- Passive associative (non-symbolic or symbolic) interaction: the dead are now associated with a specific activity at a specific place; the place symbolises the dead. Associations are made between the dead, the landscape and the social group. 'He is dead; he must be disposed of at a recognised place.' That place, however, is not modified; no energy is invested in a place, bodies are simply deposited there.
- Active associative (symbolic) interaction: as passive, but energy is now invested in the place of disposal, that is, natural features are widened, graves are excavated, and adjuncts to burials such as grave goods, stone coverings and ochre use may occur from time to time. The deliberate modification of such locales suggests specific meaning was attached to them.
- Time/space-factored associative interaction: the agency of the dead is now recognised in mortuary treatment (who gets special treatment, where and when), and mortuary activity is organised in time and space according to social rules. 'He is dead; he was an elder in life and has earned the right to be buried at the place of the elders.'

One cannot simply argue that even archaeologically observable mortuary activity was 'symbolic' in any straightforward way; arguments that grave goods are symbolic do not problematise what we mean by symbolism and get us nowhere. Scholars would probably agree that Mid Upper Palaeolithic mortuary activity had a strong symbolic character given its widespread characteristics, regional distinctions among these, repetitive patterns, 'non normal' subjects and associations with often rich grave goods including objects clearly of a symbolic nature. It is probably fair to assume that fully time/space-factored associative symbolism was in operation at this time and characterises the modern and advanced mortuary phases. Before this, activity in the modernising phase may have been structured according to active associative interactions with the dead; the variability of mortuary activity visible in the European Middle Palaeolithic and at Skhūl and Qafzeh, as well as the rare examples of elaborate behaviour such as at Regourdou, La Ferrassie, suggest clearly that the dead were associated with certain places and behaviours, and that distinct, albeit short-lived traditions of these associations arose from time to time. It is interesting in this light that there are no definable differences between modernising period burials of the Neanderthals and early modern humans and in terms of their burials 'we see no clear-cut indications that anatomically modern humans were culturally "more advanced" than Neanderthals' (d'Errico 2003, 196). One might only draw this distinction from the Early Upper Palaeolithic onwards (on the basis of human relics) or the Mid Upper

Palaeolithic (on the basis of grave goods). The appearance of burials at this time may be important. As d'Errico *et al.* (2003, 26) have suggested, 'it is difficult to imagine that a human group could excavate a grave, position the corpse in the pit, and offer funerary goods with no form of verbal exchange'. In Chapter 1 I defined burial as a process of *at least three stages;* the excavation of a grave, placement of the corpse within it, and subsequent covering of the corpse. This is organised (and in many cases I suggest difficult) behaviour, and I agree with d'Errico *et al.* how the practice could have spread within and between groups without the communication of the basic concepts. But a number of burials – for the Neanderthals in particular – reveal longer mortuary *chaînes opératoires*: it is difficult to see how the repeated burials of La Ferrassie could have been emplaced without planning, at least the groups of infants, and it is, I suggest, *impossible* that the mortuary ensemble at Le Regourdou could have been constructed without cooperation and communication of an elaborate set of beliefs. If it is correct that the corpse of a brown bear and that of a Neanderthal were deliberately buried effectively side-to-side, then this *must* invoke a deliberate conceptual association of the two.

In this light, a sharp distinction can be made between burial – which is predicated upon the communication of a set of ideas about a *chaîne opératoire* of three or more stages – and funerary caching, which need not require complex communication. This can be achieved simply by doing: demonstrating that a corpse can be hidden away. I have argued that burial arose out of funerary caching, originally as the modification of natural caches and latterly as the deliberate construction of them. This development clearly required greater communication, underpinned by active association between the living and the dead. While one may or may not be justified in calling this fully symbolic, it is certainly a major step towards it; and to those colleagues for whom 'symbolism' is a black-and-white issue, the answer to the question 'did Neanderthals possess a symbolic capacity' must, simply, be 'yes'. Furthermore, if possible cases for careful defleshing among Neanderthal communities are demonstrated beyond reasonable doubt, this *must* also be taken as evidence of a degree of symbolic activity, as anything beyond nutritional cannibalism must be symbolic in nature.

Before the modernising period, passive associative interactions may be inferred at least during the later parts of the archaic phase, for example, including the repeated deposition of bodies at the Sima de los Huesos. These interactions clearly continued on into the Middle Palaeolithic, although increasingly alongside more active interactions. Before the Middle Pleistocene, and certainly prior to the emergence of the genus *Homo,* it is difficult to infer interactions beyond emotional. While there may have been some significance of points in the landscape – such as the AL-333 hill – that would point to passive associations between the landscape and the dead, parsimonious interpretations would restrict such behaviour to emotive (and thus non-symbolic) interactions. Although it is obviously difficult to recognise the behavioural manifestation of emotive interactions in the archaeological record, it is possible that this level of interaction has a considerable antiquity given the extent to which chimpanzee mothers can carry around their dead offspring. It could be, in fact, that emotive interactions have been part of core mortuary behaviour from the evolution of the hominoids.

When did the dead become symbols? Symbolic constructions underpin all mortuary activities in the present day, no matter what communities indulge in them. I have argued above that 'breaking down' the data into a set of increasingly complex concepts provides an heuristic for approaching the mortuary data. From this it can certainly be said that mortuary activity was fully symbolically structured after 30,000 BP, possibly beforehand; and that a degree of symbolic underpinning is evident in Middle Palaeolithic burial back to ~100,000 BP. By way of conclusion, a small set of working suggestions can be forwarded:

- Only at the end of the Pleistocene did what we recognise as 'normal' ways of thinking of the dead originate. These arise from 'agricultural' thinking and resulted, in some places and times, in formal cemeteries as territorial markers.
- By the Late Upper Palaeolithic, mortuary activity was functioning in the wider symbolic realm, alongside art. A trend towards increasing fragmentation of the body is observable, paralleled in art, personal ornamentation and corpse processing. This *must* indicate that mortuary ritual at the time was embedded in widespread cultural beliefs.
- By the Mid Upper Palaeolithic the increasing social differentiation between individuals was increasingly reflected in burials (and probably in whether or not individuals were buried in the first place). Complex interactions between the living and the dead correspond to widespread, probably continent-wide, traditions, superimposing regional traditions on these.
- By the Early Upper Palaeolithic, the relics of the dead were in circulation. Despite the lack of burials outside of Africa during this period, this suggests that symbolic interactions with the dead had come about by this time.
- Among the Neanderthals and early modern humans, associative interaction with the dead is evident, at least in some places and in some periods. The active assocation probably required a degree of symbolism, at least in its more complex organisation.
- The association of the dead with places in the landscape has an antiquity stretching back at least to the Middle Pleistocene. It is the first archaeologically recognisable cultural association of the dead.
- Before this one might expect variable expressions of core mortuary activities back into the Miocene. One should expect these to have varied culturally, as other behaviours vary among modern chimpanzee groups.

And that takes us back to where we began, with a death in a storm. Recall the sympathy and empathy, and the care with which a mother treated her dying infant. We have come a long way since the Miocene, although this touching observation that I used to begin a comparison with chimpanzees reminds us that, in terms of mortuary activities at least, we are not that different after all.

NOTES

1 From the Greek god, Cronos (Latin Saturn). Having castrated his father, Cronos consumed his children (conceived with his sister, Rhea) as he believed that one of them would overcome him. Finally he was deceived by Rhea into swallowing a stone wrapped in cloth. The vomiting that this induced caused him to regurgitate his swallowed children, one of whom succeeded in overcoming him (Hammond and Scullard 1984).

2 Mourn: *v. t.* to grieve, to be sorrowful. Grief: *n.* sorrow, distress, great mourning, affliction. Sorrow: *n.* Pain of mind, grief, sadness, affliction. Definitions from *Chambers 20th Century Dictionary*.

3 Although there are serious arguments that challenge the *c.*120ka BP antiquity of Tabun C1, not least because Garrod was uncertain of its stratigraphic attribution (see Bar-Yosef 2000).

4 According to Oakley *et al.* (1971, 162) they are of an adult female, and include: cranium, mandible, cervical vertebrae I-VI, 2 scapulae, 2 clavicles, 2 humeri, 1 ulna and 2 femora. It has been suggested on palaeopathological grounds that the bones may belong to more than one individual, although on the basis of the similar sizes of the lower epiphyses it is likely that they do belong to one individual (Defleur 1993, 94).

5 Such double standards in the way archaeologists are paradigmatically drawn to Neanderthal and modern humans are still in force. Belfer-Cohen and Hovers (1992) have made the point with regard to the Levant. See also Roebroeks and Corbey 2000.

6 Although it should be noted that Hayden (1993, 121) upholds the possibility of the intentional placement of 'at least some of the bear bones' at Regourdou, which seems highly plausible as discussed in the text. More modern claims for 'bear cults' are also open to question: For example, 'some uncertainty surrounds' the recovery of bear skulls covered by leg bones and elongated limestone pieces from the Mousterian levels of Upper Cave near Kataisi, Eastern Georgia (Lubin 1997, 146).

7 This notion obviously breaks down from at least 27,000 BP, for several millennia after which some anatomically modern humans were buried in open air settlements in which bone artefacts were exceptionally well preserved. It is an obvious point to state that many Middle Palaeolithic open sites preserve bone, and that human remains are rare on them. On such Middle Palaeolithic open and aven sites where relatively complete animal carcasses are found, e.g. Mauran, Haute-Garonne (David and Farizy 1999), La Cotte, Jersey (Scott 1986), La Borde and Coudoulous, Lot (Brugal 1999), Wallertheim, Germany, where a number of bones were found in articulation (Gaudzinski 1999a. 1999b), one would by Gargett's logic expect to find Neanderthal skeletons. For Germany, only ten sites have yielded

Neanderthal remains, half of which are open sites (Turner *et al.* 2000; Street *et al.* 2006).

8 That is, Western European (French), Central European (Croatian) and Near Eastern (Israel) groups. One might add a fourth Central Asian group, i.e. including Kiik-Koba, Mezmaiskaya Cave and Teshik Tash.

9 Estimated on the basis of dental development using 14 crowns of deciduous teeth. Formation of the occlusal surface of the second deciduous molar was incomplete and the remaining teeth do no exhibit neck and root development (Golovanova *et al.* 1999, 81).

10 The radiocarbon history of the Red Lady is a good reflection of the improvement of AMS radiocarbon dating methodology at Oxford. Bones from the skeleton have been dated several times in the Oxford laboratory. An initial measurement, made in the 1980s, suggested an age ~18,000 BP, thought by many as odd given it was close to the Last Glacial Maximum during which time Britain seems to have been totally depopulated. Later measurements suggested ages closer to ~25–27,000 BP (Aldhouse-Green and Pettitt 1998). The current ultrafiltrated measurements place it a little earlier, but the resulting age range is still fully consistent with a Gravettian attribution. I hope that no one will drill further holes in the poor man.

11 My own view is that this statement pertains in Europe down to ~29,000 BP, at which time burials were inhumed at Paviland and Kostenki 14.

12 One possible French Mid Upper Palaeolithic burial is the adult from Combe-Capelle (Dordogne) that has often been assigned on stratigraphic grounds to the *Périgordien Ancien* but this is highly controversial and the burial – excavated in 1909 – could be much younger. See discussion in May 1986, 40.

13 The child has attracted most attention due to the debate as to whether it is, or is not, a Neanderthal modern hybrid. Although it is fully *Homo sapiens,* researchers differ as to whether meaningful traits shared with the Neanderthals are visible on the skeleton. I am not concerned with this issue here; see Duarte *et al.* 1999, papers in Zilhão and Trinkaus 2002a, and Bayle *et al.* 2010 for useful discussions of this debate.

14 I use here the Italian site names but French names have been used in the past (the caves were also referred to as the Mentone Caves): Grotta del Caviglione/Grotte du Cavillon, Grotta dei Fanciulli/Grotte des Enfants, Grotta del Principe/Grotte du Prince. Barma Grande and Baousso da Torre (alternatively Bausu da Ture) remain the same.

15 The cave is named after the burials of two infants. These are of Epigravettian age and are discussed in Chapter 7.

16 It is worth noting that in the oft-published photograph of the (reconstructed) double burial the female's head has been turned to side from its originally down-facing position, so as to show what were originally thought to be negroid traits on the face (Formicola 1991).

17 One should disregard the previous date of 14,990 ± 80 BP (CAMS 7641) on BG2 as it was performed in the infancy of the technique and given that collagen preservation is low in all of the Barma Grande skeletons is almost certainly an underestimate. See Mussi 2001b and Formicola *et al.* 2004 for further justification for rejecting this measurement.

18 Evidence of gnawing is not present as far as one can tell, although no detailed taphonomic studies were carried out and the remains were destroyed towards the end of the Second World War.

19 Radiocarbon dates for items from Cultural Layer 3 are erroneously young.

20 These were considered to be male and female respectively on the basis of hip bone morphology. Wider observations on the skeletons concur with this, and recent

DNA analyses of the individuals are in accord with the attribution, although independent replication of the results in a separate laboratory would be desirable (Henry-Gambier 2008). See discussion in Formicola and Buzhilova 2004.

21 Although being British I would obviously like to see it demonstrated that this was a Welsh innovation: I challenge anyone to demonstrate clearly that it was *not*!

22 The remains are currently being reanalysed and several discrepancies with the existing analysis have been noted and the interpretation of the site may change (J. Orschiedt pers. comm.).

23 Twenty-nine per cent of the sample (from Le Placard, Isturitz and Roc de Sers) are not attributable with confidence to a particular phase of the Magdalenian, although it is probable that the former belong to the early phase as noted in the text.

24 The partial remains of four individuals apparently recovered from Late Magdalenian contexts in two caves of the Döbritz cave system, Kniegrotte and Urdhöhle (Bach 1974) have been shown by direct AMS ^{14}C dating to be Holocene in age (Street et al. 2006).

25 The date is surprisingly young for a burial with clear Magdalenian associations (Vanhaeren and d'Errico 2001). The inventory of shell associated with the burial does, however, match with Final Magdalenian and Azilian shell inventories from occupation horizons at La Madeleine and other sites (Vanhaeren and d'Errico 2001, 225), and three sites in the region have furnished Final Magdalenian assemblages of this age (ibid., 227).

26 The most likely diagnosis of the reason for the dwarfism is acromesomelic dysplasia (Frayer et al. 1987). This is a form of dysplasia similar to the chondrodystrofic form that was diagnosed by Frayer and coworkers in an earlier paper albeit with a later date (Frayer et al. 1988) (V. Formicola pers. comm.).

27 Estimates of the human MNI at Taforalt vary from this figure (Mariotti et al. 2009), to 86 (a previous researcher) and 170 (the excavator). The actual number is between 40 and 86, probably closer to 40 (ibid., 349), still an impressive number.

28 An Early to Mid Holocene assemblage type of the Maghreb derived from the Epipalaeolithic.

REFERENCES

Akazawa, T. and Muhesen, S. (eds) (2002) *Neanderthal Burials: Excavations of the Dederiyeh Cave, Afrin, Syria: Studies in Honour of Hisashi Suzuki.* Kyoto: International Research Center for Japanese Studies.

Akazawa, T., Muhesen, S., Ishida, H., Kondo, O. and Griggo, C. (1999) New discovery of a Neanderthal child burial from the Dederiyeh Cave in Syria. *Paléorient* 25(2): 129–42.

Akazawa, T., Muhesen, S., Kondo, O., Dodo, Y., Yoneda, M. *et al.* (2002a) Neanderthal burials of the Dederiyeh Cave. In Akazawa, T. and Muhesen, S. (eds) *Neanderthal Burials: Excavations of the Dederiyeh Cave, Afrin, Syria: Studies in Honour of Hisashi Suzuki.* Kyoto: International Research Center for Japanese Studies, pp. 75–90.

Akazawa, T., Muhesen, S., Dodo, Y., Ishida, H., Kondo, O. *et al.* (2002b) A summary of the stratigraphic sequence. In Akazawa, T. and Muhesen, S. (eds) *Neanderthal Burials: Excavations of the Dederiyeh Cave, Afrin, Syria. Studies in Honour of Hisashi Suzuki.* Kyoto: International Research Center for Japanese Studies, 15–32.

Aldhouse-Green, S. H. R. (2000a) (ed.) *Paviland Cave and the 'Red Lady': A Definitive Report.* Bristol: Western Academic and Specialist Press.

Aldhouse-Green, S. H. R. (2000b) Artefacts of ivory, bone and shell. In Aldhouse-Green, S. H. R. (ed.) *Paviland Cave and the 'Red Lady': A Definitive Report.* Bristol: Western Academic and Specialist Press, pp. 115–32.

Aldhouse-Green, S. H. R. (2000c) Climate, ceremony, pilgrimage and Paviland: the 'Red Lady' in his palaeoecological and technoetic context. In Aldhouse-Green, S. H. R. (ed.) *Paviland Cave and the 'Red Lady': A Definitive Report.* Bristol: Western Academic and Specialist Press, pp. 227–46.

Aldhouse-Green, S. H. R. (2001) Ex Africa aliquid semper novi: the view from Pontnewydd. In Milliken, S. and Cook, J. (eds) *A Very Remote Period Indeed: Papers on the Palaeolithic Presented to Derek Roe.* Oxford: Oxbow, pp. 114–19.

Aldhouse-Green, S. H. R. and Pettitt, P. B. (1998) Paviland Cave: contextualizing the Red Lady. *Antiquity* 72(278): 756–72.

Alexeeva, T. and Bader, N. (eds) (1998) *Upper Palaeolithic Site Sungir: Graves and Environment.* Moscow: Scientific World.

Alexeeva, T. and Bader, N. (2000) *Homo Sungirensis. Upper Palaeolithic Man: Ecological and Evolutionary Aspects of the Investigation.* Moscow: Scientific World.

Allain, J., Desbrosse, R., Kozłowski, J. and Rigaud, A. (1985) Le Magdalénien à Navettes. *Gallia Préhistoire* 28: 37–124.

Alt, K. W., Pichler, S., Vach, W., Klima, B., Vlček, E. and Sedlmeier, J. (1997) Twenty-five thousand-year-old triple burial from Dolní Věonice: an Ice-Age family? *American Journal of Physical Anthropology* 102: 123–31.

Anderson, J. R., Gillies, A. and Lock, L. C. (2010) Panthanatology. *Current Biology* 20(8): R349–51.

Andrews, P. and Fernández-Jalvo, Y. (1997) Surface modifications of the Sima de los Huesos fossil humans. *Journal of Human Evolution* 33: 191–217.

Andrews, P. and Fernández-Jalvo, Y. (2003) Cannibalism in Britain: taphonomy of the Creswellian (Pleistocene) faunal and human remains from Gough's Cave (Somerset, England). *Bulletin of the Natural History Museum London* 58: 59–81.

Anikovich, M. V. (2005) The chronology of Paleolithic sites in the Kostienki-Borschevo area. *Archaeology, Ethnology & Anthropology of Eurasia* 3(23): 70–86.

Archambeau, M. and Archambeau, C. (1991) Les figurations humaines parietals de la Grotte des Combarelles. *Gallia Préhistoire* 33: 53–81.

Arensberg, B. and Tillier, A. M. (1983) A new Mousterian child from Qafzeh (Israel): Qafzeh 4a. *Bulletin et Mémoires de la Société Anthropologique de Paris* 10: 61–9.

Aronson, J. L. and Taieb, M. (1981) Geology and palaeography of the Hadar hominid site, Ethiopia. In Rapp, G. and Vondra, C. F. (eds) *Hominid Sites: Their Geologic Settings*. Boulder, CO: Westview, pp. 165–95.

Arsuaga, J. L., Martínez, I., Gracia, A., Carretero, J. M., Lorenzo, C. and García, N. (1997a) Sima de los Huesos (Sierra de Atapuerca, Spain), the site. *Journal of Human Evolution* 3: 109–27.

Arsuaga, J. L., Martínez, I., García, A. and Lorenzo, C. (1997b) The Sima de los Huesos crania (Sierra de Atapuerca, Spain): a comparative study. *Journal of Human Evolution* 33(2/3): 219–81.

Arsuaga, J. L., Carbonell, E. and Bermúdez de Castro, J. M. (2003) *The First Europeans: Treasures from the Hills of Atapuerca*. New York: American Museum of Natural History/Junta de Castilla y León.

Atran, S. (2006) The scientific landscape of religion: evolution, culture, and cognition. In Clayton, P. (ed.) *The Oxford Handbook of Religion and Science*. Oxford: Oxford University Press, pp. 407–29.

Aujoulat, N., Geneste, J.-M., Archambeau, C., Delluc, M., Duday, H. and Gambier, D. (2001) La Grotte ornée de Cussac (Dordogne), observations liminaires. *Paléo* 13: 9–18.

Aujoulat, N., Geneste, J.-M., Archambeau, C., Delluc, M., Duday, H. and Henry-Gambier, D. (2002) La Grotte ornée de Cussac – Le Buisson-de-Cadouin (Dordogne): premières observations. *Bulletin de la Société Préhistorique Française* 99(1): 129–37.

Baales, M. and Street, M. (1998) Late Palaeolithic backed point assemblages in the Northern Rhineland: current research and changing views. *Notae Praehistoricae* 18: 77–92.

Bach, H. (1974) Menschliche skelettreste aus Kniegrotte und Urdhöhle. In Feustel, R. (ed.) *Die Kniegrotte*. Weimar: Böhlaus Nachfolger, pp. 202–6.

Bachechi, L., Fabbri, P.F. and Mallegni, F. (1997) An arrow-caused lesion in a Late Upper Palaeolithic human pelvis. *Current Anthropology* 38(1): 135–40.

Backer, A. M. (1993) Spatial distributions at La Roche à Pierrot, Saint-Césaire: changing uses of a rockshelter. In Lévêque, F., Backer, A. M. and Guilbaud, M.

275

(eds) *Context of a Late Neanderthal: Implications of Multidisciplinary Research for the Transition to Upper Paleolithic Adaptations at Saint-Césaire, Charente-Maritime, France.* Madison, WI: Prehistory Press, pp. 105–27.

Backer, A. M. and Guilbaud, M. (eds) (1993) *Context of a Late Neanderthal: Implications of Multidisciplinary Research for the Transition to Upper Palaeolithic Adaptations at Saint-Cézaire, Charente-Maritime, France.* Madison, WI: Prehistory Press.

Bader, O. (1978) *Sungir Upper Palaeolithic Site.* Moscow: Nauka.

Bader, N. O. and Mikhajlova, L. A. (1998) *Upper Palaeolithic Site Sungir (Graves and Environment).* Moscow: Scientific World.

Bahn, P. (1986) No sex please, we're Aurignacians. *Rock Art Research* 3(2): 99–120.

Bartolomei, G., Broglio, A., Guerreschi, A., Leonardi, P., Peretto, C. and Sala, B. (1974) Una sepoltura epigravettiana nel deposito pleistoceno del Riparo Tagliente in Valpantena (Verona). *Rivista di Scienze Preistoriche* 29: 101–52.

Barton, N., Bouzouggar, A., Humphrey, L., Berridge, P., Collcutt, S. *et al.* (2008) Human burial evidence from Hattab II Cave and the question of continuity in Late Pleistocene–Holocene mortuary practices in northwest Africa. *Cambridge Archaeological Journal* 18(2): 195–214.

Bar-Yosef, O. (1988) Evidence for Middle Palaeolithic symbolic behaviour: a cautionary note. In Otte, M. (ed.) *L'Homme de Néanderthal*, volume 5, *La Pensée*. Liège: ERAUL 32, pp. 11–16.

Bar-Yosef, O. (1998) The Natufian culture in the Levant: theshold to the origins of agriculture. *Evolutionary Anthropology* 6(5): 159–77.

Bar-Yosef, O. (2000) The Middle and Early Upper Palaeolithic in Southwest Asia and neighbouring regions. In Bar-Yosef, O. and Pilbeam, D. (eds) *The Geography of Neanderthals and Modern Humans in Europe and the Greater Mediterranean.* Cambridge, MA: Peabody Museum Bulletin 8: 107–56.

Bar-Yosef, O. (2002) The Upper Paleolithic revolution. *Annual Review of Anthropology* 31: 363–93.

Bar-Yosef, O. and Callander, J. (1999) The woman from Tabun: Garrod's doubts in historical perspective. *Journal of Human Evolution* 37: 879–85.

Bar-Yosef, O. and Vandermeersch, B. (1993) Modern humans in the Levant. *Scientific American* April: 64–70.

Bar-Yosef, O., Laville, H., Meignen, L., Tillier, A.-M., Vandermeersch, B. *et al.* (1988) La Sépulture Néandertalienne de Kébara (Unité XII). In Otte, M. (ed) *L'Homme de Néanderthal*, volume 5, *La Pensée*. Liège: ERAUL, pp. 17–24.

Bar-Yosef, O., Vandermeersch, B., Arensburg, B., Belfer-Cohen, A., Goldberg, P. *et al.* (1992) The excavations in Kebara Cave, Mt Carmel. *Current Anthropology* 33(5): 497–550.

Bar-Yosef Mayer, D., Vandermeersch, B. and Bar-Yosef, O. (2009) Shells and ochre in Middle Palaeolithic Qafzeh Cave, Israel: indications for modern behaviour. *Journal of Human Evolution* 56: 307–14.

Bayle, P., Macchiarelli, R., Trinkaus, E., Duarte, C., Mazurier, A. and Zilhão, J. (2010) Dental maturational sequence and dental tissue proportions in the early Upper Palaeolithic child from Abrigo do Lagar Velho, Portugal. *Proceedings of the National Academy of Sciences (USA)* 107(4): 1338–42.

Bayle des Hermens, R. de (1972) Le Magdalénien final de la Grotte du Rond du Barry, Commune de Polignac (Haute-Loire). *Congrès Préhistorique de France XIXe session, Auvergne, 1969*, pp. 37–57.

Begouen, H., Begouen, L. and Vallois, H. (1936) Une pendeloque faite d'un fragment de mandibule humaine (epoque Magdalenienne). *Comptes Préhistorique de France* 12: 559–64.

Belfer-Cohen, A. and Hovers, E. (1992) In the eye of the beholder: Mousterian and Natufian burials in the Levant. *Current Anthropology* 33(4): 463–71.

Bermúdez de Castro, J. M. and Nicolás, E. (1997) Palaeodemography of the Atapuerca-SH Middle Pleistocene hominid sample. *Journal of Human Evolution* 33(2/3), 333–55.

Bermúdez de Castro, J. M., Arsuaga, J. L., Carbonell, E., Rosas, A., Martínez, I. and Mosquera, M. (1997) A hominid from the Lower Pleistocene of Atapuerca, Spain: possible ancestor to Neanderthals and modern humans. *Science* 276: 1392–5.

Bermúdez de Castro, J. M., Martinón-Torres, M., Carbonell, E., Sarmiènto, S., Rosas, A. *et al.* (2004) The Atapuerca sites and their contribution to the knowledge of human evolution in Europe. *Evolutionary Anthropology* 13: 25–41.

Bermúdez de Castro, J. M., Pérez-González, Martinón-Torres, M., Gómez-Roblez, A., Rosell, J. *et al.* (2008) A new Early Pleistocene hominin mandible from Atapuerca-TD6, Spain. *Journal of Human Evolution* 55: 729–35.

Bietti, A. and Molari, C. (1994) The Upper Pleistocene deposits of the Arene Candide cave (Savona, Italy): general introduction and stratigraphy. *Quaternaria Nova* IV, 9–27.

Billy, G. (1992) La morphologie de l'homme de Chancelade. Un siècle de controverses. In Rigaud, J.-P., Laville, H. and Vandermeersch, B. (eds) *Le Peuplement Magdalénien. Paléogéographie, Physique et Humaine.* Paris: Editions du C.T.H.S., pp. 71–77.

Binant, P. (1991) *La Prehistoire de la Mort.* Paris: Editions Errance.

Binford, L. R. (1971) Mortuary practices: their study and potential. In Brown, J. A. (ed.) *Approaches to the Social Dimensions of Mortuary Practices.* Society for American Archaeology Memoir 25, pp. 208–43.

Biro, D., Humle, T., Koops, K., Sousa, C., Hayashi, M. and Matsuzawa, T. (2010) Chimpanzee mothers at Bossou, Guinea carry the mummified remains of their dead infants. *Current Biology* 20(8): R351–2.

Bischoff, J. L., Shamp, D. D., Aramburu, A., Arsuaga, J. L., Carbonell, E. and Bermudez de Castro, J. M. (2003) The Sima de los Huesos hominids date to beyond U/Th equilibrium (>350kyr) and perhaps to 400–500kyr: new radiometric dates. *Journal of Archaeological Science* 30: 275–80.

Blanchard, R., Peyrony, D. and Vallois, H. V. (1972) *Le Gisement de la Squelette de Saint-Germain-la-Rivière.* Paris: Archives de l'Institut de Paléontologie Humaine Mémoire 34.

Boaz, N., Ciochon, R. L., Xu, Q. and Liu, J. (2004) Mapping and taphonomic analysis of the *Homo erectus* loci at Locality 1, Zhoukoudian, China. *Journal of Human Evolution* 46: 519–49.

Bocquentin, F. and Bar-Yosef, O. (2004) Early Natufian remains: evidence for physical conflict from Mount Carmel, Israel. *Journal of Human Evolution* 47: 19–23.

Bocquet-Appel, J.-P. and Arsuaga, J.-L. (1999) Age distributions of hominid samples at Atapuerca (SH) and Krapina could indicate accumulation by catastrophe. *Journal of Archaeological Science* 26: 327–38.

Boesch, C. (2008) Why do chimpanzees die in the forest? The challenges of understanding and controlling for wild ape health. *American Journal of Primatology* 70: 722–76.

Boesch, C. and Boesch-Achermann, H. (2000) *The Chimpanzees of the Taï Forest: Behavioural Ecology and Evolution.* Oxford: University Press.

Boesch, C., Marchesi, P, Marchesi, N., Fruth, B. and Joulian, F. (1994) Is nut cracking in wild chimpanzees a cultural behaviour? *Journal of Human Evolution* 26: 325–38.

Bonifay, E. (1964) La Grotte du Régourdou (Montignac, Dordogne): stratigraphie, et industrie lithique Moustérienne. *Anthropologie (Paris)* 68: 49–64.

Bonifay, E. (2008) La site du Régourdou (Montignac-sur-Vézère, Dordogne): et la problem de la signification des sépultures Neandertaliennes. *Bulletin de la Société d'Études et de Recherches Préhistoriques des Eyzies* 57: 25–31.

Bonifay, E. and Vandermeersch, B. (1965) Dépots rituels s'ossements d'ours dans le gisement moustérien du Régourdou (Montignac, Dordogne). *Actes du Vie Congrès UISPP*, Rome, 1962, pp. 136–42.

Bordes, F. (1972) *A Tale of Two Caves.* New York: Harper & Row.

Bosinski, G. and Schiller, P. (1998) Représentations féminines dans la Grotte du Planchard (Vallon Pont d'Arc, Ardèche) et les figures féminines du type Gönnersdorf dans l'art pariétal. *Bulletin de la Société Préhistorique de l'Ariège Pyrénées* 53, 99–140.

Bosinski, G., d'Errico, F. and Schiller, P. (2001) *Die Gravierten Frauendarstellunden von Gönnersdorf.* Stuttgart: Franz Steiner Verlag.

Bouyssonie, A., Bouyssonie, L. and Bardon, L. (1908) Découverte d'un squelette humain Moustérien à la bouffia de la Chapelle-aux-Saints (Corrèze). *Anthropologie (Paris)* 19: 513–18.

Bouzouggar, A., Barton, N., Vanhaeren, M., d'Errico, F., Collcutt, S. *et al.* (2007) 82,000 year-old shell beads from North Africa and implications for the origins of modern human behavior. *Proceedings of the National Academy of Science (USA)* 104(24): 9964–9.

Bowler, J. M. and Thorne, A. G. (1976) Human remains from Lake Mungo. Discovery and excavation of Lake Mungo III. In Kirk, R. L. and Thorne, A. G. (eds) *The Origins of the Australians.* Canberra: AIAS, pp. 1217–38.

Bowler, J. M., Jones, R., Allen, H. and Thorne, A. G. (1970) Pleistocene human remains from Australia: a living site and human cremation from Lake Mungo, western New South Wales. *World Archaeology* 2: 39–60.

Bowler, J. M., Johnston, H., Olley, J. M., Prescott, J. R., Roberts, R. G. *et al.* (2003) New ages for human occupation and climatic change at Lake Mungo, Australia. *Nature* 421: 837–40.

Boyer, P. (2008) Religion: bound to believe? *Nature* 455: 1038–9.

Braun, I. (2005) Die kunst des Schweizerischen Jungpaläolothikums (Magdalénien). *Helvetia Archaeologica* 141/2: 41–65.

Bresson, F. (2000) Le squelette du Roc-de-Cave (Saint-Cirq-Madelon, Lot). *Paleo* 12: 29–60.

Brinch Petersen, E. (2006) Manipulation of the Mesolithic body. In Piek, J. and Terberger, T. (eds) *Frühe Spuren der Gewalt – Schädelverletzungen und Wundversorgung an Prähistorischen Menschenresten aus Interdisziplinärer Sicht.* Schwerin: Landesamt fur Kultur und Denkmalpflege, pp. 43–50.

Broglio, A. (1995) Les sépultures Épigravettiens de la Vénétie (Abri Tagilente et Abri Villabruna). In Otte, M. (ed.) *Nature et Culture.* Liège: ERAUL 68, pp. 647–69.

Brugal, J.-P. (1999) Middle Palaeolithic subsistence on large bovids: La Borde and Coudoulous (Lot). In Gaudzinski, S. and Turner, E. (eds) *The Role of Early Humans in the Accumulation of European Lower and Middle Palaeolithic Bone Assemblages*. Bonn: RGZM Verlag, pp. 263–5.

Buckland, W. (1823) *Reliquiae Diluvianae, or Observations on the Organic Remains contained in Caves, Fissures, and Diluvial Gravel and on Other Geological Phenomena, attesting the Action of an Universal Deluge.* London: John Murray.

Buisson, D. and Gambier, D. (1991) Façonnage et gravures sur des os humains d'Isturitz (Pyrénées-Atlantiques). *Bulletin de la Société Préhistorique Française* 88(6): 172–7.

Bygott, J. D. (1972) Cannibalism among wild chimpanzees. *Nature* 238: 410–11.

Capitan, L. and Peyrony, D. (1912a) Station préhistorique de La Ferrassie, commune de Savignac-du-Bugue (Dordogne). *Revue Anthropologique* 22: 29–50.

Capitan, L. and Peyrony, D. (1912b) Trois nouveaux squelettes humains fossiles. *Revue Anthropologique* 22: 439–42.

Capitan, L. and Peyrony, D. (1921) Nouvelles foilles à La Ferrassie (Dordogne). *Association Française pour l'Avancement des Sciences*, Strasbourg 1920, pp. 540–2.

Capitan, L. and Peyrony, D. (1928) *La Madeleine: son Gisement, Son Industrie, ses Oevres d'Art.* Paris: E. Nourry.

Cardini, L. (1942) Nuovi documenti sull'antichità dell'uomo in Italia: reperto umano del Paleolitico superiore nella Grotta delle Arene Candide. *Razza e Civiltà* 3: 5–25.

Cardini, L. (1980) *La Necropoli Mesolitica delle Arene Candide (Liguria).* Memorie dell'Instituto Italiano di Paleontologia Umana 3, pp. 9–31.

Cartailhac, E. (1889) *La France Préhistorique d'après les Sépultures et les Monuments.* Paris: Alcan.

Chamberlain, A. and Parker Pearson, M. (2001) *Earthly Remains: The History and Science of Preserved Human Bodies.* London: British Museum Press.

Chapman, R. (1981) The emergence of formal disposal areas and the 'problem' of megalithic tombs in prehistoric Europe. In Chapman, R., Kinnes, I. and Randsborg, K. (eds) *The Archaeology of Death.* Cambridge: Cambridge University Press, pp. 71–81.

Chase, P. C. and Dibble, H. L. (1987) Middle Palaeolithic symbolism: a review of current evidence and interpretation. *Journal of Anthropological Archaeology* 6: 263–96.

Chatters, J. C. (in press) Patterns of Death and the Peopling of the Americas. In Jimenez Lopez, J. C. *et al. Proceedings of III Symposio International 'El Hombre Temprano en America'*. Mexico City: National Museum of Anthropology.

Chauvière, F.-X. (2001) La collection Chaplain-Duparc des Musée du Mans: nouveaux éléments d'interprétation pour 'la sépulture Sorde 1' de Duruthy (Sorde-l'Abbaye, Landes). *Paleo* 13: 89–110.

Clark, J. D., Beyene, Y., WoldeGabriel, G., Hart, W. K., Renne, P. R. *et al.* (2003). Stratigraphic, chronological and behavioural contexts of Pleistocene *Homo sapiens* from Middle Awash, Ethiopia. *Nature* 423: 747–52.

Colleter, R. and Hinguant, S. (2006) Un vestige osseux humain isolé dans la couche tardiglaciaire de la Grotte Rochefort (Saint-Pierre-sur-Erve, Mayenne). *Bulletin de la Société Préhistorique Française* 103: 793–9.

Conard, N. J., Grootes, P. M. and Smith, F. H. (2004) Unexpectedly recent dates for human remains from Vogelherd. *Nature* 430: 198–201.

Cook, J. (1991) Comment to Stiner/White and Toth. *Current Anthropology* 32(2): 126–7.

Cooke, H. B. S., Malan, B. D. and Wells, L. H. (1945) Fossil man in the Lebombo Mountains, South Africa: the 'Border Cave', Ingwavuma District, Zululand. *Man* 45: 6–13.

Coppola, D. and Vacca, E. (1995) Les supultures paléolithiques de la Grotte de Sainte Marie d'Agnano à Ostuni (Italie). In Otte, M. (ed.) *Nature et Culture. Actes du Colloque Internationale de Liège 13–17 Décembre 1993*. Liège: ERAUL 68, pp. 795–808.

Corchón Rodríguez, M. (1998) Nuevas representations de anthropomorfos en el Magdaleniense Medio Cantábrico. *Zephyrus* 51: 35–60.

Courtenay, J. and Santow, G. (1989) Mortality of wild and captive chimpanzees. *Folia Primatologica* 52: 167–77.

Coward, F. and Gamble, C. (2008) Big brains, small worlds: material culture and the evolution of the mind. *Philosophical Transactions of the Royal Society B* 363: 1969–79.

Cowgill, L. W., Trinkaus, E., and Zeder, M. A. (2007) Shanidar 10: A Middle Palaeolithic lower distal limb from Shanidar Cave, Iraqi Kurdistan. *Journal of Human Evolution* 53: 213–23.

Cullen, T. (1995) Mesolithic mortuary ritual at Franchthi Cave, Greece. *Antiquity* 69: 270–89.

Currant, A. P., Jacobi, R. M. and Stringer, C. B. (1989) Excavations at Gough's Cave, Somerset 1986–87. *Antiquity* 63: 131–6.

D'Amore, G., di Marco, S., Tartarelli, G., Bigazzi, R. and Sineo, L. (2009) Late Pleistocene human evolution in Sicily: comparative morphometric analysis of Grotta di San Teodoro craniofacial remains. *Journal of Human Evolution* 56: 537–50.

Darwin, C. (1871) *The Descent of Man*. London: John Murray.

David, F. and Farizy, C. (1999) Mauran (Haute-Garonne, France). In Gaudzinski, S. and Turner, E. (eds) *The Role of Early Humans in the Accumulation of European Lower and Middle Palaeolithic Bone Assemblages*. Bonn: RGZM Verlag, pp. 267–78.

Day, M. (1986) *Guide to Fossil Man* (Fourth Edition). London: Cassell.

Debénath, A. (1988) Recent thoughts on the Riss and Early Würm lithic assemblages of La Chaise de Vouthon (Charente, France). In Dibble, H. and Montet-White, A. (eds) *Upper Pleistocene Prehistory of Western Eurasia*. Philadelphia: University of Pennsylvania University Museum, pp. 85–94.

Debénath, A. (2000) Le peuplement préhistorique du Maroc: donées récentes et problèmes. *L'Anthropologie* 104: 131–45.

Debénath, A. and Jelínek, A. (1998) Nouvelles fouilles à La Quina: resultants preliminaires. *Gallia Préhistoire* 40: 29–74.

Defleur, A. (1993) *Les Sépultures Moustériennes*. Paris: CNRS Editions.

Defleur, A., Dutour, O., Valladas, H. and Vandermeersch, V. (1993) Cannibals among the Neanderthals. *Nature* 362: 214–22.

Defleur, A., White, T., Valensi, P., Slimak, L. and Crégut-Bonnoure, E. (1999) Neanderthal cannibalism at Moula-Guercy, Ardèche, France. *Science* 286: 128–131.

Delluc, B. and Delluc, G. (1981) La Grotte ornée de Comarque a Sireul (Dordogne). *Gallia Préhistoire* 24: 1–97.

Delporte, H. (1976) Les sépultures moustériennes de La Ferrassie. In Vandermeersch, B. (ed.) *Les Sépultures Néanderthaliennes*. Nice: Union Internationale des Sciences Préhistoriques et Protohistoriques IXᵉ Congrès, pp. 8–11.

D'Errico, F. (1991) Comment to Stiner/White and Toth. *Current Anthropology* 32(2): 127–8.

D'Errico, F. (2003) The invisible frontier: a multiple species model for the origin of behavioural modernity. *Evolutionary Anthropology* 12: 188–202.

D'Errico, F. and Vanhaeren, M. (2000) Mes morts et les morts de mes voisins. Le mobilier funéraire de l'Aven des Iboussières et l'identification de marqueurs culturels à l'Épipalaeolithique. In *Les Dernier Chasseurs-Cuilleurs d'Europe Occidental. Actes du Colloque International de Besançon, Octobre 1998.* Besançon: Presses Universitaires Franc-Comtoises, pp. 325–42.

D'Errico, F., Henshilwood, C., Lawson, G., Vanhaeren, M., Tillier, A.-M. *et al.* (2003) Archaeological evidence for the emergence of language, symbolism, and music – an alternative multidisciplinary perspective. *Journal of World Prehistory* 17(1): 1–70.

De Villiers, H. (1973) Human skeletal remains from Border Cave, Ingwavuma District, KwaZulu, South Africa. *Annals of the Transvaal Museum* 28: 229–56.

Díez, J. C., Fernández-Jalvo, Y., Rosell, J. and Cáceres, I. (1999) Zooarchaology and taphonomy of Aurora stratum (Gran Dolina, Sierra de Atapuerca, Spain). *Journal of Human Evolution* 37: 623–52.

Dodo, Y., Kondo, O., Muhesen, S. and Akazawa, T. (1998) Anatomy of the Neanderthal infant skeleton from Dederiyeh Cave, Syria. In Akazawa, T., Aoki, K. and Bar-Yosef, O. (eds) *Neandertals and Modern Humans in Western Asia.* New York: Plenum, 323–38.

Drucker, D. G. and Henry-Gambier, D. (2005) Determination of the dietary habits of a Magdalenian woman from Saint-Germain-la-Rivière in southwestern France using stable isotopes. *Journal of Human Evolution* 49: 19–35.

Duarte, C. (2002) The burial taphonomy and ritual. In Zilhão, J. and Trinkaus, E. (eds) *Portrait of the Artist as a Child: The Gravettian Human Skeleton from the Abrigo do Lagar Velho and Its Archaeological Context.* Lisbon: Trabalhos de Arqueologia 22, pp. 187–201.

Duarte, C., Maurício, J., Pettitt, P. B., Souto, P., Trinkaus, E. and Zilhão, J. (1999) An earlier Upper Palaeolithic human skeleton from the Abrigo do Lagar Velho (Portugal) and modern human emergence in Iberia. *Proceedings of the National Academy of Sciences (USA)* 96, pp. 7604–9.

Dunbar, R. (1988) *Primate Social Systems.* New York: Cornell University Press.

Dunbar, R. (1994) *Primate Social Systems.* London: Chapman & Hall.

Einwögerer, T., Friesinger, H., Händel, M., Neugebauer-Maresch, C., Simon, U. and Teschler-Nicola, M. (2006) Upper Palaeolithic infant burials. *Nature* 444: 285.

Einwögerer, T., Händel, M., Neugebauer-Maresch, C., Simon, U. and Teschler-Nicola, M. (2008) The Gravettian infant burials from Krems-Wachtberg, Austria. In Bacvarov, K. (ed.) *Babies Reborn: Infant/Child Burials in Pre- and Protohistory.* Oxford: BAR International series 1832, pp. 15–19.

Fabbri, F. (1992) Le peuplement Épigravettian de l'Italie. In Rigaud, J.-P., Laville, H. and Vandermeersch, B. (eds) *Le Peuplement Magdalénien. Paléogéographie, Physique et Humaine.* Paris: Editions du C.T.H.S., pp. 79–84.

Falguères, C., Bahain, J.-J., Yokoyama, Y., Arsuaga, J. L., Bermúdez de Castro, J. M. *et al.* (1999) Earliest humans in Europe: the age of TD6 Gran Dolina, Atapuerca, Spain. *Journal of Human Evolution* 37: 343–52.

Farrand, W. R. (1979) Chronology and palaeoenvironment of prehistoric Levantine sites as seen from sedimentological studies. *Journal of Archaeological Science* 6(4): 369–92.

Fennell, K. J. and Trinkaus, E. (1997) Bilateral femoral and tibial periostitis in the La Ferrassie 1 Neanderthal. *Journal of Archaeological Science* 24: 985–95.

Ferembach, D. (1956) Notes sur quelques dents humaines trouvées dans le gisement des Vachons (Charente). *Cahiers Préhistorique de France* 15: 310–12.

Fernández-Jalvo, Y. and Andrews, P. (2001) Atapuerca, le conte des deux sites. *L'Anthropologie* 105: 223–6.

Fernández-Jalvo, Y., Carlos Diez, J., Cáceres, I. and Rosell, J. (1999) Human cannibalism in the Early Pleistocene of Europe (Gran Dolina, Sierra de Atapuerca, Burgos, Spain). *Journal of Human Evolution* 37: 591–622.

Feustel, R. (1970) Statuettes féminines Palélithiques de la République Démocratique Allemande. *Bulletin de la Société Préhistorique Française* 67: 12–16.

Formicola, V. (1988a) The triplex burial of Barma Grande (Grimaldi, Italy). *Homo* 39: 130–43.

Formicola, V. (1988b) The male and the female in the Upper Paleolithic burials from Grimaldi caves. *Bulletin du Musée d'Anthropologie Préhistorique de Monaco* 31: 41–8.

Formicola, V. (1989) The Upper Palaeolithic burials of Barma Grande, Grimaldi, Italy. In Giocobini, G. (ed.) *Hominidae: Proceedings of the 2nd International Congress of Human Paleontology*. Milan: Jaca, pp. 483–6.

Formicola, V. (1991) Le sepolture Paleoltiche dei Balzi Rossi. *Le Scienze* 280: 76–85.

Formicola, V. (2007) From the Sungir children to the Romito dwarf. Aspects of the Upper Palaeolithic funerary landscape. *Current Anthropology* 48(3): 446–53.

Formicola, V. and Buzhilova, A. (2004) Double child burial from Sunghir (Russia): pathology and inferences for Upper Palaeolithic funerary practises. *American Journal of Physical Anthropology* 124: 189–98.

Formicola, V., Pontrandolfi, A. and Svoboda, J. (2001) The Upper Palaeolithic triple burial of Dolní Věstonice: pathology and funerary behaviour. *American Journal of Physical Anthropology* 115: 372–9.

Formicola, V., Pettitt, P. B. and del Lucchese, A. (2004) A direct AMS radiocarbon date on the Barma Grande 6 Upper Paleolithic skeleton. *Current Anthropology* 45(1): 114–18.

Formicola, V., Pettitt, P. B., Maggi, R. and Hedges, R. E. M. (2005) Tempo and mode of formation of the Late Epigravettian necropolis of Arene Candide Cave (Italy): evidence from the direct radiocarbon dates of the skeletons. *Journal of Archaeological Science* 32: 1598–602.

Fosse, P. (1999) Cave occupation during Palaeolithic times: man and/or hyena? In Gaudzinski, S. and Turner, E. (eds) *The Role of Early Humans in the Accumulation of European Lower and Middle Palaeolithic Bone Assemblages*. Bonn: RGZM Verlag, p. 88.

Foucher, P., Tisnerat, N., Valladas, H., Duday, H. and Gachina, J. (1995) Le squelette repute Aurignacien de la Grotte du Bouil Bleu à la Roche-Courbon, Saint-Porchaire (Charente-Maritime). Révision de l'âge-datation directe par la method du carbone 14 (S. M. A.). *Bulletin de la Société Préhistorique Française* 92(4): 443–4.

Frayer, D. W., Horton, W. A., Macchiarelli, R. and Mussi, M. (1987) Dwarfism in an adolescent from the Italian Late Upper Palaeolithic. *Nature* 330: 60–2.

Frayer, D. W., Macchiarelli, R. and Mussi, M. (1988) A case of chondrodystrophic dwarfism in the Italian Late Upper Palaeolithic. *American Journal of Physical Anthropology* 75: 549–65.

REFERENCES

Freeman, L. and González-Echegaray, J. (1970) Aurignacian structural features and burials at Cueva Morin. *Nature* 226: 722–6.

Friday, A. E. (2000) Human evolution: evidence from DNA sequencing. In Jones, S., Martin, R. and Pilbeam, D. (eds) *The Cambridge Encyclopaedia of Human Evolution*. Cambridge: Cambridge University Press, pp. 316–21.

Gambier, D. (1989) Fossil hominids from the Early Upper Palaeolithic (Aurignacian) of France. In Mellars, P. and Stringer, C. B. (eds) *The Human Revolution: Behavioural and Biological Perspectives on the Origin of Modern Humans*. Princeton, NJ: Princeton University Press, pp. 298–320.

Gambier, D. (1990) Practiques funéraires au Paléolithique Supérieur en France: les sépultures primaires. *Bulletins et Mémoires de la Société s'Anthropologie de Paris* 2(3–4): 19–28.

Gambier, D. (1992) Les populations Magdaléniens en France. In Rigaud, J.-P., Laville, H. and Vandermeersch, B. (eds) *Le Peuplement Magdalénien. Paléogéographie, Physique et Humaine*. Paris: Editions du C.T.H.S., pp. 41–51.

Gambier, D. and Lenoir, M. (1991) Les vestiges humains du Paléolithique Supérieur en Gironde. *Bulletin de la Société d'Anthropologie du Sud-Ouest* 26: 1–31.

Gambier, D., Valladas, H., Tisnérat-Laborde, N., Arnold, M. and Bresson, F. (2000) Datation de vestiges humains présumés du Paléolithique Supérieur par la méthode du carbone 14 en spectrométrie de masse par accélerateur. *Paleo* 12: 201–12.

Gamble, C. (1993) *Timewalkers: The Prehistory of Global Colonisation*. London: Alan Sutton.

Gamble, C. (1999) *The Palaeolithic Societies of Europe*. Cambridge: Cambrige University Press.

Gamble, C. and Roebroeks, W. (1999) The Middle Palaeolithic: a point of inflection. In Roebroeks, W. and Gamble, C. (eds) (1999) *The Middle Palaeolithic Occupation of Europe*. Leiden: University Press and European Science Foundation, pp. 1–21.

Gamble, C., Davies, W., Pettitt, P., Richards, M. and Hazelwood, L. (2005) The archaeological and genetic foundations of the European population during the Lateglacial: implications for 'agricultural thinking'. *Cambridge Archaeological Journal* 15(2): 193–223.

García, N., Arsuaga, J. L. and Torres, T. (1997) The carnivore remains from the Sima de los Huesos Middle Pleistocene site (Sierra de Atapuerca, Spain). *Journal of Human Evolution* 33(2/3), 155–74.

Gargett, R. H. (1989) Grave shortcomings: the evidence for Neanderthal burial. *Current Anthropology* 30: 157–90.

Gargett, R. H. (1999) Middle Palaeolithic burial is not a dead issue: the view from Qafzeh, Saint-Cézaire, Kebara, Amud and Dederiyeh. *Journal of Human Evolution* 37: 27–90.

Gargett, R. H. (2000) A response to Hover's, Kimbel's and Rak's argument for the purposeful burial of Amud 7. *Journal of Human Evolution* 39: 261–6.

Garralda, M. D. (1992) Les Magdaléniens en Espagne: anthropologie et context paléoécologique. In Rigaud, J.-P., Laville, H. and Vandermeersch, B. (eds) *Le Peuplement Magdalénien. Paléogéographie, Physique et Humaine*. Paris: Editions du C.T.H.S., pp. 63–70.

Garrod, D. A. E. and Bate, D. M. A. (1937) *The Stone Age of Mount Carmel*, volume 1 *Excavations at the Wadi-el-Mughara*. Oxford: Clarendon Press.

Gaudzinski, S. (1999a) Results of faunal analysis from the 1927–8 excavation at Wallertheim (Rheinhessen, Germany) and their implications for our knowledge of Middle Palaeolithic subsistence. In Gaudzinski, S. and Turner, E. (eds) *The Role of Early Humans in the Accumulation of European Lower and Middle Palaeolithic Bone Assemblages.* Bonn: RGZM Verlag, pp. 279–90.

Gaudzinski, S. (1999b) A contribution to the knowledge of the Early Weichselian open-air site of Wallertheim (Rheinhessen/Germany). In Brugal, J. Ph., David, F., Enloe, J. G. and Jaubert, J. (eds) *Le Bison: Gibier et Moyen de Subsitence des Hommes du Paléolithiques aux Paléoindiens des Grandes Plaines.* Antibes: Éditions APDCA, pp. 281–300.

Gély, B. and Morand, P. (1998) Le sépultures épipalaeolithiques de l'Aven des Iboussières à Malataverne (Drôme, France): prémiers resultats. *Ardèche Archéologie* 15: 13–18.

Geneste, J.-M. (1989) Economie des resources lithiques dans le Moustérien du sud-ouest de la France. In Otte, M. (ed) *L.Homme de Néanderthal*, volume 6 *La Subsistence.* Liège: ERAUL, pp. 75–97.

Giacomo, G. and de Lumley, M.-A. (1988) Les fossils humains de la Caverna delle Fate (Finale, Ligurie Italienne) et la définition des caractères Neanderthaliens au début du Würm. In Trinkaus, E. (ed.) *L'Homme de Neanderthal*, volume 3 *L'Anatomie.* Liège: Etudes et Recherches Archéologiques de l'Université de Liège 30, pp. 53–65.

Gibbons, A. (2003) Oldest members of *Homo sapiens* discovered in Africa. *Science* 300: 1641.

Gieseler, W. (1977) Das Jungpaläolothische skelett von Neuessing. *Festschrift 75 Jahre Anthropologie.* Munich: Anthropologische Staatsammlung München, pp. 39–51.

Gietz, F. J. (2001) *Spätes Jungpaläolithikum und Mesolithikum in der Burghöhle Dietfurt an der oberen Donau.* Materialhefte zur Archäologie in Baden-Württemberg; 60. Stuttgart: Konrad Theiss.

Gillespie, R. (2002) Dating the first Australians. *Radiocarbon* 44(2): 455–72.

Gillespie, R. and Roberts, R. G. (2000) On the reliability of age estimates for the human remains at Lake Mungo. *Journal of Human Evolution* 38: 727–32.

Golovanova, L. V., Hoffecker, J., Kharitonov, V. M. and Romanova, G. P. (1999) Mezmaiskaya Cave: a Neanderthal occupation in the Northern Caucasus. *Current Anthropology* 40(1): 77–86.

Goodall, J. (1971) *In the Shadow of Man.* London: Collins.

Goodall, J. (1977) Infant killing and cannibalism in free-living chimpanzees. *Folia Primatologica* 28: 259–82.

Goodall, J. (1986) *The Chimpanzees of Gombe: Patterns of Behaviour.* Cambridge, MA: Harvard University Press.

Goodall, J. (1990) *Through a Window: My Thirty years with the Chimpanzees of Gombe.* Boston: Houghton Mifflin Company.

Graziosi, P. (1963) Pupasidero (Prov. Cosenza). *Rivista di Scienze Preistoriche* 18: 315.

Grün, R. and Beaumont, P. (2001) Border Cave revisited: a revised ESR chronology. *Journal of Human Evolution* 40: 467–82.

Grün, R., Stringer, C. B. and Schwarcz, H. P. (1991) ESR dating from Garrod's Tabun Cave collection. *Journal of Human Evolution* 20: 231–48.

Grün, R., Stringer, C., McDermott, F., Nathan, R., Porat, M. *et al.* (2005) U-Series and ESR analyses of bones and teeth relating to the human burials from Skhūl. *Journal of Human Evolution* 49: 316–34.

Habgood, P. J. and Franklin, N. R. (2008) The revolution that didn't arrive: a review of Pleistocene Sahul. *Journal of Human Evolution* 55: 187–222.

Hamai, M., Nishida, T., Takasaki, H. and Turner, L. A. (1992) New records of within-group infanticide and cannibalism in wild chimpanzees. *Primates* 33(2): 151–62.

Hammond, N. G. L. and Scullard, H. H. (1984) *The Oxford Classical Dictionary*. Oxford: Clarendon Press.

Hardy, M. (1891) La station quaternaire de Raymondon à Chancelade (Dordogne) et la sépulture d'un chasseur de rennes. *Bulletin de la Société Historique et Archeologique du Périgord* 18: 65–89, 121–35, 195–212.

Harrold, F. (1980) A comparative analysis of Eurasian Palaeolithic burials. *World Archaeology* 12(2): 195–211.

Harvati, K., Gunz, P. and Grigorescu, D. (2005) Cioclovina (Romania): affinities of an early modern European. *Journal of Human Evolution* 53: 732–46.

Hauser, O. (1909) Découverte d'un squelette du type du Néandertal sous l'Abri Inférieur de Moustier. *L'Homme Préhistorique* 7(1): 178–9.

Haverkort, C. M. and Lubell, D. (1999) Cut marks on Capsian human remains: implications for Maghreb Holocene social organisation and palaeoeconomy. *International Journal of Osteoarchaeology* 9: 147–69.

Hayden, B. (1993) The cultural capacities of Neanderthals: a review and re-evaluation. *Journal of Human Evolution* 24: 113–46.

Heim J.-L. (1976) *Les Hommes Fossiles de La Ferrassie*. I. Paris: Masson, pp. 3–8.

Heim, J.-L. (1992) Le crâne magnalénien du Rond-du-Barry (Haute-Loire). In Rigaud, J.-P., Laville, H. and Vandermeersch, B. (eds) *Le Peuplement Magdalénien. Paléogéographie, Physique et Humaine*. Paris: Editions du C.T.H.S., pp. 53–61.

Henry-Gambier, D. (2001) *La Sépulture des Enfants de Grimaldi (Boussé-Roussé, Italie). Anthropologie et Palethnologie des Populations de la Fin du Paléolithique Supérieur*. Paris: CTHS, Réunion des Musées Nationaux.

Henry-Gambier, D. (2002) Les fouilles de Cro-Magnon (Les-Eyzies-de-Tayac, Dordogne): nouvelles données sur leur position chronologique et leur attribution culturelle. *Paleo* 14: 201–4.

Henry-Gambier, D. (2003) Évolution des practiques funéraire en Italie au Paléolithique Supérieur. In Vialou, D., Renault-Miskovsky, J. and Patou-Mathis, M. (eds) *Comportements des Hommes du Paléolithique Moyen et Supéreur en Europe: Territoires et Millieux*. Liège: ERAUL 111, pp. 213–29.

Henry-Gambier, D. (2006) Les sépultures de Sorde-l'Abbaye (Landes). In Dachary, M. (ed.) *Les Magdaléniens à Duruthy. Qui Étaient Ils?* Hastingues: Centre Départemental du Patrimoine, pp. 67–73.

Henry-Gambier, D. (2008) Practiques funéraires des populations Gravettiennes en Europe: bilan des données et interprétations. *Paleo* 20: 1–39.

Henry-Gambier, D. and Sacchi, D. (2008) La Crouzade V–VI (Aude, France): un des plus anciens fossiles d'anatomie moderne en Europe Occidental. *Bulletin et Mémoires de la Société d'Anthropologie de Paris* 20: 79–104.

Henry-Gambier, D. and White, R. (2006) Modifications artificielles des vestiges humains de l'Aurignacien Ancien de la Grotte des Hyènes (Brassempouy, Landdes). Quelle signification? In Cabrera Valdés, V., Bernaldo de Quirós Guidotti, F. and Maíllo Fernández, J. M. (eds) *En El Centenario de la Cueva de El Castillo: El Ocaso de los Neandertales*. Madrid: Ministerio de Educacion, pp. 73–88.

Henry-Gambier, D., Bruzek, J., Murail, P. and Houët, F. (2002) Révision du sexe du squelette Magdalénien de Saint-Germain-la-Rivière. *Paleo* 14: 205–12.

Henry-Gambier, D., Maureille, B. and White, R. (2004) Vestiges humains des niveaux de l'Aurignacien ancien du site de Brassempouy (Landes). *Bulletin et Mémoires de la Société d'Anthropologie de Paris* 6: 49–87.

Henry-Gambier, D., Beauval, C., Airvaux, J., Aujoulat, N., Baratin, J. F. and Buisson-Catil, J. (2007) New hominid remains associated with gravettian parietal art (Les Garennes, Vilhonneur, France). *Journal of Human Evolution* 53(6): 747–50.

Henshilwood, C. and d'Errico, F. (2009) Ochre, symbolism and the Middle Stone Age: examining the evidence from the Western Cape, South Africa. Pre-circulated paper for the *Homo symbolicus* symposium, Cape Town.

Henshilwood, C. and Marean, C. (2003) The origin of modern human behavior. Critique of the models and their test implications. *Current Anthropology* 44: 627–51.

Henshilwood, C., d'Errico, F. and Watts, I. (2009) Engraved ochres from the Middle Stone Age levels at Blombos Cave, South Africa. *Journal of Human Evolution* 57(1): 27–47.

Henshilwood, C., d'Errico, F., Vanhaeren, M., van Niekerk, K. and Jacobs, Z. (2004) Middle Stone Age shell beads from South Africa. *Science* 304: 404.

Hershkovitz, I., Speirs, M. S., Frayer, D., Nadel, D., Wish-Baratz, S. and Arensburg, B. (1995) Ohalo II H2: a 19,000 years-old skeleton from a water-logged site at the Sea of Galilee, Israel. *American Journal of Physical Anthropology* 96: 215–34.

Hertz, R. (1960) A contibution to the study of the collective representation of death. In Needham, R. and Needham, C. (eds) *Death and the Right Hand*. New York: Free Press, pp. 27–86.

Hill, K., Boesch, C., Goodall, J., Pusey, A., Williams, J. and Wrangham, R. (2001) Mortality rates among wild chimpanzees. *Journal of Human Evolution* 40: 437–50.

Höck, C. (1993) Die frauenstatuetten des Magdalénien von Gönnersdorf und Andernach. *Jahrbuch des Römisch-Germanischen Zentralmuseums Mainz* 40: 253–316.

Hovers, E. (2001) Territorial behaviour in the Middle Paleolithic of the southern Levant. In Conard, N. J. (ed.) *Settlement Dynamics of the Middle Paleolithic and Middle Stone Age*. Tübingen: Kerns Verlag, pp. 123–52.

Hovers, E. and Belfer-Cohen, A. (in press) Insights into early mortuary practises of *Homo*. In Tarlow, S. and Nilsson Stutz, L. (eds) *The Oxford Handbook of the Archaeology of Death and Burial*. Oxford: Oxford University Press.

Hovers, E., Kimbel, W. H., and Rak, Y. (2000) The Amud skeleton – still a burial. Response to Gargett. *Journal of Human Evolution* 39: 253–60.

Hovers, E., Ilani, S., Bar-Yosef, O. and Vendermeersch, B. (2003) An early case of color symbolism: ochre use by modern humans in Qafzeh Cave. *Current Anthropology* 44(4): 491–522.

Hovers, E., Rak, Y., Lavi, R. and Kimbel, W. H. (1995) Hominid remains from Amud cave in the context of the Levantine Middle Palaeolithic. *Paléorient* 21: 47–61.

Hrdy, S. (1979) Infanticide among animals: a review, classification, and examination of the implications for the reproductive strategies of females. *Ethology and Sociobiology* 1: 13–40.

Hrdy, S. Blaffer (1999) *Mother Nature: Natural Selection and the Female of the Species*. London: Chatto & Windus.

Hublin, J.-J. (2000) Modern/Non modern human interactions: a Mediterranean perspective. In Bar-Yosef, O. and Pilbeam, D. (eds) *The Geography of Neanderthals and Modern Humans in Europe and the Greater Mediterranean.* Harvard, MA: Peabody Museum Bulletin 8: 157–82.

Huntington, R. and Metcalf, P. (1979) *Celebrations of Death: the Anthropology of Mortuary Ritual.* Cambridge: Cambridge University Press.

Irish, J. D., Bratlund, B., Schild, R., Kolstrup, E., Królik, H. *et al.* (2008) A late Magdalenian perinatal human skeleton from Wilczyce, Poland. *Journal of Human Evolution* 55: 736–40.

Jacobi, R. M. (2005) Some observations on the lithic artefacts from Aveline's Hole, Burrington Combe, North Somerset. *Proceedings of the University of Bristol Spelaeological Society* 23(3): 267–95.

Jacobi, R. M. and Higham, T. F. G. (2008) The 'Red Lady' ages gracefully: new ultrafiltration AMS determinations from Paviland. *Journal of Human Evolution* 55: 898–907.

Jacobi, R. M. and Higham, T. F. G. (2009) The early Lateglacial re-colonisation of Britain: new radiocarbon evidence from Gough's Cave, southwest England. *Quaternary Science Reviews* 28: 1895–913.

Janson, C. H. and Van Schaik, C. P. (2000) The behavioural ecology of infanticide by males. In Van Schaik, C. and Janson, C. H. (eds) *Infanticide by Males and its Implications.* Cambridge: Cambridge University Press, pp. 469–94.

Johanson, D. C. and Edey, M. (1981) *Lucy: The Beginnings of Mankind.* New York: Simon & Schuster.

Johanson, D. and Shreeve, J. (1989) *Lucy's Child: The Discovery of a Human Ancestor.* London: Penguin.

Johanson, D. C., Taieb, M. and Coppens, Y. (1982) Pliocene hominids from the Hadar formation, Ethiopia (1973–1977): stratigraphic, chronologic, and paleo-environmental contexts, with notes on hominid morphology and systematics. *American Journal of Physical Anthropology* 57: 373–402.

Keele, B. F., Holland Jones, J., Terio, K. A., Estes, J. D., Rudicell, R. S. *et al.* (2009) Increased mortality and AIDS-like immunopathology in wild chimpanzees infected with SIVcpz. *Nature* 460: 515–19.

Keith, A. (1925) A discovery as wonderful as that of Tutankhamen's tomb: Prof. D. K. Absolon's new revelation of prehistoric culture 20,000 years ago. *The Illustrated London News,* 31 October, 848.

Klein, R. (1999) *The Human Career.* Chicago: Chicago University Press.

Klima, B. (1988) A triple burial from the Upper Palaeolithic of Dolní Věstonice, Czechoslovakia. *Journal of Human Evolution* 16, 831–5.

Klima, B. (1995) *Dolní Věstonice II.* Liège: ERAUL 73.

Kolen, J. (1999) Hominids without homes: on the nature of Middle Palaeolithic settlement in Europe. In Roebroeks, W. and Gamble, C. (eds) *The Middle Palaeolithic Occupation of Europe.* Leiden: University Press and European Science Foundation, pp. 139–75.

Kolosov, Y. G. (1996) Comments on the dating of Zaskal'naya VI. In Hedges, R. E. M., Housley, R. A., Pettitt, P. B., Ramsey, C. B. and Van Klinken, G. J. (eds) *Radiocarbon dates from the Oxford AMS system: Archaeometry* Datelist 21. *Archaeometry* 38(1): 190.

Kosłowski, S. K. and Sachse-Kosłowska, E. (1993) Maszycka Cave: a Magdalenian site in Southern Poland. *Jahrbuch der Römisch-Germanischen Zentralmuseums Mainz* 40, pp. 115–205.

Kuhn, S. L., Stiner, M. C., Reese, D. S. and Güleç, E. (2001). Ornaments of the earliest Upper Paleolithic: new insights from the Levant. *Proceedings of the National Academy of Sciences (USA)* 98: 7641–6.

Kuijt, I. (1996) Negotiating equality through ritual: a consideration of Late Natufian and Prepottery Neolithic A period mortuary practices. *Journal of Anthropological Archaeology* 15: 313–36.

Kurtén, B. (1976) *The Cave Bear Story: Life and Death of a Vanished Animal*. New York: Columbia University Press.

Kuzmin, Y. V., Burr, G. S., Jull, A. J. T. and Sulerzhitsky, L. D. (2004) AMS ^{14}C age of the Upper Palaeolithic skeletons from Sungir site, Central Russian Plain. *Nuclear Instruments and Methods in Physics Research* B 223–4: 731–4.

Lalueza Fox, C. (1995) Restos humanos de nivel Solutrense de la Cueva de Nerja (Málaga). *Zephyrus* XLVIII: 289–97.

Larsson, L. (2004) The Mesolithic period in southern Scandinavia with special reference to burials and cemeteries. In Saville, A. (ed.) *Mesolithic Scotland and its Neighbours. The Early Holocene Prehistory of Scotland, its British and Irish Context, and some Northern European Perspectives*. Edinburgh: Society of Antiquaries of Scotland, pp. 371–92.

Lee, R. and DeVore, I. (1968) *Man the Hunter*. New York: Aldine.

Le Mort, F. (1985) Un exemple de modification intentionnelle: la dent humaine perforée de Saoint-Garmaine-la-Rivière (Paléolithique Supérieur). *Bulletin de la Société Préhistorique Française* 82(6): 190–2.

Le Mort, F. (1988) Le décharnement du cadavre chez le Néanderthaliens: quelques examples. In Otte, M. (ed.) *L'Homme de Néanderthal*, volume 5 *La Pensée*. Liège: ERAUL 32, pp. 43–55.

Le Mort, F. (1989) Traces de décharnement sur les ossements néandertaliens de Combe-Grenal (Dordogne). *Bulletin de la Société Préhistorique Française* 86: 79–97.

Le Mort, F. and Gambier, D. (1992) Diversité du traitement des os humains au Magdalénien: un exemple particulier, le cas du gisement du Placard (Charente). In Rigaud, J.-P., Laville, H. and Vandermeersch, B. (eds) *Le Peuplement Magdalénien. Paléogéographie, Physique et Humaine*. Paris: Editions du C.T.H.S., pp. 29–40.

Lévêque, F., Backer, A. M. and Guilbaud, M. (1993) *Context of a Late Neanderthal. Implications of Multidisciplinary Research for the Transition to Upper Paleolithic Adaptations at Saint-Césaire, Charente-Maritime, France*. Madison, WI: Prehistory Press.

Lewin, R. (1987) *Bones of Contention: Controversies in the Search for Human Origins*. New York: Simon & Schuster.

Lorblanchet, M. (1995) *Les Grottes Ornées de la Préhistoire*. Paris: Éditions Errance.

Lorblanchet, M. (2001) Cussac, fantastique Grotte grave de la Préhistoire. *Archéologia* 381: 4–8.

Lourandos, H. (1997) *Continent of Hunter–Gatherers: New Perspectives on Australian Prehistory*. Cambridge: Cambridge University Press.

Lozano-Ruiz, M., Bermúdez de Castro, J. M., Martinón-Torres, M. and Sarmiento, S. (2004) Cut marks of fossil human anterior teeth of the Sima de los Huesos site (Atapuerca, Spain). *Journal of Archaeological Science* 31: 1127–35.

Lubin, V. P. (1997) Human use of caves in the Caucasus. In Bonsall, C. and Tolan-Smith, C. (eds) *The Human Use of Caves*. Oxford: British Archaeological reports International series 667, pp. 144–9.

Lubbock, J. (1865) *Pre-Historic Times* (First Edition). London: Williams & Norgate.

Lumley, H. de (1972) Les Néanderthaliens. In H. de Lumley (ed.) *La Grotte de L.Hortus (Valflaunès, Hérault)*. Marseilles: Université de Provence, pp. 375–86.

McBrearty, S. and Brooks, A. (2000) The revolution that wasn't: a new interpretation of the origin of modern human behaviour. *Journal of Human Evolution* 39: 453–563.

McCown, T. D. and Keith, A. (1939) *The Stone Age of Mount Carmel* Volume II *The Fossil Human Remains from the Levalloiso-Mousterian*. Oxford: Clarendon Press.

McDermott, F., Grün, R., Stringer, C. B. and Hawkesworth, C. J. (1993) Mass-spectrometric U-Series dates for Israeli Neanderthal/Early Modern hominid sites. *Nature* 363: 252–4.

McGrew, W. (1992) *Chimpanzee Material Culture: Implications for Human Evolution*. Cambridge: Cambridge University Press.

Madelaine, S., Maureille, B., Cavanhié, N., Couture-Veschambre, C., Bonifay, E. et al. (2009) Nouveaux restes humaines Moustériens rapportés au squelette Néanderthalien de Regourdou 1 (Regourdou, Commune de Montignac, Dordogne, France). *Paleo* 20: 101–14.

Mariani-Costantini, R., Ottini, L., Caramiello, S., Palmirotta, R., Mallegni, F. et al. (2001) Taphonomy of the fossil hominid bones from the Acheulian site of Castel di Guido near Rome, Italy. *Journal of Human Evolution* 41: 211–25.

Mariotti, V., Bonfiglioli, B., Facchini, F., Condemi, S. and Belcastro, M. G. (2009) Funerary practises of the Iberomaurusian population of Taforalt (Tafoughalt; Morocco, 11–12,000 BP): new hypotheses based on a grave by grave skeletal inventory and evidence of deliberate human modification of the remains. *Journal of Human Evolution* 56: 340–54.

Marks, J. (2000) Chromosomal evolution in primates. In Jones, S., Martin, R. and Pilbeam, D. (eds) *The Cambridge Encyclopaedia of Human Evolution*. Cambridge: Cambridge University Press, pp. 298–302.

Marks, J. (2003) *What it Means to Be 98% Chimpanzee*. Berkeley: University of California Press.

Martin, Y. (2007) The engravings of Gouy: France's northernmost decorated cave. In Pettitt, P. B., Bahn, P., Muñoz, F. J. and Ripoll, S. (eds) *Palaeolithic Cave Art at Creswell Crags in European Context*. Oxford: Oxford University Press, pp. 140–93.

Matsuzawa, T. (2003) *Jokro: the Death of An Infant Chimpanzee* (DVD film with associated leaflet). Kyoto: Primate Research Insititute.

Matsuzawa, T., Sakura, O., Kimura, T., Hamada, Y. and Sugiyama, Y. (1990) Case report on the death of a wild chimpanzee. *Primates* 31(4): 635–41.

Maureille, B. (2002a) A lost Neanderthal neonate found. *Nature* 419: 33–4.

Maureille, B. (2002b) La redécouverte du nouveau-né Néandertalien Le Moustier 2. *Paleo* 14, 221–38.

Maureille, B. and Peer, P. van (1998) Une donné peu connue sur la sépulture du premier adulte de La Ferrassie (Savignac-de-Miremont, Dordogne). *Paleo* 10: 291–301.

Maureille, B. and Tillier, A.-M. (2008) Répartition géographique et chronologique des sépultures néandertaliennes. In *Première Humanité: Gestes Funéraires des Néandertaliens*. Les Eyzies-de-Tayac: Musée National de Préhistoire, pp. 66–74.

Maureille, B. and Vandermeersch, B. (2007) Les Sépultures Néandertaliennes. In *Les Néandertaliens: Biologie et Cultures*. Paris: Éditions du CTHS (*Documents Préhistoriques* 23), pp. 311–22.

May, S. (1986) *Les Sépultures Préhistoriques: Étude Critique*. Paris: Éditions du Centre National de la Recherche Scientifique.

Meignen, L. (ed) (1993) *L'Abri des Canalettes: Un Habitat Moustérien sur les Grands Causses (Nant, Aveyron): Fouilles 1980–1986*. Paris: CNRS monograph 10.

Mellars, P. A. (1989) Major issues in the emergence of modern humans. *Current Anthropology* 30, 349–85.

Mellars, P. A. (1990) *The Emergence of Modern Humans*. Edinburgh: University Press.

Mellars, P. A. (1996) *The Neanderthal Legacy*. Princeton, NJ: University Press.

Mellars, P. A. and Stringer, C. B. (1989) *The Human Revolution*. Edinburgh: University Press.

Mercier, N., Valladas, H., Joron, J.-L., Lévêque, F. and Vandermeersch, B. (1991) Thermoluminescence dating of the late Neanderthal remains from Saint-Césaire. *Nature* 351, 737–8.

Mercier, N., Valladas, H., Bar-Yosef, O., Vandermeersch, B., Stringer, C. and Joron, J.-L. (1993) Thermoluminscence date for the Mousterian burial site of Es-Skhūl, Mount Carmel. *Journal of Archaeological Science* 20: 169–74.

Millard, A. R. and Pike, A. W. G. (1999) Uranium-Series dating of the Tabun Neanderthal: a cautionary note. *Journal of Human Evolution* 36: 581–5–5.

Mitani, J. C., Watts, D. P. and Muller, M. N. (2002) Recent developments in the study of wild chimpanzee behaviour. *Evolutionary Anthropology* 11: 9–25.

Movius, H. L. (1975) *Excavation of the Abri Pataud, Les Eyzies (Dordogne)*. Cambridge, MA: Harvard University Peabody Museum of Archeology and Ethnology.

Mulvaney, J. and Kamminga, J. (1999) *Prehistory of Australia*. Washington, DC: Smithsonian Institution Press.

Mussi, M. (1986) On the chronology of the burials found in the Grimaldi caves. *Antropologia Contemporanea* 9(2): 95–104.

Mussi, M. (1988) Continuité et discontinuité dans le practiques funéraires au Paléolithiques: le cas de l'Italie. In Otte, M. (ed) *L.Homme de Néanderthal*, volume 5 *La Pensée*. Liège: ERAUL 32, pp. 93–107.

Mussi, M. (1995) Rituels funéraires dans les sepultures Gravettiens des grottes de Grimaldi et de la Grotte delle Arene Candide: un mise au point. In Otte, M. (ed.) *Nature et Culture*. Liège: ERAUL 68, pp. 833–46.

Mussi, M. (1999) The Neanderthals in Italy: a tale of many caves. In Roebroeks, W. and Gamble, C. (eds) *The Middle Palaeolithic Occupation of Europe*. Leiden: University Press.

Mussi, M. (2001a) *Earliest Italy: An Overview of the Italian Paleolithic and Mesolithic*. New York: Kluwer and Plenum.

Mussi, M. (2001b) Comment to Riel-Salvatore, J. and Clark, G. A. Grave markers: Middle and Early Upper Palaeolithic burials and the use of chronotypology in contemporary Paleolithic research. *Current Anthropology* 42(4): 467–8.

Mussi, M. (2003) East and south of the Alps: the MUP funerary and artistic record of Italy and Moravia compared. In Svoboda, J. and Sedláčková, L. (eds) *The Gravettian Along the Danube*. Pavlov: Dolní Věstonice Studies 11, pp. 252–69.

Mussi, M., Frayer, D. W. and Macchiarelli, R. (1989) Les vivants et les morts. Les sepultures du Paleolithique Superieur en Italie et leur interpretation. In Hershkovitz, I. (ed.) *People and Culture in Change: Proceedings of the Second Symposium on Upper Palaeolithic, Mesolithic and Neolithic Populations of Europe and the Mediterranean Basin*. Oxford: BAR International Series 508, pp. 435–58.

Mussi, M., Cinq-Mars, J. and Bolduc, P. (2000) Echoes from the mammoth steppe: the case of the Balzi Rossi. In Robroeks, W., Mussi, M., Svoboda, J. and Fennema, K. (eds.) *Hunters of the Golden Age: the Mid Upper Palaeolithic of Eurasia 30,000 – 20,000 BP.* Lieden: University Press, 105–24.

Nadel, D. (1994) Levantine Upper Palaeolithic-Early Epipalaeolithic burial customs: Ohalo II as a case study. *Paléorient* 20/1: 113–21.

Nadel, D., Lengyel, G., Cabellos Panades, T. Bocquentin, F., Rosenberg, D. *et al.* (2008a) The Raqefet Cave 2008 excavation season. *Journal of the Israel Prehistoric Society* 39: 21–61.

Nadel, D., Lengyel, G., Bocquentin, F., Tsatskin, A., Rosenberg, D. *et al.* (2008b) The late Natufian at Raqefet Cave: the 2006 excavation season. *Journal of the Israel Prehistoric Society* 38: 59–131.

Narr, K. J. (1977) Das rätsel von Neuessing bemerkungen zu dem skelettfund aus de Mittleren Klause. *Festschrift 75 Jahre Staatsammlung München*, pp. 53–6.

Negrino, F. and Starnini, E. (2003) Patterns of lithic raw material exploitation in Liguria from the Palaeolithic to the Copper Age. *Préhistoire du Sud-Ouest* supplement 5: 235–43.

Nespoulet, R., Chiotti, L., Henry-Gambier, D., Agsous, S., Lenoble, A. *et al.*, with the collaboration of Grimaud-Hervé, D., Marquer, L., Patou-Mathis, M., Pottier, C., Vannoorenberghe, A. and Verez, M. (2008) L'occupation humaine de l'Abri Pataud (Les Eyzies-de-Tayac, Dordogne) il y a 22,000 ans: problématique et résultats préliminaires des fouilles du niveau 2. *Mémoire XLVII de la Société Préhistorique Française*, pp. 325–34.

Neugebauer-Maresch, C. (2003) Erste ergebnisse der neuen grabungen in Krems-Hundssteig in Rahmen eines projektes der Österr. Akademie der Wissenschaften. *Preistoria Alpina* 39: 165–73.

Neuville, R. (1951) *Le Paléolithique et le Mésolithique du désert de Judée.* Archives de l'Institut de Paléontologie Humaine, Mémoire 24. Paris: Masson.

Nishida, T. and Kawanaka, K. (1985) Within-group cannibalism by adult male chimpanzees. *Primates* 26(3): 274–84.

Nishida, T., Takasaki, H. and Takahata, Y. (1990) Demography and reproductive profiles. In Nishida, T. (ed.) *The Chimpanzees of the Mahale Mountains: Sexual and Life History Strategies.* Tokyo: Tokyo University Press, pp. 63–97.

Norikoshi, K. (1982) One observed case of cannibalism among wild chimpanzees of the Mahale Mountains. *Primates* 23(1): 66–74.

Nunn, C. L. and Van Schaik, C. P. (2000) Social evolution in primates: the relative roles of ecology and intersexual conflict. In Van Schaik, C. and Janson, C. H. (eds) *Infanticide by Males and its Implications.* Cambridge: Cambridge University Press, pp. 388–412.

Oakley, K. P., Campbell, B. G. and Molleson, T. I. (1971) *Catalogue of Fossil Hominids* Part II: *Europe.* London: British Museum (Natural History).

Oliva, M. (1996) Mladopaleoliticky hrob Brno II jako přispěvek k počtkům šamanismu. *Archeologické Rozhledy* XLVIII (3): 353–83.

Oliva, M. (2000a) Les practiques funéraires dans le Pavlovien Morave: revision critique. *Préhistoire Européenne* 16–17: 191–214.

Oliva, M. (2000b) The Brno II Upper Palaeolithic burial. In Roebroeks, W., Mussi, M., Svoboda, J. and Fennema, K. (eds) *Hunters of the Golden Age. The Mid Upper Palaeolithic of Eurasia 30,000–20,000 BP.* Leiden: University of Leiden, pp. 143–53.

Oliva, M. (2005) *Palaeolithic and Mesolithic Moravia*. Brno: Moravian Museum.

Orschiedt, J. (1997) Der nachweis einer sekundärbestattung aud dem Magdalénien der Brillenhöhle, Alb-Donae-Kreis (Baden-Württemberg). *Archäologisches Korrespondenzblatt* 27: 193–206.

Orschiedt, J. (2002) Secondary burial in the Magdalenian: the Brillenhöhle (Blauberen, Southwest Germany). *Paleo* 14: 241–56.

Orschiedt, J. (2008) Der fall Krapina – neue ergebnisse zur frage von kannibalismus beim Neanderthaler. *Quartär* 55, 63–81.

Otte, M. (1996) *Le Paléolithique Inférieur et Moyen en Europe*. Paris: Armand Collin.

Ovchinnikov, I., Götherström, A., Romanova, G. P., Kharitonov, V. M., Lidén, K. and Godwin, W. (2000) Molecular analysis of Neanderthal DNA from the Northern Caucasus. *Nature* 404: 490–3.

Pales, L. and Saint Péruse, M. Tassin de (1976) *Les Gravures de la Marche. II: Les Humaines*. Paris: Éditions Ophrys.

Palma di Cesnola, A. (1974) Su alcune recent scoperti nei livelli Gravettiani della Grotta Paglicci (Promontorio del Gargano). *Zephyrus* XXV: 65–79.

Pap, I., Tillier, A.-M., Arensburg, B. and Chech, M. (1996) The Subalyuk Neanderthal remains (Hungary): a reexamination. *Annales historico-Naturales Musei Nationalis Hungarici* 88: 233–270.

Pardoe, C. (1988) The cemetery as symbol. The distribution of prehistoric aboriginal burial grounds in southeastern Australia. *Archaeology in Oceania* 23: 1–16.

Parés, J. M. and Pérez-González, A. (1999) Magnetochronology and stratigraphy at Gran Dolina section, Atapuerca (Burgos, Spain). *Journal of Human Evolution* 37: 325–42.

Parker Pearson, M. (1999) *The Archaeology of Death and Burial*. Stroud: Sutton.

Patou-Mathis, M. (1997) Analyses taphonomiques et paleoethnographique du materiel osseux de Krapina (Croatie): nouvelles données sur la faune et les restes humaines. *Préhistoire Européenne* 10: 63–90.

Pearson, O. M., Royer, D. F., Grine, F. E. and Fleagle, J. G. (2008) A description of the Omo I postcranial skeleton, including newly discovered fossils. *Journal of Human Evolution* 55: 421–37.

Pestle, W., Colvard, M. and Pettitt, P. (2006) AMS dating of a recently discovered juvenile human mandible from Solutré (Saône-et-Loire, France). *Paleo* 18, 285–92.

Pettitt, P. B. (1997) High resolution Neanderthals? Interpreting Middle Palaeolithic intra site spatial patterning. *World Archaeology* 29(2): 208–24.

Pettitt, P. B. (2000) Neanderthal lifecycles: developmental and social phases in the lives of the last archaics. *World Archaeology* 31(3): 351–66.

Pettitt, P. B. (2002) The Neanderthal dead: exploring mortuary variability in Middle Palaeolithic Eurasia. *Before Farming* 1. Available online: www.waspjournals.com/ Beforefarming (accessed 8 September 2010).

Pettitt, P. B. (2006) The living dead and the dead living: burials, figurines and social performance in the European Mid Upper Palaeolithic. In Gowland, R. and Knüsel, C. (eds) *Social Archaeology of Funerary Remains*. Oxford: Oxbow, pp. 292–308.

Pettitt, P. B. (2007) Cultural context and form of some of the Creswell images: an interpretative model. In Pettitt, P. B., Bahn, P., Muñoz, F. J. and Ripoll, S. (eds) *Palaeolithic Cave Art at Creswell Crags in European Context*. Oxford: Oxford University Press, pp. 112–39.

Pettitt, P. B. (in press) The living as symbols, the dead as symbols: the scale and pace of symbolism over the course of hominin evolution. In Henshilwood, C. and d'Errico, F. (eds) *Homo symbolicus.* Bergen: University of Bergen Press.

Pettitt, P. B. and Bader, N. O. (2000) Direct radiocarbon dates for the Sunghir Mid Upper Palaeolithic burials. *Antiquity* 74: 269–70.

Pettitt, P. B. and Trinkaus, E. (2000) Direct radiocarbon dating of the Brno 2 Gravettian human remains. *Anthropologie (Brno)* 38: 149–50.

Pettitt, P. B., van der Plicht, J., Bronk Ramsey, C., Monge Soares, A. M. and Zilhão, J. (2002) The radiocarbon chronology. In Zilhão, J. and Trinkaus, E. (eds) *Portrait of the Artist as a Child: the Gravettian Human Skeleton from the Abrigo do Lagar Velho and Its Archaeological Context.* Lisbon: Trabalhos de Arqueologia 22, pp. 132–8.

Pettitt, P. B., Richards, M. P., Formicola, V. and Maggi, R. (2003) The Gravettian burial known as 'The Prince' ('Il Principe'): new evidence for his age and diet. *Antiquity* 77: 15–19.

Peyrony, D. (1930) Le Moustier: ses gisements, ses industries, ses couches géologiques. *Revue Anthropologique* 40: 48–76, 155–76.

Peyrony, D. (1934) La Ferrassie: Moustétien – Périgordien – Aurignacien. *Préhistoire* 3: 1–92.

Pickering, T. R., White, T. D. and Toth, N. (2000) Brief communication: cut marks on a Plio-Pleistocene hominid from Sterkfontein, South Africa. *American Journal of Physical Anthropology* 111: 579–84.

Povinelli, D. (2003) *Folk Physics for Apes: the Chimpanzee's Theory of How the World Works.* Oxford: Oxford University Press.

Pusey, A., Williams, J. and Goodall, J. (1997) The influence of dominance rank on the reproductive success of female chimpanzees. *Science* 277: 828–31.

Radosevich, S. C., Retallack, G. J. and Taieb, M. (1992) Reassessment of the paleoenvironment and preservation of hominid fossils from Hadar, Ethiopia. *American Journal of Physical Anthropology* 87: 15–27.

Radovčic, J. (1988) *Dragutin Gorjanovic-Kramberger and Krapina Early Man.* Zagreb: Hrvatski Pridoslovni Muzei.

Rak, Y., Kimbel, W. H. and Hovers, E. (1994) A Neanderthal infant from Amud Cave, Israel. *Journal of Human Evolution* 26: 313–24.

Ramirez Rozzi, F. V., d'Errico, F., Vanhaeren, M., Grootes, P. M., Kerautret, B. and Dujardin, V. (2009) Cut marked human remains bearing Neanderthal features and modern human remains associated with the Aurignacian at Les Rois. *Journal of Anthropological Sciences* 87: 153–85.

Richards, M. P, Pettitt, P. B., Stiner, M. C. and Trinkaus, E. (2001) Stable isotope evidence for increasing dietary breadth in the European Mid Upper Paleolithic. *Proceedings of the National Academy of Sciences (USA)* 98(11), pp. 6528–32.

Riel-Salvatore, J. and Clark, G. A. (2001) Grave markers: Middle and Early Upper Palaeolithic burials and the use of chronotypology in contemporary Paleolithic research. *Current Anthropology* 42(4): 449–79.

Rightmire, G. P. (1979) Implications of Border Cave skeletal remains for later Pleistocene human evolution. *Current Anthropology* 20(1): 23–35.

Rightmire, G. P. and Deacon, H. J. (2001) New human teeth and Middle Stone Age deposits at Klasies River, South Africa. *Journal of Human Evolution* 41: 535–44.

Rightmire, G. P., Deacon, H. J., Schwartz, J. H. and Tattersall, I. (2005) Human foot bones from Klasies Main Site, South Africa. *Journal of Human Evolution* 50: 96–103.

Rink, W. J., Schwarcz, H. P., Smith, F. H. and Radovčic, J. (1995) ESR ages for Krapina hominids. *Nature* 378: 24.

Ripoll López, S. (1988/9) Representaciones femininas de la Cueva de Altamira (Santillana del Mar, Cantabria). *Ars Praehistorica* 7/8: 69–86.

Rivière, E. (1887) *De l'Antiquité de l'Homme dans les Alpes-Maritimes.* Paris: Ballière.

Roche, J. (1976) La découverte de La Chapelle-aux-Saints et son influence dans l'évolution des idées concernant le psychisme de néandertaliens. In Vandermeersch, B. (ed.) *Les Sépultures Néanderthaliennes.* Nice: Union Internationale des Sciences Préhistoriques et Protohistoriques IXe Congrès, pp. 13–23.

Roebroeks, W. and Corbey, R. (2000) Periodisations and double standards in the study of the Palaeolithic. In Roebroeks, W., Mussi, M., Svoboda, J. and Fennema, K. (eds) *Hunters of the Golden Age.* Leiden: University Press and European Science Foundation, pp. 77–86.

Roebroeks, W., Mussi, M., Svoboda, J. and Fennema, K. (eds) (2000) *Hunters of the Golden Age: the Mid Upper Palaeolithic of Eurasia 30,000–20,000 BP.* Lieden: University Press.

Ronen, A. (1976) The Skhūl burials: an archaeological review. In Vandermeersch, B. (ed.). *Les Sépultures Néanderthaliennes.* Nice: Union Internationale des Science Préhistoriques et Protohistoriques IXe Congrès, pp. 27–40.

Rosas, A., Martínez-Maza, C., Bastira, M., García-Tabernero, A., Lalueza-Fox, C. *et al.* (2006) Paleobiology and comparative morphology of a late Neanderthal sample from El Sidrón, Asturias, Spain. *Proceedings of the National Academy of Sciences (USA)* 103(51), pp. 19266–71.

Rosendahl, W., Maureille, B. and Trinkaus, E. (2003) Rediscovery of the Badegoule 5 skeletal remains (Badegoule, Le Lardin-Saint-Lazare, Dordogne, France). *Paleo* 15: 273–8.

Rougier, H., Milota, Ş., Rodrigo, R., Gherase, M., Sarcin, L. *et al.* (2007) Peştera cu Oase 2 and the cranial morphology of early modern Europeans. *Proceedings of the National Academy of Sciences (USA)* 104(4), pp. 1165–70.

Roussot, A. (1965) *Cent Ans de Préhistoire en Périgord.* Bordeaux: Musée d'Aquitaine.

Russell, M. (1987) Mortuary practice at the Krapina Neanderthal site. *American Journal of Physical Anthropology* 72: 381–97.

Russell, M. and Le Mort, F. (1986) Cut marks on the Engis 2 Calvaria? *American Journal of Physical Anthropology* 69: 317–23.

Sacchi, D. (2003) *Le Magdalénien. Apogée de l'Art Quaternaire.* Paris: La Maison des Roches.

Sakura, H. (1970) State of the skeletons of the Amud Man in situ. In Suzuki, H. and Takai, F. (eds) *The Amud Man and His Cave Site.* Tokyo: University Press, pp. 117–22.

Schick T. and M. Stekelis (1977) Mousterian assemblages in Kebara Cave, Mount Carmel. *Eretz-Israel* 13: 97–149.

Schmitz, R. and Thissen, J. (2000) First archaeological finds and new human remains at the rediscovered site of the Neanderthal type specimen. In Orscheidt, J. and Weniger, G. (eds) *Neanderthals and Modern Humans, Discussing the Transition: Central and Eastern Europe from 50,000–30,000 BP*. Mettmann: Neanderthal Museum, pp, 267–74.

Schmitz, R., Serre, D., Bonani, G., Feine, S., Hillgruber, F. *et al.* (2002) The Neanderthal type site revisited: interdisciplinary investigations of skeletal remains from the Neander Valley, Germany. *Proceedings of the National Academy of Sciences (USA)* 99(20), pp. 13342–7.

Schulting, R. J. (1996) Antlers, bone pins and flint blades: the Mesolithic cemeteries of Téviec and Hoëdic, Brittany. *Antiquity* 70: 335–50.

Schulting, R. J. (2005) '. . . Pursuing a rabbit in Burrington Combe': new research on the Early Mesolithic burial cave of Aveline's Hole. *Proceedings of the University of Bristol Spelaeological Society* 23(3), pp. 171–265.

Schulting, R. J., Trinkaus, E., Higham, T., Hedges, R. E. M., Richards, M. and Cardy, B. (2005) A Mid-Upper Palaeolithic human humerus from Eel Point, South Wales, UK. *Journal of Human Evolution* 48: 493–505.

Schwarcz, H. and Rink, J. (1998) Progress in ESR and U-Series chronology of the Levantine Palaeolithic. In Akazawa, T., Aoki, K. and Bar-Yosef, O. (eds) *Neanderthals and Modern Humans in Western Asia*. New York: Plenum, pp. 57–67.

Schwarcz, H. P., Grün, R., Vandermeersch, B., Bar-Yosef, O., Valladas, H. and Tchernov, E. (1988) ESR dates for the hominid burial site of Qafzeh in Israel. *Journal of Human Evolution* 17: 733–7.

Schwarcz, H., Buhay, W. M., Grün, R., Valladas, H., Tchernov, E. *et al.* (1989) ESR dating of the Neanderthal site, Kebara Cave, Israel. *Journal of Archaeological Science* 16: 653–61.

Scott, J. and Marean, C. W. (2009) Paleolithic hominin remains from Eshkaft-e Gavi (southern Zagros Mountains, Iran): description, affinities, and evidence for butchery. *Journal of Human Evolution* 57(3): 248–59.

Scott, K. (1986) The large mammal fauna. In Callow, P. and Cornford, J. M. (eds) *La Cotte de St. Brelade 1961–1978. Excavations by CBM McBurney*. Norwich: Geo Books, pp. 109–38.

Semal, P., Rougier, H., Crevecoeur, I., Jungels, C., Flas, D. *et al.* (2008) New data on the late Neanderthals: direct dating of the Belgian Spy fossils. *American Journal of Physical Anthropology* 138(4): 421–8.

Shang, H., Tong, H., Zhang, S., Chen, F. and Trinkaus, E. (2007) An early modern human from Tianyuan Cave, Zhoukoudian, China. *Proceedings of the National Academy of Sciences (USA)* 104(16), pp. 6573–8.

Shea, J. J. (2001) The Middle Paleolithic: early modern humans and Neanderthals in the Levant. *Near Eastern Archaeology* 64: 38–64.

Sibley, C. G. (2000) DNA–DNA hybridisation in the study of primate evolution. In Jones, S., Martin, R. and Pilbeam, D. (eds) *The Cambridge Encyclopaedia of Human Evolution*. Cambridge: Cambridge University Press, pp. 313–15.

Sieveking, A. (1971) Palaeolithic decorated bone discs. In Sieveking, G. de G. (ed.) *Prehistoric and Roman Studies*. London: British Museum, pp. 206–29.

Simpson, J. J. and Grün, R. (1998) Non-destructive gamma spectrometric U-series dating. *Quaternary Science Reviews* 17: 1009–22.

Singer, R. and Wymer, J. (1982) *The Middle Stone Age at Klasies River Mouth in South Africa*. Chicago: University of Chicago Press.

Sinitsyn, A. (1996) Kostenki 14 (Markina Gora): data, problems, and perspectives. *Préhistoire Européenne* 9: 273–313.

Sinitsyn, A. (2004) Les sepultures de Kostenki: chronologie, attribution culturelle, rite funéraire. In Otte, M. (ed.) *La Spiritualité: Actes du Colloque de la Commission 8 de l'UISPP*. Liège: ERAUL 106, pp. 237–44.

Sinitsyn, A., Allsworth-Jones, P. and Housley, R. (1996) Kostenki 14 (Markina Gora): new AMS dates and their significance within the context of the site as a whole. *Préhistoire Européenne* 9: 269–71.

Smirnov, Y. A. (1989) Intentional human burial: Middle Palaeolithic (Last Glaciation) beginnings. *Journal of World Prehistory* 3: 199–233.

Soffer, O. (1985) *The Upper Paleolithic of the Central Russian Plain*. New York: Academic Press.

Soffer, O., Vandiver, P., Klima, B. and Svoboda, J. (1993) The pyrotechnology of performance art: Moravian venuses and wolverines. In Knecht, H., Pike-Tay, A. and White, R. (eds) *Before Lascaux: The Complex Record of the Early Upper Palaeolithic*. Boca Raton: CRC Press, pp. 259–75.

Soficaru, A., Doboş, A. and Trinkaus, E. (2006) Early modern humans from the Peştera Muierii, Baia de Fier, Romania. *Proceedings of the National Academy of Sciences (USA)* 103(46), pp. 17196–201.

Soficaru, A., Petrea, C., Doboş, A. and Trinkaus, E. (2007) The human cranium from the Peştera Cioclovina Uscată, Romania. Context, age, taphonomy, morphology and paleopathology. *Current Anthropology* 48(4): 611–19.

Solecki, R. S. (1963) Prehistory in Shanidar Valley, northern Iraq. *Science* 139: 179–93.

Solecki, R. S. (1972) *Shanidar: the Humanity of Neanderthal Man*. London: Allen Lane, The Penguin Press.

Sommer, D. J. (1999) The Shanidar IV 'flower burial': a re-evaluation of Neanderthal burial ritual. *Cambridge Archaeological Journal* 9(1): 127–9.

Soressi, M., Jones, H. L., Rink, W. J., Maureille, B. and Tillier, A.-M. (2007) The Pech de l'Azé Neanderthal child: ESR, uranium-series, and AMS ^{14}C dating of its MTA Type B context. *Journal of Human Evolution* 52: 455–66.

Speth, J. D. and Tchernov, E. (1998) The role of hunting and scavenging in Neanderthal procurements strategies. In Akazawa, T., Aoki, K. and Bar-Yosef, O. (eds) *Neanderthals and Modern Humans in Western Asia*. New York: Plenum, pp. 223–39.

Spiess, A. E. (1979) *Reindeer and Caribou Hunters: An Archaeological Study*. New York: Academic Press.

Stepanchuk, V. (1998) The Crimean Palaeolithic: genesis and evolution between 140–30kyr BP. In Otte, M. (ed.) *Préhistoire d'Anatolie: Genèse de deux Mondes*. Liège: ERAUL 85, pp. 261–300.

Stone, T. and Cupper, M. L. (2003) Last Glacial Maximum ages for robust humans at Kow Swamp, southern Australia. *Journal of Human Evolution* 45: 99–111.

Straus, L. G. (1991) The Early Upper Palaeolithic of Southwest Europe: Cro-Magnon adaptations in the Iberian peripheries. In Mellars, P. A. (ed.) *The Emergence of Modern Humans: An Archaeological Perspective*. Edinburgh: Edinburgh University Press, pp. 276–302.

Street, M., Terberger, T. and Orschiedt, J. (2006) A critical review of the German Paleolithic hominin record. *Journal of Human Evolution* 51: 551–79.

Stringer, C. (1998) Chronological and biogeographic perspectives on later human evolution. In Akazawa, T., Aoki, K. and Bar-Yosef, O. (eds) *Neanderthals and Modern Humans in Western Asia*. New York: Plenum, pp. 29–37.

Stringer, C. and Gamble, C. (1993) *In Search of the Neanderthals*. London: Thames & Hudson.

Sulerzhitski, L., Pettitt, P. B. and Bader, N. O. (2000) Radiocarbon dates on the remains from the settlement Sungir. In Alexeeva, T. and Bader, N. (eds) *Homo Sungirensis. Upper Palaeolithic Man: Ecological and Evolutionary Aspects of the Investigation.* Moscow: Scientific World, p. 34.

Suzuki, H. and Takai, F. (eds) (1970) *The Amud Man and His Cave Site.* Tokyo: Tokyo University Press.

Svoboda, J. (1988) A new male burial from Dolní Věstonice. *Journal of Human Evolution* 16: 827–30.

Svoboda, J. (ed.) (1991) *Dolní Věstonice II Western Slope.* Liège: ERAUL 54.

Svoboda, J. (2008) The Upper Palaeolithic burial area at Předmostí: ritual and taphonomy. *Journal of Human Evolution* 54(1): 15–33.

Svoboda, J. A., Ložek, V. and Vlček, E. (1996) *Hunters Between East and West: The Palaeolithic of Moravia.* New York: Plenum.

Svoboda, J. A., van der Plicht, J. and Kuželka, V. (2002) Upper Palaeolithic and Mesolithic human fossils from Moravia and Bohemia (Czech Republic): some new ^{14}C dates. *Antiquity* 76: 957–62.

Taborin, Y. (1993) *La Parure en Coquillage au Paléolithique.* Paris: XXIXe Supplément à Gallia Préhistoire.

Takahata, Y. (1985) Adult male chimpanzees kill and eat a male newborn infant: newly observed intragroup infanticide and cannibalism at Mahale national park, Tanzania. *Folia Primatologica* 44: 161–70.

Taylor, T. (2002) *The Buried Soul: How Humanity Invented Death.* Boston, MA: Beacon Press.

Tchernov, E. and Valla, F. F. (1997) Two new dogs, and other Natufian dogs, from the southern Levant. *Journal of Archaeological Science* 24: 65–95.

Teleki, G. (1973) Group response to the accidental death of a chimpanzee in Gombe National Park, Tanzania. *Folia Primatologia* 20: 81–94.

Terberger, T. (2006) Gewalt bei prähistorischen wildbeutern Mitteleuropas? Ein diskussionsbeitrag. In Piek, J. and Terberger, T. (eds) *Frühe Spuren der Gewalt – Schädelverletzungen und Wundversorgung an Prähistorischen Menschenresten aus Interdisziplinärer Sicht.* Schwerin: Landesamt fur Kultur und Denkmalpflege, pp, 129–54.

Teschler-Nicola, M. and Trinkaus, E. (2001) Human remains from the Austrian Gravettian; the Willendorf femoral diaphysis and mandibular symphysis. *Journal of Human Evolution* 40: 451–65.

Teschler-Nicola, M., Weiser, W., and Prossinger, H. (2004) Two human deciduous teeth found in a Gravettian excavation site near Stillfried/March, Lower Austria. *Homo* 54: 229–39.

Thorne, A. G. and Macumber, P. G. (1972) Discoveries of Late Pleistocene man at Kow Swamp, Australia. *Nature* 238: 316–9.

Thorne, A. G., Grün, R., Mortimer, G., Spooner, N. A., Simpson, J. J. *et al.* (1999) Australia's oldest human remains: age of the Lake Mungo 3 skeleton. *Journal of Human Evolution* 36: 591–612.

Tillier, A.-M. (1995) Paléoanthropologie et practiques funéraires au Levant Méditerranéen Durant le Paléolithique Moyen: le cas des sujets non-adultes. *Paléorient* 21(2): 63–76.

Tillier, A.-M. (2008) Early deliberate child burials: bioarchaeological insights from the Near Eastern Mediterranean. In Bacvarov, K. (ed.) *Babies Reborn: Infant/ Child Burials and Pre- and Protohistory*. Oxford: BAR international series 1832, pp. 3–14.

Tillier, A.-M., Arensburg, B., Vandermeersch, B. and Chech, M. (2003) New human remains from Kebara Cave (Mount Carmel). The place of the Kebara hominids in the Levantine Mousterian fossil record. *Paléorient* 29(2): 35–62.

Tillier, A.-M., Mester, Z., Bocherens, H., Henry-Gambier, D. and Pap, I. (2009) Direct dating of the 'Gravettian' Balla child's skeleton from Bükk Mountains (Hungary): unexpected results. *Journal of Human Evolution* 56: 209–12.

Tosello, G. (2003) *Pierres Gravées du Périgord Magdalénien: Art, Symboles, Territoires*. Paris: XXXVI supplément á Gallia Préhistoire.

Tournepiche, J.-F. (1994) Un Neanderthalien devore par des hyenes? La Grotte de Rochelot (Saint Armand de Bonnieure, Charente). *Paleo* 6: 319–21.

Tournepiche, J.-F. and Couture, C. (1999) The hyena den of Rochelot Cave (Charente, France). In Gaudzinski, S. and Turner, E. (eds) *The Role of Early Humans in the Accumulation of European Lower and Middle Palaeolithic Bone Assemblages*. Bonn: RGZM Verlag, pp. 89–101.

Tournier, J. (1898) La grotte des Hoteaux (Ain). Sépulture de l'âge du renne. *Comptes Rendus du 4e Congrès du Science International*, pp. 150–65.

Trinkaus, E. (1983) *The Shanidar Neanderthals*. New York: Academic Press.

Trinkaus, E. (1995) Neanderthal mortality patterns. *Journal of Archaeological Science* 22: 121–42.

Trinkaus, E. and Holliday, T. (2000) The human remains from Paviland Cave. In Aldhouse-Green, S. H. R. (ed.) *Paviland Cave and the 'Red Lady': a Definitive Report*. Bristol: Western Academic and Specialist Press, pp. 141–204.

Trinkaus, E. and Jelínek, J. (1997) Human remains from the Moravian Gravettian: the Dolní Věstonice 3 postcrania. *Journal of Human Evolution* 33: 33–82.

Trinkaus, E. and Pettitt, P. B. (2000) The Krems-Hundssteig 'Gravettian' human remains are Holocene. *Homo* 51: 258–60.

Trinkaus, E. and Shipman, P. (1993) *The Neanderthals: Changing the Image of Mankind*. London: Jonathan Cape.

Trinkaus, E., Jelínek, J. and Pettitt, P. B. (1999) Human remains from the Moravian Gravettian: the Dolní Věstonice 35 femoral diaphysis. *Anthropologie (Brno)* 37: 167–75.

Trinkaus, E., Svoboda, J., West, D. L., Sládek, V., Hillson, S. W. *et al.* (2000) Human remains from the Moravian Gravettian: morphology and taphonomy of isolated elements from the Dolní Věstonice II site. *Journal of Archaeological Science* 27: 1115–32.

Trinkaus, E., Formicola, V., Svoboda, J., Hillson, S. W., and Holliday, T. W. (2001) Dolní Věstonice 15: pathology and persistence in the Pavlovian. *Journal of Archaeological Science* 28: 1291–308.

Trinkaus, E., Moldovan, O., Milota, Ş., Bîlgîr, A., Sarcina, L. *et al.* (2003) An early modern human from the Peştera cu Oase, Romania. *Proceedings of the National Academy of Sciences (USA)* 100(20), pp. 11231–36.

Trinkaus, E., Svoboda, J., Wojtal, P., Nyvltová Fiškakova, M. and Wilczynski, J. (2009) Human remains from the Moravian Gravettian: morphology and taphonomy of additional elements from Dolní Věstonice II and Pavlov I. Published online at *International Journal of Osteoarchaeology* 2009, DOI: 10.1002/oa.1088.

Tsukahara, T. (1993) Lions eat chimpanzees: the first evidence of predation by lions on wild chimpanzees. *American Journal of Primatology* 29: 1–11.

Turner, E., Street, M., Henke, W. and Terberger, T. (2000) Neanderthaler or cave bear? A re-appraisal of the cranium fragments from the Wildscheuer Cave in Hessen, Germany. *Notae Praehistoricae* 20: 21–33.

Turq, A. (1989) Le squelette de l'enfant du Roc-de-Marsal: les données de la fouille. *Paléo* 1: 47–54.

Vacca, E. and Coppola, D. (1993) The Upper Palaeolithic burials at the cave of Santa Maria di Agnano (Ostuni, Brindisi): preliminary report. *Rivista di Antropologia* 71: 275–84.

Valladas, H., Reys, J. L., Joron, J. L., Valladas, G., Bar-Yosef, O. and Vandermeersch, B. (1988) Thermoluminescence dating of Mousterian 'Proto Cro-Magnon' remains from Israel and the origin of modern man. *Nature* 331: 614–16.

Valladas, H., Mercier, N., Froget, L., Hovers, E., Joron., J.-L. *et al.* (1999) TL dates for the Neanderthal site of the Amud Cave, Israel. *Journal of Archaeological Science* 26: 259–68.

Vallois, H. (1971) Le crane trépané magdalénien de Rochereil. *Bulletin de la Société Préhistorique Française* 68: 485–95.

Valoch, K. (2001) Da Magdalénien in Mähren. *Jahrbuch des Römisch-Germanischen Zentralmuseums Mainz* 48: 103–59.

Valoch, K. (2007) Kosenki on Don, an extraordinary proof of the Upper Palaeolithic settlement stability. *Acta Musei Moraviae* XCII: 53–70.

Vandermeersch, B. (1965) Position stratigraphique et chronologique relative des restes humains du Paléolithique du Sud-Ouest de la France. *Annales de Paléontologie* 51: 69–126.

Vandermeersch, B. (1969) Découvert d'un objet en ocre avec traces d'utilisation dans le Moustérien de Qafzeh (Israël). *Bulletin de la Société Préhistorique Française* 66: 157–8.

Vandermeersch, B. (1981) *Les Hommes Fossiles de Qafzeh (Israel)*. Paris: Cahiers de Paléontologie.

Vandermeersch, B. (1993) Was the Saint-Césaire discovery a burial? In Lévêque, F., Backer, A. M. and Guilbaud, M. 1993. *Context of a Late Neanderthal. Implications of Multidisciplinary Research for the Transition to Upper Paleolithic Adaptations at Saint-Cézaire, Charente-Maritime, France*. Madison, WI: Prehistory Press, pp. 129–31.

Van Gennep, A. (1960) *The Rites of Passage*. London: Routledge & Kegan Paul.

Vanhaeren, M. and d'Errico, F. (2001) La parure de l'enfant de La Madeleine (Fouille Peyrony). Un nouveau regard sur l'enfance au Paléolithique Supérieur. *Paleo* 13: 201–40.

Vanhaeren, M. and d'Errico, F. (2002) The body ornaments associated with the burial. In Zilhão, J. and Trinkaus, E. (eds) *Portrait of the Artist as a Child: The Gravettian Human Skeleton from the Abrigo do Lagar Velho and Its Archaeological Context*. Lisbon: Trabalhos de Arqueologia 22, pp. 154–86.

Vanhaeren, M. and d'Errico, F. (2003) Le mobilier funéraire de la Dame de Saint-Germain-la-Rivière (Gironde) et l'origine Paléolithique des inégalités. *Paleo* 15: 195–238.

Vanhaeren, M., d'Errico, F., Stringer, C., James, S. L., Todd, J. A. and Mienis, H. K. (2006) Middle Palaeolithic shell bead in Israel and Algeria. *Science* 312: 1785–8.

Van Schaik, C. P. and Janson, C. H. (2000) Infanticide by males: prospectus. In Van Schaik, C. and Janson, C. H. (eds) *Infanticide by Males and its Implications.* Cambridge: University Press, pp. 1–6.

Van Schaik, C. P., Ancrenaz, M., Borgen, G., Galdikas, B., Knott, C. D. *et al.* (2003) Orangutan cultures and the evolution of material culture. *Science* 299: 102–5.

Vercellotti, G., Alciati, G., Richards, M. P. and Formicola, V. (2008) The Late Upper Palaeolithic skeleton Villabruna 1, Italy: a source of data on biology and behavior of a 14,000 year-old hunter. *Journal of Anthropological Sciences* 86: 143–63.

Vercoutère, C., Giacobini, G. and Patou-Mathis, M. (2008) Une dent humaine perforée découverte en context Gravettien ancient à l'Abri Pataud (Dordogne, France). *L'Anthropologie* 112: 273–83.

Vermeersch, P. (2002) Two Upper Palaeolithic burials at Nazlet Khater. In Vermeersch, P. M. (ed.) *Palaeolithic Quarrying Sites in Upper and Middle Egypt.* Leuven: Egyptian Prehistory Monographs 4, pp. 273–82.

Vermeersch, P. M., Paulissen, E., Gijselings, G. and Janssen, J. (1986) Middle Palaeolithic chert exploitation pits near Qena (Upper Egypt). *Paléorient* 12(1): 61–5.

Vermeersch, P. M., Paulissen, E., Stokes, S., Charlier, C., Van Peer, P. *et al.* (1998) A Middle Palaeolithic burial of a modern human at Taramsa Hill, Egypt. *Antiquity* 72: 475–84.

Verna, C., Hublin, J.-J., Debénath, A., Jelínek, A. and Vandermeersch, B. (2010) Two new hominin cranial fragments from the Mousterian levels at La Quina (Charente, France). *Journal of Human Evolution* 58: 273–8.

Verpoorte, A. (2001) *Places of Art, Traces of Fire. A Contextual Approach to Anthropomorphic Figurines in the Pavlovian (Central Europe, 29–24kyr BP).* Leiden: Archaeological Studies of Leiden University 8.

Verpoorte, A. (n.d.) What's in the bones: the importance of disarticulated human remains in the Upper Palaeolithic of Europe. Unpublished manuscript.

Verworn, M., Bonnet, R. and Steinmann, G. (1919) Der Diluviale Menschenfund von Obercassel bei Bonn. Wiesbaden.

Vilotte, S. and Henry-Gambier, D. (2010) The rediscovery of two Upper Palaeolithic skeletons from Baousso da Torre Cave (Liguria, Italy). *American Journal of Physical Anthropology* 141: 3–6.

Wadley, L. (1997) Where have all the dead men gone? Stone Age burial practices in South Africa. In Wadley, L. (ed.) *Our Gendered Past: Archaeological Studies of Gender in Southern Africa.* Johannesburg: Witwatersrand University Press, pp. 107–33.

Wadley, L. (2001) What is cultural modernity? A general view and a South African perspective from Rose Cottage Cave. *Cambridge Archaeological Journal* 11: 201–11.

Webb, S. G. and Edwards, P. C. (2002) The Natufian human skeleton remains from Wadi Hammeh 27 (Jordan). *Paléorient* 28(1): 103–24.

Welté, A.-C. and Cook, J. (1993) Un décor exceptionnel (silhouette feminine stylisée) sur godet de pierre de la Grotte du Courbet (France). *Comptes Rendu de l'Academie Scientifique de Paris* 315 Séries II, pp. 1,133–8.

Wendorf, F. and Schild, R. (1986) *The Wadi Kubbaniya Skeleton: A Late Palaeolithic Burial from Southern Egypt.* Dallas, TX: Southern Methodost University Press.

White, M. J. and Pettitt, P. B. (2009) The demonstration of human antiquity: three rediscovered illustrations from the 1825 and 1846 excavations in Kent's Cavern (Torquay, England). *Antiquity* 83: 758–68.

White, R. (1982) Rethinking the Middle/Upper Palaeolithic transition. *Current Anthropology* 23: 169–92.

White, R. (1993) Technological and social dimensions of 'Aurignacian-Age' body ornaments across Europe. In Knecht, H., Pike-Tay, A. and White, R. (eds) *Before Lascaux: the Complex Record of the Early Upper Palaeolithic*. Boca Raton, FL: CRC Press, pp. 277–99.

White, R. (1995) Ivory personal ornaments of Aurignacian age: technological, social and symbolic perspectives. In Hahn, J. (ed.) *le Travail et Usage de l'Ivoire au Paléolithique Supérieur*. Rome: Istituto Poligrafico e Zecca dello Stato, pp. 29–62.

White, R., Henry-Gambier, D. and Normand, C. (2003) Human tooth ornaments from the French early Aurignacian: implications for the early Upper Palaeolithic treatment of the dead. Paleoanthropology Society abstracts, available online at www.paleoanthro.org.

White, T. D. (1986) Cut marks on the Bodo cranium: a case of prehistoric defleshing. *American Journal of Physical Anthropology* 69: 503–9.

White, T. D. and Johanson, D. C. (1989) The hominid composition of Afar Locality 333: some preliminary observations. In Giacobini, G. (ed.) *Hominidae: Proceedings of the 2nd International Congress of Human Paleontology, Turin, September 28-October 3 1987*. Milan: Jaca, pp. 97–102.

White, T. D. and Toth, N. (1991) The question of ritual cannibalism at Grotta Guattari. *Current Anthropology* 32(2): 118–34.

White, T. D., Asfaw, B., DeGusta, D., Gilbert, H., Richards, G. D. *et al.* (2003) Pleistocene *Homo sapiens* from Middle Awash, Ethiopia. *Nature* 423: 742–7.

Whiten, A., Goodall, J., McGrew, W. C., Nishida, T., Reynolds, V. *et al.* (1999) Cultures in chimpanzees. *Nature* 399: 682–5.

Wild, E. M., Teschler-Nicola, M., Kutschera, W., Steier, P., Trinkaus, E. and Wanek, W. (2005) Direct dating of Early Upper Palaeolithic human remains from Mladeč. *Nature* 435: 332–5.

Williams, J. M., Lonsdorf, E. V., Wilson, M. L., Schumacher-Stankey, J., Goodall, J. and Pusey, A. E. (2008) Causes of death in the Kasakela chimpanzees of Gombe. *American Journal of Primatology* 70: 766–77.

Wrangham, R. W. (1999) Evolution of coalitionary killing. *Yearbook of Physical Anthropology* 42: 1–30.

Wüller, B. (1999) *Die Ganzkörperbestattungen des Magdalénien*. Köln: Rudolf Habelt.

Zilhão, J. (2005) Burial evidence for the social differentiation of age classes in the Early Upper Palaeolithic. In Vialou, D., Renault-Miskovsky, J. and Patou-Mathis, M. (eds) *Comportements des Hommes du Paléolithique Moyen et Supérieur en Europe. Actes du Colloque du G. D. R. 1945 du CNRS, Paris, 8–10 Janvier 2003*. Liège: ERAUL 111, pp. 231–41.

Zilhão, J. and Almeida, F. (2002) The archaeological framework. In Zilhão, J. and Trinkaus, E. (eds) (2002a) *Portrait of the Artist as a Child: The Gravettian Human Skeleton from the Abrigo do Lagar Velho and Its Archaeological Context*. Lisbon: Trabalhos de Arqueologia 22, pp. 29–57.

Zilhão, J. and Trinkaus, E. (eds) (2002a) *Portrait of the Artist as a Child: The Gravettian Human Skeleton from the Abrigo do Lagar Velho and Its Archaeological Context.* Lisbon: Trabalhos de Arqueologia 22.

Zilhão, J. and Trinkaus, E. (2002b) Social implications. In Zilhão, J. and Trinkaus, E. (eds) *Portrait of the Artist as a Child: The Gravettian Human Skeleton from the Abrigo do Lagar Velho and Its Archaeological Context.* Lisbon: Trabalhos de Arqueologia 22: 519–41.

INDEX

abandonment: definition 9
advanced mortuary developmental phase
  265
AL-333 (Hadar, Ethiopia) 42–5
Amud (Israel) 86–7, 92, 99, 101, 102,
  118, 128, 129
Anzik 1 (USA) 259
Arch Lake (USA) 259
archaic mortuary phase 264
Arene Candide (Italy) 162, 182–4, 250,
  251–3
Arnold Cave (USA) 259
Atapuerca (Spain): Gran Dolina 47–9;
  Sima de los Huesos 49–55
Australopithecines 42–5
Avdeevo (Russia) 214
Aveline's Hole (England) 259
Azilian 218

Badegoule (France) 218
Badegoulian 218
Balzi Rossi (Italy) *see* Grimaldi
Baousso da Torre (Italy) 164, 174, 176
Baradostian 144–5
Barma Grande (Italy) 162–3, 180–2,
  213
Bédeilhac Cave (France) 223
binding 201
Bodo (Ethiopia) 49
Bonn-Oberkassel (Germany) 226,
  246–7
Border Cave (South Africa) 72–3
Bouil Bleu, Grotte du (France) 147
Brassempouy (France) 146
Brillenhöhle (Germany) 221–2

Brno (Czech Republic) 157–8, 193–4
Bruniquel (France) 228, 234, 236
Burghöhle Dietfurt (Germany) 220

caching *see* funerary caching
cairn covering: definition 9
cannibalism *see* Cronos compulsions
Cap Blanc (France) 228, 234, 238
Capsian 256
Castel di Guido (Italy) 55
Castillo, El (Spain) 220
Cave, Roc-de- (France) 218, 228
Caviglione, Grotta del (Italy) 165, 174,
  176
Cavillon, Grotte du (Italy) *see*
  Caviglione, Grotta del
cemetery: Africa 254–7; Australia
  257–9; definition 10; European
  Epipalaeolithic 251–3; evolution
  and 263; Late Pleistocene 249–59;
  Natufian 253–4; North America
  259; sedentism and 249
Chaffaud (France) 223
Chancelade (France) 229, 234, 238, 241
Chapelle-aux-Saints, La (France) 79, 84,
  110–11
chimpanzees: aggression as cause of
  death 14; Bambou's death 26–31;
  compassion 24–6; Cronos
  compulsions and infanticide among
  15–22; curation of Jokro 22–4; death
  of Olly's infant at Gombe 1; disease
  as cause of death 13, 23; infant
  responses to death of mothers 25–6;
  morbidity 35–8; Pansy's death 31–2;

303

Made in the USA
Monee, IL
30 August 2020

40456153R20177